BIRDS
of BRITAIN
and EUROPE

AA Publishing

Produced by AA Publishing

© Automobile Association Developments Limited 1997.
Reprinted 1998, 2001, 2003, 2005, 2006, 2007, 2008

Published by AA Publishing (a trading name of
Automobile Association Developments Limited,
whose registered office is Fanum House, Basing
View, Basingstoke, Hampshire RG21 4EA;
registered number 1878835).

Find out more about AA Publishing at
www.theAA.com/travel

ISBN-10: 0-7495-4666-2 (HB with CD)
ISBN-13: 978-0-7495-4666-3 (HB with CD)
ISBN-10: 0-7495-1587-2 (HB)
ISBN-13: 978-0-7495-1587-4 (HB)

A CIP catalogue record for this book is available from
the British Library.

The contents of this book are believed correct at the
time of printing. Nevertheless, the publishers cannot
be held responsible for any errors or omissions or for
changes in the details given in this book or for the
consequences of any reliance on the information
provided by the same. This does not affect your
statutory rights. We have tried to ensure accuracy in
this book, but things do change and we would be
grateful if readers would advise us of any inaccuracies
they may encounter.

Contributing authors: Paul Sterry (consultant editor),
Andrew Cleave, Andy Clements, Peter Goodfellow
Designer: Stuart Perry Associates
Artists: Richard Allen, Norman Arlott, Trevor Boyer,
Hilary Burn, John Cox, Dave Daly, John Gale, Robert
Gillmor, Peter Hayman, Ian Lewington, David Quinn,
Darren Rees, Chris Rose, Christopher Schmidt
Maps: Advanced Illustration, Congleton
© Automobile Association Developments Limited 1997

Printed and bound in Dubai by Oriental Press

A03896

Contents

The Birds

INTRODUCTION

THIS book is a visual and practical celebration of Europe's rich and diverse birdlife. Europe is a wonderful arena for birdwatching, and from Jan Mayen Island to the Bosphorus offers a host of 'hotspots' to watch birds, both native species and vagrants to the region. 'Europe' here is the great land mass bordered on the east by the Urals, the Caspian Sea and the Persian Gulf, and all the lands around the Mediterranean Sea. The birds selected are all native and naturalised species – residents and migrants – as well as the most regularly encountered vagrants from America and Asia. The birds are presented in standard evolutionary order, although, to make best use of the beautiful illustrations, a few species may be out of strict sequence.

Illustrations

Specially commissioned from some of Europe's finest bird artists, the full-colour illustrations provide an accurate and striking portrait of each species. The plumages and poses shown are those that the observer is most likely to encounter. Feature pages throughout the book compare easily confused species.

Factfile

A clearly laid-out fact panel contains all the practical background information that the reader might need for reference for each species and for direct comparison between species. All the essential basic information concerning the physical attributes of the species is included here, together with details on habitat.

Species Descriptions

Each panel contains a full but concise description of the bird, highlighting key features and the main differences from similar species. All plumages are described (although not all forms of the species are illustrated), and, where appropriate, species descriptions are complemented by the picture captions.

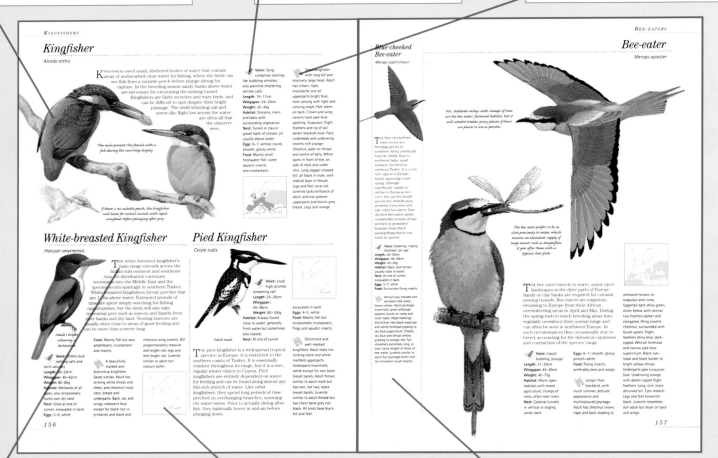

Background Text

This provides an interesting and useful insight into the life of each bird. The emphasis varies from species to species, in some cases covering distinctive behaviour or characteristics, or key identification features; in other cases the focus might be on the species' distribution or migration habits.

Maps

Clear, colour-coded maps show the range of each bird throughout the year:

  green – present all year
  yellow – present in summer
  blue – present in winter

Maps for birds with complex migration habits are also marked with directional arrows.

Rarities

Very unusual or localised birds and key vagrants are presented in side panels in smaller type. The information is provided in the same format as for main entries but there is no distribution map for vagrant birds. Further pages throughout the book show a selection of other, rarer vagrants.

BIRD TOPOGRAPHY AND FUNCTION

STRUCTURE AND SKELETON

Fundamentally, a bird's skeleton is like any other vertebrate's, but the basic plan has been greatly modified to cope with flight. Central to this is the fusion of many bones to form a cage around the vital organs and to brace the body, especially on landing. Another key feature is the keel, a flattened projection on the breastbone, where the wing muscles are attached. Devoid of feathers, the bird's body is angular and bony, but with a sleek covering of feathers most flying birds become beautifully streamlined. Reducing wind drag is essential as flying is an energetic means of locomotion: a bird must expend energy to prevent itself from falling and to propel itself forward.

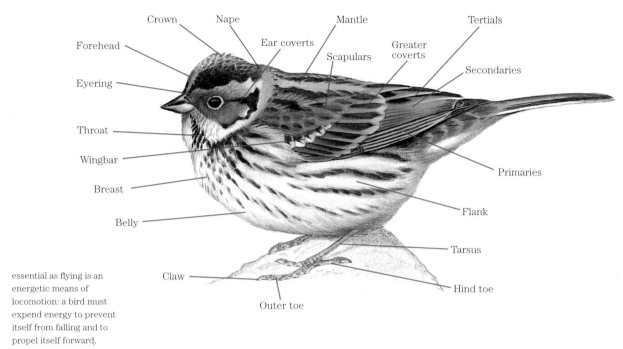

Crown · Nape · Mantle · Tertials · Forehead · Ear coverts · Greater coverts · Scapulars · Secondaries · Eyering · Throat · Wingbar · Breast · Belly · Claw · Outer toe · Primaries · Flank · Tarsus · Hind toe

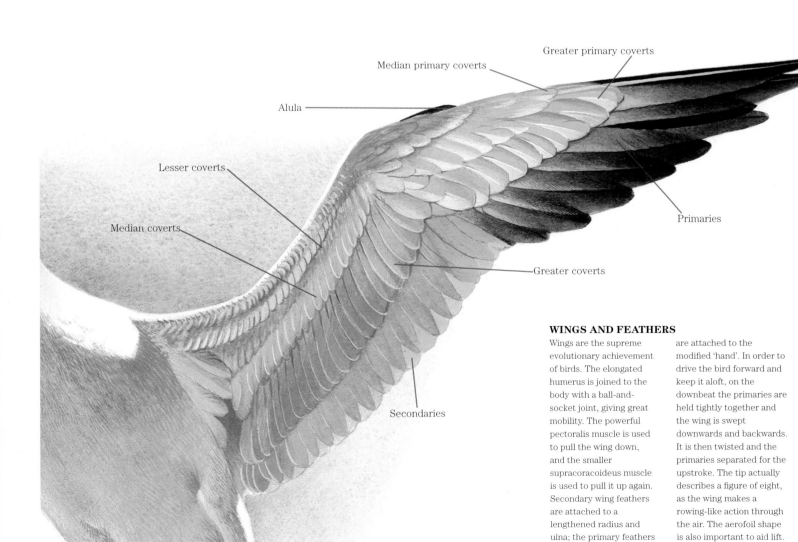

Greater primary coverts · Median primary coverts · Alula · Lesser coverts · Median coverts · Primaries · Greater coverts · Secondaries

WINGS AND FEATHERS

Wings are the supreme evolutionary achievement of birds. The elongated humerus is joined to the body with a ball-and-socket joint, giving great mobility. The powerful pectoralis muscle is used to pull the wing down, and the smaller supracoracoideus muscle is used to pull it up again. Secondary wing feathers are attached to a lengthened radius and ulna; the primary feathers are attached to the modified 'hand'. In order to drive the bird forward and keep it aloft, on the downbeat the primaries are held tightly together and the wing is swept downwards and backwards. It is then twisted and the primaries separated for the upstroke. The tip actually describes a figure of eight, as the wing makes a rowing-like action through the air. The aerofoil shape is also important to aid lift.

5

BIRD TOPOGRAPHY AND FUNCTION

BILLS

A bird's bill (sometimes called its beak) is an extension of its jaw. It has two parts, the upper and lower mandibles, both covered in a horny, protective layer of skin.

Whimbrel
The long bills of waders like the whimbrel are sensitive probes, and the unusual bill of the avocet sifts small animals from mud and water as it is waved from side to side.

Puffin
The familiar, brightly coloured bill of the puffin is used to attract a mate, and its razor-sharp edge is good for gripping fish.

Eider
Some bills are incredibly strong. That of the eider has a hook at the end which helps it crack open crabs and assorted shellfish.

Green Woodpecker
Woodpeckers use their bills to chisel into wood, and also to 'drum' instead of singing, hitting the bill tip hard and very fast against a dead branch to produce a resonant drumming.

Kestrel
Birds of prey and owls have hooked bills for tearing skin and flesh. Falcons have a notch near the bill tip which is used to kill prey by biting into the neck.

FEET

The legs and feet of birds are little more than skin-covered bones with a few tendons. Most of the muscles are hidden away at the top of the leg. Legs are usually scaly or leathery, but some are feathered: to give protection in birds of prey, to act as insulation in some birds, such as ptarmigan, or to reduce wind noise in owls. As with bills, a bird's leg and foot design reflects

its lifestyle, and leg length is largely determined by how much, and in what, it walks. Aerial birds have very poorly developed legs and can often barely walk.

Whimbrel
Wading in water and walking on dry land require long legs but unspecialised feet, as demonstrated by the whimbrel. The rear toe is often absent or reduced.

Eider
Waterbirds, like the eider, have partial or complete webs between their toes, creating effective paddles. The puffin has, in addition, sharp claws to help in digging its nesting burrow.

Serin
Passerines have a tendon along the back of the leg to curl the toes automatically as the leg is bent, keeping the bird on its perch with little effort. Claws are often long to give extra grip.

Kestrel
The feet of the kestrel and other birds of prey have long toes, widely spread, with rough soles and sharp claws to catch and hold live prey securely.

FEATHERS

Feathers evolved from the scales of birds' reptilian ancestors, and are unique to birds. They are astonishingly light, yet strong, and while they are vital for flight they are also

used for camouflage, advertising, insulation and waterproofing. The main feathers are the contour feathers that give the bird its outline. Downy feathers and semi-plumes lie under

these and provide insulation. Filo-plumes are usually thin, hair-like feathers that are very specialised and may be sensory. Bristles occur around the bills, nostrils and eyes of many birds. Colour is produced by pigments, or by iridescence created by the feather's surface structure, or by reflections from pigment inside the feather. Feathers wear out and must period-ically be shed and replaced through moulting. All birds moult at least once a year, usually after breeding and before migration.

EYES AND SENSES

Birds are very visually biased creatures and many have largely dispensed with the senses of taste, smell and touch. Their eyesight, however, is often superb, and their hearing, too, can be far better than a human's. They also appear to be sensitive to magnetism, although how they use it to help them navigate is unknown. Birds' eyes are big. In fact,

at 5cm across, an ostrich's eye is the largest of any land animal. The bigger the eye the more light-sensitive cells it can contain, which results in vision that is not telescopic compared to the human eye's, but is up to eight times clearer. This is important for all birds, but particularly for hunters like buzzards, which can spot prey a kilometre below them. Birds' eyes are

usually sited on the side of the head for good all-round vision, but predatory birds have eyes pointing forward to increase binocular vision, vital for accurately judging distances. All birds have good hearing, but it is especially well developed in those active at night. Smell is important in only a few species; taste is generally very poor.

BODY LINES

Birds for which flight is important on a day-to-day basis, such as the passerines and birds of prey, conform closely to

the ideal streamlined shape when seen from the side in flight. The neck is short or well covered in feathers, giving a bluntish front end; the breast is deep because of the keel; and the pelvic bones are extended forward; there is then a gentle tapering of the

abdomen and tail. The bulk of the body weight is centrally positioned, helped by the skull's being very light and the legs' being brought forward due to the position of the pelvis. The cigar or torpedo shape is the most streamlined: rounded at the nose but

tapering gently towards the rear. The tapering is particularly important as it helps prevent eddies of air from forming, which would increase drag. The best shape, giving the least drag, is a streamlined torpedo about 4.5 times as long as its maximum diameter.

The streamlined shape is not just good for flying: it translates perfectly to a swimming lifestyle. Puffins appear to 'fly' underwater, their streamlined bodies every bit as effective here as in the air.

FIELDCRAFT

WHERE AND WHEN TO WATCH BIRDS

Europe's seasons have a marked influence on bird behaviour, distribution and, in the case of migratory species, their presence or absence. Breeding activity is generally at its peak between March and June, and migration is best observed around coasts in April and May, and again from August to October. Outside the breeding season, many birds form flocks, some of which comprise mixed species. The weather and the time of day also have a serious influence on bird behaviour. Once fully aware of the implications of these factors, the birdwatcher will avoid wasting time and can, on occasions, use it to his or her advantage.

HABITAT

With a few exceptions, each species of European bird is adapted to a particular habitat and to specific niches within this environment. Dippers, for example, are found almost exclusively on fast-flowing rivers while woodpeckers are always associated with woodland. Being aware of these limitations can help the birdwatcher in a number of ways. When trying to identify a mystery bird, for example, taking note of the habitat can help exclude many species on the grounds of habitat choice. Interestingly, birds on migration and out of their normal range favour habitats similar to those chosen on their breeding or overwintering grounds. You would be unlikely to find a migrating spotted crake or little stint anywhere other than beside a freshwater pool, or a migrating shearwater anywhere but over the sea. The coast acts like a magnet for many species of birds, and estuaries have a particular lure. At low tide, vast expanses of mudflats are exposed, revealing rich feeding grounds for waders and wildfowl, and invariably distant observation opportunities for birdwatchers.

EQUIPMENT

Buy a young ornithologist a bad pair of binoculars and her or she could be put off birdwatching for life. Some of the cheapest models even seem to create the illusion of making the image appear smaller than that seen with the naked eye, and flimsy models soon get broken or mis-aligned. Binoculars allow easy observation of distant birds and also add to the enjoyment of seeing birds at close quarters. Some birdwatchers are satisfied just to watch birds, but, for the more dedicated, taking notes and obtaining some form of visual record is essential. Those with artistic ability can make field sketches but, for most, photography is the answer. Taking basic record shots may seem easy but the discerning photographer will soon notice a world of difference between a beginner's picture and one taken by a seasoned photographer. However, with practice, almost anyone can take rewarding pictures.

A knowledge of a bird's appearance, calls, distribution and behaviour all aid identification among closely related species such as these tits

BIRD BEHAVIOUR AND SIGNS

Experienced birdwatchers can often tell a great deal about a bird just from looking at its behaviour. A bird anxiously scolding the observer during the breeding season, for example, is likely to have a nest near by and its territory should be vacated as soon as possible. A vulture circling lower and lower is likely to have spotted a carcass and will soon come in to land to feed, attracting a stream of others after it. The bird's environment also tells a tale: a boulder in a river or an isolated post on open moorland whitewashed with droppings, for example, is likely to be used as a regular perch by a dipper and a merlin respectively. Patient and distant observation of the site may yield good views of the birds.

WHAT TO LOOK FOR

It will not take too many trips to realise that identification of species new to the observer is not always easy, even if the bird in question is seen really well. One way to improve your chances of identification is to become practised in knowing which are the most important characteristics to look for. Of course, these vary from species to species but, generally speaking, groups of birds such as waders or gulls have features in common which are of particular significance. Thus, among the wheatears, the shape of the black and white markings on the rump and tail are by far the most important features to look for. With the ducks, however, the shape and length of the bill and colour of the speculum are of more importance.

MIGRATION

Birds go to incredible lengths to avoid harsh winter weather: Arctic terns migrate 17,000km each way between their Arctic nesting areas and their wintering grounds in the Antarctic; whooper swans have been seen at altitudes over 8km; and birds as small as finches may travel up to 600km in a day. Migration is the key to the success of many species. Those that have evolved to breed in one area and overwinter somewhere else are able to exploit habitats that would be otherwise unavailable to them. Birds are excellent navigators: their internal 24-hour clock ensures that they can navigate during the day by the sun, and at night by the stars. Evidence also suggests that some species can detect and respond to the Earth's magnetic field, using it to determine north and south.

CONSERVATION

Birds have suffered badly at the hands of man. From the extinction of the ancient, giant moas of New Zealand to infamous extinctions of more modern times, whole species have been wiped out. Island populations have been especially badly hit, as such birds are often fearless of man and sometimes flightless. There is a growing awareness of the need to conserve all life, and birds have often been the focus of conservation efforts. Effective conservation requires information, both to assess the need for conservation and to monitor the effectiveness of measures already in place.

Red-throated Diver

Gavia stellata

Except in very good light the red throat patch appears dark, almost black; it is the last part of summer plumage lost in autumn

Winter bird and summer bird, right

THE red-throated diver is widespread across northern Europe, although it occurs at comparatively low densities. In much of its European habitat, breeding is limited to small lakes and pools within flying distance of the sea, where it feeds. Shy and easily disturbed at the nest, it is protected by law in many countries. Red-throated divers are superbly adapted to life on water and only venture on to land during the breeding season. In winter, they generally favour inshore waters but can still be difficult to spot, partly because they swim buoyantly but low in the water, and partly because they dive regularly for extended periods.

In territorial disputes rival males glide across surface of water calling loudly, in 'snake', 'penguin race' and 'plesiosaur' ceremonies

Voice: Only heard during breeding season: goose-like calls; deep, rhythmic quacking in flight; song rapidly repeated 'kwuk-uk-uk'
Length: 53–69cm
Wingspan: 110cm
Weight: 1.2–1.6kg
Habitat: Breeds on northern coastal pools; overwinters around coasts
Nest: A shallow depression in waterside vegetation

Eggs: 1 or 2; dark, speckled brown
Food: Mostly fish but occasionally crabs or shrimps

Sexes similar. Dagger-like bill and red eyes. In breeding season both sexes have red throat, black and white striping on nape and otherwise grey head and neck. Dark-brown back and white underparts. In winter, upperparts grey-brown with white speckling on back and white underparts. Juvenile similar to winter adult but with grubbier appearance to underparts. Swims low in water with superficially shag-like appearance but head and bill have characteristic upward tilt. Looks goose-like in flight with neck outstretched; in winter, looks very pale in flight.

Black-throated Diver

Gavia arctica

summer bird

Winter bird

INVARIABLY seen on water, the black-throated diver swims buoyantly and dives smoothly, unlike the superficially similar shag, which has a leaping dive. It breeds from May to August and favours large lakes, where it can both nest and feed. After nesting, black-throated divers move mainly to the coast and in winter disperse to inshore waters of western Europe and the eastern Mediterranean. Following gales or severe winter weather, individual birds sometimes turn up on inland reservoirs elsewhere in Europe.

Territorial displays may involve spectacular rushes across the water with wings raised, before the bird rears up with its neck arched back

Voice: Only heard during breeding season: raven-like croaks and wailing calls
Length: 58–73cm
Wingspan: 120cm
Weight: 2–3kg
Habitat: Breeds on large lakes; overwinters around coasts
Nest: Depression in waterside vegetation, often on an island
Eggs: 1 or 2; olive-brown with black spots
Food: Almost exclusively fish

Sexes similar: grey head and neck with black throat and black and white stripes on side of neck and under chin. Sides of breast have black and white stripes that grade into black on back and upperparts; distinctive white chequerboard pattern on back. In winter, bill grey with black tip; plumage dark on upperparts and pale on underparts. Throat and cheeks often look conspicuously white; white patch on flanks at waterline. Juvenile similar to winter adult, although upperparts not clean white.

Great Northern Diver

Gavia immer

THE great northern diver breeds mainly in North America, where it is known as the common loon. In Europe, its breeding range is limited to Iceland. During the breeding season its eerie wails seem to capture the spirit of the lonely north and the large, still lakes on which it breeds. In contrast, winter often finds this species on some of the roughest waters in Europe. Perfectly at home in a gale, the birds dive almost continuously in search of flatfish and crabs. On calm days the great northern, like other divers, can sometimes be observed rolling over on its side in order to preen all its feathers.

Voice: Only heard during breeding season: loud, eerie wailing calls
Length: 69–91cm
Wingspan: 135cm
Weight: 3–4kg
Habitat: Breeds on large lakes; overwinters in sandy bays and around rocky coasts
Nest: Depression in waterside vegetation
Eggs: 1 or 2; greenish-brown with dark spots
Food: Mainly fish but some crustaceans

Size and markings make breeding-plumage bird distinctive; sexes are similar. Bill, head and neck black except for band of narrow, white stripes on side of neck and under chin. Eyes red. Underparts white. Upperparts black except for tiny white spots and white chequerboard pattern on back; also black and white stripes on side of breast. Bill is large and grey with black tip, and neck often shows dark band on sides. Juvenile similar to winter adult but with dirtier appearance to white underparts and pale fringes to feathers on upperparts. In flight shows large wingspan and feet.

In summer (top) adult has spangled appearance and black head. Winter bird (bottom) has mainly dark upperparts and white underparts; when at rest on the water, head and bill are held horizontal

White-billed Diver

Gavia adamsii

THE white-billed diver is a breeding bird of the high Arctic. In Europe it is mainly seen as a winter visitor; reasonable numbers regularly spend the winter off the coast of Norway and smaller numbers penetrate the northern North Sea. Unlike the great northern diver, which prefers large lakes for nesting, the white-billed diver is found beside a variety of water bodies, some quite small, in the breeding season. In the winter months it prefers waters that are further from land than its near relative does. This predilection presumably explains why this is such a difficult bird to observe.

In winter, upperparts mostly dark brown and underparts white; head and neck grubby brown with dark smudge on side of neck and behind eye; face whitish

Voice: Wailing calls on breeding ground, similar to great northern; otherwise silent
Length: 75–91cm
Wingspan: 150cm
Weight: 5–6kg
Habitat: Breeds on high Arctic coastal lakes; overwinters in coastal waters
Nest: Mound of vegetation beside water

Eggs: 1 or 2; olive with dark spots
Food: Mainly fish but also some crustaceans

Superficially similar to great northern diver except for bill, which is large, dagger-like and pale yellow. Head and bill characteristically held with upward tilt. In breeding plumage, head and neck are black except for band of narrow, white stripes on sides of neck and under chin. Upperparts mostly black except for white chequerboard effect on back and scattering of small white spots. Underparts white except for black and white stripes on side of breast. Juvenile similar to winter adult (see caption).

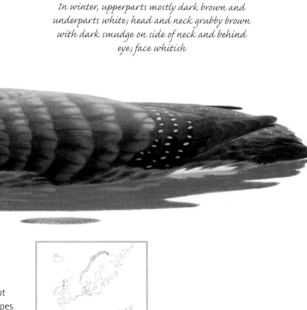

Great Crested Grebe

Podiceps cristatus

REAT crested grebes occur patchily across much of central and southern Europe, their precise distribution being determined by the presence or absence of suitable wetland habitats. In freezing conditions the birds are forced to abandon their chosen lakes and occur in small numbers around the coasts of western Europe. The sight and sound of great crested grebes displaying in spring is one of the highlights of the birdwatcher's calendar. During these ceremonial displays they exhibit a wide range of curious antics. Head-shaking, penguin dances with bills full of water plants, and ritual preening are all part of the varied show, which is usually accompanied by noisy outbursts from the excited birds.

In the penguin dance the birds raise themselves from the water breast to breast, feet paddling furiously, and swing their heads from side to side

During the head-shaking display the crest is raised to make the bright colouring as obvious as possible

The fluffy, striped young often take rides on the backs of their parents.

Ear tufts are lost in winter; bird always appears paler than red-necked grebe

Voice: Barking 'rah-rah-rah' and a clicking 'kek'; most vocal in spring
Length: 46–51cm
Wingspan: 85–89cm
Weight: 800–1,400g
Habitat: Breeds on lakes, gravel pits and slow-flowing rivers; occasionally on the sea in winter
Nest: Floating heap of water plants secured to surrounding vegetation
Eggs: 3–4; white but generally stained reddish by vegetation from nest
Food: Mainly fish but some aquatic insects and molluscs

Elegant waterbird with slender neck. Sexes similar. At a distance can look black and white. In breeding season has pink bill, white face, black cap and large, showy, orange-chestnut and brown ear tufts. Nape and back brown but underparts white. In winter, loses ear tufts and has mainly brownish upperparts and white underparts; black cap appears above level of eye and contrasts with white face. Bill pink. Juvenile in early autumn is stripy but resembles winter adult by late autumn (see captions). In flight, shows white wedges on leading and trailing edges of innerwing in all plumages.

Pied-billed Grebe

Podilymbus podiceps

Little Grebe

Tachybaptus ruficollis

Young birds have striped appearance

In summer looks mainly dark brown except for bright chestnut on neck and face

THE pied-billed grebe occurs throughout most of America in suitable habitats. Vagrant birds in Europe are usually first noted in late autumn and often stay for long periods, sometimes even weeks or months; some have even stayed long enough to acquire breeding plumage. Although vagrant pied-billed grebes sometimes seem indifferent to humans, most are rather retiring in their habits, keeping close to cover and partially submerging when alarmed.

Voice: Vagrants to Europe generally silent
Length: 32–35cm
Wingspan: 58–62cm
Weight: 300–500g
Habitat: Freshwater wetlands with emergent vegetation
Nest: Does not nest in region
Eggs: Does not nest in region
Food: Mainly fish but also some aquatic invertebrates

Small, dumpy grebe with proportionately longer neck and larger head than superficially similar little grebe. Bill noticeably bulky for size of head. Sexes similar. Tail short with powder-puff of white undertail feathers. Adult in breeding plumage (seldom seen in region) has largely grey-brown plumage; upperparts darker than underparts. Bill pale pinkish-grey except for striking vertical black band midway along length. Throat and chin black. Adult in winter loses black markings. In flight, adults show uniformly grey-brown upperwings at all times.

THROUGHOUT most of its range the little grebe is resident, but birds from eastern Europe and southern Scandinavia are migratory. Within their resident range, little grebes often move in the autumn from small areas of water to larger lakes less likely to freeze over; prolonged cold spells in winter may force birds to move to the coast. Little grebes are excellent swimmers underwater, propelling themselves along using the lobed toes on their long feet. The feet are set well back on the body, which helps their swimming but hinders their ability to walk on land.

Voice: High-pitched, whinnying trill
Length: 25–29cm
Wingspan: 40–44cm
Weight: 140–230g
Habitat: Shallow-edged lakes, ponds, slow-flowing rivers and canals
Nest: Floating tangle of aquatic vegetation attached to water plants
Eggs: 4–6; white but usually stained reddish

Food: Small fish, water shrimps, aquatic insects

Small, dumpy bird with powder-puff appearance to body feathers. Feathers at rear end are often fluffed up. Yellow-green legs and lobed feet sometimes visible in clear water. Shows lime-green patch at base of bill, which is dark with pale tip. In winter, appears paler brown but darker on cap, nape and back. Tail end is whitish; white patch at base of bill.

Slavonian Grebe

Podiceps auritus

On a calm winter day, a good view will reveal a compact and sleek bird that looks distinctly black and white in strong sunlight

The spectacular orange-yellow eyestripe and tufts of breeding plumage birds are prominent in mating displays

SLAVONIAN grebes nest in loose colonies on shallow, reedy lakes. A visit to a colony in May is well worthwhile, with plenty of bird activity to see. Displaying pairs engage in 'water rush' dances, swimming upright, each holding water plants in its bill, and racing across the water along parallel routes. In northwest Europe Slavonian grebes are most familiar as coastal winter visitors to sheltered bays and estuaries. Because of their small size and frequent dives, however, they can be difficult to spot in rough winter seas.

Voice: Various screams and cries heard at nest
Length: 31–38cm
Wingspan: 60–65cm
Weight: 350–450g
Habitat: Breeds on well-vegetated lakes and pools; overwinters on coastal waters
Nest: Floating aquatic vegetation anchored to surrounding vegetation
Eggs: 4–5; white but usually stained reddish
Food: Fish

A beautiful bird in breeding plumage, when neck, underparts and flanks are brick red and head black except for striking orange-yellow feathering from eye to ear tufts. Bill black with white tip, and eyes red. Back black, with small white tuft of feathers at rear end. In winter, appears mainly black and white and most easily confused with black-necked grebe. Cap is black, leading to narrow, black line on nape which widens on back of neck. Black back and white underparts. In flight, shows white patches on leading and trailing edges of innerwing; patch on leading edge is small.

Black-necked Grebe

Podiceps nigricollis

In winter birds fish in the breakers, floating buoyantly over the waves

Summer plumage has an attractive sheen to it; golden-yellow plumes on cheeks more straggly and unkempt-looking than on slavonian grebe

THE breeding range of the black-necked grebe shows little overlap with the Slavonian grebe, but its precise distribution is necessarily patchy, given the habitat requirements of nesting birds. Larger lakes in western Europe sometimes hold breeding colonies, and the species nests sporadically in Britain. In winter, its range is similar to that of the Slavonian grebe. Unlike other members of the family, black-necked grebes are often seen gathered in small flocks outside the breeding season. This alone is not enough to identify the species but the characteristic upward-tilted bill and head are distinctive even at a distance or in silhouette. Black-necked grebes are adept swimmers and seem perfectly at home even on comparatively rough seas. Severe winds or cold spells will, however, force birds to seek more sheltered feeding spots or fly to new areas altogether.

Voice: Chittering trill
Length: 28–34cm
Wingspan: 55–60cm
Weight: 250–400g
Habitat: Breeds on shallow, well-vegetated ponds; overwinters on coastal waters
Nest: Floating or grounded mound of vegetation
Eggs: 4–5; white but invariably stained brownish
Food: Fish

Superficially similar to Slavonian grebe but with steep forecrown, upturned bill and upward-tilted head and bill. Sexes similar. Adult in summer plumage has black head, neck and back. Underparts brick red. Eyes red with orange-yellow feather tufts behind them. In winter has mostly dark upperparts and white underparts. Black cap looks more complete than it does on Slavonian grebe, while neck appears greyer and generally more grubby. In flight, shows white wedge on trailing edge of innerwing only.

Red-necked Grebe

Podiceps grisegena

Distant winter-plumage birds can look deceptively diver-like, but their habit of jumping at the surface when they dive helps to identify them

During the breeding season the white cheeks and red neck are distinctive

FOR most birdwatchers in western Europe, the red-necked grebe is most familiar as a winter visitor that appears in September and October and often stays into March or April. Red-necked grebes often breed in loose colonies, but despite this they can be hard to see at this time of year, partly because of their choice of well-vegetated lakes and partly because of their retiring nature when nesting. Outside the breeding season, when they occur on open water, they can be easier to see, although their extended dives and the distances travelled underwater mean that views are all too brief and relocation is a frustrating business.

Voice: During breeding season utters cackling and ticking sounds, and loud wails; otherwise silent
Length: 40–50cm
Wingspan: 80–85cm
Weight: 500–800g
Habitat: Breeds on shallow lakes with abundant water plants; overwinters mainly on coastal waters
Nest: Floating mound of aquatic vegetation secured to surrounding water plants
Eggs: 4–5; white but usually stained reddish
Food: Small fish, aquatic insects, shrimps

Most easily confused with great crested grebe, but smaller and more compact. Sexes similar. During breeding season, adult very distinctive with black-tipped yellow bill, white face, black cap and brick-red neck. In winter loses red neck, although a hint may remain in autumn birds. Black cap extends down to level of eye. White cheeks look conspicuous and black-tipped yellow bill still a good feature. Juveniles have stripy heads but soon resemble winter adults. In flight, shows white wedges on leading and trailing edges of innerwing; less extensive than in great crested grebe.

Black-browed Albatross

Diomedea melanophris

Throughout the year, black-browed albatrosses, especially sub-adult birds, range widely across the southern oceans, and it is presumably these individuals that reach European Atlantic waters. Most sightings come from northwest Europe, with the majority having been seen off Britain and Ireland. Several records refer to birds that have spent several months, and sometimes even successive seasons, among nesting gannets. Size alone is usually a good indicator of identity, as is the effortless, gliding flight pattern with stiffly held wings and infrequent wingbeats.

Voice: Generally silent at sea
Length: 90cm
Wingspan: 220–240cm
Weight: 3kg
Habitat: Open oceans
Nest: Does not breed in region
Eggs: Does not breed in region
Food: Fish, squid, crustaceans

Immense seabird. Unmistakable when seen well but, at a distance, plumage pattern superficially similar to that of adult great black-backed gull or immature gannet. Sexes similar. Seen in flight, wings look disproportionately long. Upperwings and mantle appear all dark. Body pure white except for black 'eyebrow' line above eye and darkish tail feathers. Legs dull pink. Bill long, large and yellowish-orange. Juvenile similar to adult but with dull pink bill; sub-adult birds have dark-tipped yellow bill but otherwise identical to adult.

Fulmar

Fulmarus glacialis

Rapid wingbeats alternate with low gliding over water

Nests on sea cliffs, invariably in the company of other seabird species

Over the last hundred years the fulmar's range has expanded dramatically and today it occurs across much of the north Atlantic as far south as northern France. Throughout much of its range, the fulmar nests on sea cliffs. Non-breeding birds often range far out to sea, especially during the winter months, but established nesting birds linger in the vicinity of the colony for much of the year. The fulmar's stiff-winged flight pattern enables it to ride updraughts on cliffs as easily as it glides over the waves. Large groups tend to gather around trawlers and fish-processing ships. These long-lived birds usually pair for life and couples greet one another by bobbing and bowing their heads and cackling loudly.

Voice: Loud cackling and crooning at nest, grunts and cackles in feeding flocks; otherwise silent
Length: 45–50cm
Wingspan: 102–112cm
Weight: 600–800g
Habitat: Coastal waters, especially near cliffs
Nest: In colonies on cliff ledges; occasionally on ground or buildings
Eggs: 1; white
Food: Offal, crustaceans, fish, carrion

Sexes similar. Superficially gull-like but distinguished by stiff-winged flight and large tube-nostrils. Adults have white head with dark smudge through eye. Bill comprises horny plates and has hooked tip and tube-nostrils. Wings relatively narrow and pointed; upperwing blue-grey and underwing white. Back and rump grey. Underparts white. Rarely seen northern birds look all grey.

Cory's Shearwater

Calonectris diomedea

Larger-headed and appears more front-heavy than great shearwater

The species appears further north towards the end of the breeding season when sea temperatures rise; there are regular sightings off the French coast, and off Cornwall and southern Ireland

Cory's shearwater is common throughout its breeding range and, like other shearwaters, it favours isolated rocky islands for nesting. Strong onshore breezes improve the likelihood of these seabirds coming close to land, and windy conditions also allow the observer to see their impressive aerobatic skills. With hardly a wingbeat, they ride the gusts and eddies, sometimes rising to considerable heights in the process. This immediately distinguishes them from other shearwaters, which seldom fly more than a few metres from the surface of the sea.

Voice: Wails and coughing screams on breeding ground; otherwise silent
Length: 45–55cm
Wingspan: 100–125cm
Weight: 600–900g
Habitat: Breeds on islands; otherwise at sea
Nest: In burrows
Eggs: 1; white
Food: Fish, squid

Large shearwater, most easily confused with great shearwater but lacks that species' black cap and white nape band. Sexes similar. Bill proportionately large and yellow with black tip; colour seen only at close range. Upperparts brownish except for darker wingtips and black tail; scaly effect caused by pale feather edges. At close range, faint pale base to tail sometimes visible. Underparts white except for leading and trailing edges to wings, which are dark, and brown face.

Great Shearwater

Puffinus gravis

LIKE its cousin, the sooty shearwater, the great shearwater breeds in the southern hemisphere during the northern winter, and only passes through coastal waters of northwest Europe from July to September. A pelagic trip to the edge of the continental shelf at the right time of year offers the best chances of seeing good numbers of great shearwaters. The prospects of encountering this species closer to shore are less certain, especially since the numbers visiting the region vary greatly from year to year. Onshore gales in late August or early September probably offer the best chances for observation from land.

It takes a very severe storm to force a great shearwater off course – this species shows masterful control in strong winds

Voice: Silent within its European range
Length: 45–50cm
Wingspan: 100–115cm
Weight: 750–900g
Habitat: Mostly far out to sea; occasionally close to land
Nest: Does not breed in region
Eggs: Does not breed in region
Food: Fish, squid

Noticeably larger than Manx shearwater. Invariably seen in flight on stiffly held wings. Sexes similar. Seen from above, dark cap is clearly separated from grey-brown mantle by white nape band. Upperwings and back dark, but pale feather edging to mantle and wing coverts visible in good light. White-tipped uppertail coverts produce white-rumped effect. Underparts white except for dark bands on underwing and dark undertail feathering.

Sooty Shearwater

Puffinus griseus

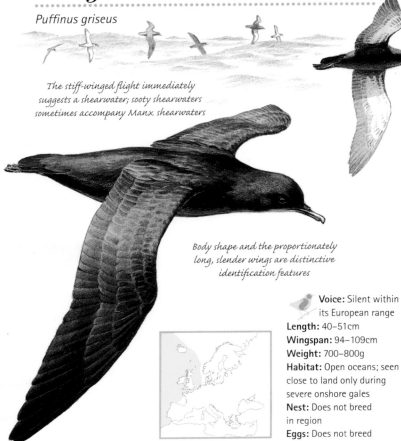

The stiff-winged flight immediately suggests a shearwater; sooty shearwaters sometimes accompany Manx shearwaters

Body shape and the proportionately long, slender wings are distinctive identification features

THE sooty shearwater breeds on islands in the southern oceans, then embarks on a daunting clockwise journey around the south and north Atlantic, reaching Europe by late summer. Intrepid birdwatchers who venture out to the edge of the continental shelf between July and October will find that sooty shearwaters are not uncommon. Onshore winds down west-facing coasts of northwest Europe offer the likeliest opportunities of seeing them on land, although sooty shearwaters also pass through the North Sea in good numbers. You will probably need a telescope to see one clearly.

Voice: Silent within its European range
Length: 40–51cm
Wingspan: 94–109cm
Weight: 700–800g
Habitat: Open oceans; seen close to land only during severe onshore gales
Nest: Does not breed in region
Eggs: Does not breed in region
Food: Squid, fish

Invariably seen in flight; appears all dark except at close range or in very good light; however, identification is straightforward. Larger and longer-winged than Manx shearwater. Body is cigar-shaped and bill long and thin compared with other shearwater species. Sexes similar. Body and upperwing are dark sooty-brown. Underwings are mostly dark but show a pale, silvery stripe along their length that can be conspicuous in good light.

BOAT trips round the Canary Islands or Madeira, especially between April and October, are most likely to yield sightings of little shearwaters. After severe westerly or southwesterly gales they are sometimes seen from headlands in southern Spain, occasionally even on the Mediterranean side of the Straits of Gibraltar. This species is also recorded annually off English and Irish headlands. The little shearwater's flight is generally rather direct and low with fast, fluttering wingbeats giving them a passing resemblance to a puffin.

Voice: Screaming churrs heard at nesting colonies; silent at sea
Length: 27–28cm
Wingspan: 60–65cm
Weight: 200–230g
Habitat: Nests on island sea cliffs; otherwise always at sea
Nest: In rock crevice
Eggs: 1; white
Food: Small fish and crustaceans

Small seabird, nearly always seen in flight. Superficially similar to, but appreciably smaller than Manx shearwater. Sexes similar. Adult has white underparts including underwing; undertail coverts white in race *baroli* from Madeira and Canary Islands but dark in race *boydi* from Cape Verde Islands. Upperparts including upperwing blackish-brown, appearing very dark in most conditions. Wings proportionately shorter than those of Manx shearwater, resulting in more whirring flight action. Juvenile post-fledging indistinguishable from adult at sea.

Mediterranean Shearwater

Puffinus yelkouan

Both races of this species are widespread in the Mediterranean but are seldom seen by birdwatchers at the nest, as they nest in burrows and only return to land after dark. Remote islands and dangerous cliffs are favoured sites. Mediterranean shearwaters range widely and can easily be seen from ferries and headlands. The birds often favour inshore waters for feeding, often settling briefly in areas where shoals of small fish are moving at the surface, and sometimes making shallow plunge-dives to feed.

Voice: Raucous cackles at breeding colonies; otherwise silent
Length: 33–38cm
Wingspan: 80–89cm
Weight: 350–400g
Habitat: Breeds on inaccessible islands and cliffs; otherwise seen at sea
Nest: In burrows
Eggs: 1; white
Food: Small fish, squid

Usually seen flying in long lines, low over water. Short, cigar-shaped body and narrow, stiffly held wings. Upperparts sooty-brown. Underparts and underwing whitish in race *yelkouan* but buffish or dusky in race *mauretanicus*. Both races have dark undertail feathering distinguishing them from similar Manx shearwater. At close range, legs can be seen projecting beyond tail.

Wilson's Storm-petrel

Oceanites oceanicus

Wilson's storm-petrels breed on exposed rocky stretches around the Antarctic. In Europe, large numbers are found from June to September in the Bay of Biscay, and smaller numbers off the Isles of Scilly. They are seldom seen within sight of land except during severe weather. Wilson's storm-petrels are often easy to identify with certainty: their habit of pattering on the water with their long legs is distinctive and birds sometimes appear to stand still when facing into the wind.

Voice: Silent in region
Length: 16–18cm
Wingspan: 40–42cm
Weight: 35–45g
Habitat: Always seen at sea in region
Nest: Does not breed in region
Eggs: Does not breed in region
Food: Small fish, squid and crustaceans

Tiny seabird, usually appearing all dark except for white rump. Sexes similar. Adult at all times has mainly sooty-black plumage except for broad, white rump. Dark upperwings show broad, sandy-brown panel on secondary coverts. In direct flight, legs are clearly seen to project beyond tip of tail. Tail square-ended. When pattering on water to feed, yellow webs sometimes visible in good light at close range.

In summer it is quite easy to see Manx shearwaters from ferries and headlands in northwest Europe. Their burrowing nesting habits and the fact that they only return to the colony after dark, however, mean they are hard to see on land. During the day, the shearwaters are seen out to sea in long lines, banking from side to side and revealing alternately their dark upperwings and pale underwings. Wherever feeding is good, sizeable groups or 'rafts' gather to feed; the birds also mass in large numbers around their breeding islands at dusk.

Voice: Excited cackling noises at breeding colonies; otherwise silent
Length: 30–38cm
Wingspan: 76–89cm
Weight: 400–520g
Habitat: Breeds on offshore islands; otherwise seen at sea
Nest: In burrows
Eggs: 1; white
Food: Small fish, squid

Usually seen flying low over water. Sexes similar. At a distance, appears all black above and all white below. Body cigar-shaped and wings comparatively narrow and pointed. Tube-nostrils only visible at very close range. Upperparts almost black. Underparts white, including undertail feathering. Underwing white except for dark margin. Flies on stiffly held wings except in very calm conditions, when rapid wingbeats interspersed with long glides are used.

Manx Shearwater

Puffinus puffinus

Manx shearwaters are well-adapted seabirds, but are barely able to shuffle along on land

European Storm-petrel

Hydrobates pelagicus

European storm-petrels (often referred to simply as storm-petrels) breed on remote, rocky islands and cliffs. The tiny birds are sometimes seen from ferry crossings, where they occasionally linger and follow in the wake of the boat. European storm-petrels also congregate around fishing vessels to feed on the offal. This habit is exploited by pelagic birdwatching trips that use 'chum' (fish offal) to attract the birds.

When the bird is feeding its flight can look fluttering; it also uses its feet to patter on the water

Voice: Churring and hiccuping from burrow; otherwise silent
Length: 14–18cm
Wingspan: 36–39cm
Weight: 25–30g
Habitat: Nests on sea cliffs and islands; otherwise at sea
Nest: In crevice or burrow
Eggs: 1; white
Food: Plankton

A tiny seabird, superficially recalling house martin. Plumage usually appears all black except for conspicuous white rump. At close range, brownish edges to wing covert feathers may be revealed as pale bands, and white band on underwing sometimes visible. Legs black and trailing and bill black and slender, bearing delicate tube-nostrils.

In direct flight the wingbeats are strong and regular

Leach's Storm-petrel

Oceanodroma leucorhoa

Erratic flight path recalls shearwater one minute and tern the next

Does not patter its feet as often as European storm-petrel, but legs may be dangled

Wɪᴛʜɪɴ its European range, Leach's storm-petrel occurs from May to October, the winter months being spent in the oceans of the southern hemisphere. For most European birdwatchers, the best opportunities for seeing this species come with the arrival of gales in September and October. If these happen to coincide with southerly autumn movements of Leach's storm-petrels down the coasts of northwest Europe, the birds sometimes pass quite close to land. Sometimes large numbers of birds are driven by severe weather and a few appear inland.

Voice: Agitated churrs and hiccups at nest; otherwise silent
Length: 19–22cm
Wingspan: 45–48cm
Weight: 40–50g
Habitat: Breeds on remote islands; otherwise at sea
Nest: In burrow
Eggs: 1; white
Food: Plankton, small fish

Slightly larger than European storm-petrel, with distinctly forked tail visible at close range. Wings relatively long and pointed. Plumage can appear all black. In good light, however, head, back and wing coverts look smoky-grey; trailing edge of coverts shows pale feathering, producing a transverse wingbar. No pale bar on underwing. Rump conspicuously white; at close range, narrow grey bar revealed down centre. Varied flight pattern distinctive. Sometimes glides like shearwater then engages in darting, fluttering or hovering flight. Direct flight confident and powerful.

Gannet

Morus bassanus

Juvenile

Body shape distinctive even from a distance

Adult bird

Adult with chick

Tʜᴇ gannet is Europe's largest breeding seabird. Gannets are a common sight off many west-facing headlands along the coast of northwest Europe. On most days they will simply stream by in long lines, but now and again birdwatchers may be lucky enough to see them feeding. If conditions are particularly good, and shoals of mackerel or herring are near the surface, gannets may gather in large numbers. They plunge-dive from a considerable height, folding their wings right back just before they enter the water.

Voice: 'Arr', 'urrah', heard at colonies; otherwise silent
Length: 87–100cm
Wingspan: 165–180cm
Weight: 2.5–3.5kg
Habitat: Breeds colonially on islands and inaccessible cliffs; otherwise at sea
Nest: Pile of vegetation, seaweed and flotsam
Eggs: 1; pale blue and chalky, later whitish and stained
Food: Fish

Large size and black and white adult plumage distinctive. Adult looks all white except for yellow-buff head, black wingtips and dark legs. Feet webbed; at close range, pale blue visible along toes. Bill dagger-like and pale blue-grey. Juvenile is dark brown, speckled with pale spots; acquires white adult plumage over five years or so, the upperwing and back being the last to lose immature feathering. Flight pattern includes long glides on outstretched wings, deep, powerful wingbeats in direct flight and characteristic plunge-dive feeding method.

Madeiran Storm-petrel

Oceanodroma castro

Mᴀᴅᴇɪʀᴀɴ storm-petrels are invariably associated with remote and often inaccessible islands. They are highly pelagic and are seldom seen within sight of land. Breeding colonies are visited only after dark and the birds nest deep in rock crevices. Identification at sea is perhaps best achieved by observing the birds' behaviour. Their flight is less fluttering and bat-like than that of the European storm-petrel and less erratic and variable than that of Leach's storm-petrel; and they do not habitually patter their feet on the water.

Voice: Purring calls at nest; silent at sea
Length: 20cm
Wingspan: 45cm
Weight: 35–45g
Habitat: Breeds on remote islands; otherwise at sea
Nest: In crevice between rocks on cliffs
Eggs: 1; white
Food: Small crustaceans, fish and squid

Tiny seabird, often appears all black except for white rump. Very similar to Wilson's and European storm-petrels. Sexes similar. Seen in flight, dark upperwings show faint pale band across secondary coverts (much less conspicuous than on Leach's and Wilson's storm-petrels). Tail slightly forked but often looks square-ended; all-dark legs do not obviously project beyond tail in flight as is the case with Wilson's storm-petrels. White rump appears smaller and more rectangular than on other storm-petrels. Juvenile similar to adult.

Pygmy Cormorant

Phalacrocorax pygmeus

Pygmy cormorants are colonial nesters and will often join colonies of other waterbirds. Here they are difficult to see, since they prefer to nest among the dense reeds for cover. Birdwatchers are more likely to see them swimming low in the water or perched on dead branches, either during the day, with wings outstretched, or at roost. Sometimes, however, pygmy cormorants can be seen soaring on rising thermals.

Voice: Croaking calls at nest; otherwise silent
Length: 45–55cm
Wingspan: 80–90cm
Weight: 600–750g
Habitat: Shallow, reed-fringed lowland lakes
Nest: In trees or reedbeds
Eggs: 3–4; pale green with chalky coat
Food: Fish

Sexes similar. Compared with cormorant, head and neck look proportionately short and tail looks proportionately long; these features are most noticeable in flight. Adult has mostly dark plumage except for chocolate-brown head. In breeding plumage, shows white flecks on head, breast and mantle. In winter, adult has whitish throat. Juvenile has brownish upperparts and paler underparts, belly and throat looking almost white.

WHEN seen in flight, the robust body and broad wings of the cormorant give the bird a rather goose-like appearance. By contrast, on the water and at a distance cormorants can resemble divers. They swim low in the water, with their heads tilted slightly upwards, and dive frequently and often for extended periods. Their adaptations to an aquatic life include modifications to the feather barbs, allowing air to escape and water to penetrate the plumage. Although this means they can swim underwater efficiently, it also soon results in waterlogged plumage. Birds are often seen perched on posts with wings outstretched.

Voice: Guttural croaks at nest and roost; otherwise silent
Length: 80–100cm
Wingspan: 130–160cm
Weight: 2.5–3.5kg
Habitat: Breeds colonially, mainly around coasts in western Europe but on inland lakes elsewhere; overwinters mainly around sheltered coasts but also on inland waters

Nest: Pile of twigs, seaweed and flotsam in coastal nesters; in trees or reedbeds in some parts
Eggs: 3–4; chalky white
Food: Fish, especially flatfish and eels

Adult looks dark at a distance; at close range, has scaly appearance due to oily greenish-brown feathers on upperparts

having dark margins. Race *sinensis* has white throat but also shows white feathering on nape and side of head. Both *carbo* (see illustration) and *sinensis* races have white thigh patches in breeding season. Much of white feathering lost outside summer months. Juvenile brown and scaly; looks palest on underparts.

Cormorant

Phalacrocorax carbo

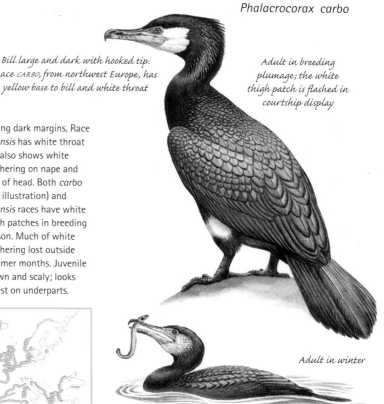

Bill large and dark with hooked tip. Race CARBO, from northwest Europe, has yellow base to bill and white throat

Adult in breeding plumage; the white thigh patch is flashed in courtship display

Adult in winter

Shag

Phalacrocorax aristotelis

UNLIKE its cousin, the cormorant, the shag is an entirely maritime bird, favouring deeper waters and rockier coasts than its relative. Shags are largely year-round residents, with adult birds staying faithful to the particular stretch of shore where they nest each year. In early spring adult birds engage in head- and neck-rubbing courtship displays, and are constantly adorning their large, untidy nests with some new piece of seaweed or flotsam, including items such as plastic bags and baler twine. The early start to nesting ensures that the young birds are in the nest when fish stocks are most productive.

Voice: Grunts and clicks
Length: 65–80cm
Wingspan: 90–105cm
Weight: 1.8–1.9kg
Habitat: Rocky coasts
Nest: Heap of seaweed and vegetation on sheltered rocky ledge
Eggs: 3; pale blue with chalky deposit
Food: Fish, mainly sand eels and herrings

Smaller than superficially similar cormorant and seldom seen in similar habitats. Sexes similar. In poor light, adult looks all dark. At close range, breeding birds have oily-green plumage, bottle-green eyes, yellow gape and upturned crest. In winter, crest and sheen are lost or less obvious. Lores feathered on shag, bare on cormorant. Juvenile is pale brown with white chin; Atlantic birds have brown underparts but those from Mediterranean have white on belly. In flight, has proportionately shorter and more rounded wings than cormorant and faster wingbeats.

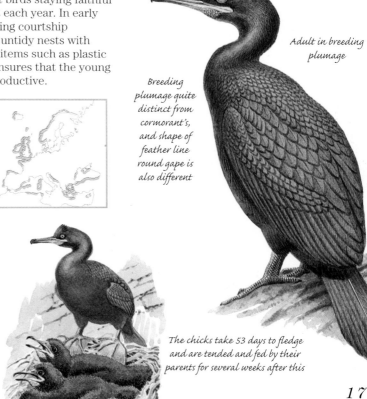

Adult in breeding plumage

Breeding plumage quite distinct from cormorant's, and shape of feather line round gape is also different

The chicks take 53 days to fledge and are tended and fed by their parents for several weeks after this

Grey Heron

Ardea cinerea

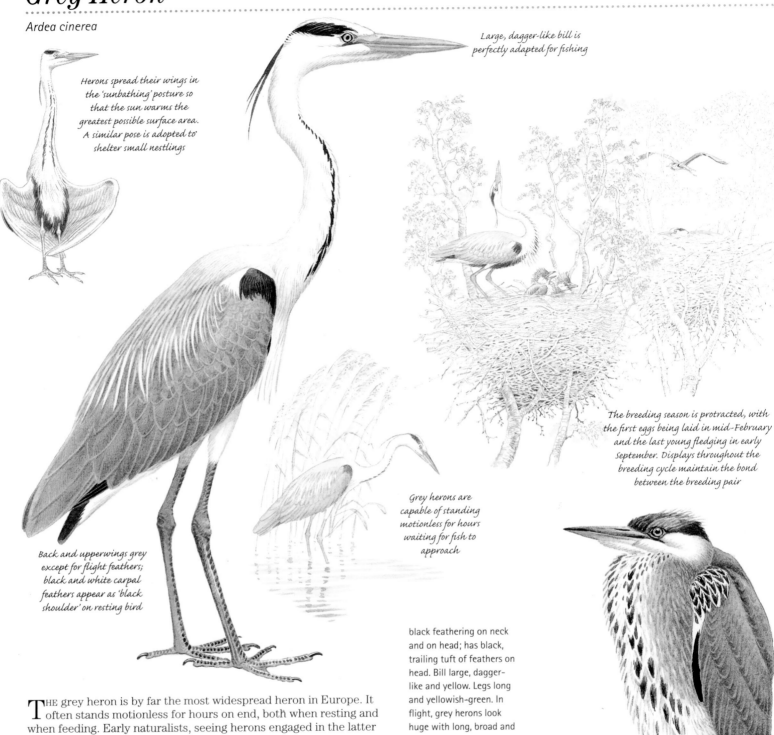

Herons spread their wings in the 'sunbathing' posture so that the sun warms the greatest possible surface area. A similar pose is adopted to shelter small nestlings

Large, dagger-like bill is perfectly adapted for fishing

The breeding season is protracted, with the first eggs being laid in mid-February and the last young fledging in early September. Displays throughout the breeding cycle maintain the bond between the breeding pair

Back and upperwings grey except for flight feathers; black and white carpal feathers appear as 'black shoulder' on resting bird

Grey herons are capable of standing motionless for hours waiting for fish to approach

THE grey heron is by far the most widespread heron in Europe. It often stands motionless for hours on end, both when resting and when feeding. Early naturalists, seeing herons engaged in the latter pursuit, ascribed fish-attracting properties to the birds' legs. Of course, this is not the case and patience is the only secret they employ for their wait-and-see fishing. Grey herons will also stalk their prey on occasion, using a slow, deliberate pace followed by a lightning strike of the bill. After a successful fish catch, grey herons usually preen. If the head or neck feathers are coated with fish scales and mucus, they are rubbed against powdery feathers on the chest. The powder makes preening easier.

black feathering on neck and on head; has black, trailing tuft of feathers on head. Bill large, dagger-like and yellow. Legs long and yellowish-green. In flight, grey herons look huge with long, broad and rounded wings. Wingbeats slow and leisurely, and head and neck held kinked and pulled in. Legs held outstretched with toes held together.

Juvenile similar to adult but underparts more grubby and streaked; black and white head markings less distinct

Voice: Call a loud and harsh 'frank'; young birds at nest give pig-like squeals
Length: 90–98cm
Wingspan: 175–195cm

Weight: 1.1–1.7kg
Habitat: Wetland; sometimes on coasts
Nest: Colonial; tangled stick construction in tree
Eggs: 4–5; pale blue

Food: Fish, frogs and other aquatic animals

Adult head, neck and underparts mostly whitish, except for

Purple Heron

Ardea purpurea

In flight, head is held in snake-like kink, and long, trailing legs show hind toes cocked upwards

Adult bird with eel

ALTHOUGH seldom seen as well as or as often as the grey heron, the purple heron is nevertheless a locally common summer visitor to southern and central Europe wherever its rather specific habitat requirements can be met. It also occurs as a vagrant north and west of its breeding range. Patient and prolonged observation of reedbeds where purple herons are known to occur offers the best chances of good views. The bird blends in well with its reedbed surroundings and is reluctant to venture out into the open. In flight, it keeps close to the tops of the reeds and soon drops back into cover.

Voice: 'Kraank' call sometimes used, but mostly silent
Length: 78–90cm
Wingspan: 120–150cm
Weight: 600–1,200g
Habitat: Extensive wetlands, especially in dense reedbeds
Nest: Colonial; platform of reeds built in reedbeds

Eggs: 4–5; pale bluish-green
Food: Fish, frogs and other aquatic animals

Most attractively marked heron. Slightly smaller than grey heron, with more slender head and neck. Adult plumage appears mostly purplish-grey. Head and neck orange to buff, with black stripe along length down each side. Long breast feathers appear streaked and underparts look dark on standing bird. Upperparts purplish-grey. Juvenile appears more uniformly buffish-brown. In flight, adult upperwings look purplish-brown with black flight feathers; underwings look grey, except for dark maroon band forming leading edge.

Does not stand about in the open as much as grey heron, but is often flushed from the dense vegetation it favours

Night Heron

Nycticorax nycticorax

Juvenile bird

Adult has black bill, black crown and large, red eyes

Relatively slow wingbeats make flight action seem almost mechanical

THE night heron is a summer visitor to Europe, present from April to September; because of its colonial nesting habits, detailed maps show its precise distribution in tight groups. Although a few birds overwinter in the Mediterranean region, the vast majority migrate to tropical Africa. The species occurs as a vagrant north and west of the breeding range. As the name suggests, the night heron is most active after dark. Outside the nesting period, hunched-up night herons can sometimes be seen in semi-colonial daytime roosts in trees, with long lines of flying birds leaving at dusk for their feeding grounds. They can sometimes be observed feeding in shallow water as the light fades.

Voice: Raven-like 'kwaak' flight call
Length: 60–65cm
Wingspan: 105–110cm
Weight: 550–700g
Habitat: Wetlands
Nest: Colonially, usually in trees, twig platform

Eggs: 3–5; pale blue
Food: Fish, amphibians and insects

Sexes similar. Adult face, neck and underparts pale grey; whitish on forecrown and around base of bill. Back black and wings grey, the contrast most noticeable in flight. In breeding plumage sports long, white head plumes. Legs yellowish except at start of breeding season, when pinkish. Immature has black-tipped yellow bill and dark-brown plumage adorned with large, pale spots. Underparts streaked.

Bittern

Botaurus stellaris

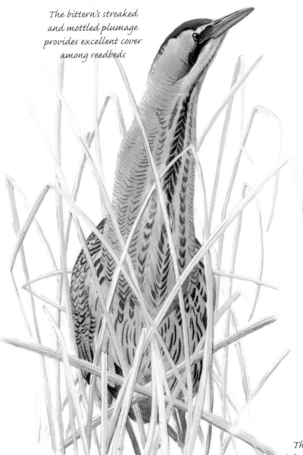

The bittern's streaked and mottled plumage provides excellent cover among reedbeds

In flight, the brown plumage and rounded wings can make the bittern resemble a large woodcock or owl

BITTERNS are far more easily heard than seen: the male's loud, booming call can be heard up to 5km away on calm spring evenings in the vicinity of their reedbed habitat. Most birdwatchers have to satisfy themselves with brief views of birds flying low over the reeds and dropping into cover after a limited period in the air. During extreme winter weather, however, bitterns do occasionally venture out into the open or are forced to move to wetland areas, where their camouflaged plumage is not effective. Damage done to wetlands has caused bittern numbers to decline markedly, and their range to shrink.

This species' skulking and secretive behaviour and excellently camouflaged plumage make it very difficult to observe: the best option for those seeking good views is to visit a reedbed reserve with hides, but even there patience and luck will be needed

Voice: During breeding season, male utters deep, resonant booming, 3–4 times in 5–6 seconds; otherwise silent
Length: 70–80cm
Wingspan: 125–135cm
Weight: 900–1,500g
Habitat: Reedbeds; rarely in other wetland habitats – except during cold weather
Nest: On ground among reeds
Eggs: 5–6; olive-brown
Food: Mainly fish, occasionally frogs

Sexes similar. Large bird with mottled and marbled buffish-brown plumage. Darker streaks, barring and arrow-shaped markings afford excellent camouflage against reedbed. Neck long but often held in hunched posture. Cap and nape dark and shows dark moustachial stripe. Bill large, dagger-like and yellowish. Legs and feet yellowish-green with very long toes. When alarmed adopts motionless, upright posture with head and neck stretched skywards. In flight, often looks owl-like, with long and broad brown wings; trailing legs and forward-pointing head and bill clearly visible.

American Bittern

Botaurus lentiginosus

IT IS most likely that American bitterns recorded in Europe come from northeast coastal North America and have got caught up in westerly weather systems in late autumn. Most European vagrants have been seen in October or November although some of these birds have then stayed for several weeks in the same location. The American bittern is far more likely to venture into the open and give good views than its European cousin. At such times, attention should be paid to the plumage to be sure of identification.

Voice: Croaking call sometimes uttered in flight; otherwise silent in region
Length: 70–80cm
Wingspan: 110–120cm
Weight: 350–450g
Habitat: Wetlands with abundant emergent vegetation
Nest: Does not breed in region
Eggs: Does not breed in region
Food: Fish, amphibians, aquatic insects etc

Superficially very similar to bittern; requires good views for certain identification. Sexes similar. Adult has brown, streaked plumage, generally darker above than below. White throat is well marked with large, reddish-brown streaks. Cap reddish-brown, not blackish as in bittern. Shows conspicuous black face patches and, in flight, striking black flight feathers (absent in bittern). Bill dagger-like and dull yellow; legs yellow-green. Juvenile plumage similar to that of adult but lacks black facial markings; these acquired in first winter.

Little Bittern

Ixobrychus minutus

Although unobtrusive and easily overlooked, little bitterns are common summer visitors to Europe

Adult male

Pale upperwing panels can best be seen in flight. Flight action consists of jerky, rapid wingbeats and prolonged glides

Adult male

THE little bittern is much easier to see than its larger cousin. Vigilant scanning of a suitable reedbed or wetland within the species' range will normally produce flight views, since little bitterns take to the wing regularly. Lucky observers may even see them clamber up reed stems to scrutinise the intruder before taking off in alarm. They then characteristically drop back down into the vegetation after a comparatively short flight. The little bittern occurs as a spring vagrant outside its normal breeding range and has even nested in Britain.

Voice: Mostly silent but frog-like calls heard during breeding season; 'kerk' flight call
Length: 35–38cm
Wingspan: 53–56cm
Weight: 140–150g

Habitat: Reedbeds and other well-vegetated wetlands
Nest: Pile of vegetation among reeds
Eggs: 5–6; white
Food: Fish, frogs and aquatic insects

Male has black-tipped yellow bill, greyish face, black cap and orange-buff, streaked underparts. Back and flight feathers black, contrasting with buffish-white wing coverts forming pale panel.

Upperwing features most striking in flight. Female has much more subdued version of male's plumage, with reddish-buff face and underparts and streaked, brown back. Juvenile heavily streaked.

Squacco Heron

Ardeola ralloides

PRESENT in the region from April to September, most European squacco herons then migrate to tropical Africa. Vagrants appear north of the breeding range in Europe, most records referring to overshooting spring migrants. At first glance, a flying squacco heron could be mistaken for a breeding-plumage cattle egret. On closer inspection, the extensive buffish upperparts of the heron soon distinguish it, as do the species' habits. Unlike the more gregarious cattle egret, the squacco heron is generally a solitary bird, feeding by stealth in shallow wetland margins. When nesting, however, pairs often join large mixed colonies of other heron and egret species.

Voice: Harsh croaks heard in breeding season; otherwise silent
Length: 45–47cm
Wingspan: 80–90cm
Weight: 250–350g
Habitat: All sorts of wetlands

Nest: Colonial; twig platforms built in trees
Eggs: 4–6; greenish-blue
Food: Fish, amphibians, aquatic insects

Sexes similar. In breeding plumage crown and nape streaked, feathers on lower nape being long and plume-like. Underparts white. Bill greenish with black tip and eyes yellow. Legs greenish-orange. In flight, shows pure white wings and back. In non-breeding plumage, adult has dull-brown upperparts and streaked head and neck. Still strikingly white in flight. Bill yellowish with black tip. Juvenile similar to non-breeding adult.

In breeding plumage, standing bird looks mainly orange-buff with reddish tinge to back

Little Egret

Egretta garzetta

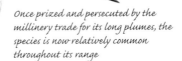

Once prized and persecuted by the millinery trade for its long plumes, the species is now relatively common throughout its range

Legs long and black, contrasting with yellow feet

W HEREVER large, shallow lakes or coastal wetlands are found in southern Europe, you are likely to find little egrets present during the summer. Furthermore, the species' range is expanding and it now occurs regularly in southern Britain. A hunched-up roosting little egret may not inspire much admiration, but when striding purposefully through the shallows on its long legs, or poised motionless, waiting for a fish to pass by, it is a most elegant bird: it will stab at prey with unerring accuracy. On some occasions, the birds appear to shuffle their feet in front of them, apparently to disturb resting or hiding prey into tell-tale movement.

In flight, head and neck held in hunched-up posture

Voice: Harsh 'khaah' and other grating sounds heard at colony; otherwise mostly silent
Length: 55–65cm
Wingspan: 88–95cm

Weight: 400–550g
Habitat: Shallow lakes and wetlands; also coastal lagoons and saltpans
Nest: Colonial; twig platform in tree or among reeds

Eggs: 3–5; greenish-blue
Food: Fish, amphibians and other aquatic animals

The most common pure-white, heron-like bird in Europe. Sexes alike. Slender and elegant appearance, with long neck. Bill long, dark and dagger-like. Bare skin at base of bill yellowish in breeding season but otherwise darker. Also sports long head plumes in breeding season. Appearance remains similar throughout year. In flight, shows broad, rounded wings and trails its long legs behind it.

Cattle Egret

Bubulcus ibis

During the brief breeding season the feathers on the nape, mantle and breast have a warm, buffish tinge

I N EUROPE the cattle egret's breeding range is limited mainly to southern and southwestern parts of the Iberian peninsula, although the number of records of individuals or small flocks north of its usual range is increasing. In contrast with the wait-and-see approach to feeding adopted by many herons and egrets, cattle egrets are far more active. This is especially true when flocks join herds of cattle or sheep. Ever alert, the birds keep pace with the animals in order to spot frogs and insects disturbed by their progress. Mornings and evenings see long lines of birds flying to and from their night-time tree roosts and favoured feeding areas.

Voice: During breeding season, utters barking 'aak' and other calls; otherwise silent
Length: 48–52cm
Wingspan: 90–95cm
Weight: 300–350g
Habitat: Cultivated land and grassland, often alongside animals; also follows ploughs
Nest: Colonial; platform of twigs or reeds or in tree
Eggs: 4–5; whitish
Food: Insects, invertebrates, small mammals, frogs, etc, disturbed by progress of herd animals

A stocky, white bird with a characteristic bulging throat. Sexes similar. Plumage pure white except during brief period of breeding season. Bill dagger-like and proportionately large; at height of breeding season pinkish-orange but otherwise yellow. Legs dull yellowish-green except, briefly, during breeding season, when pinkish-orange. In flight, wings broad and rounded, and legs trailing; neck held in typical hunched-up posture, giving large-headed appearance.

Dalmatian Pelican

Pelecanus crispus

DELIBERATE destruction by fishermen and wetland drainage have severely depleted the Dalmatian pelican's numbers. They are often seen in the company of white pelicans, both on migration through the region and at feeding or nesting sites. Like their relatives, Dalmatian pelicans sometimes engage in group feeding, a dozen or more birds forming a semi-circle and driving fish into the shallows. More than 1kg is consumed each day by a single bird and fish up to 45cm can be swallowed.

Voice: Hissing and grunting calls heard at colony; otherwise silent
Length: 160–175cm
Wingspan: 280–290cm
Weight: 10.5–11.5kg
Habitat: Shallow freshwater lakes
Nest: Mound of twigs and vegetation
Eggs: 2; white
Food: Fish

Similar in proportions and size to white pelican but slightly larger. White plumage has blue-grey tinge; sports a back-curled mane in the form of curly feathers. Bill long and large and throat sac orange-yellow in breeding season but pink at other times. Legs grey in all plumages. In flight, adult seen from below has uniformly greyish-white wings, easily separating it from white pelican. Seen from above, primary flight feathers are black, contrasting with otherwise pale plumage. Juvenile has more uniformly greyish-white underwing in flight than white pelican. A consummate flier, able to soar and glide with ease.

Great White Egret

Egretta alba

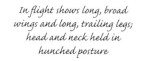

In flight shows long, broad wings and long, trailing legs; head and neck held in hunched posture

GREAT white egrets have a very limited breeding range in the Region, but occur as vagrants as far north and west as Britain. Although they are colonial nesters, they tend to be solitary or are seen, at most, in small groups at other times. The leisurely way in which great white egrets wade through deep water differs from the more active approach often adopted by their smaller cousins. Birds also stand motionless for extended periods, stabbing or lunging with their bills at the crucial moment. As well as fish and frogs, great white egrets also include mammals such as voles as well as water snakes in their diet.

Voice: Grating 'kraak' heard at colony and roost; otherwise silent
Length: 85–102cm
Wingspan: 140–170cm
Weight: 1–1.5kg
Habitat: Extensive wetlands and large, reed-fringed lakes
Nest: Colonial; pile of reeds or twigs in reedbeds or bushes
Eggs: 3–5; pale blue
Food: Fish, amphibians and other aquatic animals

Distinctly larger than little egret, with which it sometimes occurs, and with rather more statuesque proportions. Plumage pure white at all times; shows long, lacy plumes on lower back in breeding season.

Bill black in breeding season but yellow at other times; patch of yellow skin at base of bill present at all times. Legs long; yellow in breeding season on adult but dark greenish-yellow at other times and in juvenile.

White Pelican

Pelecanus onocrotalus

The white pelican is especially impressive in flight

ATRIP to northern Greece in spring offers the best opportunities for seeing this imposing species in Europe. With its long, broad wings, the white pelican is every bit as proficient at soaring and thermalling as birds of prey. Birds are sometimes seen circling above their breeding grounds or in migrating flocks of several hundred individuals. They are also well adapted to an aquatic life, their webbed feet enabling them to propel themselves along quickly. White pelicans are easily disturbed at their colonial nesting grounds.

The capacious throat sac is used to engulf whole shoals of fish if feeding conditions are good

Large, white waterbird. Often seen swimming in flocks when adult plumage looks all white, except for black wingtips. In good light, plumage can be seen to be tinged yellowish. Bill large and very long. Throat sac yellow to orange and shows bare patch of pink skin around eyes. Robust legs and webbed feet orange-yellow. From below, adult shows black flight feathers that contrast with otherwise white plumage. Juvenile has brownish plumage and yellow throat sac; shows brown flight feathers and brown leading edge to wing.

Voice: Grunts, growls and mooing calls heard at nest; otherwise silent
Length: 140–170cm
Wingspan: 275–290cm
Weight: 10–11kg
Habitat: Shallow, lowland lakes and river deltas
Nest: Mound of twigs and vegetation in reedbeds or on islands
Eggs: 2; white
Food: Fish

White Stork

Ciconia ciconia

ANYONE who has visited bird migration hotspots at the Bosphorus in Turkey or the Straits of Gibraltar in southern Spain will have lasting memories of migrating storks. Designed for soaring flight, the species favours narrow isthmuses, where thermals give enough lift to glide over the cooler seas. Flocks of more than 10,000 are not unknown and tens of thousands pass through each day when conditions are good. White storks are easy birds to see during the breeding season. They invariably favour small towns and villages, nesting on rooftops or churches and even taking to man-made platforms provided for them.

Adult in flight

Bill-clapping display of nesting adults

Voice: Mostly silent; non-vocal bill-clapping at nest
Length: 100–115cm
Wingspan: 155–165cm
Weight: 3–4kg
Habitat: Feeds in wetlands and fields adjacent to towns and villages
Nest: Arrangement of twigs on rooftop; occasionally in tree
Eggs: 3–5; white
Food: Fish, frogs, small mammals, insects

Unmistakable, given size and markings. Sexes similar. Standing, adult head, neck, back and underparts white; can look rather grubby. Wingtips black. Bill long, dagger-like and bright red. Legs long and red. In flight, soars impressively on long, outstretched wings, which look square-ended and have 'fingers' of primaries projecting. Body white except for black flight feathers when seen from above and below. Juvenile similar to adult but colour of bill and legs duller.

Black Stork
Ciconia nigra

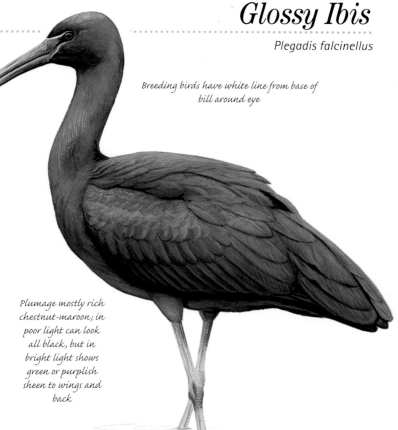

Bird has long, dagger-like, red bill, and a ring of bare, red skin around eye

THE black stork is a rare breeding bird in Europe. Most European birds migrate to tropical Africa, where they are present from September to March, but some birds from the Iberian peninsula appear to be year-round residents. Especially when nesting, the black stork can be a shy and retiring bird that is difficult to see. In this respect, its habits contrast markedly with its cousin, the white stork. Most observations are of birds feeding in large, open wetlands and marshes, where they keep a wary eye on goings-on. They are also often seen in flight, their ability to soar, thermal and glide being essential for such long-distance migrants. Families tend to migrate together, about a month after the white stork.

In eastern Europe the black stork can sometimes be seen feeding side by side with its white relative, but it is generally shyer and harder to observe; it is only seen in any numbers on migration

Voice: Variety of soft calls; also non-vocal bill clattering at nest
Length: 95–100cm
Wingspan: 145–150cm
Weight: 3kg
Habitat: Forested wetlands
Nest: Twig and branch platform built in tree
Eggs: 3–5; white
Food: Fish, frogs and other small animals

Sexes similar. From behind, plumage of adult looks all black; in good light, oily sheen also visible. From other views, white underparts can be seen. Legs long and red. In flight, has huge, broad wings, which look square-ended with 'fingers' of primaries showing; plumage all black except for white underparts

extending to innerwing. Juvenile similar to adult but plumage browner and legs and bill dull greenish.

Glossy Ibis
Plegadis falcinellus

Breeding birds have white line from base of bill around eye

THE glossy ibis is found in its European breeding range mainly from May to August; birds then tend to disperse widely before embarking on autumn migration, and individuals sometimes turn up north and west of their normal range. From a distance, the glossy ibis looks like a cross between a curlew and a heron. It strides through the shallows, probing for mainly invertebrate food in the muddy margins. Feeding areas are not necessarily near roosting or nesting sites, so small flocks are often seen in flight at dawn and dusk. Their distinctive flight silhouette and habit of flying in a trailing line make them comparatively easy to identify.

Plumage mostly rich chestnut-maroon; in poor light can look all black, but in bright light shows green or purplish sheen to wings and back

Voice: Crow-like 'kra-kra' sometimes heard near nest, but mostly silent
Length: 55–65cm
Wingspan: 80–95cm
Weight: 550–650g
Habitat: Wetlands
Nest: Colonial; twig platform built in bush or reedbed
Eggs: 4–5; blue-green

Food: Aquatic insect larvae and other aquatic animals

Waterbird with distinctive shape, even in silhouette. Pinkish bill large, long and curved downwards, and head rather large and bulbous in proportion to long neck. Non-breeding birds have pale streaks on head and

neck. In flight, head and neck held outstretched and legs trail.

Spoonbill

Platalea leucorodia

Spoonbills fly in long lines, their outline and rapid wingbeats making them relatively easy to identify

ALTHOUGH the spoonbill's breeding range extends in a wide band across central Asia, and includes much of the Indian sub-continent, it is a distinctly local species in Europe at shallow lowland lakes and coastal lagoons. In the winter months, birds from southeast Europe tend to move to coastal wetlands around the shores of the eastern Mediterranean; those from the Netherlands move down the Atlantic coast of northwest Europe. Out of their normal range, spoonbills are usually seen singly or in small parties, but around breeding colonies sizeable groups sometimes feed together.

Voice: Mostly silent; occasional grunting sounds at nest
Length: 80–90cm
Wingspan: 115–130cm
Weight: 1.4–1.9kg
Habitat: Shallow lakes, coastal lagoons
Nest: Colonial; pile of twigs or reeds in reedbed or bush
Eggs: 3–4; white with small, reddish spots
Food: Small aquatic insects, fish, molluscs, crustaceans

Sexes similar. Resting birds often have bill tucked in and so can be mistaken for little egrets. Feeding birds distinctive, and identified by bill shape and feeding method, when bill is swept from side to side. Adult plumage all white, although can look rather grubby; shows buffish-yellow on breast in breeding season and long plumes on nape. Legs long and black, and bill long and flattened with spoon-shaped tip. In flight, carries head and neck outstretched and legs trailing. Immature has black wingtips.

Easy to tell from white egrets even at a distance because small groups keep tightly together and are constantly, if slowly, on the move

The spoonbill's flat-tipped bill is ideally suited for filtering out small water animals from soft sediment or the water column

In Europe spoonbills are under threat from marsh draining and pesticides; they are also sensitive to disturbances at breeding time

Greater Flamingo

Phoenicopterus ruber

In flight, wings show black flight feathers and rosy-pink coverts; head and neck held outstretched and legs trailing

FLAMINGOS are notoriously fickle in their breeding habits, only attempting to nest if feeding conditions are perfect and sometimes not even trying to breed in any given area for several years. Outside the breeding season, flocks of flamingos range widely around the Mediterranean, from Cyprus to northern Greece and from the Camargue to Andalucia. Individual birds seen out of their normal range are invariably escapes from captivity and are often the conspicuously red-kneed Caribbean race. Flocks of flamingos feed in close formation and interact with one another regularly; the groups are also very noisy.

Voice: Flocks utter 'kaa-haa' calls
Length: 125–145cm
Wingspan: 140–165cm
Weight: 3–4kg
Habitat: Shallow brackish lagoons and saline lakes
Nest: Colonial; mud platform
Eggs: 1; white but usually stained
Food: Mainly small, aquatic invertebrates

Large and unmistakable bird both standing and in flight. Adult plumage mainly pale pink but can look very washed out. Black-tipped pink bill is downcurved and banana-shaped. Neck very long and usually held in 'S' shape. Body compact and rounded. Juvenile is pale grey-brown with dark legs and black-tipped grey bill.

Legs of adult (seen here) extremely long and pinkish-red; juvenile's are about two-thirds the length of the adult's

The bill is used to filter out animals from the surface of the water: the head and neck are held downwards while the upside-down bill is swept from side to side

27

Mute Swan

Cygnus olor

In flight wingbeats are deep and powerful; the wings make a unique humming sound that serves the same purpose as other species' contact calls

Nᴏʀᴛʜᴡᴇꜱᴛ Europe is the focus for the region's mute swans, the species being particularly widespread in Britain and Ireland. In spring, aggressive males engage in spectacular 'busking' displays with arched wings, their competitive spirits sometimes leading to serious fights. Watch the adult swans for any length of time and you will see them feeding. They sometimes graze in shallow water and up-end in deeper water, using their long necks to uproot water plants. Unfortunately, they are prone to ingest fishermen's lost lead weights, which cause serious poisoning; abandoned fishing lines and hooks can also be a threat.

Voice: Hoarse trumpeting, snorting and hissing calls; non-vocal wing noise in flight
Length: 145–160cm
Wingspan: 210–235cm
Weight: 8–13kg
Habitat: Lakes, slow-flowing rivers, wet meadows and sheltered coasts
Nest: Mound of vegetation beside water
Eggs: 5–8; greenish, chalky
Food: Mainly water plants; some small invertebrates

Adult has all-white plumage although neck sometimes stained buffish. Bill is orange-red with large black knob at base. Juvenile buffish-brown with grubby-pink bill; acquires adult feathering during first winter. When swimming, adult and juvenile hold neck in a more graceful 'S' shape than other swans. Sometimes flies in 'V' formation or diagonal lines.

The mute swan's long neck allows it to exploit deeper water than geese or dabbling ducks

Male swans are aggressive in the breeding season, chasing off intruders by flying, then swimming quickly towards them ; this is called 'busking'

Bewick's Swan

Cygnus columbianus

Fʀᴏᴍ October to March Bewick's swans can be found at traditional sites, which are coastal or lowland wetlands, from Denmark to Britain and Ireland. If especially cold weather spreads west during the winter, birds are sometimes forced to move ahead of it in order to continue feeding. On some traditional sites, individual birds can be recognised by their unique bill patterns. Watch a flock of Bewick's swans for a while and you will notice that small family parties, comprising two adults and two or three youngsters, tend to stick together; this bond lasts throughout the winter, the parties having migrated from their high Arctic breeding grounds together as well.

Voice: Varied, soft or loud musical, bugling calls; far-carrying
Length: 115–125cm
Wingspan: 180–210cm
Weight: 4–8kg
Habitat: Breeds on remote tundra areas outside region; overwinters on flood meadows, saltmarsh and shallow lakes
Nest: Mound of vegetation on hummock
Eggs: 3–5; white
Food: Roots, shoots, aquatic plants, grain

Smallest swan in Europe. Adult has all white plumage. Legs black and bill black with irregularly shaped yellow patch at base; yellow does not extend beyond nostrils. Juvenile is buffish-grey and has black-tipped pink bill, fading to white at base; distinguished from juvenile whooper swan by its smaller size, and bill size and shape, but more importantly by association with adult birds.

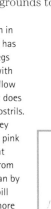

Bewick's swans that visit Europe in the winter breed in the northeast Arctic

Bewick's swans are invariably seen in flocks; young birds are greyer and have pink and black bills

Whooper Swan

Cygnus cygnus

The adult whooper swan is essentially pure white

Tʜᴇ sight and sound of an overwintering flock of whooper swans is a memorable one. Flying in 'V' formation flocks through flurries of snowflakes, or swimming through rising mists on a part-frozen loch, they appear far more at ease with wintry conditions than most human observers. As with Bewick's swans, with which they seldom mix, family units remain together within the looser associations of winter flocks.

Voice: Loud, trumpeting or bugling calls
Length: 145–160cm
Wingspan: 220–240cm
Weight: 8–14kg
Habitat: Breeds on northern lakes and marshes; winters on flood meadows, stubble fields and lochs
Nest: Mound of vegetation, lined with down

Eggs: 3–5; white but stained
Food: Aquatic vegetation; increasingly on grain in stubble fields during winter

Much larger than superficially similar Bewick's swan and with proportionately longer neck. Adult has all white plumage, black legs and black bill with yellow patch at base; area of yellow larger than on Bewick's; wedge-shaped and extends beyond nostrils. Juvenile is pinkish-buff with black-tipped, pinkish bill, grading to white at base. Similar to juvenile Bewick's: best identified by larger size and association with adult birds.

Bewick's swan smaller and shorter-necked than whooper

Whooper swan large and long-necked

Mute swan raises pointed tail

Juvenile Bewick's swan

Juvenile whooper swan

Greylag Goose

Anser anser

Pairs mate for life and remain together all year round; families overwinter together

Breeding birds in Britain and Ireland are mainly resident but numbers are augmented by tens of thousands of winter migrants from Iceland. Elsewhere in Europe the winter range extends to coastal marshes around the Mediterranean

THE precise natural distribution of greylag geese in Europe is now difficult to determine, since introductions and feral populations have confused the situation. Although some feral populations of greylag geese can be approachable, they are generally wary of man – justifiably so, as they are often persecuted and shot. If danger threatens, all the heads in a feeding flock will go up and, if the alarm continues, the birds may take to the air, running along the ground to take off. They fly on powerful wingbeats and the flock will sometimes engage in surprisingly aerobatic dives and plunges. Generally speaking, wintering flocks will not be found far from water, to which they retreat without hesitation should the need arise.

Voice: Clattering clamour in flight, less bugling than other grey geese
Length: 75–90cm
Wingspan: 150–180cm
Weight: 3–4kg
Habitat: Arable land, marshes, lakes
Nest: Sheltered depression on ground, among vegetation
Eggs: 4–6; creamy-white
Food: Grass, spilt crops, growing cereals

Large, stoutly built goose with mainly grey-brown plumage. Most adult birds seen in western Europe have orange bills; eastern birds have pinkish bills. Legs pink in all adult birds. Shows pale margins to feathers on back. Lower belly and undertail white. Some birds have a few dark feathers on belly. In flight, shows grey on forewing, lower back and tail.

In flight the pale grey area on the forewing is visible above and below; it is more obvious than on any other grey goose

Juvenile similar to adult but duller and appears more irregularly barred on upperparts

During the 'triumph ceremony' pairs lower their necks and cackle at each other, avoiding beak-to-beak confrontation. The ceremony is performed throughout the year

White-fronted Goose

Anser albifrons

THE white-fronted goose occurs in two races: the Siberian race *albifrons* overwinters in east and southeast Europe and also occurs along the coast of northwest Europe and southern England; the Greenland race, numbering some 20,000 birds, overwinters in Ireland, Scotland and Wales. Although difficult to approach closely in most parts of their European overwintering range, the species is afforded special protection in a few areas, where hides allow the quarrelsome antics of busy feeding flocks to be watched at close quarters. Startled geese take to the air in huge, noisy flocks, flying in 'V' formations or chevrons.

Voice: Flocks utter musical ringing, laughing and yodelling calls; hissing and yapping calls on ground and non-vocal 'creaking' wings on taking to air
Length: 65–78cm
Wingspan: 130–165cm
Weight: 1.5–2.5kg
Habitat: Breeds on boggy tundra; overwinters on water meadows and near estuaries
Nest: Vegetation-lined depression on hummock
Eggs: 5–6; very pale buff
Food: Grass, roots, other vegetation

Large goose, which, as adult, has white forehead not extending above eye. Siberian race *albifrons* has pinkish bill, while Greenland race *flavirostris* has orange-yellow bill. Plumage generally grey-brown, with underparts paler, but with variable black bands and crescents on belly; undertail white. Juvenile similar to adult but lacks white forehead. In flight, looks comparatively long-winged and more agile than greylag.

Juvenile

White-fronted geese are very wary of intruders and take to the air in huge, noisy flocks if alarmed

Adult bird

Lesser White-fronted Goose

Anser erythropus

ALTHOUGH small flocks of lesser white-fronted geese can be found by travelling to southeast Europe in the winter, birdwatchers from northwest Europe also stand a reasonable chance of finding a stray bird among flocks of white-fronted geese. One or two turn up most winters at Slimbridge in southern England, and small numbers also occur in mainland European flocks. However, actually picking an individual bird out of a flock of several thousand birds is very difficult. Size alone is not a good enough feature for certain identification, because white-fronts are very variable themselves. Patient scanning of the flock can give a good view of the bird's head: the white blaze on the forehead and bright yellow eyering immediately attract attention.

Voice: High-pitched yelping calls
Length: 55–65cm
Wingspan: 120–135cm
Weight: 1.5–2.5kg
Habitat: Breeds on tundra; overwinters on meadows and fields
Nest: Vegetation-lined mound on tundra hummock
Eggs: 4–6; off-white
Food: Plant material

Superficially similar to white-fronted goose, but more compact and appreciably smaller when seen side by side. Bill on adult relatively small and pinkish-orange. White forehead extends above eye, which has conspicuous yellow eyering; white forehead absent in juvenile and eyering dull. Plumage on all birds mostly grey-brown, darker than white-front, with dark markings on paler belly. Undertail white. In flight, has fast wingbeats and very hard to tell from white-front.

The lesser white-front's head markings are distinctive, but as they spend much of their time with their heads down feeding, these features can be difficult to spot

Adult

Bean Goose

Anser fabalis

The bean goose is a particularly nervous bird in winter and favours large, open fields, where the flock can keep wary eyes open for danger; although similar in colouring to other geese, this species has very distinctive orange legs, a characteristic common to both races

IN EUROPE, there are two races of bean goose: *rossicus*, which nests at more northerly latitudes on open tundra, and *fabalis*, which favours taiga or boreal forest at slightly lower latitudes. Both races are migratory, moving south and east in autumn. Some winter in lowland areas, others around arable land and wetlands. They favour traditional sites, some of which have varying degrees of protection from hunting. When danger threatens, birds are quick to take to the air and are more able to rise in a near-vertical manner than many other goose species.

Voice: Calls include a nasal cackle
Length: 65–80cm
Wingspan: 150–175cm
Weight: 2–4kg
Habitat: Breeds on tundra and in northern forests; in winter, on arable and stubble fields
Nest: Mound of vegetation, lined with down
Eggs: 4–6; buffish but stained
Food: Grasses and cereal grains

Can generally be identified by chocolate-brown appearance, particularly on head and neck, and proportionately long neck. Bill dark with variable orange markings: in race *rossicus* orange limited to near bill tip, but in race *fabalis* orange much more extensive. Legs of both races orange. In flight, upperwings look all dark. Lower back is brown, separated from white-edged brown tail by white band at base.

Pink-footed Goose

Anser brachyrhynchus

The characteristic pink legs of this species are much duller in juvenile; the variable pink patch on the bill makes this goose very similar in appearance to the bean goose in poor light

smaller than white-fronted goose (below left)

THE pink-footed goose is essentially an Arctic breeding species, with the entire world population migrating to northwest Europe in September and October. During the day, the birds usually feed on coastal fields, including a wide variety of plant material in their diet. As dusk approaches, they take to the air in vast flocks, streaming overhead in noisy skeins towards the safety of their saltmarsh roost on the shores. The species is still persecuted by hunters in some areas, as well as having to endure the rigours of the brief Arctic summer when breeding; in some bad seasons, few or sometimes no young are reared by entire breeding groups.

Voice: Musical disyllabic or trisyllabic honking; also high-pitched, sharp 'wink-wink'
Length: 60–75cm
Wingspan: 135–170cm
Weight: 1.8–3kg
Habitat: Breeds on uplands or tundra; in winter, on fields, roosting on estuaries or lakes

Nest: Mound of vegetation on hummock or ledge; sometimes colonial
Eggs: 3–5; white
Food: Plant material; in winter, mainly stubble or grass

Smaller than superficially similar bean goose and with proportionately shorter neck and smaller bill. Bill dark with variable patch of pink, usually in the form of a band, near tip. Head and neck usually dark brown, breast and flanks paler brown and back greyish. Legs pink, although much duller in juvenile. In flight, wings look pale grey except for darker flight feathers; back and tail also paler than on bean goose.

Canada Goose

Branta canadensis

INTRODUCED to Europe in the 17th century, Canada geese seem to favour semi-urban or even man-made habitats and most birds are residents. Unlike their wild North American cousins, they are generally tolerant of human observers and flock behaviour can often be studied at close quarters. It soon becomes apparent that winter flocks in particular have an organised hierarchy. Within the flock, large family groups dominate smaller ones and show considerable aggression towards one another; not surprisingly, single birds come right at the bottom of the pecking order.

Voice: Loud, resonant honking calls, usually two notes 'gor-rronk'; also a variety of other trumpeting notes
Length: 90–100cm
Wingspan: 150–180cm

Weight: 4–5kg
Habitat: Ornamental lakes, flooded gravel pits and nearby meadows
Nest: Pile of leaves and vegetation, usually near water
Eggs: 5–6; cream or white
Food: Roots, stems, leaves, etc of aquatic and waterside plants

Europe's largest goose. Head and neck black, except for contrasting white patch on face. Plumage on back and underparts brown, except for white on undertail and black flight feathers; upperparts can look rather barred. Yellow-buff goslings follow parents. Juvenile birds duller than adults but soon indistinguishable.

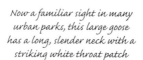

Now a familiar sight in many urban parks, this large goose has a long, slender neck with a striking white throat patch

Barnacle Goose

Branta leucopsis

IN EUROPE, the attractive barnacle goose is seen as a winter visitor, arriving in October and departing in March. Studies have shown that distinct populations are represented within the breeding range, with little mixing or overlap between them. The sight of feeding flocks of these strikingly marked birds is memorable enough, but their flights at dawn and dusk are even more remarkable.

Voice: Short, sharp bark; repeated as yapping chorus by flocks
Length: 60–70cm
Wingspan: 135–145cm
Weight: 1.5–2kg
Habitat: Breeds on tundra; overwinters on coastal grassland and saltmarshes
Nest: Mound of vegetation on cliff ledge or island
Eggs: 4–5; greyish-white
Food: Plant material, including roots and seeds

The colours of these glossy black and white birds contrast even more in flight

A small, compact goose. Bill and eye black. Adults have white face and black neck. Back barred black and grey; underparts white. Legs and feet black. Juvenile has more blotched face and greyer chest. In flight, looks very black and white; flight feathers black, and shows conspicuous white rump when seen from above.

Barnacle geese are the subjects of much controversy at their winter grounds on Islay, where they prefer the meadow-grasses in fields 'improved' for sheep rearing

Brent Goose

Branta bernicla

The white rear of the brent goose is best seen in flight; the white neck patch is more of a stripe, and far less prominent than that on the Canada goose

VISIT almost any sizeable estuary on Europe's North Sea coast between October and February and you are likely to find large flocks of brent geese. Feeding out on the mudflats, they are unobtrusive, especially on dull days. Contact calls give their presence away, however, and they frequently take to the air when disturbed or in search of alternative feeding grounds. In late winter, when food supplies on the estuaries may be exhausted, flocks increasingly visit nearby arable land and grassland prior to the long migration back to their high Arctic breeding grounds.

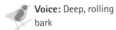 **Voice:** Deep, rolling bark
Length: 55–60cm
Wingspan: 110–120cm
Weight: 1.5–2kg
Habitat: Breeds on tundra; in winter, on saltmarsh and coastal grassland
Nest: Mound of vegetation on island or hummock in water
Eggs: 3–5; off-white
Food: Plant material, particularly eelgrass in winter

A small, dark goose. Adult has all-black head and neck except for white neck patch. Back and wings dark grey-brown except for black flight feathers. Rear end white, most noticeable in flight, but tail dark. Legs and feet black. Race *bernicla* has dark belly; race *hrota* has pale-grey belly. Juvenile has pale-edged feathers on back and lacks white neck; adult characteristics acquired during winter.

Snow Goose

Anser caerulescens

The distinctive black wingtips of the snow goose are easily noticeable when the bird is in flight

TWO races of snow goose are recognised and distinguished mainly on size. The western race, *A. c. caerulescens*, is smaller than the eastern race, *A. c. atlanticus*; the blue colour phase is only common in *atlanticus* snow geese. Sightings in Europe invariably refer to white-phase birds. The species is recorded almost annually in north-west Europe, especially in Britain and Ireland, with birds usually being found among flocks of other wintering geese, notably white-fronted geese. The birds could, however, be escapes and not truly wild.

The western race of snow goose, seen here in the adult white phase, is smaller than its eastern counterpart

Voice: Loud cackling honks uttered in flight
Length: 70–75cm;
Wingspan: 140–150cm
Weight: 2.5–3.5kg
Habitat: Breeds on tundra; overwinters on wetlands and grasslands
Nest: Does not breed in region
Eggs: Does not breed in region
Food: Seeds and plant roots and shoots

Relatively small but distinctive goose, seen in two colour phases. Sexes similar but male larger than female. Adult white phase is pure white except for black primaries and greyish upperwing primary coverts. Adult blue phase has white head and neck and variable amounts of white on otherwise dark bluish-grey body plumage. Immature white phase has pale greyish-brown upperparts and dirty-grey underparts. Immature blue phase has brownish plumage, paler on underparts. Both colour phase juveniles have greyish legs and bill and black primaries. Immatures of both phases resemble adults by first spring. Beware confusion with escapes from captivity including domestic white goose and Ross's goose; latter superficially similar but appreciably smaller with relatively short, stubby bill.

Egyptian Goose

Alopochen aegyptiacus

IN EUROPE, the Egyptian goose has a long-established feral population in East Anglia, in England; solitary individuals seen elsewhere are assumed to be escapes from captivity. Watch the birds for long enough and you are likely to see evidence of their aggressive behaviour towards one another. This antagonism sometimes extends to other species, so Egyptian geese do not usually mix closely with other wildfowl species. Birds often feed in more lush vegetation than do other ducks and geese, and sometimes only their heads can be seen above the grass. Rather surprisingly, they sometimes perch in trees.

Voice: Mostly silent
Length: 65–73cm
Wingspan: 135–155cm
Weight: 1.5–2kg
Habitat: Seldom far from water, usually in fields and marshes
Nest: Mound of vegetation under bush or in hole
Eggs: 8–9; off-white
Food: Mainly leaves and seeds of grass and cereal crops

Superficially similar to ruddy shelduck but with distinctive markings. Adult has pinkish bill and legs. Head and neck pale except for dark patch through eye and dark collar. Breast and underparts buffish-brown but with dark chestnut patch on belly. Back usually rufous-brown but sometimes greyish-brown. Juvenile is more uniformly buffish-brown, without clear markings on head or belly; legs and bill dull brown. In flight, adults show striking white forewing patches on both upper and underwing surfaces, green speculum and black flight feathers.

THE red-breasted goose is a far from common species, and declining. It often nests in surprisingly accessible sites, which, it might be supposed, would be vulnerable to attack by ground predators. Nests are frequently placed close to peregrines'; the geese presumably acquire protection from the falcon's vigorous defence of its own nest. A decline in peregrine numbers may have something to do with the red-breasted goose's own shrinking population, although persecution and habitat loss must surely be factors too. It occurs as a rare but regular vagrant among flocks of brent and white-fronted geese in northwest Europe.

Voice: High-pitched, disyllabic call
Length: 53–56cm
Wingspan: 115–135cm
Weight: 1–1.5kg
Habitat: Breeds on tundra; in winter, on steppe or sometimes arable land
Nest: Mound of vegetation; usually built near bird of prey nest
Eggs: 4–5; whitish
Food: Plant material

A small but beautifully marked goose. Adult has complicated pattern of red, white and black on head, neck and breast. Back, wings and belly mostly black but shows conspicuous white stripe on flanks. Rear end white except for tail; white is most striking in flight. Juvenile similar to, but duller than, adult.

Red-breasted Goose

Branta ruficollis

The striking looking red-breasted goose is a rare but regular straggler to parts of western Europe; individual birds are invariably found among flocks of brent, barnacle or white-fronted geese

Bar-headed Goose

Anser indicus

The bar-headed goose looks well balanced in flight; it can often be found amongst flocks of other species of wild geese

AS A breeding species, the bar-headed goose is confined to Tibet, Ladakh and southeastern Russia. In autumn, flocks of geese fly south to overwintering grounds in northern India and Pakistan. It is unlikely that truly wild bar-headed geese ever reach Europe, but they are not infrequently seen as escapes in the wild, often among flocks of wild geese (usually Canada geese or grey geese) or ducks. Bar-headed geese also occur in feral breeding populations in parts of Scandinavia.

This quite large and weighty bird takes its name from the distinctive dark bars on its crown, a feature lacking on juvenile birds

Voice: Honking calls uttered in flight
Length: 70–80cm;
Wingspan: 140–150cm
Weight: 3–4kg
Habitat: Grassland and wetlands
Nest: Mound of vegetation
Eggs: 4–5; whitish
Food: Seeds, plant roots and shoots

Distinctively marked goose. Sexes similar. Adult has mainly pale grey-brown plumage on body. Head white except for two dark, transverse bars on crown. Neck dark brown with bold white stripe down side. Bill and legs orange-yellow. Juvenile similar to adult but lacks bars on head, crown being greyish-brown not white. Plumage acquires adult characters by first winter.

Comparing Grey Geese

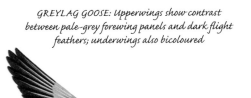

BEAN GOOSE: Similar to pink-footed but longer-necked with more uniformly dark wings; white tail band narrower than on pink-footed

SEEN at a distance grey geese can be a challenge to identify. Close attention should be paid to the overall colour of the birds in question, markings on the head, and leg and bill colour. In flight, the degree of contrast between the dark flight feathers and the rest of the wing is crucial. The best way to learn grey goose identification is to observe feeding flocks of known species and then take careful note when they take to the wing.

GREYLAG GOOSE: Upperwings show contrast between pale-grey forewing panels and dark flight feathers; underwings also bicoloured

PINK-FOOTED GOOSE: Dark head and neck contrast with pale-grey back and mostly pale-grey upperwings; seen from below; head, neck and underwings appear uniformly dark; rump darker than greylag's

LESSER WHITE-FRONTED GOOSE: Superficially very similar to white-fronted, but slightly smaller

WHITE-FRONTED GOOSE: Flight feathers darker than rest of upperwing when viewed from above but contrast never as striking as in greylag and pink-footed; adult has black belly patches

BEAN GOOSE: Larger and proportionately longer-necked than pink-footed; contrast between head and neck and rest of body never so noticeable as in pink-footed

GREYLAG GOOSE: Bulky; appears uniformly grey-brown but head and neck slightly paler than rest of body; legs pink and bill pinkish-orange

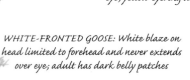

LESSER WHITE-FRONTED GOOSE: Smaller than white-fronted, with more dainty bill and white on forehead extending back over eye; yellow eyering diagnostic at close range

WHITE-FRONTED GOOSE: White blaze on head limited to forehead and never extends over eye; adult has dark belly patches

PINK-FOOTED GOOSE: Striking contrast between brown head and neck and greyish back; bill appears dark at a distance but shows small, variable amount of pink

Comparing Ducks in Flight

D UCKS seen at a distance and in flight can often be frustratingly difficult to identify. Observers should concentrate on the overall body proportions, the relative size and the presence of any distinctive colours or patterns on the body and, more particularly, on the wing speculum. Female ducks are generally more of a challenge to identify than males, but fortunately a clue to their identity can often be gained from their association with males of their kind.

WIGEON: Compact and rather dumpy. Male shows conspicuous white patch on leading edge of inner upperwing and white belly; stern looks strikingly black and white. Female lacks conspicuous markings on wings but shows pale belly. Outside breeding season invariably seen in single-species flocks

MALLARD: Both sexes show bright, iridescent blue speculum on innerwing, bordered on leading and trailing edges by narrow white border; underwings appear uniformly whitish. Body of female is uniformly brown and streaked, while that of male shows clear colour demarcations between head, neck and body

GADWALL: Body plumage of male appears uniformly grey except for black stern and bill; wings show diagnostic white speculum, defined and bordered by black. Female similar to female mallard but has pale belly and suggestion of white on speculum

PINTAIL: Male's elongated shape is diagnostic; equally striking are black and yellow stern and dark head, contrasting with white sides to neck and white belly. Female also looks elongated but appears buffish-brown. Both sexes have indistinct speculum bordered by prominent white bands; underwings variably mottled with brown

SHOVELER: Male's green, white, orange and black body plumage is striking, as is proportionately large bill; upper surface of innerwing shows blue leading edge separated from green speculum by white band. Female has front-heavy proportions of male but uniformly mottled brown plumage; underwing appears whitish

TEAL: Tiny duck, which, when alarmed, rises almost vertically from water. Head of male can look dark when seen against sky; it contrasts with paler, grey body plumage. Female appears uniformly grey-brown in flight. Both sexes show pale underwing and green speculum bordered by white on leading and trailing edges

GARGANEY: Poor flight views can lead to confusion with teal but male's striking head pattern is diagnostic. Pattern on male's upperwing similar to that of male shoveler with pale-blue leading edge separated from green speculum by white band. Female's wing pattern similar to male's but colours less intense; body plumage brown but paler on belly

POCHARD: Appears bulky and thick-set. Male distinctive with grey wings and belly, black stern and neck and reddish head. Female's pattern less contrasting than male's but head and neck always dark and clearly demarcated from paler belly and wings

TUFTED DUCK: Male in particular looks strikingly black and white, white appearing on belly and on extended wingbar. Female similar to male but contrast between dark and light elements of plumage less sharp

Shelduck

Tadorna tadorna

The bright colours of this striking species can be seen to great effect in flight

THROUGHOUT much of its European range, the shelduck is an essentially coastal bird. It breeds along much of the north-west European coast, from northern France to Norway, and is common around Britain and Ireland. Visiting the coast in spring, it always seems slightly odd to see a shelduck emerge from an abandoned rabbit burrow: where rabbits are common, this is a favourite nesting site. Nesting birds will aggressively drive off others of their own species and will even attack young from different parents. After breeding has finished, shelduck often congregate in favoured, traditional sites to moult all their flight feathers.

A hole in a tree is a convenient nesting site for the shelduck

Voice: Male whistles; female utters deep, quick quacks
Length: 60–70cm
Wingspan: 110–130cm
Weight: 1–1.3kg
Habitat: Mostly coastal on sandy and muddy shores; also inland on flooded gravel pits and marshes
Nest: In burrow or hole in tree
Eggs: 8–10; white
Food: Mainly molluscs or crustaceans sieved from mud

Adult has bright red bill and legs. Head and upper neck dark green; can look all dark in some lights. Rest of plumage comprises patches of white and black with conspicuous orange-chestnut breast band. Male has red knob at base of bill, while female shows pale feathering at bill base instead; sexes similar in other plumage respects. Juvenile is mottled and marbled brown and white; shows dull pink legs and bill. In flight, adult looks conspicuously black and white.

Although the shelduck can be aggressive when nesting, the adult bird will show care and devotion to its own ducklings, and long lines of black and white youngsters can be seen following the female across shallow estuaries

A large and distinctively marked bird, the smaller female lacks the bill knob of the male

Ruddy Shelduck

Tadorna ferruginea

LIKE its cousin, the shelduck, the ruddy shelduck is a hole-nesting species. Underground burrows are favoured, although birds are not averse to using holes in trees or unexpected locations such as derelict buildings. The young ducklings, which leave the burrow soon after hatching, can feed on their own almost immediately, but are guided and protected by both parents until able to fend for themselves. Family groups are seldom found far from water, to which they retreat if danger threatens.

Voice: Noisy; flight call 'ang' or rolling 'aarl'
Length: 61–67cm
Wingspan: 120–145cm
Weight: 1.1–1.5kg
Habitat: Variety of wetland habitats including river deltas
Nest: In burrows or holes in trees
Eggs: 8–9; white
Food: Plant material and small invertebrates

An attractive and distinctive duck. Sexes similar. Adult has dark bill, eyes and legs. Head and upper neck buffish with clear demarcation from orange-brown body. In breeding season, only the male has black collar separating buff and orange plumage; sexes similar in other plumage respects. At rest, black wingtips can be seen. In flight, wings are strikingly black and white, the black being confined to the flight feathers. Juvenile similar to adult but duller.

Mallard

Anas platyrhynchos

The mallard's resident and winter ranges include almost the whole of western Europe, except for the higher mountains; the breeding population is difficult to assess, but an estimated 1.5 million birds overwinter in northwest Europe, 750,000 in Britain alone

Adult male

Adult female

The mallard is probably one of the most familiar wildfowl species in western Europe, often seen being fed by humans in urban parks and on ponds; ducklings are capable swimmers almost immediately after hatching

The eclipse plumage of the male, although similar to the female, shows a more reddish breast

Male and female mallards are easily distinguished, but the bright orange legs are common to both sexes

M ALLARDS can be found in almost any freshwater habitat and are occasionally seen around the coast as well. On urban lakes and at beauty spots where they are fed, mallards seem to have lost most of their connections with the wild. They are often tame and respond to human visitors not by fleeing but by pestering them for scraps of bread. Under more natural conditions, mallards can be seen feeding by dabbling in the shallows or up-ending to feed on the bottom mud. The small, fluffy ducklings swim almost from the moment they hatch.

Voice: Female gives familiar quack; male a weak nasal note
Length: 50–65cm
Wingspan: 80–100cm
Weight: 950–1,300g
Habitat: Almost anywhere with water
Nest: Usually a depression on the ground
Eggs: 9–13; bluish-green
Food: Omnivorous; an opportunistic feeder

brown plumage; shows black stern and white tail. Female has orange-yellow bill and rather uniform brown plumage. Eclipse male similar to female but more reddish on breast. In flight both sexes show white-bordered blue speculum.

Male has yellow bill, green head showing sheen in good light, chestnut breast and otherwise mostly grey-

Teal

Anas crecca

The teal breeds throughout much of northern Europe, and also occurs in North America as a separate subspecies

Female

Male

The teal's winter range extends south of its breeding range and includes most of western and southern Europe; some populations in northwestern Europe are year-round residents

DESPITE being widely hunted in much of its range, the teal is still one of Europe's commonest ducks. Except in areas where they are protected from hunting pressures, teal are wary of man and quick to take to the air, rising almost vertically from the water when alarmed. They fly off rapidly with whirring wingbeats and swerving flight patterns, flocks sometimes having a wader-like jizz. When undisturbed, the birds feed in very shallow water, thrusting their bills ahead of them into the soft mud as they walk.

Voice: Distinctive, high-pitched, chirping 'krick'
Length: 34–38cm
Wingspan: 58–65cm
Weight: 240–360g
Habitat: Shallow fresh water when nesting; in winter, on flood meadows or saltmarshes
Nest: On ground, in cover
Eggs: 8–11; off-white
Food: Seeds, invertebrates

The region's smallest duck. Male has attractive orange-brown head with large green patch from eye to nape, bordered with creamy-yellow stripe. Back and flanks show grey vermiculation and underparts white. Black-bordered, creamy-yellow patches on sides of stern. Female and juvenile have grey-brown plumage; best identified by size and association with male. In flight, all birds show green speculum and white underwing.

Marbled Duck

Marmaronetta angustirostris

Although marbled ducks are migratory in parts of their range, their movements in Europe are unpredictable and perhaps have more to do with changes in water level in favoured habitats than with seasons alone

WITH a decreasing range and population, the marbled duck is now a rare bird in Europe, holding out only in southern Spain, where fewer than 100 pairs breed each year. Marbled ducks are difficult birds to see, since they favour the cover of dense emergent vegetation and are also rather shy and retiring. Perhaps the best chances of getting a glimpse of the species can be had by visiting the Coto Doñana or Ebro Delta in Spain. Although marbled ducks will take to the wing, they seldom fly far and soon drop back into cover. They occasionally venture across open water but spend lengthy periods on shady waterside perches.

Voice: Mostly silent
Length: 40–42cm
Wingspan: 63–67cm
Weight: 400–550g
Habitat: Shallow, well-vegetated pools and lakes; freshwater and saline
Nest: Shallow depression in dense cover
Eggs: 7–14; off-white
Food: Plant material and some invertebrates

Despite subdued colouring, an attractive duck. Sexes similar. Plumage ground colour is grey-brown but covered with pale buff spots; these are particularly large and striking on breast, belly and back. Bill dark and shows dark smudge through eye. In flight has rather uniform brown wings.

Wigeon

Anas penelope

Males in particular are well marked in flight

Female

DURING the breeding season, wigeon are retiring and favour rather inaccessible wetlands; consequently, the species is difficult to see well at this time of year. From late August until April, however, flocks of wigeon move south to spend the winter on coastal marshes and estuary saltmarshes, where they are much more visible. At low tide, the birds waddle across the oozing mud in a rather ungainly manner, feeding on eelgrass and algae. As the tide advances, they up-end in the shallows to feed.

Male

Voice: Male utters whistling 'whee-OO'; female gives grating purr
Length: 45–51 cm
Wingspan: 75–85cm
Weight: 600–900g
Habitat: Breeds on northern lakes and wetlands; in winter, on saltmarshes and coastal grassland
Nest: On ground in cover
Eggs: 6–12; pale buff
Food: Plant material, mainly eelgrass and algae

An attractive dabbling duck. Male can look drab in dull light. In good light, reveals orange head with yellow forecrown. Breast pinkish, and back and flanks covered with soft, grey vermiculation. Underparts white and stern black. In water, appears to have black and white rear end. Female has mainly brown plumage with white belly and dark feathering around eye. In flight male shows conspicuous white patch on upper surface of innerwing.

The wigeon is one of the most attractive European ducks, the plumage of the male being subtle rather than gaudy

Garganey

Anas querquedula

When alarmed, garganey rise steeply from the water; their flight is direct and fast, without the swerves and twists that characterise teal flight

THE garganey is unique among European ducks, being a summer visitor to the region; most breeding garganey from Europe overwinter in tropical Africa. The first migrants start to appear on wetlands in southern Europe in February and March, continuing northwards after feeding for a few days. They can be unobtrusive, favouring the cover of vegetation to open water. Occasionally, however, they are seen moving slowly through the shallows, using their bills to pick up aquatic insect larvae or tear off plant buds, shoots or roots.

Voice: Male utters characteristic mechanical-sounding rattle; female gives quiet quack
Length: 37–41cm
Wingspan: 60–65cm
Weight: 320–500g
Habitat: Shallow wetlands and flooded meadows
Nest: On ground, in thick tussock
Eggs: 8–9; light brown
Food: Aquatic insects and plants

and neck otherwise reddish-brown. Breast brown, flanks grey and shows long, trailing black, blue-grey and white feathers on back. Female similar to female teal and best distinguished by association with male. In flight, blue forewing and green speculum of both sexes can be seen.

Male is distinctive with broad, white crescent-shaped stripe over eye leading back to nape. Cap dark but head

Female

The arrival of small parties of garganey on marshes in the region is a sure sign that spring is on the way

Male

Gadwall

Anas strepera

Outside the breeding season, from August to April, gadwall are invariably found in flocks and identification of the females is far easier when male and female ducks are seen within the same flock than when females are alone; the species often associates freely with coots

Adult female

Adult male has dark grey bill and head, and buffish-grey neck and back with black stern

AS A breeding bird, the gadwall occurs rather locally in western Europe, with perhaps just a few thousand pairs breeding at latitudes from northern Britain south to southern Spain. A few hundred pairs breed in Iceland, but the species becomes much more common across its central Asian breeding range, and gadwall are also common breeding birds in northwest North America. The breeding population could not possibly account for the species' abundance in Europe during winter – over 10,000 birds in north-west Europe, and perhaps 40,000 throughout mainland Europe and the Mediterranean.

Voice: Male utters nasal 'mair'; female gives quiet quack
Length: 45–55cm
Wingspan: 85–95cm

Weight: 600–900g
Habitat: Breeds on wetlands with open water; in winter, on lakes and marshes
Nest: On ground beside water
Eggs: 8–12; pale pink
Food: Seeds, plants and insects

and brown plumage. Juvenile resembles dull adult female. Both sexes are easily identified when swimming if flash of white speculum is revealed. This latter feature very obvious in flight, when white underwing also noticeable.

At first glance, a rather drab duck. Close views of male in good light reveal grey plumage comprising intricate vermiculation. Female recalls female mallard with yellow bill

Pintail

Anas acuta

Adult female

In flight both sexes look particularly long-bodied

Adult male

Tails are raised upright in display

In winter pintails feed on a tiny mollusc called the laver spire shell, found on mudflats

Eclipse male

IN WESTERN Europe, the pintail is a local and rather scarce breeder. In winter it is a different story, with some 50,000 birds present in northwest Europe, mostly in coastal districts, and 250,000 in the Mediterranean region. Even when seen from a distance, a male pintail is easily identified by its gleaming white neck and breast, and long tail. Often seen in pairs or small groups in winter, pintails are comparatively shy and unobtrusive wild birds, seldom accustomed to the close presence of humans. Although they often feed on coastal wetlands, they are also seen on mudflats in winter.

Voice: Male utters quiet whistle; female gives short quacks
Length: 51–66cm
Wingspan: 80–95cm
Weight: 750–1,000g
Habitat: Open areas with shallow water
Nest: Hollow on ground, usually in the open
Eggs: 7–9; yellowish
Food: Variety of plant and animal material

Male is an elegant duck with chocolate-brown head and white on underparts and on front of neck, forming narrow stripe up side of face. Flanks grey and black with elongated feathers. Stern is buff and black, with long tail often characteristically cocked upwards. Female has dark-grey bill and largely brown plumage with long-bodied appearance. Juvenile resembles dull adult female.

Wood Duck

Aix sponsa

Adult male

Adult female

The female's white chest markings can make her easily confused with the female mandarin

ALTHOUGH widespread and common in North America, with many populations being migratory, the wood duck has not been recorded naturally in Europe, where, however, it frequently escapes from collections. It favours the cover of tree roots and overhanging branches to forage for food and is generally most active at dawn and dusk; the hours of daylight are often spent sitting on branches well above the water.

Voice: Mostly silent
Length: 40–50cm
Wingspan: 68–74cm
Weight: 550–650g
Habitat: Wetlands
Nest: Does not breed naturally in the region
Eggs: Does not breed naturally in the region
Food: Plant material and some invertebrates

Male unmistakable and showy, with red bill and green head showing white stripes. When swimming, deep red breast shows vertical white stripe; flanks buff and back dark. Female superficially similar to female mandarin, with grey-brown plumage and large, white spots on breast and flanks. White 'spectacle' around eye extends down head, to a lesser extent than on female mandarin, and white at base of bill and chin is less extensive.

Mandarin

Aix galericulata

Mandarins are inclined to perch in trees, and nest in large tree-holes – usually positioned where the young ducklings can leap straight from their nest into the water.

THE strange-looking mandarin has its true range in eastern Asia, as its oriental name implies. In Europe, it is a popular bird in captivity and many sightings are in fact escapes. Although disregarded by many serious birdwatchers, the mandarin has established several feral breeding populations in Britain – mainly in southern and central England, but also in southern Scotland. Despite its gaudy appearance, the mandarin can be difficult to locate since pairs or small groups tend to feed among marginal vegetation and under overhanging trees.

Voice: Mostly silent
Length: 41–49cm
Wingspan: 68–75cm
Weight: 450–600g
Habitat: Wooded rivers and lakes
Nest: Hole in tree
Eggs: 9–12; white
Food: Plant material and some invertebrates

Male is extremely distinctive with long mane of dark feathers on cap and nape, broad, pale stripe above eye and radiating orange feathers on neck and breast. Underparts and back dark but flanks orange and shows sail-like feathers at rear end; undertail white. Female mainly grey-brown with white belly and larger white spots on neck and breast. Shows conspicuous white 'spectacle' around eye, and white throat and base to bill.

Adult male

Adult female

Shoveler

Anas clypeata

In flight and on the water the shoveler has a somewhat front-heavy appearance

SHOVELERS are difficult birds to observe during the breeding season, although pairs are sometimes seen performing aerobatic display flights above suitable territories. They are easier to watch at wetland reserves in winter, when small groups often gather to feed in the shallows. Continually on the move, feeding shovelers walk slowly forward, using their bills to sieve food from the mud. Given the small size of the animals and plant debris on which they feed, it is not surprising that an almost constant intake of food is required.

Voice: Quiet 'tuc' uttered by male; female quacks
Length: 44–52cm
Wingspan: 70–85cm
Weight: 400–850g
Habitat: Shallow water
Nest: Depression in ground
Eggs: 9–11; buff
Food: Mostly small invertebrates but some plant matter

An unusual duck, the most distinctive feature of both sexes being the broad, flattened bill. Male has green head with sheen in good light. Bright orange belly provides striking contrast with otherwise white breast and flanks. Back and stern dark and bill black. Female has mottled brown plumage. Bill dark but with lower edges orange. In flight, both sexes show blue forewing separated by white band from green speculum.

Eclipse male

The characteristic shovel-like bill is ideal for scooping up food

Adult female

Adult male

Pochard

Aythya ferina

From September to March perhaps as many as 250,000 pochards are found in northwest Europe, some 80,000 of which occur in Britain alone

Adult female

he wings of both sexes look similar in flight; the male's contrasting dark head and neck and pale belly are distinctive, while the female's belly is much paler than the rest of the underparts

Outside the breeding season, pochards are invariably seen in flocks, some of which can be quite sizeable. Birds of this species mix freely with tufted ducks and spend much of their time diving for food. A large proportion of their diet comprises plant material such as seeds and shoots, which are most readily found in shallow waters; this explains the pochard's fondness for the margins of well-vegetated lakes and flooded gravel pits. As a rule, pochards tend not to become accustomed to people, although birds that are fed on urban lakes may prove to be exceptions.

Voice: Harsh, growling notes
Length: 42–49cm
Wingspan: 72–82cm
Weight: 800–1,200g
Habitat: Well vegetated pools in summer but open water in winter
Nest: On ground near water
Eggs: 8–10; greenish
Food: Water plants, seeds and invertebrates

Male is attractive and distinctive. Bill relatively long and black with broad, grey band across middle. Rounded head is reddish-orange and neck and breast are black. Underparts and back grey with intricate vermiculations. Stern black. Female has mottled brown and grey-brown plumage, mostly grey on back. Bill pattern and head shape as male. Usually shows pale 'spectacle' around eye. In flight, wings of both sexes appear rather uniform; belly of female looks pale.

Adult male

Red-crested Pochard

Netta rufina

The pale underwing and broad white stripes on the upperwing are pronounced in flight

Adult male pochard (front) with adult male red-crested pochard

As a European breeding bird, the red-crested pochard has a very local and patchy distribution, centred mainly on eastern and southeastern Europe and the Iberian peninsula

Adult male

Irrespective of their origins, red-crested pochards are exciting birds to find anywhere in Europe. It often comes as a surprise to birdwatchers new to the species that this is a diving duck, an activity which it performs with great ease. Red-crested pochards also feed in the shallows, however, and frequently up-end to feed in the manner of a pintail or mallard. In most parts of its natural range, the species is seen in pairs or small flocks, and is wary of man. An isolated, extralimital bird that is tolerant of people is likely to be an escape.

Adult female

Voice: Mostly silent
Length: 53–57cm
Wingspan: 85–88cm
Weight: 900–1,200g
Habitat: Fresh water with extensive cover; in winter, on lakes and flooded gravel pits
Nest: In dense cover or waterside vegetation
Eggs: 8–10; pale green
Food: Mostly plant material

has pink-tipped dark bill. Cap and nape dark brown but cheeks and throat conspicuously pale. Plumage otherwise brown. Eclipse male resembles female but retains red bill. In flight, both sexes show pale underwing and broad, white stripes on upperwing.

Male is attractive and distinctive. Bill bright red. Head orange-brown and neck and body feathers mostly black except for grey-brown back and white flanks. Female

Scaup

Aythya marila

In flight the scaup, with its white wingbars, looks very similar to the tufted duck

Adult female

T HE scaup's breeding range in Europe includes northern Scandinavia and its Baltic coasts. Although harsh winter weather may force small parties of scaup to visit coastal gravel pits and lagoons, they are primarily sea ducks that are quite at home in shallow, fairly sheltered waters. Here, they spend much of the day diving for molluscs, with birds bobbing to the surface for a few seconds before embarking on another dive. Because they are relatively shallow divers, however, their feeding patterns are influenced by the tide and flocks may also spend extended periods on the surface.

Adult male

Voice: Harsh, grating 'karr-karr' while flying
Length: 42–51cm
Wingspan: 72–83cm
Weight: 900–1,200g
Habitat: Breeds on coastal tundra; in winter in shallow, coastal waters
Nest: Close to tundra pools
Eggs: 8–11; pale grey
Food: Mainly molluscs

Male is superficially similar to male tufted duck. Can look black, grey and white

at a distance, but rounded head has green gloss in good light. Bill grey with black nail at tip and yellow iris. Neck, breast and stern black, belly and flanks white and back soft grey with fine vermiculations. Female has mainly brown plumage but with yellow iris and conspicuous white patches at base of bill and on forehead and cheek. In flight, both sexes show white wingbars.

Eclipse male

In winter scaup are known to occur locally in parts of the eastern Mediterranean, the Black Sea and on large, ice-free inland lakes in central Europe

Tufted Duck

Aythya fuligula

F ROM September to March, some 500,000 tufted ducks move into northwest Europe, mostly from their main breeding range in northern Europe, boosting the numbers of resident birds. Watch a winter flock of tufted ducks for any length of time and you will soon discover how difficult it is to estimate numbers. Each bird dives frequently and often for considerable lengths of time, also covering a considerable distance while swimming underwater. In many parts of their range, tufted ducks have benefited from the increase in man-made water bodies such as reservoirs and flooded gravel pits.

Voice: Various harsh, growling notes
Length: 40–47cm
Wingspan: 68–73cm
Weight: 600–1,000g
Habitat: Open water, including rivers
Nest: On ground near water but well hidden
Eggs: 8–11; greenish-grey
Food: Mainly molluscs and aquatic insects but some plant material

Male is very distinctive, looking black and white at a distance. In good light, dark feathering has sheen. Bill is

grey with white band towards end, and has black tip. Iris yellow and head bears crest feathers which can be raised. Female has mostly brown plumage, slightly paler on belly and flanks. Bill pattern similar to that of male and iris yellow. Head bears short tuft of feathers, giving it a rather square outline. Some females have white patch at base of bill; this never as extensive as on female scaup. Eclipse male similar to female. In flight, both sexes show white wingbar.

The tufted duck's winter range extends to southern Europe wherever suitable habitats can be found

Adult female

Adult male

Eclipse male

The increase in suitable habitats for the tufted duck explains its success; its winters are spent in large flocks on open water

Ferruginous Duck

Aythya nyroca

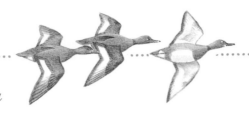

In flight the ferruginous duck looks slim and sports a gleaming white wingbar

Ferruginous with tufted ducks

B OTH during the breeding season and in winter, ferruginous ducks usually prove more difficult to find than most other diving ducks. The main reason for this elusiveness is their liking for the cover of marginal vegetation, particularly overhanging trees and shrubs, with which they blend in well. As a consequence, they are often found on surprisingly small bodies of water, much smaller than those favoured by their relatives.

Adult female

Adult male

As with many other extralimital records of wildfowl, there is a possibility of 'escaped' birds being recorded

Voice: Female utters high-pitched, repeated 'karri'
Length: 38–42cm
Wingspan: 63–67cm
Weight: 500–650g
Habitat: Shallow, well-vegetated lakes and pools
Nest: On ground near water
Eggs: 8–10; pale buff
Food: Mainly plant material but some invertebrates

Male has rather uniform chocolate-brown plumage with dark back and very conspicuous white stern. Bill grey with dark tip; eye has white iris. Female similar to male but duller and with brown iris. Juvenile similar to female but lacks white stern. In flight, looks slimmer than tufted duck and shows striking white wingbar; underwings pale.

Ruddy Duck

Oxyura jamaicensis

The presence of foaming water indicates the male's chest-beating display

Adult female

The male ruddy duck can be distinguished by its bright-blue bill

I N POOR light and at a distance, a feeding ruddy duck might be mistaken for a little grebe: it also tends to dive frequently and bob up to the surface a few seconds later. In good light, however, ruddy ducks of both sexes are distinctive. In the spring, males display by rattling their bills and chest-beating, the result being a froth of bubbles surrounding their chests at water level. During the breeding season, ruddy ducks are rather retiring; they are easier to see in winter, when small flocks sometimes gather in more open areas of water.

This species appeared on the European birdwatching scene in the late 1950s when a small number of unpinioned birds escaped from the Wildfowl and Wetland Trust reserve at Slimbridge

Voice: Mostly silent
Length: 35–43cm
Wingspan: 53–62cm
Weight: 500–700g
Habitat: Well vegetated ponds, lakes and reservoirs
Nest: Well hidden near water
Eggs: 6–10; whitish
Food: Mainly aquatic insect larvae; also seeds

A so-called 'stifftail' duck which often lives up to its name by raising its relatively long tail in the air. Male has mainly orange-brown plumage but with black cap, white face and bright-blue bill; stern white. Female has mainly grey-brown plumage but similar, distinctive outline. Often shows pale cheeks broken by dark line from base of bill. Seldom seen in flight.

White-headed Duck

Oxyura leucocephala

T HE white-headed duck is one of Europe's rarest waterbirds, having its last stronghold in the south of Spain; even here, not many more than ten pairs are thought to breed. The white-headed duck possesses one of the strangest bills of any duck and often swims with its bristly tail cocked in the air. The bird is, however, an excellent swimmer and diver, covering surprisingly long distances underwater and staying submerged for half a minute or more in its quest for water plants.

Voice: Mostly silent
Length: 43–48cm
Wingspan: 62–70cm
Weight: 550–800g
Habitat: Shallow, well vegetated lakes and pools; both freshwater and brackish
Nest: Woven platform of reeds
Eggs: 5–10; whitish
Food: Plant material and small aquatic animals

A 'stifftail' duck, superficially similar to, but larger than, ruddy duck. Male is distinctive with white head, black cap and eye and disproportionately large blue bill with strangely swollen base. Body plumage mainly brown. Female has brown body plumage and bill similar in shape to male's but dark grey in colour. Head shows dark brown cap down to level of eye and white face with dark line running from base of bill.

Vagrant Ducks from North America

FEMALE: Mainly brown plumage, paler and mottled on face; 'spectacle' shows in good light

MALE: Blackish head, neck, breast and back; crown peaked but not tufted; greyish flanks separated from black breast by white vertical stripe; distinctive bill pattern

RING-NECKED
DUCK
AYTHYA COLLARIS

LESSER SCAUP ('AYTHYA AFFINIS): Buoyant diving duck; very similar to scaup but smaller with smaller bill with only small black tip; has peaked, not rounded, head. Female and juvenile essentially brown

Male

SURF SCOTER (MELANITTA PERSPICILLATA): All birds show proportionately large, flat-topped head and large bill that is continuation of forehead. Male all black except for white patches on nape and foreneck and diagnostic bill pattern. Female and juvenile uniform brown except for pale patches on head

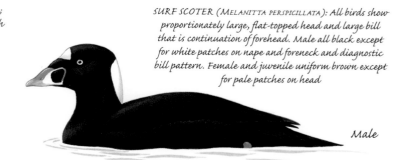

Male

AMERICAN WIGEON (ANAS AMERICANA): Superficially similar in all plumages to corresponding plumages of wigeon. Adult male has yellow crown, green mask, pinkish-grey mantle and pinkish-buff underparts. Female and juvenile mainly reddish-brown with mottled grey head

Male

BLUE-WINGED TEAL (ANAS DISCORS): Similar to garganey. Male has blue-grey head and conspicuous white crescent in front of eye; plumage mottled brown with dark spots. Female, eclipse male and juvenile mottled grey-brown; recall female teal but larger with longer bill and white patch at base of bill

Male

BLACK DUCK (ANAS RUBRIPES): Large and robust dabbling duck, superficially similar to female mallard. Male has chocolate-brown body with paler feather edges, and pale grey-brown head. Eclipse male similar but with olive bill. Female and juvenile similar with olive bill and brown legs

Male

GREEN-WINGED TEAL (ANAS CRECCA CAROLINENSIS): Tiny dabbling duck. Male has chestnut head with glossy green patch, pinkish-buff breast, mostly white underparts, grey-brown upperparts and grey flanks. Female and juvenile indistinguishable from female teal

Male

47

Eider

Somateria mollissima

The female has a plain, barred appearance; 'eiderdown' comes from her breast, with the best-quality down being produced a few days before the eggs hatch

Adult male is easily identified, being only duck with white breast and back and black underparts and stern

EIDERS are engaging birds to watch during the breeding season. Early on, the males perform crooning and cooing calls, throwing their heads and necks back in the process. Having mated, the females move ashore to nest on undisturbed beaches and grassland; their plumage affords them amazing camouflage while sitting on the eggs. When the young hatch, they are immediately led by the mother to the sea, where they often join with ducklings from other broods to form large 'crèches'. These are overseen by numerous 'aunties', who pay very close attention to their charges. Eiders feed on bottom-dwelling marine creatures and dive to reach them.

A distinctive coastal duck with dumpy body and wedge-shaped bill following line of forehead. Mature male is unmistakable, with black and white markings on body; also shows lime-green markings on head and pink flush to breast. Full plumage not acquired until fourth year. Female has mottled brown plumage, looking rather barred on flanks. In flight, both sexes look heavy and ponderous with slightly drooping neck. Flies low over the water in lines.

Voice: Male utters humorous 'ah-whooo' during breeding season; otherwise silent
Length: 50–71cm
Wingspan: 80–105cm
Weight: 1.5–2.5kg
Habitat: Coastal waters, usually close to shore
Nest: On ground, often exposed; lined with down
Eggs: 4–6; greenish-grey
Food: Mainly molluscs, especially mussels

Juvenile

Immature male, first autumn

Immature male, first winter

adult male, eclipse

Adult male, breeding

Despite its heavy, dumpy appearance, the eider is adept at walking on land

Adult male

THE spectacled eider seldom ventures south of the Arctic Circle, its range extending mainly across eastern Siberia and Alaska. Nevertheless, the species has been recorded as an extremely rare vagrant to northern Scandinavia; birds spotted further south in Europe are likely to be escapes. Even at a distance, the extent of black on the underparts and the pale-looking head of the male can be used to distinguish the species from male common eider. Distant views of female birds require more care although the contrast between the pale eye patch and the dark lores is distinctive.

Voice: Generally silent
Length: 54–56cm
Wingspan: 85–90cm
Weight: 1.5–1.7kg
Habitat: Breeds on tundra; otherwise in Arctic seas
Nest: Does not breed in region
Eggs: Does not breed in region
Food: Freshwater and marine invertebrates

Adult male has black breast and underparts. Upperparts mainly white except for dark rump; flight feathers black. Head shows black 'spectacle' line around eye bordered in front and behind by dull-green patches of feathers. Bill orange-pink. Adult female has essentially brown plumage with darker barring. Head shows conspicuous pale patch around eye, corresponding to 'spectacle' of male; bordered at front by dark feathering on lores. Bill dark grey. Eclipse male and juvenile similar to adult female. Immature male takes three years to acquire full adult plumage.

King Eider

Somateria spectabilis

Female similar to female eider but smaller with proportionately shorter bill

Mature male has two sickle-shaped 'sails' on back

Kᴵɴɢ eiders breed in the high Arctic, but overwinter further south; they are found at this time around the coasts of northern Norway, and a few turn up every winter among eider flocks off the Scottish coast. At the end of the breeding season, king eiders gather in often sizeable flocks, first to move to moulting grounds and then to migrate to their overwintering quarters. These flocks remain together throughout the winter, when the birds feed in sheltered, coastal waters. Although king eiders will feed in the shallows, they are capable of dives of 15m or more, mainly in search of bivalve molluscs on the seabed. They mix freely with eiders.

Voice: Male utters cooing calls during courtship; otherwise mostly silent
Length: 48–63cm
Wingspan: 85–100cm
Weight: 1.4–1.8kg
Habitat: Breeds on Arctic tundra; in winter, on northern coasts
Nest: Open ground, usually beside water
Eggs: 4–5; olive
Food: Mainly molluscs and crustaceans

Mature adult male has red bill expanded at base into basal knob. Head proportionately large with square outline; marked with pale blue-grey and green, the areas of colour outlined in black. Rest of body plumage black and white. Female similar to female eider with mottled and barred brown plumage; pale on cheeks and around eye.

Steller's Eider

Polysticta stelleri

Female has dark brown plumage but bill size and head outline similar to male

Sᴛᴇʟʟᴇʀ's eiders are present off the north Norway coast throughout the year, and small numbers overwinter regularly in the Baltic. Rare vagrants appear further south and west to Scotland. The rather bizarre-looking plumage of the male Steller's eider is put to good use when courting a female. The head and neck are often stretched and thrown back, lifting the breast out of the water. During this process, the eye cannot help but follow the black spot on the side of the breast. Outside the breeding season, the species is extremely sociable, and the coasts of north Norway offer the best opportunities for observation in Europe. The tight flocks feed off rocky shores and the birds often all dive together with ease. The gregarious nature of Steller's eider may explain why vagrant individuals are invariably found among flocks of eiders rather than on their own.

Voice: Mostly silent; non-vocal whistling sound made by wings in flight
Length: 43–47cm
Wingspan: 70–75cm
Weight: 500–800g
Habitat: Breeds on Arctic tundra; in winter, on sheltered coasts
Nest: On ground, close to water
Eggs: 6–8; pale olive
Food: Mainly molluscs and crustaceans

Mature adult male is unmistakable. At closer range, rounded head has green feather patches on forehead and rear of crown; has black under chin and as collar. Belly has pinkish-orange tinge, variable in intensity, and a circular black mark on side of flanks, which is visible at water level when swimming. For description of adult female, see caption.

Adult male's body plumage mainly black and white, especially from a distance

Common Scoter

Melanitta nigra

Female

Male

IN THE winter months, the common scoter becomes widespread in European coastal waters, with an estimated million birds occurring in the region. In areas where they are common in the winter, common scoters form large flocks. They dive well, often in search of molluscs such as mussels and cockles; they also swim buoyantly, sometimes with their tails cocked upwards. They favour inshore waters and tend to avoid particularly rough areas. During the breeding season, common scoters are distinctly wary of man and become very secretive.

Voice: Mostly silent but male utters quiet whistles in breeding season
Length: 44–54cm
Wingspan: 80–90cm
Weight: 700–1,300g
Habitat: Breeds on upland moors and tundra; in winter, around coasts
Nest: On ground, near water
Eggs: 6–8; cream to buff
Food: Mainly aquatic insect larvae in breeding season; in winter, dives for molluscs

A classic sea duck that can look all dark at a distance. Male has black plumage with black and yellow bill. Female has dark-brown plumage but much paler cheeks that show up well even at a distance or in flight. Invariably seen in flocks outside breeding season. Migrating flocks seen flying low over water, sometimes in lines but also in more tightly bunched packs with trailing stragglers.

Velvet Scoter

Melanitta fusca

Immature male (top) lacks white eye patch of adult male (bottom) and has little yellow on bill

Like common scoters, flying birds look bulky; however, the white wing patch is immediately distinctive

SEEN in good light, velvet scoters are stunning birds. Although they do sometimes form small, one-species flocks of 20 or 30 birds, they are also seen during the winter in the company of common scoters. Seen side by side, velvet scoters are appreciably larger, and are perhaps closer in size and bulk to eiders. They swim lower in the water and their greater size means they have more difficulty in taking to the air than their relatives; in flight, they look rather thick-set. Individual birds sometimes turn up inland during the winter months on reservoirs and flooded gravel pits, and they can be surprisingly tame.

Female

Voice: Male utters whistling call in breeding season and female has grating call; silent at other times
Length: 51–58cm
Wingspan: 90–100cm
Weight: 1.2–1.8kg
Habitat: Breeds on coastal moors and tundra; in winter, in coastal waters
Nest: On ground, near water
Eggs: 7–9; buff
Food: Mainly molluscs and crustaceans

Male has all-black plumage but is readily identified, even when among common scoters, by conspicuous white eye and white patch below eye. Bill black and yellow. Female has brown plumage with white patches between eye and base of bill and behind eye. In flight, both sexes show extremely conspicuous white wing patches; these are occasionally visible on swimming birds.

Male

Harlequin Duck

Histrionicus histrionicus

Breeding male

Female

I N EUROPE, just 3,000 pairs of harlequin ducks are found in Iceland, and they do not move far in winter. In summer, they favour white-water areas where rivers crash and tumble over boulders and rocks. Here they plunge fearlessly into the torrent in search of insect larvae and other invertebrates. In the winter, the coastal waters they favour can be no less challenging, although they seldom venture far from land; harlequins will also spend long periods resting on rocks above high tide.

Voice: Occasionally utters high-pitched squeals but otherwise mostly silent
Length: 38–45cm
Wingspan: 63–69cm
Weight: 500–700g
Habitat: In summer, on fast-flowing rivers; in winter, around coasts
Nest: On ground, near water
Eggs: 5–7; off-white
Food: Mainly aquatic insect larvae in summer; in winter, mainly molluscs

Male is attractive and distinctive. Plumage mainly a mixture of blue and deep red with bold white stripes and spots on head and body. Female has more subdued, dark-brown plumage with white patch between base of bill and eye, and white spot behind eye. Eclipse male similar to female. All birds fly low over the water with fast, whirring wingbeats.

Long-tailed Duck

Clangula hyemalis

L ONG-TAILED ducks are invariably seen in flocks outside the breeding season. They often favour the very roughest of waters and easily ride the breakers in windswept bays. They dive with ease and for long periods, members of a flock sometimes diving and surfacing together. Flocks are restless, however, and regularly fly off a few hundred yards or further afield in search of better feeding. Because they are constantly on the move, long-tailed ducks are vulnerable to oil pollution.

Voice: Very vocal, males having musical calls
Length: 40–47cm + male tail length
Wingspan: 73–79cm
Weight: 600–800g
Habitat: Breeds on tundra; overwinters on sea coasts
Nest: On ground, close to water
Eggs: 6–9; greenish-buff
Food: Mainly molluscs and crustaceans

An attractive sea duck with a distinctive outline. Plumage a mixture of black, white and brown but varies throughout year. Male has dark bill with pink band and long central tail feathers, often cocked upwards. In summer, head, neck and breast dark except for white patch around eye. Shows brown back and white underparts. In winter, male has much more white in plumage, face having buff flush and dark cheeks. Female lacks male's long tail and has grey bill. In summer, upperparts mostly brown and underparts white. In winter, body brown but head white with variable dark markings.

Winter female (below) has variable plumage, but dark cheek patches useful identifier

Outside the breeding season long-tailed ducks range widely around coasts in northwestern Europe; winter populations in the southern Baltic are among the most important for this species

Winter male

Summer female

Summer male

Juvenile

First-winter males

Juvenile generally resemble female, but first-winter males have the drake's bicoloured bill and the beginnings of the long tail

Goldeneye

Bucephala clangula

Displaying male

In flight both sexes show white patches on upper surface of innerwing

Note characteristic head shape and relatively small bill of both sexes

Female

Male

IN NORTHWEST Europe the goldeneye is best known as a winter visitor, with more than 200,000 birds visiting the region between October and March. Within their usual overwintering range, goldeneye are usually seen in flocks. They spend much of the time diving; when swimming buoyantly at the surface, the birds look hunch-necked with rounded heads. However, the sight of birds perched in trees or flying into or out of their tree-hole nest sites can be surprising. In many areas, goldeneye readily take to the provision of appropriately placed nest boxes.

Voice: Creaking display call but otherwise silent
Length: 42–50cm
Wingspan: 65–80cm
Weight: 800–1,000g
Habitat: Breeds beside northern, wooded lakes; in winter on lakes and reservoirs, occasionally on coasts
Nest: In tree-hole
Eggs: 8–11; bluish-green
Food: Aquatic molluscs, crustaceans and insect larvae

Superb diving duck with peaked-cap profile to head, readily seen even in silhouette. Male has dark head with greenish sheen, white circular patch at base of bill and yellow eye. Body plumage mostly white except for dark back and stern. Female has reddish-brown head and dark grey bill with pink patch near tip. Body plumage grey-brown except for paler underparts and white neck.

Smew

Mergus albellus

OUTSIDE the breeding season, small parties of smew are generally found on coastal lagoons or reservoirs, although they also occur on large, ice-free lakes from central Europe south to the Balkans. They are hardy birds and it usually takes severe conditions in mainland Europe to force them to move. During the breeding season, smew are more difficult to observe, partly because of their favoured tree-hole nest sites. Old abandoned holes excavated by black woodpeckers are often chosen, and the species will also take to nest boxes.

Most birds seen in western Europe in winter are 'redheads', comprising both young birds and almost identical females; they are often seen with goldeneyes

Female

Male

Voice: Mainly silent
Length: 38–44cm
Wingspan: 55–70cm
Weight: 600–900g
Habitat: In breeding season, favours wooded lakes; in winter, on lakes, reservoirs and sheltered coasts and estuaries
Nest: In tree-holes; nest boxes
Eggs: 7–9; pale buff
Food: Mainly small fish; some insect larvae

Small sawbill duck with narrow, serrated-edged bill. Male is distinctive and attractive with mainly white plumage but with black lines on body, around eye and on back; at close range, fine grey markings visible on flank. Female has grey-brown plumage, reddish-brown cap and white cheeks and chin. Immature drake resembles female. In flight, both sexes show white bars on wings.

Barrow's Goldeneye

Bucephala islandica

Male

Female

THE vast majority of the world's Barrow's goldeneye are found in the Pacific northwest of North America; in Europe, the species is represented by the thousand or so pairs that breed in Iceland and nowhere else. These are considered resident and only move towards the coast when forced to do so by freezing conditions. The males court the females in May with much bobbing of heads, splashing and diving. Individual birds sometimes turn up in northwest Europe, but these may be escapes.

Voice: Grunting calls accompany courting male's display; otherwise silent
Length: 42–52cm
Wingspan: 67–85cm
Weight: 900–1,300g
Habitat: Breeds on Arctic lakes and rivers; in winter, on more coastal Arctic lakes and rivers and sometimes actually in coastal waters
Nest: In rock crevice or tree-hole
Eggs: 8–11; bluish
Food: Aquatic insects, crustaceans and molluscs

Similar to goldeneye but distinguished, even in silhouette, by steep, rounded forehead and relatively short, broad bill. Male has dark head with purple gloss and white crescent shape in front of yellow eye. Underparts mainly white and upperparts and stern dark; back shows small patches of white. Female has dark-brown head with yellow eye. Body plumage mainly grey-brown and underparts paler. In flight, both sexes show less white on innerwing than goldeneye does.

Red-breasted Merganser

Mergus serrator

FROM April to July red-breasted mergansers can be found on suitable water bodies throughout Scandinavia and more locally in northern Britain, Ireland and Iceland. Thereafter the birds move to coastal waters around northwest Europe. Seen at a distance in the winter, a lone red-breasted merganser could be mistaken for a grebe, with its slender neck and ragged head outline. At close range, the bill shape and colour are distinctive. Observers are unlikely, however, to be able to see the serrated edges, which grip slippery fish prey, and after which this species and its near relatives are called 'sawbills'. The fish-eating habits of the red-breasted merganser has caused it to be persecuted in some parts of its breeding range because it is perceived as a threat to commercial fishing.

Male (below left) has dark-green head with untidy tufts, white neck and reddish-brown breast; female (below right) has red bill and reddish head

Voice: Mostly silent
Length: 52–58cm
Wingspan: 70–85cm
Weight: 900–1,200g
Habitat: Breeds on clear, northern lakes and rivers; in winter, mainly in coastal waters
Nest: On ground, well hidden
Eggs: 8–10; buff to olive
Food: Mainly fish

Slim-bodied duck with long, narrow sawbill. Male has red bill, legs and eyes. Underparts grey and finely marked, and.back black and white. Female body plumage mainly grey-brown, although underparts paler. In flight, both sexes show white on innerwing; less extensive on female and divided by black bar.

'Loafing' birds occasionally gather on shingle beds during the winter months

Goosander

Mergus merganser

IN EUROPE goosanders nest mainly in the far north, although isolated populations also breed in Switzerland and Germany; their winter range is rather wider. Goosanders swim buoyantly and winter groups often cruise in unison with great ease and at surprising speed across the water. They dive well and frequently, sometimes returning to the surface to consume their prey if the fish is particularly large. In late winter and early spring, when they have returned to their breeding grounds, male goosanders perform solitary or group displays, their antics including head-stretching and bobbing and water-rushing, where the male shoots rapidly across the surface of the water.

In flight female shows undivided white speculum and male shows entire white innerwing

Eclipse male resembles female

Female

Male

Voice: Ringing calls uttered by displaying male; otherwise silent
Length: 58–66cm
Wingspan: 82–96cm
Weight: 1.1–1.7kg
Habitat: Breeds beside northern lakes and rivers; in winter, favours lakes, reservoirs, flooded gravel pits and sheltered coasts
Nest: In tree-hole or sometimes rock crevice; will take to nest boxes
Eggs: 8–11; whitish
Food: Fish

A large, attractive sawbill duck. At a distance, male can look black and white. At closer range and in good light, head has greenish gloss and white on body plumage suffused with pink. Bill red; lower back and tail grey. Female similar to female red-breasted merganser but has more elegant, reddish-brown head. Throat and neck white; body plumage mainly grey-brown with underparts paler.

Egyptian Vulture

Neophron percnopterus

PRESENT in the region from April to September, Egyptian vultures are associated with warm climates and are perhaps easiest to see in central and southern Spain. They favour eroded sandstone gorges or towering mountain slopes and, from mid-morning onwards, they soar to great heights on the rising thermals. By vulture standards, the Egyptian vulture has a comparatively small, weak bill, which means that it is often obliged to feed on the scraps left over by other scavengers at a carcass; in some parts of its range it scavenges at rubbish dumps.

Egyptian vultures are invariably seen in flight, circling above a mountain peak or riding the updraughts of a high cliff face

Voice: Mostly silent
Length: 60–70cm
Wingspan: 155–180cm
Weight: 1.8–2.2kg
Habitat: Mountainous regions
Nest: Cliff ledge or cave
Eggs: 2; dirty white
Food: Scavenges at carcasses but also takes rubbish

In flight, silhouette recalls a miniature lammergeier with its wedge-shaped tail; wings proportionately broader and shorter than that species'. Sexes similar. Seen from below, adult has black flight feathers that contrast with otherwise rather grubby white plumage; at close range, black-tipped yellow bill, bald yellow face and yellow or pink legs visible. Juvenile similar shape to adult but all dark; full adult plumage acquired gradually over four years or so.

Lammergeier

Gypaetus barbatus

SOMETIMES referred to as the bearded vulture, the lammergeier is Europe's scarcest and most local vulture species. It is found in the western Pyrenees, on Corsica and in northern Greece, with a total population of 50 to 100 pairs. Extremely fortunate observers may see one feeding. Although lammergeiers will readily feed at a fresh carcass if the opportunity arises, they also have an amazing alternative means of getting a meal of bone marrow. Holding a large bone firmly in their bill, they take to the air and rise to a considerable height. When they are above a suitable flat rock the bone is dropped and shatters on impact. The lammergeier then retrieves the pieces and swallows them whole.

One of the most majestic vultures in flight

Eggs: 1–2; warm buff with darker markings
Food: Scavenges bones and flesh from fresh carcasses

A very distinctive bird of prey with very long and comparatively narrow wings and a long, wedge-shaped tail. Seen in good light, adults show orange-buff head and underparts; wings and tail black. At close range, black patch around orange eye can be seen along with black moustache-like feathers. Juvenile has similar flight silhouette to adult but is all dark.

Voice: Mostly silent
Length: 100–115cm
Wingspan: 265–280cm
Weight: 4.5–6.5kg
Habitat: Mountainous regions, often near gorges and ravines
Nest: Cliff ledge or cave

Black Vulture

Aegypius monachus

Even at the great heights favoured by this species, its immense size is still apparent from a distance, especially when it is joined by smaller birds of prey such as booted eagles or is mobbed by ravens; it dwarfs both these species

THE black vulture is Europe's largest bird of prey and also one of its rarest. Although it was probably never numerous, persecution by farmers has reduced its numbers in the region to a few hundred pairs, the majority of these being found in central southern Spain. Given its size, it is not surprising that the black vulture takes precedence over other scavengers at a carcass. With its powerful bill and strong neck muscles, it can tear open the hide of even the largest animal, something which other, smaller vultures are not able to do; in this respect, black vultures do their cousins a favour by initiating the scavenging process.

Voice: Mostly silent
Length: 100–110cm
Wingspan: 250–290cm
Weight: 7–11kg
Habitat: Seen at towering heights over all sorts of broken terrain, especially near mountains
Nest: Twig platform built in tree
Eggs: 1; white with reddish streaks
Food: Carrion

Flight silhouette distinctive with long, broad and parallel-sided wings, which are square-ended but show splayed 'fingers' of primary feathers; soars with wings held flat. Head appears relatively small and tail is usually slightly fanned. Sexes similar. Plumage mostly dark brown but invariably appears all black because of distance at which most birds are seen. Seen at close range, has huge, black-tipped bill and bald head and neck with ruffled collar of feathers. Juvenile difficult to separate from adult in the field.

Griffon Vulture

Gyps fulvus

ALTHOUGH reduced in range and numbers, the griffon vulture is by far the commonest vulture of the region and, in most of its range, is a year-round resident. Given its size and usual indifference to man, it is also the easiest to see, especially when tens or even hundreds rise in spiralling fashion on a single thermal. Griffon vultures are most numerous and widespread in the Iberian peninusla but they also occur in the eastern Mediterranean and a few birds still persist on Sicily. In contrast to their rather grizzly feeding habits, these are majestic birds in flight, able to soar for hours on end with hardly a wingbeat.

When standing, looks hunched up with wings almost touching the ground

Voice: Utters croaking calls near nest or roost; silent in flight
Length: 95–105cm
Wingspan: 260–280cm
Weight: 7–10kg
Habitat: Warm, mountainous regions
Nest: Pile of twigs on inaccessible cliff ledge
Eggs: 1; whitish
Food: Carrion

Large, broad-winged vulture. Sexes similar. Adult has buffish-brown body plumage contrasting with dark flight feathers; contrast visible from above and below in flight and on perched birds. Head and neck bald and whitish but sometimes stained; has collar of ruffled feathers. In flight, looks small-headed and short-tailed. Wings long and broad, narrowing towards tips and showing pale barring against brown underwing coverts; soars with wings held in shallow 'V'. Juvenile generally similar to adult but underwing coverts rather pale with dark barring.

Being dependent on rising thermals, griffon vultures are seldom seen in the air before ten in the morning

Golden Eagle

Aquila chrysaetos

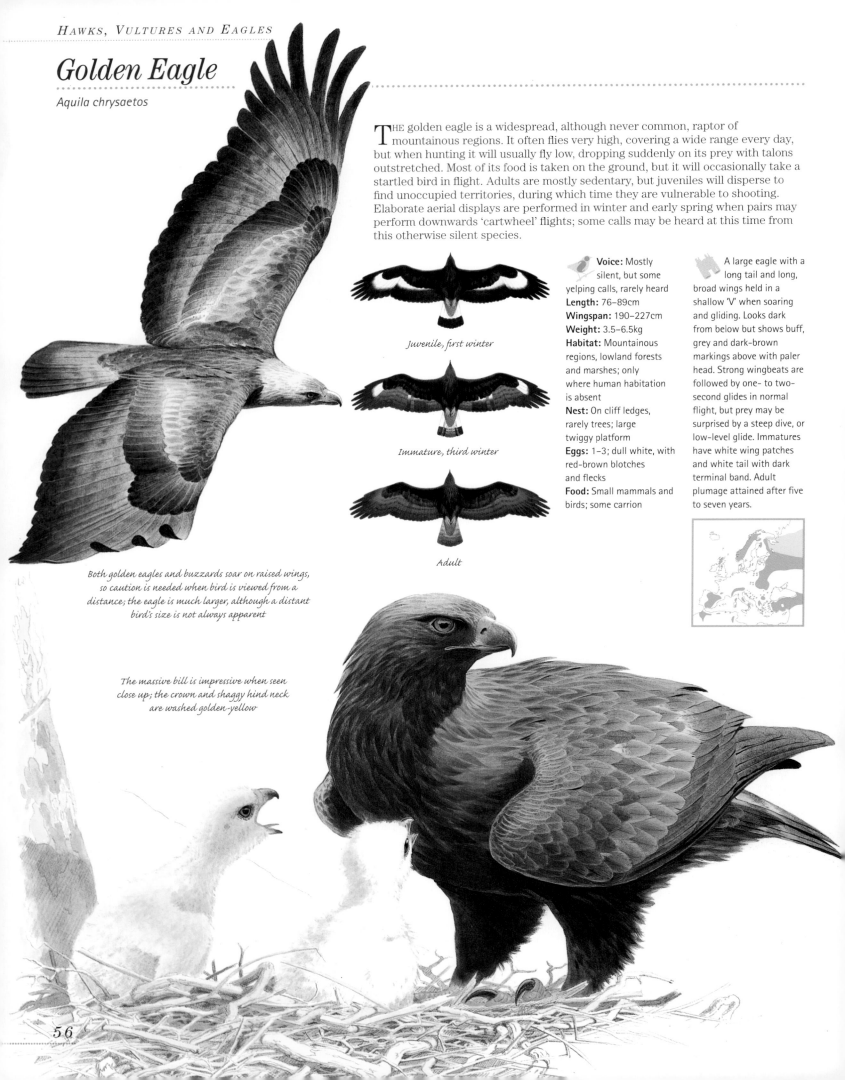

THE golden eagle is a widespread, although never common, raptor of mountainous regions. It often flies very high, covering a wide range every day, but when hunting it will usually fly low, dropping suddenly on its prey with talons outstretched. Most of its food is taken on the ground, but it will occasionally take a startled bird in flight. Adults are mostly sedentary, but juveniles will disperse to find unoccupied territories, during which time they are vulnerable to shooting. Elaborate aerial displays are performed in winter and early spring when pairs may perform downwards 'cartwheel' flights; some calls may be heard at this time from this otherwise silent species.

Juvenile, first winter

Immature, third winter

Adult

Voice: Mostly silent, but some yelping calls, rarely heard
Length: 76–89cm
Wingspan: 190–227cm
Weight: 3.5–6.5kg
Habitat: Mountainous regions, lowland forests and marshes; only where human habitation is absent
Nest: On cliff ledges, rarely trees; large twiggy platform
Eggs: 1–3; dull white, with red-brown blotches and flecks
Food: Small mammals and birds; some carrion

A large eagle with a long tail and long, broad wings held in a shallow 'V' when soaring and gliding. Looks dark from below but shows buff, grey and dark-brown markings above with paler head. Strong wingbeats are followed by one- to two-second glides in normal flight, but prey may be surprised by a steep dive, or low-level glide. Immatures have white wing patches and white tail with dark terminal band. Adult plumage attained after five to seven years.

Both golden eagles and buzzards soar on raised wings, so caution is needed when bird is viewed from a distance; the eagle is much larger, although a distant bird's size is not always apparent

The massive bill is impressive when seen close up; the crown and shaggy hind neck are washed golden-yellow

Greater Spotted Eagle

Aquila clanga

Juvenile heavily spotted

GREATER spotted eagles are still fairly common in parts of their eastern European range. Vast tracts of undisturbed forest are not essential to them, and in fact small copses and scattered woodland will sometimes serve as a breeding site, provided that wetland areas lie close by. The bird's leisurely flight on downward-bowed wings can give the impression of a much larger bird. Although carrion can feature quite heavily in this species' diet, it also catches live prey in active, low-level flight. In favoured hunting areas, small numbers of eagles can sometimes be found perched on nearby posts and trees, waiting for a feeding opportunity to arise.

Adult

Voice: Yapping call heard near nest
Length: 62–75cm
Wingspan: 160–180cm
Weight: 1.6–2.2kg

Habitat: Forest and scattered woodland close to wetland areas
Nest: Stick construction built in tree
Eggs: 1–3; white, sometimes with reddish spotting
Food: Mammals, reptiles and birds but also carrion

Appreciably larger than lesser spotted eagle, but this not always easy to see in distant, solitary birds. Best feature for separation in flight seen from below is greyish flight feathers, which appear paler than rest of feathering on wings and body (converse true in lesser spotted eagle). Seen from above, adult plumage looks all dark; that of juvenile shows heavy white spotting on wing coverts and inner flight feathers with white 'shafts' on all primaries.

Lesser Spotted Eagle

Aquila pomarina

A REQUIREMENT for extensive and undisturbed forested areas for nesting and the juxtaposition of marshes and wet meadows for feeding inevitably limits possible breeding sites for lesser spotted eagles; degradation or destruction of both these habitats may help explain its demise. Visit one of the eastern European countries, however, and your chances of seeing this species are good. Like other similarly sized raptors, lesser spotted eagles soar effortlessly. They are often seen in low-level, rather laboured flight as well and will perch for extended periods on posts adjacent to feeding areas.

Adult

Voice: High-pitched yapping call
Length: 57–65cm
Wingspan: 135–160cm
Weight: 1.3–1.8kg
Habitat: In European breeding range, favours forests adjacent to wetlands
Nest; Stick construction built in tree
Eggs: 1–3; white, spotted with reddish-brown
Food: Mainly small mammals, but also birds and reptiles

Juvenile shows white spotting on inner flight feathers

Comparatively small eagle but with proportionately long, parallel-sided wings, which appear rather square-ended in soaring flight with 'fingers' of primaries clearly visible. Seen from below, can look all dark; in good light, flight feathers always darker than brown body feathers in both adults and juveniles, a good feature for separating from similar greater spotted eagle. Seen from above, adult shows tail and flight feathers darker than body feathers, narrow white band on base of tail and white 'shafts' on inner primaries. Juvenile similar to adult but has numerous white spots on inner flight feathers.

Bonelli's Eagle

Hieraaetus fasciatus

Bonelli's eagles often hunt in pairs along mountainsides and over rough ground, frequently using the same hunting areas every day; prey is usually captured on the ground and consists of medium-sized mammals such as rabbits and birds such as partridges; birds are also sometimes caught in flight

MOST Bonelli's eagles remain near their breeding grounds all year, but outside the breeding season juveniles will migrate south towards the Mediterranean, where they will hunt over coastal marshes and plains. Bonelli's eagles are found across southern Europe and north Africa as far as the Middle East, although they are very widely scattered and nowhere common. The nest is a very large structure, often used year after year, and may be up to 180cm high and 180cm in diameter, composed mainly of large branches up to 3cm thick, with fresh greenery added almost every day. Both sexes help with building or rebuilding the nest, which may take place over three or four months before the first egg is laid.

Voice: Shrill, piping calls
Length: 65–70cm
Wingspan: 150–170cm
Weight: 1.5–2.5kg
Habitat: Mountainous and hilly country in Mediterranean region; sometimes marshes
Nest: In tree or on cliff ledge; large, with many branches and some greenery
Eggs: 2; white, with brown and lilac spots and lines
Food: Small mammals and birds

Adults are distinctive with very pale belly, dark terminal band to long tail, and contrasting dark underwings; lesser underwing coverts are whitish and flight feathers greyish at base giving distinctive pattern, but general effect is of dark wings. A variable pale patch shows on the upper back. Sexes similar. Wingbeats are quick and shallow, with wings held level and slightly forwards when soaring. When gliding, wings are gently arched and show straight rear edge. Juveniles are pale pinkish-brown below and darker on back.

Spanish Imperial Eagle

Aquila adalberti

THE regions around the Coto Doñana in the far south of Spain are one of the Spanish imperial eagle's strongholds, and here the birds spend much of the day sitting around in trees, where they are surprisingly easy to overlook. Spanish imperial eagles soar on rising thermals to great heights but can still follow movements on the ground and descend rapidly on an unsuspecting rabbit. The species is considered by some authorities to be a race of imperial eagle and not a separate species.

Voice: Repeated, harsh barking call
Length: 75–85cm
Wingspan: 180–215cm
Weight: 2.5–3.5kg
Habitat: Open woodland and fields
Nest: Stick platform built in tree
Eggs: 2–3; white with brownish markings
Food: Mainly mammals but some carrion

Seen in flight, wings look relatively long and parallel-sided; tail not normally fanned. Adult can look all dark but in good light shows dark brown plumage and white markings on scapulars and leading edge of innerwing; crown and nape are pale buff. Juvenile has pale-brown plumage except for dark flight feathers and tail; shows heavy white spotting on upper surface of flight feathers and, in good light, teardrop spots on wing coverts.

White-tailed Eagle

Haliaeetus albicilla

A WHITE-TAILED eagle in flight is an unforgettable sight and few people can fail to be impressed by its sheer size. During the winter months, birds seldom rise to great heights, so the chances are good of getting superb views of them in low-level flight. Although white-tailed eagles will take carrion and mammals at any time of the year, during the winter they often specialise in catching ducks and geese, hence their ties with wetland habitats. When hunting, they show surprising speed and agility for such a large bird.

In many parts of their European range white-tailed eagles are year-round residents, but birds from Russia migrate south and west in the autumn

Voice: Yelping call
Length: 70–90cm
Wingspan: 200–240cm
Weight: 4–6kg
Habitat: Associated with sea coasts and extensive wetlands
Nest: Bulky mass of sticks in tree or on cliff
Eggs: 2; white
Food: Carrion, waterbirds, mammals, fish

In flight, has immense wingspan with broad, parallel-sided wings, which are square-ended with primaries resembling splayed 'fingers'. Tail relatively short and broad; white in adult birds but dark in juveniles. When seen perched, yellow legs and bill can be seen in adult; juvenile bill dark but yellow at the base. Adult head looks paler than body.

Imperial Eagle

Aquila heliaca

Immense, relatively long-winged raptor with white scapular patches

THE imperial eagle is a rare bird in Europe. It hunts in open, lightly wooded lowland areas where there are scattered tall trees for nesting. Much time is spent sitting on a low perch, sometimes even on the ground, but feeding forays are made at high altitude, often at great speed. The nest is a large, twiggy structure high in a tall tree, although very rarely it may be on a cliff ledge. This is normally a solitary bird, but very occasionally a few may be found at a good feeding spot. Its lack of fear of humans has led to it being heavily persecuted.

Voice: Deep raven-like 'gahk'
Length: 75–84cm
Wingspan: 180–215cm
Weight: 2.5–4.5kg
Habitat: Mediterranean steppe, mixed lowland habitats with some tall trees
Nest: High in large tree; twigs and branches, lined with green leaves
Eggs: 2–3; dull white, sometimes with darker flecks
Food: Small mammals and birds, waterfowl, some carrion

Adult is a very dark bird showing a creamy-buff nape and greyish tail with a dark terminal band. Wings are long and narrow and held flat when soaring, but may be slightly raised with a flat tip when gliding. Tail appears long and narrow in adults, but juveniles show a more spread tail when soaring. Juvenile brownish-red, fading to paler buff-brown with streaked breast. Juveniles take four to five years to attain adult plumage.

Osprey

Pandion haliaetus

The big stick nest is added to each year; it is usually built at the top of a pine tree

To help them grip fish osprey have specially adapted talons that are long, of equal length and spiny below; large prey are turned to face forwards before the osprey flies off, presumably to assist streamlined passage through the air

The osprey hits the water at high speed when fishing; if the fish is too large the osprey will let it go, but birds have been known to drown as a result of claws catching in bones or scales

AN OSPREY circling over a lake may resemble a large immature gull until it sights prey, when it will hover with deep, powerful wingbeats and dangling legs. It descends from its hunting flight in stages until ready to dive, which it does at high speed, sometimes disappearing below the surface before emerging with its catch. Both sexes share the care of the young, with the male doing most of the fishing while the female broods the chicks. Young birds will linger in the breeding area after the parents have migrated south, but will follow them after a month to the overwintering grounds in tropical Africa. The osprey is found, either as a breeding or overwintering bird, all around the world and is one of the most widespread birds of prey; in Europe it is confined mainly to the north and Scandinavia.

Voice: Shrill piping and yelping calls
Length: 55–69cm
Wingspan: 145–160cm
Weight: 1.1–1.65kg
Habitat: Rivers, lakes, coastal areas
Nest: Large; branches and twigs, moss lined; in tree
Eggs: 2–3; white with red-brown spots and blotches
Food: Fish

the underwing a distinctive pattern. Females and juveniles have a darker breast band on a buff background. The long tail has a broad, dark terminal band and three to four narrower dark bands.

The osprey is a large, long-winged bird of prey, looking very pale below. Dark primaries and carpal patches give

Short-Toed Eagle

Circaetus gallicus

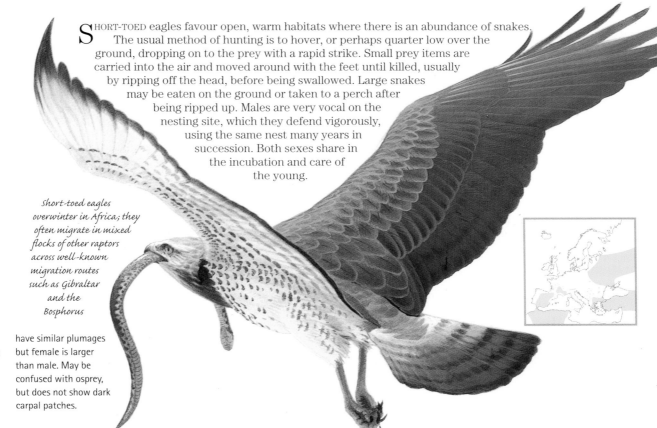

SHORT-TOED eagles favour open, warm habitats where there is an abundance of snakes. The usual method of hunting is to hover, or perhaps quarter low over the ground, dropping on to the prey with a rapid strike. Small prey items are carried into the air and moved around with the feet until killed, usually by ripping off the head, before being swallowed. Large snakes may be eaten on the ground or taken to a perch after being ripped up. Males are very vocal on the nesting site, which they defend vigorously, using the same nest many years in succession. Both sexes share in the incubation and care of the young.

Voice: Fluting calls by male, harsher notes from female
Length: 62–67cm
Wingspan: 170–185cm
Weight: 1.2–2.2kg
Habitat: Dry, open habitats, with some maquis, garigue or scattered trees
Nest: Top of low tree; deep cup of twigs, lined with green leaves
Eggs: 1; white and smooth
Food: Snakes, lizards

A large, pale raptor, usually seen hovering or using updraughts, when underparts look very white. Wings broad and quite long in proportion to body size; tail narrow and square-ended. Darker head gives hooded appearance. Sexes have similar plumages but female is larger than male. May be confused with osprey, but does not show dark carpal patches.

Short-toed eagles overwinter in Africa; they often migrate in mixed flocks of other raptors across well-known migration routes such as Gibraltar and the Bosphorus

Booted Eagle

Hieraaetus pennatus

The booted eagle can hang motionless at great height without hovering, and then dive straight down at breathtaking speed with legs extended forwards

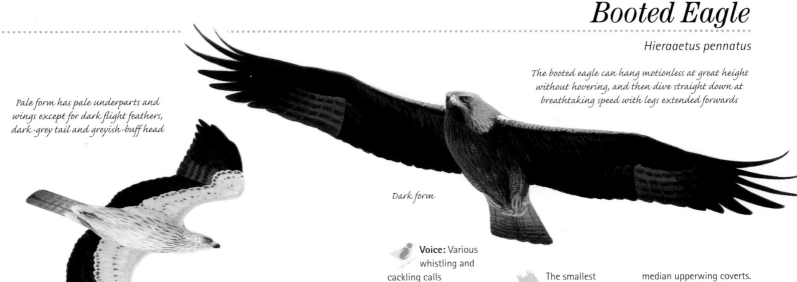

Pale form has pale underparts and wings except for dark flight feathers, dark-grey tail and greyish-buff head

Dark form

THE booted eagle is still relatively common in Spain, but is rarer elsewhere in southern and central Europe. This is one of the most vocal of the eagles, with several wader-like calls uttered near the nest site and during courtship. Booted eagles sometimes hunt in pairs, swooping one after the other on prey, which may be pursued through the branches of trees or captured on the ground. A great variety of small birds, mammals, reptiles and insects are taken, with birds usually being beheaded and plucked before being eaten.

Voice: Various whistling and cackling calls
Length: 45–50cm
Wingspan: 100–130cm
Weight: 500–1,250g
Habitat: Wooded mountain slopes, open hilly country
Nest: In tree, sometimes cliff face; large and twiggy with green leaves
Eggs: 2; dull white, rarely marked
Food: Small mammals, birds, reptiles and insects

The smallest European eagle, occurring in a pale and dark form. Dark form easily confused with black kite and juvenile Bonelli's eagle; plumage varies from red-brown to blackish-brown, with buff tail darkening towards tip. For description of pale form see caption. Both dark and pale forms show a pale 'V' on upperparts formed by median upperwing coverts. Primary feathers in outstretched wings appear as typical eagle 'fingers'.

Buzzard
Buteo buteo

Soaring effortlessly overhead, several individuals may join a single thermal and stay aloft for hours on end

From below buzzards can be highly variable, with colouring ranging from largely dark to largely white

Birds frequently perch in a hunched position on roadside telegraph poles

ALTHOUGH still common in many parts of Europe, buzzard numbers have decreased over the last century. In parts of the northwest of the range, however, there are signs that the species may be expanding its range again into formerly occupied areas. Where it is common, the buzzard often attracts attention to itself with its mewing, cat-like call. Furthermore, unlike many other large birds of prey, buzzards spend quite long periods perched on posts and dead branches in the open, often yielding good views to observers. They will also feed on the ground, searching mainly for earthworms and carrion.

Voice: Mewing 'peeioo'
Length: 50–55cm
Wingspan: 115–130cm
Weight: 700–1,200g
Habitat: Hilly country, open farmland with adjacent woodland
Nest: Stick nest built in tree or on crag
Eggs: 2–3; white or bluish
Food: Earthworms, rabbits, carrion

Medium-sized bird of prey. Sexes similar. Colour extremely variable but almost always some shade of brown. Soars on broad, rounded wings held in a 'V' angle with barred tail fanned out. Upperparts usually dark brown, although flight feathers contrastingly dark in paler birds. Seen from below, wings and tail barred, the trailing edge of wings and terminal edge of tail noticeably dark. Some birds show dark collar and dark carpal patches. At close range, black-tipped yellow bill and yellow legs visible. Almost pure white birds are occasionally seen.

Long-legged Buzzard
Buteo rufinus

THE long-legged buzzard is essentially a bird of North Africa and western central Asia; in Europe it is perhaps most easily seen in Greece and European Turkey between April and August. Compared to the common buzzard, the long-legged buzzard looks large, pale and relatively long-winged. In good light, the rufous coloration is a useful identification feature as is the uniformly pale, unbarred tail. Long-legged buzzards seem more inclined than other buzzard species to spend long periods of time perched on posts and rocks.

Voice: Mewing call, similar to that of buzzard
Length: 50–65cm
Wingspan: 130–150cm
Weight: 800–1,100g
Habitat: Arid mountainous terrain and semi-desert
Nest: Twiggy mound built on cliff ledge or crag
Eggs: 3–4; pale greenish-white with darker blotching
Food: Mainly small mammals and reptiles

Sexes similar. Adult plumage extremely variable but perched birds generally show noticeably pale head and breast; latter separated from pale vent and undertail by broad, rufous band across belly. Seen from below in flight, shows reddish-brown underwing coverts and dark carpal patches; flight feathers white but with conspicuous and contrasting black tips to primaries and black trailing edge to secondaries. From above, reddish-brown mantle and upperwing coverts contrast with dark flight feathers; tail and head look very pale. Juvenile similar to adult but with faint barring on tail and less uniform coloration overall.

Rough-legged Buzzard

Buteo lagopus

THE rough-legged buzzard's low-level flight, conspicuous white-based tail and habit of hovering make it easy to identify even at a distance. Its diet comprises mainly small mammals and it is presumably a dearth of voles and mice in some winters that forces birds to spread more widely in Europe than in good rodent years. In the Arctic, lemmings are major prey items, these creatures having three- or four-year cycles of abundance. In good years large broods of rough-legged buzzards are reared while in bad years breeding success crashes.

Like buzzard soars on raised wings, but is larger, with proportionately longer wings and tail

Voice: Similar mew to buzzard but louder and lower
Length: 50–60cm
Wingspan: 120–150cm
Weight: 700–1,200g
Habitat: Nests on tundra; in winter, on marshes, moors and downs
Nest: Stick platform, on rocky ledge if available
Eggs: 3–4; white, streaked with red
Food: Mainly small mammals; in winter, may take birds and rabbits

Superficially similar to buzzard in silhouette but slightly larger and with proportionately longer wings and tail. Like that species, the rough-legged soars on raised wings, but also regularly hovers. Seen from below, typically shows dark and white pattern: has dark belly patch, dark carpal patches on wings and tail with faint barring towards tip and broad, dark terminal band. Seen from above, conspicuous pale base to tail appears as white rump. Seen perched, dark belly often noticeable and head can look pale, especially in young birds.

White tail with dark terminal band diagnostic

Honey Buzzard

Pernis apivorus

WITHIN their breeding range, honey buzzards are comparatively easy to see in flight, since they frequently soar over the forests and woods favoured as nesting sites with characteristically flat wings. When not in the air, however, they are secretive and seldom seen, even when feeding. In certain European locations (Falsterbo in Sweden and the Bosphorus in Turkey) huge numbers of honey buzzards can be seen at migration times. They also occur as passage migrants outside their normal breeding range, particularly in spring. The species overwinters in sub-Saharan Africa.

Unlike other buzzards, soars on flat or slightly arched wings

Voice: Thin, mournful call, seldom heard
Length: 50–60cm
Wingspan: 135–160cm
Weight: 500–1,000g
Habitat: Breeds in mature woodland
Nest: In tree, often built on an existing nest
Eggs: 2; whitish with red or chocolate markings
Food: Mainly bee and wasp larvae but also other large insects and occasionally small mammals.

Colour rather variable but usually dark brown above and pale underneath with dark barring. Seen from below in flight, wings are long and broad, tail is relatively long and head proportionately long and cuckoo-like. Shows pale throat but heavy barring from neck to base of tail; tail itself has several dark bars and conspicuous dark terminal band. On wings, flight feathers have dark tips and are barred, as are coverts. Dark patches on forewing are characteristic. At close range, pale head, yellow eyes and yellow legs can be seen.

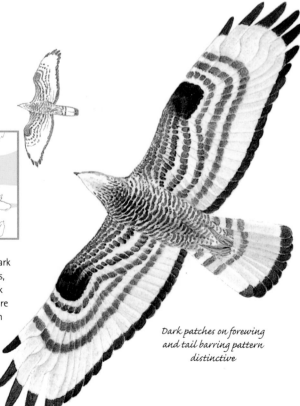

Dark patches on forewing and tail barring pattern distinctive

Marsh Harrier

Circus aeruginosus

Female's plumage (left) is mostly brown; male (right) takes at least three years to acquire pale parts of plumage

Voice: A plaintive, shrill 'kweeoo'
Length: 50–55cm
Wingspan: 115–130cm
Weight: 500–900g

Habitat: Reedbeds and wetlands; sometimes over nearby farmland
Nest: Bulky nest of reeds and twigs built among reeds
Eggs: 4–5; bluish-white, often stained
Food: Amphibians, birds and small mammals

WITH wings held in a pronounced 'V', marsh harriers quarter the reedbeds in a leisurely fashion, dropping down occasionally to catch a frog or small bird. They seldom fly more than a few feet above the height of the reeds when hunting. When courting and nesting, however, the male sometimes circles to a considerable height above his territory and will perform dramatic, stooping display flights. When the young have hatched, patient observers may even see spectacular food passes where the female takes to the air and turns upside down to receive prey from the male's talons.

Graceful bird of prey with relatively long wings and long tail. Occasionally seen perched but more usually observed in flight low over ground, often with legs dangling. Seen from above, male has dark-brown back and wing coverts, which contrast with blue-grey flight feathers and tail. Wingtips black, and head and leading edge of innerwing pale grey-buff. Seen from below, underwing blue-grey except for black wingtips, body dark brown and tail grey. Female has mostly chocolate-brown plumage except for pale-buff forehead and cap, throat and leading edge to innerwing. Juvenile resembles female but pale markings less distinct.

Hen Harrier

Circus cyaneus

Adult female and juvenile very similar

ALTHOUGH capable of rapid, direct flight, the flight pattern more usually associated with the hen harrier is a combination of leisurely wingbeats and long glides. In windy conditions, the birds seldom have to flap their wings, holding them instead in a pronounced 'V' shape. Because the hen harrier flies so low over the ground, it is easy to lose sight of when it is quartering over broken ground. Although highly territorial in the breeding season, during the winter months hen harriers will often roost communally, with up to a dozen birds flying into a chosen, sheltered spot at dusk.

Adult male mainly pale grey

Voice: Rapid, chattering 'ke-ke-ke' heard in nesting territory; otherwise silent
Length: 45–50cm
Wingspan: 100–120cm
Weight: 300–550g
Habitat: Breeds on northern and upland moors and bogs; in winter, in lowland, open terrain, often coastal
Nest: On ground, usually in heather, lined with rushes and grasses
Eggs: 4–5; bluish-white, occasionally with reddish marks
Food: Small mammals, birds and insects

Male has mainly pale-grey plumage, feathers on breast and belly being palest of all. Wingtips contrastingly black and shows conspicuous white rump in flight. At close range and when perched reveals yellow iris, black-tipped yellow bill and yellow legs. Female has brown plumage with owl-like facial disc and streaked underparts; shows conspicuous white rump in flight and strongly barred tail and underwing. Juvenile similar to female.

Pallid Harrier

Circus macrourus

Adult male

THE breeding range of the pallid harrier extends across central Asia, abutting the boundaries of Europe in the west. The species has occasionally bred in Europe in the past but is more usually encountered in the region on spring or autumn migration; most pallid harriers overwinter in sub-Saharan Africa. For certain identification, the thing that most raptor enthusiasts hope for is a clear view of a male bird. Pallid harriers are vagrants to many countries in north and northwest Europe.

Voice: Whistling calls uttered near nest; otherwise generally silent
Length: 44–46cm
Wingspan: 100–15cm
Weight: 300–400g
Habitat: Grassland
Nest: Loose pile of vegetation in scrub
Eggs: 4–5; bluish with brown blotches
Food: Small mammals, small birds, insects and reptiles

Graceful raptor usually seen in buoyant, low-level flight. Similar in all plumages to corresponding plumages of Montagu's and hen harriers. In flight, all birds show wingtips more pointed than other harriers. Adult male appears uniformly pale grey, often almost white, in flight except for conspicuous black wingtips. Lacks male hen and Montagu's harriers' dark-hooded appearance. Legs, base of bill and iris yellow. Adult female difficult to separate from adult female hen and Montagu's harriers, although seen at close range, facial pattern is more contrasting. Juvenile has reddish-brown underparts and underwing coverts; flight feathers grey-brown with contrasting dark barring. Not readily separable from juvenile Montagu's but facial markings more contrastingly dark and light.

Montagu's Harrier

Circus pygargus

Female has white rump like female hen harrier, but is smaller; wings also look more pointed

Male has greyish plumage with black wingtips and black bars on underwing

THE Montagu's harrier's favoured hunting method is to fly low over the ground, its skilled use of breezes enabling it to fly at strikingly slow speeds. A tell-tale rustle will cause it to swerve in mid-flight and plunge, talons first, to the ground. Voles and mice are important food items but lizards, insects and small birds are also eaten, particularly in southern Europe. Seen near the nest, Montagu's harriers circle and soar, pairs also performing dramatic food passes in mid-air. The species is a summer visitor to Europe and overwinters in Africa.

Voice: High-pitched 'yik-yik-yik' over breeding ground; otherwise silent
Length: 40–45cm
Wingspan: 105–120cm
Weight: 300–400g
Habitat: Uses variety of habitats during breeding season including wetlands, arable fields, young plantations, heaths and moors
Nest: On ground, lined with grasses
Eggs: 4–5; pale bluish-white with faint rusty markings
Food: Small mammals, birds, reptiles

Both sexes are superficially similar to hen harrier but wings look proportionately longer and more pointed. Male has mainly pale-grey plumage, palest on breast and belly. Seen from below, shows extensive black wingtips, two black wingbars and fainter, reddish wingbars on coverts; seen from above, has black wingtips, single black wingbar and white rump, less conspicuous than male hen harrier's. Female very similar to female hen harrier and best told by smaller white rump and wing shape. Juvenile similar to female but, seen from below, body and wing coverts reddish-orange.

Black-shouldered Kite

Elanus caeruleus

IN SPAIN and Portugal black-shouldered kites are mainly year-round residents that start nesting comparatively early in the year, sometimes in February. Although they favour open terrain, the presence of scattered trees and bushes is essential to the species. Nests are built among the branches but the trees also serve as vantage points for these keen-eyed raptors, which spend a large part of the day perched, scanning the ground below for the tell-tale movements of lizards and other prey. Nowadays, telegraph poles and overhead wires are also used as lookouts. Seen well in good light there can be no mistaking a black-winged kite. A distant flight view in poor light can be misleading, however, as the bird sometimes hovers like a kestrel or glides and quarters like a short-eared owl.

Voice: Mostly silent but utters thin scream in alarm
Length: 31–35cm
Wingspan: 75–83cm
Weight: 230g
Habitat: Dry, open country with scattered trees
Nest: Twig platform built in tree
Eggs: 3–4; buff
Food: Reptiles, small mammals and insects

Sexes similar. Upperparts mostly pale grey and underparts white. Head looks superficially owl-like and has staring red eyes with black 'eyebrows'. Has black-tipped yellow bill and yellow legs. In flight, which is buoyant and graceful, black wingtips and black on leading edge of innerwing look conspicuous. Often hovers or glides with wings in 'V' shape.

Seen perched, looks rather large-headed and short-tailed; black patch on innerwing shows as a black 'shoulder'

Black Kite

Milvus migrans

Wings relatively long and broad and held flat when circling; tail is constantly twisted in flight to assist control

Black kites are skilled low-speed aeronauts as well as consummate soaring birds

A S ITS scientific name suggests, the black kite is a migratory species and summer visitor to Europe, arriving in April or May and leaving again in August and September to overwinter in sub-Saharan Africa. Its range includes much of mainland Europe as far north as Germany; it is absent from Britain and Scandinavia as a breeding species but is seen as a rare passage migrant, mainly in spring. With eyes ever on the look-out for an easy meal, black kites glide in a leisurely manner over lakes, dipping to the surface to grasp a dead fish and making off with heavy wingbeats. In some parts of their range, black kites are associated with people, making a handsome living off discarded food and rubbish. In such circumstances, they often become bold and will visit markets and rubbish dumps with confidence.

Voice: Gull-like whinnying call
Length: 55–60cm
Wingspan: 145–165cm
Weight: 650–900g
Habitat: Wooded lakes and open country
Nest: Twig platform in tree; sometimes in loose colonies
Eggs: 2–3; white with red spotting

Food: Scavenger, but will take small mammals, insects etc

In flight most easily confused with female marsh harrier. Sexes similar. Plumage mainly dark brown and can look all black in poor light. Head rather paler than body. Has black-tipped yellow bill and yellow legs. Tail forked, but not as deeply as red kite's.

Red Kite

Milvus milvus

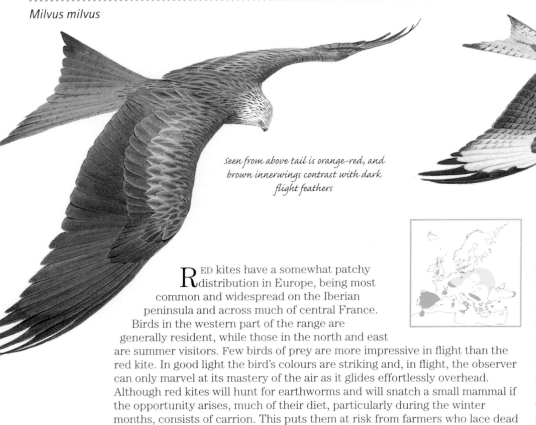

Seen from above tail is orange-red, and brown innerwings contrast with dark flight feathers

From below rusty-red body and underwing coverts contrast distinctively with pale-grey head and wing patches; wingtips are black

R ED kites have a somewhat patchy distribution in Europe, being most common and widespread on the Iberian peninsula and across much of central France. Birds in the western part of the range are generally resident, while those in the north and east are summer visitors. Few birds of prey are more impressive in flight than the red kite. In good light the bird's colours are striking and, in flight, the observer can only marvel at its mastery of the air as it glides effortlessly overhead. Although red kites will hunt for earthworms and will snatch a small mammal if the opportunity arises, much of their diet, particularly during the winter months, consists of carrion. This puts them at risk from farmers who lace dead carcasses with poisons not knowing what will come and eat them.

Voice: Shrill, quavering 'weoo-weoo-weoo'
Length: 60–65cm
Wingspan: 155–185cm
Weight: 850–1,000g
Habitat: Typically associated with wooded valleys adjacent to areas of farmland or open country
Nest: Stick and mud platform built in tree
Eggs: 3–4; whitish but variably marked
Food: Small mammals, birds, earthworms, carrion

Sexes similar. Plumage mainly reddish-brown with paler, greyish head and deeply forked tail. Has black-tipped yellow bill and yellow legs. In flight, soars effortlessly, often with wings slightly kinked forwards. Seen from below, body and leading edge of innerwing are reddish. Wings are long and show translucent pale-grey patch near tips; tail pale grey.

Levant Sparrowhawk

Accipiter brevipes

THE Levant sparrowhawk has a limited breeding range in Europe, but on migration passes through the Bosphorus in spring and autumn. Its overwintering grounds are not known, but presumed to be in Africa. Levant sparrowhawks favour warm lowland and coastal districts. Habitats chosen might include light woodland or olive groves, or farmland with only scattered trees. Levant sparrowhawks do not use mid-air surprise attacks to catch prey, but circle at low level before dropping to catch prey on the ground.

Voice: Harsh screaming call uttered near nest
Length: 33–36cm
Wingspan: 65–75cm
Weight: 170–210g (male), 220–250g (female)
Habitat: Warm, dry woodland and farmland
Nest: Twiggy structure on branch of tree
Eggs: 3–5; pale green with faint darker markings
Food: Mainly insects and lizards

Dashing raptor, superficially similar to sparrowhawk. Adult male seen in flight appears very pale underneath except for pinkish flush to breast, black wingtips and dark barring on tail. At rest, head and back appear uniformly blue-grey; shows white throat, white vent and faint pinkish barring on breast and belly. Adult female similar to adult male but barring on underparts more prominent. When seen in flight from below, black wingtips contrast with pale wings. Juvenile recalls adult female but has teardrop-shaped dark spots and streaks on breast and belly; underwings show dark barring.

Sparrowhawk

Accipiter nisus

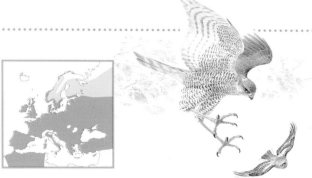

sparrowhawks catch prey either by surprise attack from a concealed perch or flight close to a woodland edge

Adult male considerably smaller than female

SPARROWHAWKS are often seen in low-level, dashing flight, but they will also occasionally soar, showing their short, rounded wings and long tail. The species has suffered greatly at the hands of man, both from the use of DDT and other agrochemicals and from sportsmen. Both these areas are now subject to tighter control, however, so we are just starting to see numbers recover. Sparrowhawks are resident across most of their range although birds from the north of the region migrate south in the autumn.

Voice: Harsh 'kek-kek-kek-kek'
Length: 30–40cm
Wingspan: 55–75cm
Weight: 100–300g
Habitat: Mixed woodland, farmland with hedgerows; increasingly in urban areas
Nest: Stick platform built in tree; may use foundation of another species' nest

Eggs: 4–5; whitish
Food: Small birds caught on the wing

Male has blue-grey upperparts and whitish underparts bearing strong reddish-orange barring on body and underwing coverts. Undertail feathers white

and tail barred. Female has grey-brown upperparts and whitish underparts with grey-brown barring. At close range, both sexes show yellow legs and black-tipped yellow bill; iris of male orange, that of female yellow. Juvenile similar to female but with streaked underparts.

Goshawk

Accipiter gentilis

Goshawks are resident across most of their range, but birds in the far north and east move south and west in the autumn

Both sexes have prominent pale supercilium above bright-yellow eye; feet and legs yellow with black talons

THE best time of year to look for goshawks is in the early spring, in the early morning, when pairs display above their territories. Birds can be seen circling and stooping, often with their white undertail feathers fluffed out like a powder puff. At other times, goshawks are generally shy and solitary, spending much of their time sitting unobtrusively in cover. When prey is sighted, however, the goshawk's flight is rapid and dashing, the bird often gliding at high speed through the trees or just above the tree canopy.

Voice: Rapid, hoarse 'gek-gek-gek' heard at nest; otherwise silent
Length: 50–60cm
Wingspan: 125–150cm
Weight: 600–900g (male); 1–1.4kg (female)

Habitat: Extensive forests, often of pine or beech
Nest: Substantial stick platform, built in tree
Eggs: 3–4; bluish-white
Food: Birds, especially pigeons, and squirrels etc

Large, dashing hawk, the female similar in size to buzzard. Smaller male can be confused with female sparrowhawk but note goshawk's bulkier body, shorter tail relative to body

size and longer wings, often held in an 'S' curve. Seen from below, both sexes look pale with grey barring on body, wings and tail; fluffy white feathers at base of tail often conspicuous. Both sexes

have rather similar grey-brown upperparts. Juvenile has streaked underparts and less uniform upperparts.

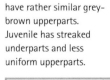

Kestrel

Falco tinnunculus

Male is colourful and distinctive

Its hovering flight distinguishes the kestrel immediately from that other common and widespread raptor, the sparrowhawk

Perched kestrels have a noticeably upright posture

Female has mainly chestnut plumage

THE kestrel is the commonest bird of prey over most of Europe. When in direct flight, the wingbeats are fast and shallow with a few glides, but the most distinctive behaviour is the ability to hover in a fixed position on rapidly beating wings or remain motionless on an updraught. When prey is spotted the kestrel drops vertically. Prey is usually carried away to be eaten on a perch. Kestrels also hunt by sitting on wires and posts, and they will stalk earthworms on the ground as well. Kestrels have excellent eyesight and can continue hunting in very low light.

Voice: Piercing 'kee-kee-kee', especially at nest site
Length: 33–39cm
Wingspan: 65–75cm
Weight: 130–300g
Habitat: Cultivated country, heaths, moorland, roadsides and towns

Nest: Old crow nests, tree-holes, cliffs and building ledges; little nest material
Eggs: 3–6; buff-white, almost covered with reddish-brown speckles
Food: Mainly small mammals; some birds, reptiles, insects

Frequently seen hovering with a characteristic long-tailed silhouette and downward-looking head. Male is colourful with spotted brick-red back, black primaries and grey tail and head. Female is more uniform with heavily spotted chestnut plumage, a barred tail and brownish streaked head. At a distance the sexes can appear similar. Juvenile resembles female but is more streaked on the underside.

Lesser Kestrel

Falco naumanni

Male has blue-grey head and unspotted chestnut back

Female has chestnut colouring and shows dark spotting on upperparts; primaries are dark

LESSER kestrels nest colonially in old buildings and on rock faces and are often seen hunting together when there is an abundance of flying insects, their favourite prey. They often nest near human habitation and show little fear unless directly persecuted. Lesser kestrels hover far less than kestrels and have a lighter, more agile flight pattern. Food may be caught on the wing in the air or pounced on, but it is normally eaten in the air. Most lesser kestrels overwinter in Africa, but a few remain near the breeding sites all year, especially those in the southern part of the range.

Voice: Rasping two- or three-note calls and trilling notes at colonies
Length: 29–32cm
Wingspan: 58–72cm
Weight: 90–200g
Habitat: Mediterranean region; cultivated country, villages

Nest: In hole in old building; colonial nester
Eggs: 3–5; white with pale yellow-red spots
Food: Insects

Small falcon with narrow wings and a longish slender tail. Male is strongly coloured with unspotted chestnut back, blue-grey innerwing and hood and pale-grey tail with dark terminal band. Female is slightly larger than male and has barred tail. Juvenile resembles female. In all birds claws are pale, not dark, as in kestrel.

Merlin

Falco columbarius

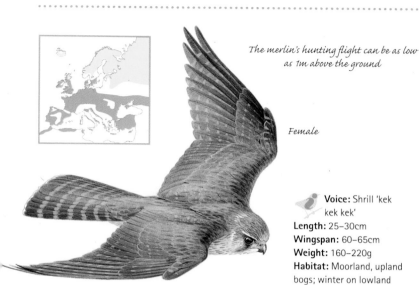

The merlin's hunting flight can be as low as 1m above the ground

Female

When not hunting the merlin will sit on a low perch where there is a sweeping view of the moorland, adopting a very upright posture

Voice: Shrill 'kek kek kek'
Length: 25–30cm
Wingspan: 60–65cm
Weight: 160–220g
Habitat: Moorland, upland bogs; winter on lowland heaths, coastal marshes
Nest: On ground in heather and bracken; sometimes in old crow nest in low tree
Eggs: 3–5; light buff with dense brown-red blotches
Food: Small birds

Male

Europe's smallest bird of prey, with a neat, light outline. Wings appear short and relatively broad but tail looks long and square-ended. Resembles small peregrine. Male is greyish-blue above with reddish-buff underside. Female is noticeably larger than male, dark brown above and strongly patterned below. Juvenile resembles female but is darker with white patches on nape.

THE merlin's small size is compensated for by its strong, dashing flight and ability to startle small birds by coming upon them suddenly from its low hunting flight. It will sometimes soar or hang in the wind high overhead and can even hover briefly, but will normally keep low down. The merlin's preferred ground nest site exposes it to danger from predators such as foxes (and in some parts of the region gamekeepers), but new birds will nest year after year in nests where the previous occupants have been destroyed. In winter most merlins move to estuaries, coastal marshes and open agricultural land where there are many small birds such as waders, pipits, finches and larks.

Hobby

Falco subbuteo

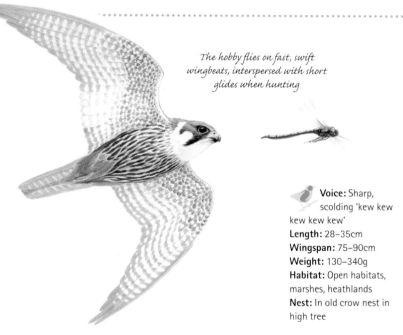

The hobby flies on fast, swift wingbeats, interspersed with short glides when hunting

Hobbies are widespread summer visitors to Europe, being most frequently seen in warm, open habitats such as heaths and extensive marshes

Voice: Sharp, scolding 'kew kew kew kew kew'
Length: 28–35cm
Wingspan: 75–90cm
Weight: 130–340g
Habitat: Open habitats, marshes, heathlands
Nest: In old crow nest in high tree
Eggs: 3; brownish-yellow with reddish spots yellowing with age
Food: Insects caught on wing; a few small birds

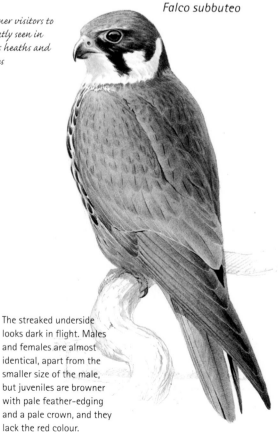

In flight, the wings look long and pointed, and the tail appears short, giving the impression of a large swift. Adult's white cheeks and moustachial stripes show well in sitting birds, as do the red 'trousers' and vent. The streaked underside looks dark in flight. Males and females are almost identical, apart from the smaller size of the male, but juveniles are browner with pale feather-edging and a pale crown, and they lack the red colour.

THE hobby is expert at catching large insects like dragonflies on the wing. The prey is seized by the talons in a downwards stoop and eaten in flight, unless it is a small bird, which will be taken to a perch and plucked. Hobbies often hunt late into the evening, when bats may also be taken. Prey is usually captured high up, not low over the ground, and a high perch is normally chosen as an observation point before making the feeding flight. Nesting occurs late in the season so that the young can take advantage of the abundance of unskilled fledgling passerines. Hobbies overwinter in sub-equatorial Africa.

Red-footed Falcon

Falco vespertinus

Red-footed falcons spend much of the day sitting still – most activity is at dusk

Adult male

Juvenile/first summer

Immature male, first spring

Immature male, late first summer

Sub-adult male, second autumn

Adult male

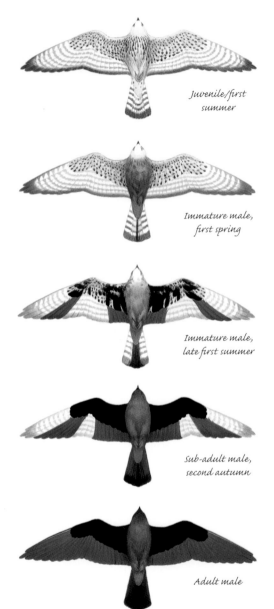

RED-FOOTED falcons are frequently seen perching on a post or overhead wire, from which short forays are made to catch prey; occasionally, however, acrobatic flights are made, sometimes to high altitudes in search of high-flying insects. Breeding usually takes place late in the season when birds such as rooks vacate their nests; nesting is often colonial and so birds are usually seen hunting together. Red-footed falcons seem indifferent to human presence and may nest in close proximity to farms or villages. Red-footed falcons are summer visitors to Europe and overwinter in southern Africa.

Voice: Highly vocal; 'kew kew kew' flight calls
Length: 28–31cm
Wingspan: 65–75cm
Weight: 130–195g
Habitat: Open heaths, cultivated land, steppe, marshland

Nest: Colonial; old rook nests
Eggs: 3–4; buff, heavily marked with spots and blotches
Food: Insects, some small birds, frogs

Adult female has bright orange-yellow head and underside

A small falcon resembling a short-tailed kestrel at a distance. Male is distinctive with dark-grey plumage, pale, silvery primaries, deep rufous-red vent and thighs and red feet, eyering and cere; immature male similar to adult male but has paler underparts and pale face and throat. Adult female has orange or pale-yellow crown and underside, and barred, dark grey upperparts. Juveniles are streaked below and have darker, blotched upperparts and a barred tail, and like female have dark eye patches resembling a highwayman's mask.

Eleonora's Falcon

Falco eleonorae

ELEONORA'S falcons are at home on isolated, windy headlands in the Mediterranean, occurring from the Balearic Islands and Morocco eastwards to Cyprus. They appear late in the season when all other migrants have already arrived and commenced breeding. They delay nesting until late in the summer so that their young can capitalise on the offspring of migrant songbirds returning south to Africa. As well as taking small birds, Eleonora's falcons will prey on large insects and occasionally bats, most prey being caught on the wing, and usually late in the day or very early in the morning. They will also hunt on clear, moonlit nights when large numbers of birds may be migrating. Eleonora's falcons overwinter in east Africa and Madagascar.

Voice: Hoarse, kestrel-like chatter; not often heard
Length: 36–42cm
Wingspan: 90–105cm
Weight: 350–400g
Habitat: Sea cliffs and headlands, arid deserts
Nest: On cliff ledge under overhang, in rock crevice or under dense bush; no nest material
Eggs: 2–3; white or pale buff with brownish markings
Food: Small birds, bats, insects

Appears rather slender and dainty but is actually larger than the hobby. Tail longer than on other small falcons. Wings long and slender, giving an angular outline in flight. Pale and dark forms occur, pale form being three times more numerous. Dark phase looks almost black in flight; pale phase shows pale cheek, dark moustachial stripe and dark, streaked underside. Underwing shows contrasting dark coverts and paler primaries in both phases. Juvenile similar to light phase adult but with buffish underparts and heavy streaks.

Dark phase bird

It has been estimated that one in every 600 birds migrating across the Mediterranean may be attacked by Eleonora's falcons

Pale phase bird

Eleonora's falcons' flight is light and acrobatic, perfect for intercepting swallows and martins, and they often give long displays over their nesting sites

Peregrine Falcon

Falco peregrinus

FOLLOWING a crash in its numbers, Europe's peregrine population is now recovering again, and birds can turn turn up in almost any habitat. Numbers are highest in northwest Europe, but peregrines breed in much of the rest of Europe where suitable cliffs for nesting occur. Prey, in the form of a medium-sized bird like a rock dove, may be spotted from a lofty perch or from the air, and once identified it will be attacked by a high-speed stoop. Near the nest, aerial food passes may be witnessed: the male will present the female with prey as part of courtship or to feed to the young.

Voice: Shrill 'kek kek kek kek'
Length: 39–50cm
Wingspan: 95–115cm
Weight: 600–1,300g
Habitat: Open, upland habitats; sea cliffs, coasts in winter
Nest: On cliff ledge, sometimes high buildings; uses abandoned bird's nests
Eggs: 3–4; creamy-buff with many reddish-brown markings
Food: Birds, mostly taken on the wing

Large falcon with a compact body shape and broad-based, pointed wings. Shallow wingbeats with springy wing tips are characteristic, as is the dramatic high-speed stoop for prey from a great height. Adult is steely grey above with a paler grey rump. Has bold facial patterning with dark moustachial stripes. Juvenile is slightly slimmer and browner than adult, with pale feather edging on mantle and bold streaking below; facial markings less distinct than on adult and cere is grey-blue, not yellow.

The flight of a peregrine across an estuary will cause panic among gulls and waders, which will take to the air with the result that one at least will end up as prey

Peregrines attack prey with a breathtaking stoop at speeds up to 240km/h

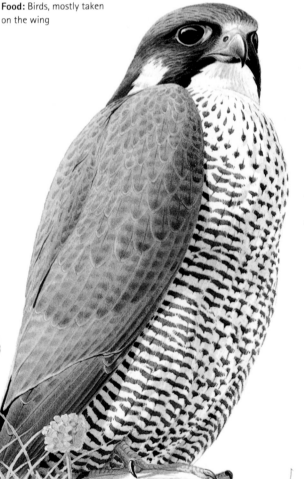

Adult is steely grey above with a paler grey rump and pale underside with dark barring

small birds are often killed by the impact of the talons, but larger birds may be taken away to a perch to be killed and eaten

Lanner Falcon

Falco biarmicus

Lanners lack the speed and agility of some falcons, but will still catch birds in flight

Adult male

Similar to peregrine, but slightly slimmer with longer tail and uniformly broad wings with more rounded wingtips. Male has a rusty nape and dark blue-brown mantle with a pale, spotted underside. The larger female is similar but has a buff nape and more boldly spotted underside. In both sexes, the moustachial stripe is less pronounced than in the peregrine. Juvenile is darker brown above than adult and more buff below with heavier brownish-black streaks. Flight feathers look pale on underwing.

THIS large falcon is rare in Europe. Lanners often hunt in pairs, covering vast areas and ones where few other birds of prey occur. They sometimes skim low over the ground to startle a ground-dwelling bird or small mammal, but they will also pursue birds through the air. Lanners normally take over the nest of another bird, often evicting resident crows or ravens. They are mostly resident, making trips to their nesting sites outside the breeding season from time to time to check for intruders.

Voice: Similar to, but quieter version of, peregrine's call
Length: 43–52cm
Wingspan: 95–115cm
Weight: 500–900g
Habitat: Mediterranean region; dry open country, mountains

Nest: Rock ledge or tree; uses old nest of crow or raven
Eggs: 3–4; dull white with yellow, red or brown blotches
Food: Birds, some small mammals, reptiles, insects

Saker Falcon

Falco cherrug

THE saker falcon may be seen circling high up with wings held straight and tail closed, or even hovering laboriously; in active flight, however, it has powerful wingbeats and may make its attack from a low-level flight path, dropping on to a small mammal at great speed. The saker favours open habitats where hunting for birds is easy. It may spend long periods on a high perch watching for prey, but it will also range over 20km from its nesting site in search of food. This is a rare bird in Europe and is normally sedentary.

Voice: Harsh 'kek kek kek' or screaming 'giak giak giak'
Length: 48–57cm
Wingspan: 110–125cm
Weight: 750–1,300g
Habitat: Open cultivated country, steppe, lightly wooded areas
Nest: On high cliff or tall tree in nest of other large bird

Eggs: 3–5; pale buff or light brown, boldly spotted with dark brown, rust and black
Food: Small mammals, some birds, lizards, large insects

Sexes similar, although females are larger than males. Adult is greyish-brown

above with pale-fringed feathers on the mantle. Head is noticeably pale with a lightly streaked crown. Underside is streaked, with the boldest markings on the flanks and 'trousers'. Most individuals show contrast on the underwing between pale flight feathers and darker coverts, although some very pale birds occur, where this is not obvious. Juvenile is generally darker than adult with bolder markings on the underside.

Gyr Falcon

Falco rusticolus

THE powerful wingbeats of the gyr falcon enable it to fly quickly, low over the ground, and flush birds that it can then pursue with ease and catch in flight. It will, however, also drop on to small mammals on the ground. It often sits on a low rock lookout between irregular feeding forays. Gyr falcons will also feed on carrion, which enables them to remain in the Arctic throughout the year, although birds from the most northerly regions will move south. Juveniles mostly disperse south to spend the winter along coasts and lowland plains.

White phase birds show hardly any spotting but do have dark wingtips

Dark phase birds occur in the southern part of the range

Voice: A hoarse 'kee-a kee-a kee-a'
Length: 55–60cm
Wingspan: 125–155cm
Weight: 1.1–1.75kg
Habitat: Arctic tundra, high mountains; high Arctic seabird colonies
Nest: On cliff ledge in nest of raven or rough-legged buzzard
Eggs: 3–4; pale yellowish-white with variable red or dark red spots
Food: Medium-sized birds, some small mammals

Some birds, mostly from high Arctic, are almost pure white, but dark lead-grey and brownish birds also occur in southern part of range. Southern birds have heavily barred plumage with pale patches and a pale forehead, darker eye patch and moustachial streak. The white underparts are heavily marked with spots and

streaks, and the underwing shows almost translucent panels contrasting with darker coverts. Adult white high Arctic forms have almost no spots except on

mantle, although dark tips to primaries can be seen; juveniles of this form are similar to adults but have black 'teardrop' marks on underparts.

73

Comparing Birds of Prey

IDENTIFYING raptors (birds of prey) in flight is decidedly challenging even for an experienced observer. Absolute size is often hard to gauge and colours can be difficult to detect when the bird is seen in silhouette against the sky. Concentrate on size relative to nearby birds of known species, the relative proportions of body, wing and tail, and any distinctive habits. Even seasoned raptor watchers have to accept that a significant proportion of sightings must remain unidentified.

SHORT TOED EAGLE: Medium-sized, pale eagle that frequently hovers on updraughts over open hillsides. Has distinct barring on tail and underwing but lacks dark carpal patches

GOLDEN EAGLE: Much larger than buzzard, with longer wings and tail and powerful bill on well-protruding head. Soars on wings raised in shallow 'V'

GRIFFON VULTURE: Easily told by immense size and flight silhouette. Broad wings can look narrow-tipped in gliding flight. Compared to eagles, tail looks proportionately short; neck appears bulging and head tiny

ELEONORA'S FALCON: Easily recognised by elegant, long-tailed, long-winged silhouette. In vicinity of nesting cliffs, often performs incredible aerobatic feats

MARSH HARRIER (male): Note wing pattern and rusty body. Like all harriers, soars and glides on raised wings

BUZZARD: Large raptor with broad wings raised in shallow 'V' when soaring; Has different wing pattern from honey buzzard, which has longer neck and tail and soars on flat wings

HEN HARRIER: Male (above) has white underparts, grey head and upper breast, black wingtips and dark trailing edge. Female (below) difficult to distinguish from female Montagu's, but note head pattern

MARSH HARRIER (female): Brown, often with yellow head and wing markings

RED KITE: Forked, reddish tail and white wing patches are best identifiers

GOSHAWK: Size difference between this species and sparrowhawk not always apparent but flight always looks heavier. Wings proportionately broader and tail shorter than sparrowhawk's

HONEY BUZZARD: Head and neck look proportionately long and narrow and generally paler than body. Typically shows dark carpal patches, extensive barring on wings and diagnostic pattern on tail. Generally soars on flat wings

OSPREY: Long wings bowed when gliding and soaring. Underbody white with large, black patches at bend of wing

GYR FALCON: Recalls peregrine but looks much bulkier, with proportionately broader wings and thick-set body. In direct flight, wingbeats much slower and more leisurely than peregrine's

RED-FOOTED FALCON (below): Plumage varies according to age and sex. Flight pattern extremely variable: sometimes hawks for insects like hobby but also hovers like kestrel

BOOTED EAGLE: Size of buzzard. Pale form (left) shows diagnostic contrast between pale head, body and underwing coverts and dark flight feathers. Dark form recalls black kite without forked tail. Soaring birds often hold wings curved slightly forwards

Adult male

LESSER KESTREL: Slightly smaller than kestrel. Hovers less frequently and wingbeats much more rapid in level flight

MONTAGU'S HARRIER: Male (right) similar to male hen harrier but note dark bars on wings. Female very similar to female hen harrier but narrower-winged

HOBBY: Wings long, narrow and pointed. Silhouette not unlike large swift. Streaked black underparts and reddish untail coverts are characteristic

MERLIN (female)

MERLIN (male): Smallest falcon, with shorter wings than other species and bold, dashing flight. Male has blue-grey upperparts and black tail band

PEREGRINE FALCON: Large falcon with thick-set body, broad-based, pointed wings and rather short tail. Note large 'moustache' and white cheeks

SPARROWHAWK: Has short, rounded wings and long tail. In flight, rapid wingbeats are interspersed with glides

KESTREL: Most characteristic feature is persistent hovering; often seen over roadside verges

Willow Grouse

Lagopus lagopus lagopus

Winter male

summer male

A plump gamebird with liver-red to grey-brown plumage in summer and white plumage in winter. Male has red wattle over eye that is more prominent in spring, when white plumage is lost from the head first; by the end of summer male is more uniformly brown, but retains white primaries and black tail feathers, which are most obvious in flight. Female white in winter, but more tawny brown in summer than male and lacks his red wattle.

THE willow grouse is a widespread gamebird of open northern forests. Most birds are residents and do not migrate except for short distances within their ranges in search of winter food and territories. The strange laughing call of the male is sometimes uttered from within the cover of birch scrub and has a startling effect on passers-by; the calls of the female are quieter and shorter. For most of the time these are quiet birds that keep themselves hidden.

Voice: A hoarse, rattling 'ko-ah-ko-ah-ko-ah'
Length: 37–42cm
Wingspan: 55–66cm
Weight: 550–640g
Habitat: Mixed forests on mountain slopes, willow scrub

Nest: On ground under low vegetation; shallow moss-lined cup
Eggs: 6–9; glossy pale yellow with reddish-brown mottlings
Food: Buds and shoots of willow and birch; young eat insects

Red Grouse

Lagopus lagopus scoticus

Nest: Shallow cup on ground under low vegetation
Eggs: 6–9; yellowish, glossy with reddish-brown mottlings
Food: Mainly heather shoots; some other plant material and insects in summer.

RED grouse are restricted to northern Britain and Ireland and are most often seen when flushed from dense heather; the low, gliding flight alternating with bursts of rapid wingbeats, and the frantic call, are all most visitors will observe. In spring, males take up territories and stand on a raised hillock to call, but females are far more secretive. In very harsh weather red grouse will move to lower ground. Males guard territories in winter to ensure an adequate food supply. Females need to feed well in the spring in order to breed successfully; they take some insect food, as do immature birds.

Voice: A hoarse, rattling 'ko-ah ko-ah ko-ah'
Length: 37–42cm
Wingspan: 55–66cm
Weight: 550–690g
Habitat: Treeless heather moorland, mountain slopes

A plump gamebird that appears uniformly dark brown both on the ground and in flight; the wings are a dark grey-brown. Male is rich reddish-brown with red wattles and white-feathered legs. Female is pale buff-brown with pale feathered legs, but lacks the male's wattles over the eyes. Juvenile is buff-brown all over with pale feather margins.

Ptarmigan

Lagopus mutus

Winter male

Spring male

Summer male

Autumn male

Ptarmigan's wings are white all year – only the body plumage changes colour

HARSH winter weather is not as much of a problem to ptarmigan as poor conditions in early summer, when the chicks are at their most vulnerable; these need a plentiful supply of insects. The variable plumage of the ptarmigan helps it to blend in with the tundra as the snow recedes. Males may be seen displaying on prominent rocks with the better camouflaged females creeping around near by. In winter, ptarmigan form flocks, moving slowly over the snow in search of food, which they find by scratching with their feet, but as the breeding season approaches the males separate to find territories.

Voice: Hoarse rattling 'karrrrrr k k k k k k'
Length: 34–36cm
Wingspan: 54–60cm
Weight: 400–550g
Habitat: Open, stony tundra, high treeless mountain slopes

Nest: Shallow scrape, sometimes sheltered by boulder; lining of moss and feathers
Eggs: 5–8; rich glossy dark red with deep-brown spots, fading to yellowish-buff with black spots
Food: Buds, shoots, berries, some insects

Slightly smaller than willow grouse, which it resembles in winter, except that male has black lores in addition to red wattles. Both sexes appear all white in winter, except for black outertail feathers seen in flight. Plumage changes gradually through spring and summer, as snow melts, to more mottled grey-brown in male, and buff-brown in female. White primaries are retained in the wings, showing prominently in flight. Newly hatched young are downy and mottled buff-brown; juveniles similar to summer female but brown with darker feather edges.

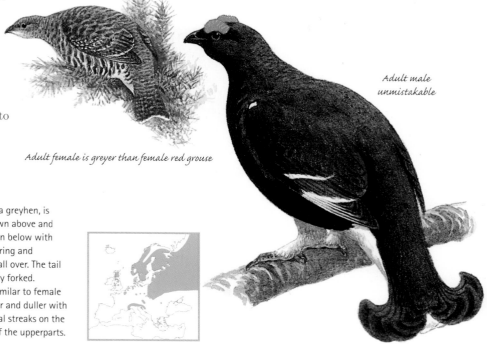

Black Grouse

Tetrao tetrix

In flight male's tail shape distinctive; female has slightly forked tail

THE black grouse prefers marginal forest areas with easy access to open areas such as bogs and moors, where it is usually seen feeding on the ground. Through the spring males may be seen displaying out in the open at dawn. When perched quietly high in a tree, however, black grouse can be very difficult to spot. Habitat loss and increased hunting have caused the numbers to drop in many regions. In much of their range black grouse remain within their territories, but in the far north harsh weather may cause them to disperse to lower areas.

Adult male unmistakable

Adult female is greyer than female red grouse

Voice: Males make cooing calls and a sudden loud 'shoo-eesh'; females cackle
Length: 40–55cm
Wingspan: 65–80cm
Weight: 800–1,250g
Habitat: Woodland close to bogs and heather moors
Nest: Shallow grass-lined scrape on ground, under low bush
Eggs: 6–11; glossy, pale buff or pale ochre with reddish-brown spots
Food: Seeds, buds, berries, shoots; young eat insects

Almost all-black male, the size of a domestic hen, has white wingbars, white shoulder patches, white underwings and white undertail coverts. The black tail has a distinctive lyre shape and is used in the communal display. Female, often known as a greyhen, is warm brown above and grey-brown below with strong barring and speckling all over. The tail is shallowly forked. Juvenile similar to female but smaller and duller with pale central streaks on the feathers of the upperparts.

Capercaillie

Tetrao urogallus

Capercaillies are sometimes flushed from their tree roosts, when the broad, rounded wings are noticeable

THIS very large grouse is the family member that is most tied to trees, and has an almost entirely vegetarian diet. It inhabits mature forests of pine, spruce, fir or larch and will also occur where there are birch and aspen; pine needles and other leaves form the major part of its diet. During courtship in the spring, males gather at display areas at dawn and emit very loud popping and clicking calls. At other times they are difficult to find, despite their large size, because of their tree-roosting habits. Large finger-sized droppings are clues to their presence. In rare cases the capercaillie has hybridised with other large grouse such as the black grouse.

Birds can be found on the ground, often in the early mornings, taking grit to help their digestion

Adult male

Voice: Very loud popping sounds, followed by 'drum roll'; various grunts and gulps
Length: 60–87cm
Wingspan: 87–125cm
Weight: 3.5–5.5kg (male), 1.5–2kg (female)
Habitat: Coniferous forest with some bogs and shrubby areas
Nest: Shallow depression on ground; sometimes old nest low in tree
Eggs: 7–11; glossy yellowish-white with scattered brown streaks
Food: Pine needles, shoots, some other leaves, berries

Both sexes are very bulky with broad wings and tails, and strong, heavy bills. Male appears dark blackish-grey at a distance, but has glossy green chest and dark-brown wing coverts and upper mantle. Large, white patches on shoulders and whitish speckles on flanks and tail break up overall dark effect. Female has rufous-brown upperparts with chestnut patch on chest and paler-brown underside. Most of plumage is heavily barred with black above and black and white below. Juvenile resembles female but is smaller and duller; young males develop distinctive plumage in their first winter, but do not reach full size until the next year.

Adult female

Hazel Grouse

Bonasa bonasia

Hazel grouse often perch in trees, and if flushed will not fly far off, usually perching in another tree near by

Adult male's underside is heavily marked with chestnut and brown blotches

THE hazel grouse is a bird of dense lowland forests, found particularly where there are damp gullies and mossy hollows rich in bilberry, birch and alder, which provide fruits, seeds and buds for food. Hazel grouse occur mainly in extensive, undisturbed lowland forests, but can be found at up to 2,000m. Becoming more scarce in France and Belgium and other parts of southern Europe, their main stronghold is now Scandinavia and northern Europe. Nests are concealed below vegetation and the eggs are incubated by the female alone. After hatching, the young leave the nest within about 24 hours and are able to feed for themselves, although the mother stays close by and broods them at frequent intervals. After three weeks they can fly and reach buds and shoots in low branches. There is no migration in winter and so dispersal is very limited.

Voice: High-pitched whistle, recalling goldcrest
Length: 35–37cm
Wingspan: 48–54cm
Weight: 370–450g
Habitat: Extensive mixed and coniferous forests
Nest: On ground, under bush; grass-lined cup
Eggs: 7–11; pale yellow-brown with darker red-brown speckles

Food: Buds, shoots, fruits; some insects in summer

A compact gamebird with a grey rump and grey tail ending in a black and white band. Male has a black chin patch, red wattle over the eye, and a short crest. Head and neck are finely barred and underside heavily blotched. Female has a warmer brown coloration overall and is generally less boldly marked.

Common Quail

Coturnix coturnix

In flight quail shows relatively long, narrow wings

Female

Male has striking dark facial markings

Usually crouches but may stand higher to peer over vegetation

Quail are very widespread in Europe in the summer, especially in the warmer parts of southern Europe

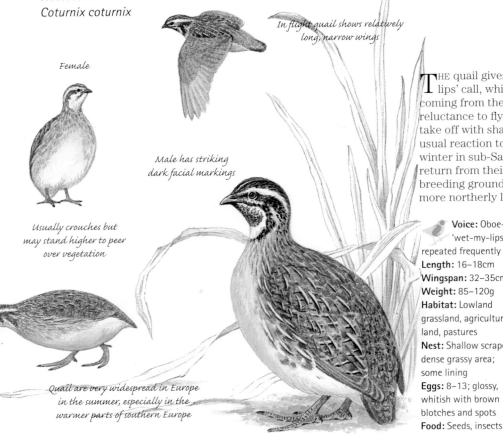

THE quail gives its presence away by the male's persistent 'wet-my-lips' call, which is heard for hours on end, particularly around dusk, coming from the ground in dense vegetation such as a cornfield. Its reluctance to fly makes it very hard to see, and only if flushed will it take off with shallow wingbeats on a rapid flight to safety. Its more usual reaction to danger is to run, or simply squat. Quails spend the winter in sub-Saharan Africa, migrating south in small flocks; on their return from their feeding grounds, quail sometimes overshoot their breeding grounds and end up in a variety of different habitats and more northerly locations than those in which they usually occur.

Voice: Oboe-like 'wet-my-lips', repeated frequently
Length: 16–18cm
Wingspan: 32–35cm
Weight: 85–120g
Habitat: Lowland grassland, agricultural land, pastures
Nest: Shallow scrape in dense grassy area; some lining
Eggs: 8–13; glossy, whitish with brown blotches and spots
Food: Seeds, insects

When flushed, rounded shape, small head and pale underside are easy to see. Male is mostly yellowish-brown with dark brown barring on the upperside, a rufous chest and dark-streaked flanks. Head markings vary, but usually show some dark chestnut markings on the crown, through the eye, and on the cheeks and throat. Female resembles male but has less striking head markings; juvenile similar to female but has barred and spotted, not streaked, flanks.

Golden Pheasant

Chrysolophus pictus

SOLITARY golden pheasants seen in Europe are invariably escapes. In a few areas in Britain, however, birds have been released in sufficient numbers to form seemingly stable feral populations. These are thought to be the only viable non-captive populations outside China. As in their native land, golden pheasants are extremely difficult to see in the mature conifer plantations they favour in Britain. They are seldom flushed and usually retreat into cover by running long before an observer could hope to detect their presence.

Voice: Male utters crowing call during breeding season; otherwise both sexes rather silent
Length: male 85–115cm; female 65–85cm
Wingspan: 65–75cm
Weight: 800–900g
Habitat: Mountain woodland and scrub in natural range; birds introduced into Europe favour conifer plantations
Nest: Shallow depression in ground
Eggs: 5–10; white
Food: Seeds, plant shoots and insects

Large, well-marked pheasant. Adult male has mainly orange-red body plumage except for yellow on crown and areas of blue and green on mantle and wings; shows conspicuous barring on nape. Tail broad and extremely long; brown with intricate pattern of fine, black lines. Adult female has roughly similar proportions to male. Body plumage mainly buffish-brown with dark barring. Juvenile similar to adult female but with shorter tail.

Pheasant

Phasianus colchicus

Adult male

ORIGINALLY introduced to Europe from Asia, pheasants are now widespread and well established. Several races are also regularly released for shooting, leading to a great variety of plumages being seen. Pheasants forage on the ground searching for plant food, but roost in trees at night. The males give a characteristic two-note crow, which can be heard up to 1.5km away, in order to establish their territory. They have a more frenzied call in response to danger and also when flying up to roost, when the whirring wingbeats may also be heard. Startled pheasants can fly rapidly upwards from a standing start, but cannot sustain this for long.

Voice: Male has two-note crow, females have quieter contact notes
Length: 53–89cm
Wingspan: 70–90cm
Weight: 750–1,350g
Habitat: Woodland, copses, farmland, large gardens and orchards
Nest: On ground beneath thick vegetation; sparse lining of leaves
Eggs: 8–15; shiny olive-brown and plain
Food: Mainly seeds, plant material; chicks take small invertebrates.

Male has brightly coloured, iridescent plumage, with red wattles and glossy green head, some showing well-developed 'ear tufts'. White collar is present in some races. Tail very long and barred. Purplish-chestnut plumage shows scalloped pattern due to bold markings on each feather. Female has paler brownish-buff plumage with strong pattern on upperparts and flanks. Barred tail is shorter. Juvenile resembles female, but with duller, less strongly marked plumage.

Lady Amherst's Pheasant

Chrysolophus amherstiae

IN ITS native China, Lady Amherst's pheasant lives in woodlands and scrub at altitudes ranging from 2,000 to 4,600m and often feeds on bamboo shoots. It has been introduced into Britain at various times since 1900 and a population has become established in a small area of the south. During the breeding season Lady Amherst's pheasant is a secretive bird, running into cover to escape from danger, so despite its colourful appearance it is difficult to find. In winter, birds gather in larger groups but are still very secretive. They fly up into trees to roost at night, settling just before dark, usually without any calls or contact notes. Males may guard one or two females, which find a very secluded site for the nest on the ground.

The male's striking neck cape is fanned out in its courtship display, but the bird's secretive habits make this difficult to observe; the wing coverts have a bluish sheen in good light

Voice: Hissing 'su-ik-ik-ik' calls at dusk roosts
Length: 60–120cm
Wingspan: 70–85cm
Weight: 600–700g
Habitat: Mixed woodland with dense undergrowth
Nest: Shallow scrape with some lining, under thick cover
Eggs: 6–11; glossy buff or creamy white
Food: Seeds, shoots, buds, roots, some insects

A very long-tailed pheasant with blue-grey legs and feet.

Male is strikingly marked with dark glossy green and white, and has a colourful yellow rump with red at the base of the tail. Females are smaller with cinnamon-brown plumage and black barring on all feathers. Juvenile is similar to adult female but duller without rufous colouring on the crown.

Red-legged Partridge

Alectoris rufa

Both sexes have red bill and legs

THE red-legged partridge prefers dry habitats, often where there is some bare ground, and avoids woodland and very wet areas. It nests on the ground and relies on finding plenty of insects when the young have first hatched. The red-legged partridge's call usually gives away its presence; it is heard when several birds are feeding in an area and need to keep in contact in dense vegetation.

Voice: Harsh repetitive 'kchoo kchoo-kchoo kchoo'
Length: 32–34cm
Wingspan: 45–50cm

Weight: 400–550g
Habitat: Open country, farmland, lowland heaths
Nest: Shallow scrape with grass lining; protected by low vegetation
Eggs: 10–16; glossy, yellow or buff with reddish or grey blotches
Food: Seeds, roots, leaves, few insects

A compact gamebird with overall greyish-brown colouring, but strongly marked flanks and head. Sexes are similar in appearance but males are larger. The head is grey and the rest of the upperparts and the chest are greyish-brown, but there is a more distinct grey band on the lower chest. The necklace meets over the bill and surrounds the white throat patch, and there is a bib of black streaks. The flanks are strongly barred with black and chestnut stripes on a white background. Juvenile lacks adult's head pattern and flank markings.

Chukar

Alectoris chukar

Adults have strongly patterned head and flanks, and red legs and bill

THE chukar can be difficult to locate when it crouches down, its greyish colouring enabling it to blend in with the background. During courtship, males show off their striped flanks to intimidate other males; they may also circle around on the ground tilting their heads and calling in order to establish dominance. Chukars rarely stray far from their home ranges, usually remaining in small groups; when flushed they fly strongly low over the ground, dropping quickly and continuing to run.

Voice: Short 'chuck' sounds; louder rhythmic call when flushed

Length: 32–34cm
Wingspan: 47–52cm
Weight: 420–550g
Habitat: Dry, rocky mountain slopes, stony plains
Nest: Shallow scrape, sheltered by rock; some lining
Eggs: 8–15; glossy, cream or buff with red-brown spots
Food: Seeds, mainly of grasses; some leaves and insects

Compact, rounded gamebird. Sexes are very similar, showing grey heads and grey-brown upperparts, and a grey chest merging into a sandy underside. The white flanks are boldly barred with black and chestnut stripes and the black eyestripe extends down the neck to join on the chest, forming a dark necklace. Juvenile similar to adult but head and flank markings less distinct.

Rock Partridge

Alectoris graeca

Rock partridges favour high mountain slopes

ROCK partridges fly only reluctantly, usually heading downhill and dropping to the ground quite quickly. They rarely stray far from their home ranges and usually live in small groups (covies). Although very similar to the chukar, the rock partridge's preference for higher ground means the species are unlikely to be confused. Its calls are more varied than the chukar's; the most frequent call is similar in pitch to the nuthatch's.

Voice: A four-note call and various shorter contact notes uttered by members of covies

Length: 32–35cm
Wingspan: 46–53cm
Weight: 500–800g
Habitat: Dry treeless mountain slopes, often south-facing
Nest: Shallow scrape, sheltered by rock; some lining
Eggs: 8–14; glossy, yellow-cream with reddish speckles
Food: Leaves, buds, shoots, seeds; some insects when young

Very similar in appearance to the chukar but chin and throat are pure white, not creamy buff, and the black necklace extends through the eyes and down to the base of the bill. Stripes on flanks are narrower and neater in appearance than on chukar, and the chest and upperparts are greyer. The general impression at a distance is of very sharply defined set of markings. Juvenile similar to adult but, like on juvenile chukar, head and flank markings are less distinct.

Barbary Partridge

Alectoris barbara

The Barbary partridge will not fly unless approached very closely

THE Barbary partridge is likely to have been introduced into its few sites in Europe, as the species is highly sedentary. This secretive bird remains concealed in low vegetation, usually running from danger to avoid breaking cover. If it does take to the air, the distinctive head pattern and horizontally held wings distinguish it from other partridges. The Barbary partridge will often feed at dawn and dusk and hide during the day; it is partly nocturnal in areas of high disturbance.

Voice: Repetitive 'kchek kchek' and other harsh calls; also curlew-like call in flight
Length: 32–34cm
Wingspan: 46–49cm

Weight: 400–500g
Habitat: Dry, open habitats with low bushes at low altitudes and mountains up to 3,000m
Nest: Shallow scrape, usually unlined
Eggs: 10–14; slightly glossy, yellow-buff with fine reddish-brown markings
Food: Leaves, shoots, seeds, some insects

Very similar to red-legged partridge, but lacks that species' striking facial markings; the face and throat are grey and there is a collar of white spots on a dark-chestnut background, but no necklace. Most distinctive feature is the crown of dark chestnut with a light-grey supercilium. The upperparts are grey-brown with a pinkish tinge and the flanks are less boldly marked than in the red-legged partridge, with bars of black, buff and white.

Grey Partridge

Perdix perdix

Gᴿᴇʏ partridges avoid very wet and very arid areas as these do not provide the nutritious plant foods they require. They use cultivated fields, tracks for dust-bathing and ditches for drinking. Like most partridges, the grey partridge is fairly sedentary, although birds will flock together in winter. In the far east and north of its range, deep snow will drive birds to move further in search of food. When alarmed they will run for cover, eventually taking flight in a flock and dropping quickly when out of danger.

Voice: Harsh 'keirr-ik keirr-ik' at night, 'pitt pitt pik pirr pik' calls when alarmed and fleeing
Length: 29–31cm
Wingspan: 45–48cm
Weight: 350–450g
Habitat: Lowland grassland, cultivated areas
Nest: Shallow depression in low, thick vegetation; grassy lining
Eggs: 10–20; glossy olive-brown
Food: Seeds, buds, leaves, shoots; young eat some insects

This bird has a dumpy, rounded appearance, its head appearing particularly round with no neck. Underparts mostly grey. From a distance, upperparts look brown and plain, although on close inspection they are finely marked with darker brown and buff. Facial colouring is brick-red, contrasting with the grey underside. In flight, distinctive rusty outertail feathers are seen. Adult has dark chestnut horseshoe-shaped patch on underside which is larger in male than female. Juvenile is browner than adult and lacks the horseshoe mark.

Female (far right) has less pronounced horseshoe mark on belly than male (right); juvenile (above) lacks the mark altogether and generally looks browner

Andalusian Hemipode

Turnix sylvatica

Unusually, the female hemipode is the more brightly coloured sex

Tʜᴇ Andalusian hemipode is a most elusive bird, keeping to the ground in thick cover unless flushed, when it will fly low for only a very short distance before dropping. Its smaller size, more striking markings, upright posture on landing and flight outline help distinguish it from the quail. The normal roles of the sexes are reversed in the Andalusian hemipode, with the male caring for the eggs and young, while the female is more brightly coloured and initiates courtship.

Voice: At dawn female gives deep 'hoo hoo hoo' resembling distant cattle
Length: 15–16cm
Wingspan: 25–30cm
Weight: 60–70g
Habitat: Dry, sandy areas with grass and scattered bushes
Nest: Shallow scrape well hidden on ground in low vegetation
Eggs: 4; glossy, pale buff or grey-white with black or red blotches
Food: Seeds, insects

A small, secretive, quail-like bird; adult has rusty-red breast and boldly black-spotted flanks. The crown is brown and finely barred and has a creamy stripe, and the upperparts are brown with darker brown bars and cream streaks. The female is more strikingly marked than the male with overall browner colouring. Juveniles are very similar to males, but at close range show more spots on the chest and white spots on the upperparts.

Black Francolin

Francolinus francolinus

Adult male

Black francolins favour partly dried-up river beds and agricultural land where there are drainage channels and thick cover

Tʜᴇ black francolin is a very difficult bird to see, but its distinctive and far-carrying seven-note call, uttered from a low mound at dawn and dusk, advertises its presence. Normally it remains in thick, low cover and is difficult to flush, but in the breeding season various calls may be heard during the day and it can sometimes be glimpsed in gaps in the vegetation.

In flight this partridge-sized bird shows dark outertail feathers and rich-brown, dark-barred wings. Male has a mostly black head and underside with white ear coverts and white flecks on the flanks. Wings are dark brown with black feather-centres, and tail is finely barred with black and white. There is a broad, chestnut collar. Female has pale head, chestnut patch on neck, and overall brown plumage with black arrow-marks on all feathers. Juvenile resembles female but has dull plumage and faint markings.

Voice: Harsh, shrill 'kek kek kek kek-ek-ek'
Length: 33–36cm
Wingspan: 50–55cm
Weight: 400–500g
Habitat: Low-lying shrubby areas near water; dried-up river beds
Nest: Shallow scrape, little lining
Eggs: 8–12; glossy, pale yellowish-brown, sometimes white-spotted
Food: Seeds, buds, roots, insects

Corncrake

Crex crex

Adult males utter their 'crex crex' call incessantly through the night and early morning

THIS very secretive bird is hard to see but is easily located by the male's far-carrying call. Although it keeps to dense cover in meadows and hayfields, the male will sometimes perch on a stone wall to call or respond to the calls of another male. Corncrakes are summer visitors to Europe, where they attempt to nest in fields before the crops are harvested. Traditional methods allowed them to do this, but modern farming has made most areas unsuitable and this is now a very rare bird, restricted to a few localities where crops are harvested late in the season.

Voice: Far-carrying, rasping 'crex crex' or 'crake crake'
Length: 27–30cm

Wingspan: 46–53cm
Weight: 130–180g
Habitat: Hay meadows, driest areas of marshes

Nest: On ground; shallow cup of leaves with slight canopy
Eggs: 8–12; slightly glossy, greyish-green with reddish-brown spots and blotches
Food: Invertebrates; some plant material

Similar in size to water rail but with shorter, yellowish-brown bill and noticeably long rusty wings when seen in flight. Upperparts of adult are grey-brown with dark centres to the feathers that form broken lines running the length of the body. Neck and supercilium are greyish, but underside is mostly brownish-buff turning to reddish-brown with white barring on the flanks. Sexes are identical apart from the lack of grey on the neck and face of the female. Juvenile resembles female but is paler, with light spots on the wing coverts and grey legs. Legs are flesh coloured, darker in juveniles than adults, and the eyes are pale brown. Flight pattern is weak and the legs dangle.

Flies low, quickly drops into cover and then runs to safety

Water Rail

Rallus aquaticus

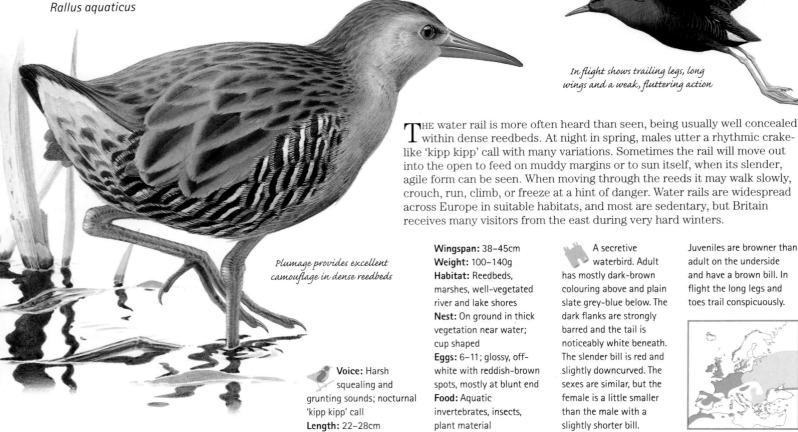

Plumage provides excellent camouflage in dense reedbeds

In flight shows trailing legs, long wings and a weak, fluttering action

THE water rail is more often heard than seen, being usually well concealed within dense reedbeds. At night in spring, males utter a rhythmic crake-like 'kipp kipp' call with many variations. Sometimes the rail will move out into the open to feed on muddy margins or to sun itself, when its slender, agile form can be seen. When moving through the reeds it may walk slowly, crouch, run, climb, or freeze at a hint of danger. Water rails are widespread across Europe in suitable habitats, and most are sedentary, but Britain receives many visitors from the east during very hard winters.

Voice: Harsh squealing and grunting sounds; nocturnal 'kipp kipp' call
Length: 22–28cm

Wingspan: 38–45cm
Weight: 100–140g
Habitat: Reedbeds, marshes, well-vegetated river and lake shores
Nest: On ground in thick vegetation near water; cup shaped
Eggs: 6–11; glossy, off-white with reddish-brown spots, mostly at blunt end
Food: Aquatic invertebrates, insects, plant material

A secretive waterbird. Adult has mostly dark-brown colouring above and plain slate grey-blue below. The dark flanks are strongly barred and the tail is noticeably white beneath. The slender bill is red and slightly downcurved. The sexes are similar, but the female is a little smaller than the male with a slightly shorter bill.

Juveniles are browner than adult on the underside and have a brown bill. In flight the long legs and toes trail conspicuously.

Spotted Crake

Porzana porzana

Spotting on plumage only visible at very close range

Adult male

WHEN seen in good light the spotted crake is not easily confused with any other small water bird but its secretive habits make it difficult to locate; the 'whiplash' call, heard mostly at night, is the best guide to its presence. Outside the breeding season, spotted crakes are normally solitary. They keep to dense vegetation along the edges of rivers and lakes that have muddy margins, finding small food items at the surface of the mud or among plant roots; they are known to take a variety of small invertebrates and some plant material.

Voice: Far-carrying 'dripping tap' call – 'hwitt hwitt'
Length: 22–24cm
Wingspan: 37–42cm
Weight: 70–100g
Habitat: Sedges and rushes bordering lakes, ponds and rivers
Nest: Cup-shaped on tussock in thick waterside vegetation
Eggs: 10–12; glossy, olive-buff with reddish-brown and grey spots
Food: Aquatic invertebrates, plant material

A small, compact water bird, which at a distance appears all dark grey-brown or greenish-brown, but in good light looks spotted. The undertail is pale buff, the short pointed bill is red at the base with a yellowish-orange tip, and the legs and feet are bright olive-green. Females resemble males but have less grey on the face and underparts, with slightly more spotting. Juveniles resemble females but lack any grey tones and have less spotting and duller, olive-coloured legs.

From behind, buff undertail is best identifier

Little Crake

Porzana parva

Little crakes are adept at walking over floating mats of vegetation

Adult male

LITTLE crakes prefer slightly deeper water than do other small crakes; they are more inclined to swim or even dive briefly and will also emerge into the open on the edges of reeds in the early mornings and at dusk. They will also sometimes climb up stems of bulrush and reedmace for short distances to reach food. Little crakes are scarce in western Europe but in central and eastern Europe they are locally common around nutrient-rich lakes.

Voice: Low accelerating croaking sounds, ending in a trill
Length: 18–20cm
Wingspan: 34–39cm
Weight: 37–60g
Habitat: Reedbeds and swamps with still water and floating vegetation
Nest: Shallow cup on raised tussock in thick waterside vegetation
Eggs: 7–9; glossy, yellow-buff with brown spots and blotches
Food: Aquatic invertebrates

Male is olive-brown above with the feathers showing dark centres and buff margins; at close range the scapulars and mantle show some pale streaks. The face and underside are slate-blue or grey with pale streaking on the rear flanks and undertail coverts, which are not as striking as in the water rail. Female is pale buff beneath, rather than grey, and has a whitish face with faint barring under the tail.

Juvenile is similar to female but is paler below; shows white supercilium and pale mottling on the chest and flanks; barring on the underside is darker than in female.

Baillon's Crake

Porzana pusilla

Adult male has slate-blue face and chest

THE Baillon's crake's normal habit is to search for food among dense water plants and it rarely emerges into the open. It swims readily and can make shallow dives, so is often found in areas of deep water in large swamps and reedbeds. The frog-like call is produced mostly by the male, but females utter shorter, rasping notes near the nest. Its secretive habits make this a very difficult bird to observe. When alarmed it flicks its tail, showing the dark underside with white barring, and also flicks its head; the red eye can appear pale against the dark cheeks.

Voice: Rasping sounds resembling a finger scratching a comb
Length: 17–19cm
Wingspan: 33–37cm
Weight: 30–50g
Habitat: Swampy areas with thick vegetation, streamsides, pond margins
Nest: On ground in thick cover next to water; cup-shaped with canopy
Eggs: 6–8; glossy, yellowish-buff with brownish streaks and spots
Food: Aquatic invertebrates, some plant material

A very small waterbird, the size of a house sparrow, with colouring resembling a water rail. Adult upperparts are rufous brown with irregular whitish spots and streaks, and the feathers have dark centres. The face and chest are deep slate-blue and unmarked, but the rear flanks and underside as far as the tail are black with white barring. The legs are a dark flesh colour or dull olive, and the bill is green. The female is almost identical to the male but the throat and chest region are paler grey. Juveniles have the same upperpart colouring as adults, but are buff-coloured below and the bill is brownish. Has weak flight with dangling legs that is characteristic of smaller crakes.

Coot

Fulica atra

Coots are widespread across Europe where suitable water bodies exist, and are resident in the south and west

AN AGGRESSIVE water bird of larger bodies of water, the coot defends a territory in spring against all comers. Coots prefer areas free of overhanging trees or steep banks and usually avoid fast rivers unless there is thick marginal vegetation. Outside the breeding season they will sometimes gather in large flocks and may be seen feeding confidently some distance away from the water's edge. They swim and dive quite well and fly freely, taking off by pattering across the water with rapidly flapping wings. This is the least retiring and secretive of the rail family, and is very confident on urban park lakes.

Nest: Platform of plant material over shallow water, hidden by tall plants
Eggs: 6–10; slightly glossy, buff with dark speckling
Food: Mainly aquatic plant material but some invertebrates also taken

black, while flanks are greyer. In flight, wings appear to have a pale margin. Juvenile is dull brown with pale face and throat, and a yellowish-grey bill.

Voice: Loud repetitive 'kowk' and explosive shrill 'pitt'
Length: 36–38cm
Wingspan: 70–80cm
Weight: 600–900g
Habitat: Larger ponds and lakes, canals, urban park lakes

A rounded, sooty-black water bird, adult with gleaming white bill and facial shield and red eye. Sexes are identical, although the male is larger than the female. At close range, head and neck are seen to be the most intensely

The greenish feet have lobes on them to aid swimming; they are large and conspicuous on land and in flight

Crested Coot

Fulica cristata

THE crested coot is a very rare bird in Europe. Where its restricted range overlaps with the coot's, it can be difficult to pick out, even in the breeding season when its 'horns' are most prominent. When the species are seen together, the crested coot seems to have a slightly longer and stiffer neck than its common cousin, and a flatter head. A strange groaning or 'mooing' call is sometimes uttered from cover. This species is not as tolerant of human presence as the coot and is also less inclined to emerge on to land to feed; it is also intolerant of colder conditions.

Adult very similar to coot but has slate-blue legs and feet

Eggs: 5–7; slightly glossy, pale grey with dark-brown speckles
Food: Mainly aquatic plants, especially roots and tubers, some invertebrates

Voice: Two-note 'clukuk' and a metallic 'croo-oo-k'
Length: 38–42cm
Wingspan: 75–85cm
Weight: 800–900g
Habitat: Large water bodies with plenty of marginal vegetation
Nest: Floating platform in shallow water, concealed by emergent vegetation

Slightly larger than the coot, but in other respects very similar. Sexes are identical. Adult has red knobs over the facial shield that can be seen at close range; at a distance they are not especially obvious and in winter they are smaller and duller than during the

breeding season. In flight, wings lack the white edge to the secondaries seen in the coot. Juvenile is drab brownish-black with a paler chin and throat, and a white centre to the belly. Adults and juveniles have slate-blue legs and feet.

Moorhen

Gallinula chloropus

Can become confident close to humans in town parks

THE moorhen has adapted well to life in a variety of wetland habitats and is as likely to be seen out in the open grassland as on a deep lake or among dense reeds. Its fluttering take-off gives way to a relatively powerful flight, and it can also climb well and seek food on overhanging branches of waterside trees. During the breeding season moorhens are rather secretive and solitary, nesting in concealed sites close to or even on the water. After breeding they may gather in larger groups in favourable feeding areas.

Voice: Varied, loud calls, including harsh 'krreck' and rhythmic 'kipp kipp kipp'
Length: 32–35cm
Wingspan: 50–55cm
Weight: 250–330g
Habitat: Wetlands, including urban park lakes, rivers, small ponds

Nest: Near water, sometimes on floating platform; untidy cup of leaves, stems
Eggs: 5–9; glossy, buff with brownish spots and blotches
Food: Aquatic and terrestrial invertebrates, plant material

At a distance adult appears all black with a red shield on the face and yellow tip to the bill. A horizontal white line along the flanks and the black and white pattern under the constantly flicked tail make confusion with any other water bird unlikely. Seen more closely in good light the plumage is black only on the head, while the rest of the upperparts are very dark brown and the underside is deep slate-grey. Before the autumn moult the worn plumage looks dusty and the white lateral line may disappear. Juveniles are brownish overall with paler flanks and chest, white chin and throat, and a buff rather than white lateral line. The undertail pattern resembles that of the adult.

Adult

The tail is flicked constantly, and when swimming the head bobs forwards with each push of the feet

Purple Gallinule

Porphyrio porphyrio

THE purple gallinule is a very scarce bird in Europe, found only in brackish marshes and areas of still water where there is ample plant material for it to feed on. It is adept at uprooting tubers and rhizomes of water plants, and can manipulate these in its feet to get at the central pith; it will also raid the nests of other waterbirds, taking eggs and chicks. Its slow walk is heron-like and it can swim or dive quite easily, sometimes emerging into open water, often at dawn or dusk. Most birds are resident and do not undertake long migrations.

Voice: Variable, deeper versions of moorhen calls, low 'chock chock'
Length: 45–50cm
Wingspan: 90–100cm
Weight: 720–900g
Habitat: Marshes, reedbeds, tracts of bulrush, brackish swamps
Nest: Large mass of leaves and stems over water in dense vegetation
Eggs: 3–5; glossy, cream with maroon or grey spots and blotches
Food: Aquatic plant roots and shoots, seeds, buds, invertebrates, frogs

Adult has violet-blue plumage with brighter blue face, and red legs, eyes and bill. Undertail is white. Sexes similar but male is larger. After breeding, the bill is duller and has dark patches. The bluest birds are those from the western Mediterranean; the Egyptian race has green tinges on the scapulars and back, and the Middle Eastern race has a green head and is paler blue. Juveniles are grey, with dull-red bill and legs and white throat.

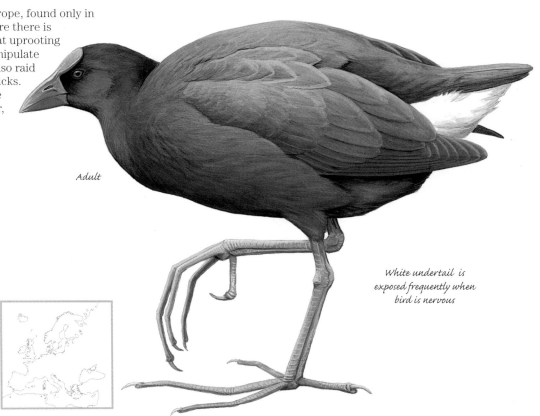

Adult

White undertail is exposed frequently when bird is nervous

Crane

Grus grus

On migration and in their winter quarters cranes form large flocks and are easier to observe than in the breeding season

Cranes search for food by walking slowly and probing with the large bill; plant material is the commonest food in winter but in the breeding season frogs, ground-nesting birds and invertebrates will also be eaten

Adult cranes are stately and imposing birds

Cranes are solitary and nervous birds during the breeding season, but the rest of the year they congregate in large flocks. They nest in wetland areas, sometimes in boggy clearings in forested areas in the far north, using sites that afford them protection from predators. The crane's elaborate dancing display is most commonly seen in spring, and involves wing-flapping, head-pointing and jumping. This sometimes precedes courtship, or may be performed by rival males. It is thought that cranes pair for life. In the autumn cranes migrate in small flocks and family groups in a tight 'V' formation to overwintering sites in Africa, India and southeast Asia; a few use traditional European sites in Portugal and Spain. There are regular stop-over sites that are mostly protected from hunting.

Voice: Loud bugling calls, plus 'kroo-krii kroo-krii' calls by pairs
Length: 110–130cm
Wingspan: 200–230cm
Weight: 4.5–6kg
Habitat: Marshes, farmland, large boggy clearings in northern forests
Nest: Large pile of vegetation with hollow top; on ground or in shallow water
Eggs: 2; slightly glossy, variable colours from buff through olive to red-brown, spotted with red or dark brown
Food: Invertebrates, small mammals, nestling birds, fruits, seeds

Adult plumage is mostly grey but the head is much darker, appearing black at a distance, with a white band extending back from the red eye and a red crown. The chest and parts of the back have a pale-rufous tinge, and the tail and overhanging cloak of secondaries are darker. Juvenile is paler grey than adult with an unpatterned head and grey, rather than black, legs. In flight it shows long wings of even width with black flight feathers and a long extended neck and trailing legs.

A very large bird of upright posture, which moves in a steady and measured way on the ground. Sexes similar.

Demoiselle Crane

Anthropoides virgo

The best chance of seeing wild demoiselle cranes in Europe is to visit Cyprus during migration time: small numbers pass through from late March to mid-April, and larger numbers in late August and early September. Views in Europe are generally of distant flying birds, so certain separation from the crane may be difficult. Size alone is not a good identifier but the demoiselle crane's neck is proportionately shorter. The greater extent of black on the neck is diagnostic, but often difficult to detect in flying birds. The demoiselle crane's call is higher pitched than its cousin's.

Voice: Grating, honking flock calls uttered on ground and in flight
Length: 80–100cm
Wingspan: 170–180cm
Weight: 2.4–2.8kg
Habitat: Steppe and upland grassland
Nest: Shallow scrape on ground
Eggs: 2; greyish-buff
Food: Mainly plant material but some invertebrates

Superficially similar to common crane but smaller. Sexes similar. Adult has mainly pale blue-grey plumage, but is black from throat and neck to breast and has broad, black supercilium bordering grey crown. White nape plumes arise from behind eye. Iris red. Black flight feathers mostly hidden at rest but conspicuous in flight. Legs dark and bill yellowish. Juvenile has grubby brownish-grey plumage and lacks adult's head and neck patterns.

Great Bustard

Otis tarda

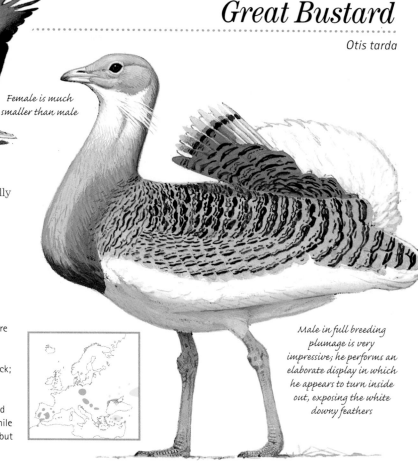

Female is much smaller than male

Normally the great bustard is a very shy bird and is difficult to observe; it keeps to open plains where it can spot danger easily and flee if necessary. The broad wings of the great bustard show a white panel in flight; this is much smaller in the female than the male, but both fly with strong, eagle-like wingbeats. Birds in the far east of Europe migrate south in the winter, but in the west of their range they disperse locally to more productive winter feeding areas. Great bustards were once widespread across Europe, but have declined considerably.

Voice: Mostly silent, but may give short, barking, alarm note
Length: 75–105cm
Wingspan: 190–260cm
Weight: 12–16kg (male), 4–8kg (female)
Habitat: Open grasslands, lowland areas, wide river valleys and plains
Nest: Shallow depression on ground in low vegetation
Eggs: 2–3; glossy, variable pale colours with brown blotches

Food: Plant material, invertebrates; few small birds and mammals in summer

Europe's heaviest bird. In the breeding season the displaying male has a bulging neck and a cocked-up tail that makes it appear even larger. Breeding males also have a strong chestnut chest band and white moustachial 'whiskers' extending back from base of bill. Outside the breeding season, male resembles female apart from his greater size. Female head and neck are grey with upperparts cinnamon-brown but strongly barred with black; the underside is white, giving the bird a three-coloured grey, brown and white appearance. Juvenile resembles adult female but has a buff neck.

Male in full breeding plumage is very impressive; he performs an elaborate display in which he appears to turn inside out, exposing the white downy feathers

Little Bustard

Tetrax tetrax

Female (above) lacks black and white neck pattern

In spring displaying male little bustards stand out in the open with their neck feathers splayed out

Male little bustards display in the spring in the open; they give short rasping calls and make short jumps into the air. In flight they resemble gamebirds or possibly mallards. The male's wings create a rhythmic whistling sound due to a short, narrow, fourth primary feather. Little bustards are commonest in southwest Europe, where they are resident year round, but there are scattered breeding sites in France and Turkey. Their preferred habitat of open grassy plains leads them to use man-made sites such as airfields and military training grounds. Little bustards are strong fliers and take to the air if disturbed; they seem to be intolerant of humans.

Voice: Snorting 'knerr' or 'pritt' calls, various grunts and whistles
Length: 40–45cm
Wingspan: 105–115cm
Weight: 600–950g
Habitat: Open grassy plains, large arable fields, grassy airfields
Nest: Shallow scrape on ground in low vegetation
Eggs: 3–4; glossy, olive-brown or green with darker streaks and spots

Food: Plant material, invertebrates

A pheasant-sized bird with sturdy legs and a small head on a long thick neck. The overall body colour is speckled grey-brown with a white underside. Adult male has a strongly patterned black and white head and neck with a grey throat. Female lacks the male's black and white patterning, but has coarse speckling on the back. In flight both sexes show white wings with black-tipped primaries and primary coverts, and a black and white tail rim. Juvenile is similar to female.

Oystercatcher

Haematopus ostralegus

Northern birds migrate south for the winter, and flocks of thousands also gather on British estuaries

Plumage is striking black and white with heavy orange bill; winter birds (right) acquire white collar

OYSTERCATCHERS are common where there are shorelines that provide molluscs such as cockles and mussels to feed on; they open the shells with their powerful bills. They also take marine worms from mud, catching them by probing with their long bills. They roost communally so are normally found in areas that provide safe high-tide roosts as well as good feeding areas. In the breeding season the flocks disperse and they spread themselves out around the coast and along broad, stony rivers, usually nesting among rocks and pebbles.

Voice: Shrill piping calls, loud 'kubeek kubeek' alarm call
Length: 40–45cm
Wingspan: 80–86cm
Weight: 450–700g
Habitat: Rocky shores, estuaries, large stony rivers, stony lake shores
Nest: Shallow scrape in the open, lined with pebbles or shells; sometimes on promontory
Eggs: 3; slightly glossy, buff-yellow with many dark spots, blotches, streaks
Food: Molluscs, marine worms; earthworms for inland birds

Adults have striking black and white plumage, a red eye, an orange-pink bill and red-pink legs. In winter, adults acquire a white chin stripe on the otherwise black neck. Newly fledged juveniles are exceptionally well camouflaged to resemble lichen-covered rocks. First-winter birds are paler than adults with a larger, white throat patch.

Avocet

Recurvirostra avosetta

In flight shows long, trailing bluish-grey legs; wing action is strong and shows off black and white wing pattern well

THE avocet uses its upcurved bill to sweep through liquid mud in search of tiny invertebrates; the side-to-side motion of the head is characteristic of this species. It prefers water about 10cm deep, a depth at which the long legs are hidden when wading. It can also swim if necessary, and frequently up-ends itself like a duck to reach deeper mud. In flight it often gives its clear, ringing call. Avocets are generally summer visitors to the coasts of northwest Europe but a few remain in overwintering sites in southwest England in mild winters.

Voice: Varied calls, including a ringing 'pleet pleet'
Length: 42–46cm
Wingspan: 77–80cm
Weight: 230–290g
Habitat: Estuaries, coastal lagoons, saltpans, shallow lakes
Nest: Shallow scrape in the open, near water; some lining of shells, stones
Eggs: 3–4; smooth, pale buff with brownish spots and blotches
Food: Small invertebrates

A unique large, black and white wader with a strongly upcurved bill and long, blue-grey legs. The plumage is predominantly white with a black head and nape and black panels on the wings, which appear as oval panels in flight. From below the avocet looks all white in flight apart from black wingtips. Sexes identical and juveniles resemble adults except that the black element of the adult plumage is brownish instead.

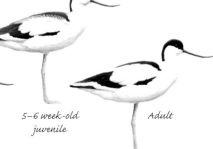

7–10-day-old chick

Newly hatched chick

3-week-old juvenile

5–6 week-old juvenile

Adult

Stone-curlew

Burhinus oedicnemus

staring yellow and black eye gives stone-curlew stern appearance

STONE-CURLEWS are largely nocturnal in their habits, giving their presence away by their eerie and far-carrying calls. During the day they rest quietly amongst low vegetation, remaining motionless even when approached closely. When flushed they fly off low over the ground with strong but shallow wingbeats, dropping into cover and running for a short distance before freezing again. Normally solitary, stone-curlews gather together in small flocks after the breeding season and before embarking on migration; in some cases there are traditional gathering sites where they may congregate before heading south. Birds in southwest Europe are residents. Changes in agriculture and increased persecution have led to a great decline in numbers in many regions.

Voice: Curlew-like flight call, and various high-pitched whistling and shrill wader-like calls at night
Length: 40–44cm
Wingspan: 77–85cm
Weight: 440–500g
Habitat: Dry, open areas, semi-desert, arable land, heaths
Nest: Shallow scrape in open position; lining of small stones, rabbit droppings
Eggs: 1–3; slightly glossy, pale buff with brownish-purple streaks and spots
Food: Soil invertebrates, small birds, mammals, frogs

A stocky wader with large, black and yellow eyes and stout, almost gull-like bill, which is black at tip. Sexes similar. Adult plumage is mostly sandy brown with darker streaks; underside is pale. At rest, wings show a white bar and dark lower edge; in flight, wings appear black with paler panels. Tail appears relatively long. When standing the tarsus joint is prominent. Juvenile resembles adult but is less boldly marked.

Black-winged Stilt

Himantopus himantopus

Adult female

Walks gracefully with delicate high steps

Adult male

THE black-winged stilt has the longest legs, proportional to its size, of any bird, although in deep water it moves much like any other wader. Its long, slender bill is used to snatch at tiny insects in the air and on emergent vegetation, and it can also be used to probe into soft mud for tiny aquatic larvae; when probing for food in deep water the stilt's head may be completely submerged. The stilts prefer areas with high invertebrate populations and may nest in loose colonies. They are not tolerant of direct human disturbance, but seem to accept the presence of visitors who do not interfere with them.

Voice: Varied short, nasal, bleating calls
Length: 35–40cm
Wingspan: 67–83cm
Weight: 140–220g
Habitat: Coastal lagoons, shallow lakes, saltpans
Nest: Shallow scrape near water, or raised platform over shallow water
Eggs: 4; smooth, pale brown with black spots and blotches
Food: Small aquatic invertebrates

A very long-legged wader with entirely black and white plumage. The wings and mantle are black and the underside is white, but the degree of black on the head is variable. In flight the white rump and long white wedge on the back show clearly, as do the trailing pink legs. The head may be all white or show varying amounts of black. The sexes are very similar except that breeding female usually shows pure white head and neck. Juvenile is paler on the mantle than adult, with sepia tinges to the darker feathers.

Dotterel

Charadrius morinellus

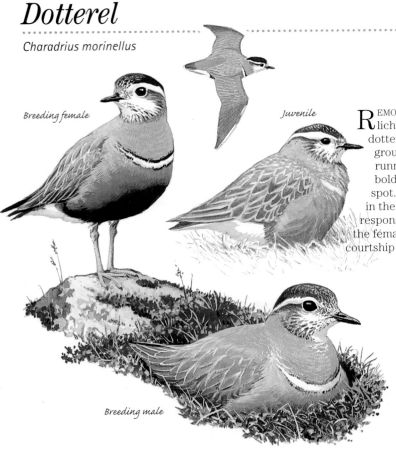

Breeding female

Juvenile

Breeding male

Remote mountain tops with sparse mosses and lichens are the preferred breeding habitat of the dotterel. It is a very confiding bird on its breeding grounds, spending most of its time on the ground, running from danger rather than flying. Despite its bold markings, the stationary bird can be hard to spot. The traditional roles of the sexes are reversed in the breeding season, with the male taking most responsibility for the care of the eggs and young; it is the female who has the brightest colours, initiates courtship and performs displays over a territory.

Voice: Soft 'pweet pweet' flight calls and trilling calls on ground
Length: 20–22cm
Wingspan: 57–64cm
Weight: 86–130g
Habitat: Dry, open mountain plateaux; overwinters on arid grasslands
Nest: Shallow scrape, often near large stone; moss or lichen lining
Eggs: 3; smooth, buff with green tinge and darker red-brown blotches and streaks
Food: Insects, small soil invertebrates

Distinctly patterned wader with no real affinity for water. In the breeding season, adult has broad, white supercilium and thin black and white chest band. Crown is very dark, framed by white eyestripes that meet on nape; face is whitish and rest of upperparts and neck are grey-brown. Chest is a rich chestnut with a darker centre and the undertail region is white. Female is generally brighter and more distinctive than male. In winter, colours fade to more uniform buff-brown with less markedly white supercilium. Juvenile resembles winter adult but has pale feather margins, which give a scalloped appearance.

Ringed Plover

Charadrius hiaticula

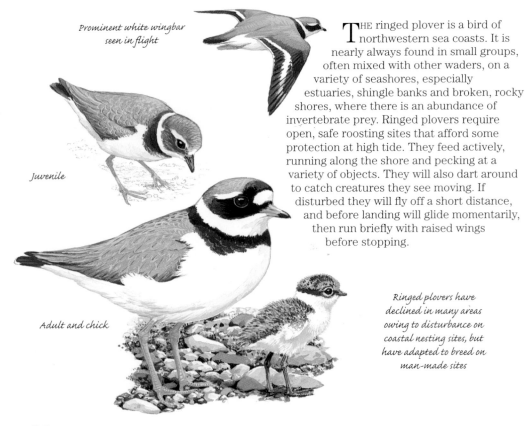

Prominent white wingbar seen in flight

Juvenile

Adult and chick

The ringed plover is a bird of northwestern sea coasts. It is nearly always found in small groups, often mixed with other waders, on a variety of seashores, especially estuaries, shingle banks and broken, rocky shores, where there is an abundance of invertebrate prey. Ringed plovers require open, safe roosting sites that afford some protection at high tide. They feed actively, running along the shore and pecking at a variety of objects. They will also dart around to catch creatures they see moving. If disturbed they will fly off a short distance, and before landing will glide momentarily, then run briefly with raised wings before stopping.

Ringed plovers have declined in many areas owing to disturbance on coastal nesting sites, but have adapted to breed on man-made sites

Voice: A quiet 'tooip' whistle, and a louder alarm 'te-lee-a te-lee-a'
Length: 18–20cm
Wingspan: 48–57cm
Weight: 54–74g
Habitat: Seashores, estuaries, large lake shores, tundra
Nest: Shallow scrape in open, near water; lining of small pebbles, shells
Eggs: 3–4; slightly glossy or dull, pale buff with black spots and blotches
Food: Invertebrates, mainly worms, molluscs, shrimps, larvae

Small, stocky wader with mostly plain colouring but striking facial markings. Upperparts of adult grey-brown and underparts pure white; in summer, legs and bill base are orange, but in winter legs are darker and bill is all dark with a yellow base to the lower mandible. Head is strikingly marked with black cheeks and black line over the brow; there is a black chest ring. In winter, black fades and looks worn. Sexes are almost identical, although some females have less distinct black markings than males. Juvenile resembles adult, but has a scalloped appearance on upperparts due to pale feather edges, and partial brownish collar. Striking white wingbars show well in flight in both adults and juveniles.

Little Ringed Plover

Charadrius dubius

In flight lack of white wingbar immediately obvious

L ITTLE ringed plovers are summer visitors to Europe, arriving on their mostly inland breeding grounds in early spring from their overwintering quarters in northern tropical Africa. They have adapted well to human activities such as gravel extraction, which expose the type of terrain they prefer to nest on. They are very secretive when nesting, but their far-carrying calls are good clues to their presence. If disturbed by a predator a nesting bird will perform an elaborate distraction display, dragging its wings or pretending to feed in order to lead attention away from the nest.

Voice: Loud 'kiu' flight call and plaintive 'krree-u krree-u'
Length: 14–15cm
Wingspan: 42–48cm
Weight: 33–48g
Habitat: Dry, open habitats, gravel beds, lake shores, and similar man-made sites
Nest: Shallow scrape on bare ground near water; some lining of stones
Eggs: 4; not glossy, buff or stone-coloured with many brown spots and streaks
Food: Insects, spiders, aquatic invertebrates

Small, slender wader. Sexes similar. Adult has dull-brown upperparts and pure white underparts with a strongly patterned head. Bright-yellow eyering stands out well against the black cheeks. Bill is all black and legs are dull orange-brown. When seen in flight the lack of any wingbar at any time is diagnostic for this species. Juvenile looks like faded version of adult with indistinct head and chest markings.

Juvenile (above) only has trace of pale line over eye

Little ringed plovers are absent from the far north and avoid densely vegetated areas and very wet habitats

Kentish Plover

Charadrius alexandrinus

M OST Kentish plovers are summer visitors to Europe, spending the winter on the west coast of Africa, although they can be found along the Mediterranean shore in winter. Like many small waders that nest on the shore, this species is subject in the breeding season to disturbance caused by human interference. It has adapted to changes in land use in some areas and has made use of saltpans and gravel extraction areas, abandoning them as they become unsuitable. Where appropriate, safe nesting areas do occur the Kentish plover can be almost colonial, with several nests being built within a short distance of each other.

Voice: Short 'kip' or 'peep' sounds
Length: 15–17cm
Wingspan: 42–58cm
Weight: 40–54g
Habitat: Lagoons, estuaries, saltpans; mainly in Mediterranean
Nest: Shallow scrape on ground, usually near water; lining of shells or pebbles
Eggs: 3; not glossy, pale buff with black streaks and spots
Food: Small worms, crustaceans, molluscs; insects when inland

Small, pale plover. Adult shows less black on head than ringed plover and neck ring is incomplete. Breeding male has chestnut crown and black patch on forehead; female has no black patch and a grey-brown crown. In winter, male resembles female, with both becoming duller in appearance. Bill and legs are black, and both sexes appear longer-legged than the ringed plover. Juvenile plainer than adult, with greyer upperparts.

In flight shows broad, white wingbar; often looks relatively large-headed and short-tailed

Male only has chestnut crown during breeding season

Lapwing

Vanellus vanellus

THE lapwing is a very agile bird in the air, performing exciting displays over its territory at the start of the breeding season. The acrobatic swoops and dives are accompanied by the typical 'pee-wit' call. It can take to the air with great ease and quickly turn to mob a predator. In winter, large flocks form near favoured feeding areas, and at the onset of snow or frost they will move south or west to find new areas. In the south and west of their range lapwings are mostly year-round residents, but in the east and north they are summer visitors only.

All adults have a long black crest but the male's is longer than the female's

Voice: Shrill 'peeoo-wit' and other more scratchy sounds
Length: 28–31cm
Wingspan: 75–85cm
Weight: 190–300g
Habitat: Wet grasslands, marshes, open pastures
Nest: In the open, slightly raised on tussock or mound; shallow scrape with lining of vegetation in wet areas
Eggs: 4; smooth, olive, brown or pale with heavy streaks and spots
Food: Soil invertebrates, especially beetles and earthworms

Adult has glossy green upperparts and all-white underparts apart from rich orange undertail coverts, seen when bird dips its head during feeding. Male is more boldly marked than female. At a distance, lapwing appears all black and white, and in flight shows long, broad, black and white wings with white tips to three outer primaries. In winter, feathers have pale margins which give a scalloped appearance to the mantle; cheeks are buff rather than white. Juvenile resembles winter adult but has shorter crest and browner chest.

In his spring display flight male rises slowly before suddenly diving down, twisting and turning as if out of control before pulling up

Lapwings are found across Europe in summer in any suitable open habitat, avoiding only very high ground and steep slopes – the presence of ground they can run over in search of food seems to be the key factor in choice of habitat

Adults vigorously defend nests against potential predators such as magpies

Male attracts female to nest site by scraping

On alighting after display flight, male often holds wings up for a few seconds

Spur-winged Plover

Hoplopterus spinosus

WHEN standing still the spur-winged plover has a curious hunched posture, but when feeding or flying it recalls the lapwing. It is sometimes possible to approach the bird quite closely, but if defending its territory it will mob intruders fearlessly. It lives in small flocks, or more usually pairs, but will mix with other similar species, such as the lapwing, in good feeding areas. Most of its time is spent on the ground, where it finds its food, and when in flight it normally keeps low.

Voice: Shrill 'peey-k peey-k peey-k' and lapwing-like calls
Length: 25–27cm
Wingspan: 65–80cm
Weight: 130–160g
Habitat: Lakesides, marshes, river deltas, dry grassland
Nest: Shallow scrape in the open, near water; sparse lining
Eggs: 4; smooth, creamy-yellow with heavy black blotches and spots
Food: Ground-living invertebrates

Sexes similar. Adult has mainly black and white underparts and buff wing coverts and back. Face and shoulders are white, and in flight the mostly white underwing shows clearly, contrasting with black tips to primaries and black belly. Upperwing has white panel between black primaries and buff mantle. Rump is white and tail has broad, black terminal band. Juvenile resembles adult but has pale margins to dark feathers, giving scalloped appearance.

Golden Plover

Pluvialis apricaria

Belly white in winter (right) and black in summer (far right)

THE golden plover is a bird of open moorlands and bogs where the vegetation is short enough to allow it to run easily. It feeds on the ground, pursuing small soil invertebrates, and takes flight only if disturbed. It will occasionally stand on a small tussock to survey its territory or use a grass clump to provide a little cover. Outside the breeding season golden plovers leave the high moorlands and move to lower levels to form flocks, sometimes mixed with lapwings, on open arable lands, grass airfields and the upper reaches of estuaries. Only in the most severe weather will they move to the seashore.

Voice: A mournful, whistling 'pyuuh' or 'pyuu pu'
Length: 26–29cm
Wingspan: 67–76cm
Weight: 150–220g
Habitat: Breeds on moorlands, bogs; overwinters on lowland pastures
Nest: Shallow scrape on tussocky ground, sparse lining
Eggs: 4; slightly glossy, greenish-olive or buff with darker streaks and blotches
Food: Soil invertebrates, some berries and seeds

Plump wader with short bill and rounded head and spangled golden-brown upperparts. In summer, male has black face and black underside separated from upperparts by broad white border. In flight it shows white underwings contrasting with black belly. Female similar to male but has far less black on underside, which is restricted to belly; face is greyer than male's and white border to the black areas is less distinct.

Northern birds (Iceland and Scandinavia) have far more black than southern birds (Britain). In winter sexes are similar, with no black on the underside and more uniform plumage overall. Juvenile paler above than adult and greyer below, lacking the golden tinge to the plumage seen in adults in all seasons.

Grey Plover

Pluvialis squatarola

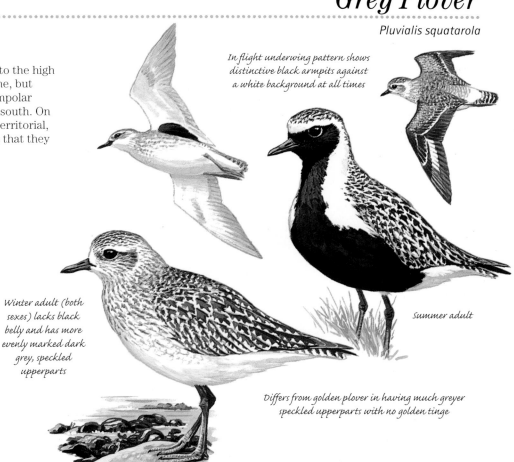

In flight underwing pattern shows distinctive black armpits against a white background at all times

Winter adult (both sexes) lacks black belly and has more evenly marked dark grey, speckled upperparts

summer adult

Differs from golden plover in having much greyer speckled upperparts with no golden tinge

IN THE breeding season the grey plover is confined to the high Arctic, nesting on open ground beyond the tree line, but usually not on the coast or on islands. It has a circumpolar distribution. In autumn the whole population heads south. On their overwintering sites grey plovers may become territorial, defending good feeding areas, and there is evidence that they remain faithful to these sites over several years.

Voice: Whistling 'pleeoo-wee'
Length: 27–30cm
Wingspan: 71–83cm
Weight: 215–300g
Habitat: Breeds on Arctic tundra; overwinters on muddy and sandy seashores
Nest: Shallow scrape on dry ground; lining of small stones
Eggs: 4; smooth, grey or buff with darker spots and blotches
Food: Soil invertebrates on breeding grounds; small molluscs, crabs, worms, etc on shore

In summer male is strikingly black below with pale head and white shoulders, and white-flecked upperparts. Female is duller than male and has greyish cheeks and grey-brown upperparts. Juvenile resembles winter adult (see caption) but with pale-buff wash to plumage.

Collared Pratincole

Glareola pratincola

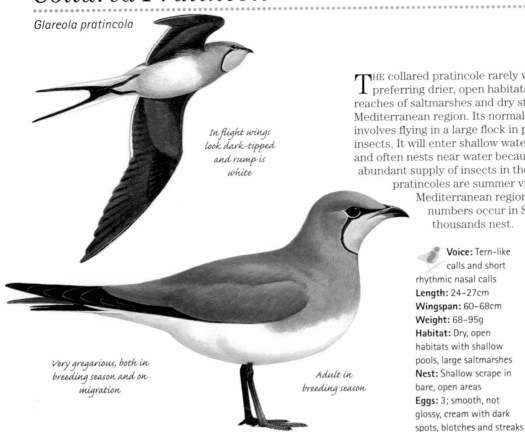

In flight wings look dark-tipped and rump is white

Very gregarious, both in breeding season and on migration

Adult in breeding season

THE collared pratincole rarely wades in water to feed, preferring drier, open habitats, such as the uppermost reaches of saltmarshes and dry steppe areas in the Mediterranean region. Its normal method of feeding involves flying in a large flock in pursuit of airborne insects. It will enter shallow water to drink and preen, and often nests near water because there may be a more abundant supply of insects in the vicinity. Collared pratincoles are summer visitors to the Mediterranean region; the greatest numbers occur in Spain, where many thousands nest.

Voice: Tern-like calls and short rhythmic nasal calls
Length: 24–27cm
Wingspan: 60–68cm
Weight: 68–95g
Habitat: Dry, open habitats with shallow pools, large saltmarshes
Nest: Shallow scrape in bare, open areas
Eggs: 3; smooth, not glossy, cream with dark spots, blotches and streaks

Food: Invertebrates, especially insects caught in flight

No other European small wader (apart from black-winged pratincole) has combination of a very short bill, forked tail and long wings. At a distance, adult upperparts appear dark sandy or olive-brown with darker primaries and tail

feathers. Underside is divided into pure white belly, light-olive chest and buff throat, clearly demarcated by thin black necklace stretching from eye to eye under chin. Gape of bill is bright red. Outside breeding season, adults have far less distinct necklace and more spotted throat and chest. Juvenile looks more speckled than adult because of pale margins to feathers; necklace is absent.

Black-winged Pratincole

Glareola nordmanni

Summer adult

As a breeding species, the black-winged pratincole is essentially a bird of steppe grassland, occurring on lowlands to the north of the Black Sea and at similar latitudes eastwards into central Asia; it occasionally breeds further west, sometimes among colonies of collared pratincoles

Voice: Churring calls at nest; squeaky call uttered in flight
Length: 25cm
Wingspan: 60–65cm
Weight: 90–100g
Habitat: Steppe grassland, usually close to water
Nest: Shallow scrape
Eggs: 4; olive green with darker spots
Food: Insects; mainly caught in flight but sometimes on ground

Superficially very similar to collared pratincole. Sexes similar. Summer adult at rest looks rather tern-like in

silhouette. Plumage essentially dark sandy brown, palest on underparts. Has creamy-buff throat outlined and bordered by black and white lines. In flight, recalls tern or outsized hirundine. Shows forked tail and white rump. Upperwings uniformly dark sandy brown, lacking white trailing edge to innerwing and contrasting dark wingtip seen in collared pratincole. Underwing all-dark, lacking reddish-brown underwing coverts of collared pratincole. Winter adult (not seen in region) has pale feather margins on upperparts, giving scaly appearance, and less clearly defined throat markings. Juvenile recalls winter adult but looks even more scaly on back and on breast.

IN WEST and northwest Europe black-winged pratincoles occur only as vagrants. The species is rarely seen on passage; a trickle of birds is noted in early autumn, however, in the eastern Mediterranean. Birds sometimes disperse in late summer prior to migrating so a trip to eastern Austria or Hungary can provide sightings. Separation from the collared pratincole can be problematic. The black underwing is diagnostic, but the collared pratincole's reddish underwing often looks dark when seen against the light. Better pointers are the black-winged pratincole's uniformly coloured upperwing, and absence of white trailing edge to secondaries.

Dunlin

Calidris alpina

Hᵁᴳᴱ flocks of dunlin congregate on the shores of western Europe in autumn and winter. They are active feeders, seen in busy flocks pecking at small food items and probing to short depths in soft mud. Occasionally whole flocks take to the air and give an exciting display, changing colour from grey to white as they wheel and turn before settling again to start feeding. Within a flock there may be some variation in appearance, birds from the southernmost breeding populations in Britain and Iceland having a smaller and less distinct belly patch and a shorter bill.

Voice: Harsh, rolling 'krreee' in flight; longer display over nest site
Length: 16–22cm
Wingspan: 35–40cm
Weight: 36–57g
Habitat: Breeds on moorlands and tundra; overwinters on estuaries, sandy shores, lake shores
Nest: Concealed in vegetation on ground; shallow scrape with some lining
Eggs: 4; slightly glossy, pale brown or olive with darker blotches
Food: Insects on tundra; small worms, shrimps, molluscs, etc on shores

Small wader. Sexes similar. In summer has black belly and mostly white underside. Upperparts are chestnut and black, neck and chest are streaked and undertail region is white. For description of winter adult, see caption. Juvenile recalls moulting adult, but black breast patch is replaced by darker streaks especially on flanks; upperparts have paler appearance than adult due to buff fringes to feathers.

Looks generally brown in flight, with distinct, narrow, white wingbar

summer male adult

Winter plumage (below) pale grey above and white below with slight grey streaking on upper breast and crown

Bill varies greatly in length according to race, but is black and slightly downcurved in all plumages

Juvenile, late summer

Juvenile, autumn

Immature, first winter

Adult male, summer

Adult (both sexes), winter

Curlew Sandpiper

Calidris ferruginea

Fᴼᴿ a brief period in summer the male curlew sandpiper has rich red coloration, but as it is a high Arctic breeder this is rarely seen. Most birds seen in western Europe occur in autumn and are in juvenile plumage; they are usually seen in mixed flocks of small waders and can be picked out by their elegant long legs and curved bill, and white rump seen in flight. Curlew sandpipers, like other small waders, are able to deposit body fat very quickly, which enables them to undertake long migrations without regular stop-overs. This bird winters mainly in tropical Africa.

Voice: A clear, ringing 'krillee' in flight
Length: 18–20cm
Wingspan: 38–45cm
Weight: 45–90g
Habitat: Breeds in high Arctic; overwinters on seashores, lakes
Nest: On dry ground, near water; shallow depression
Eggs: Number unknown; smooth, buff with many dark brown spots and blotches

Food: Insects on tundra; worms, shrimps on shores

In summer has rich red underside and dark upperparts. Fresh plumage looks 'mealy' at first owing to pale feather edges, but abecomes darker with wear. Winter adults are very pale grey above with light streaking on upper chest; underparts pure white. For description of juvenile see caption. In all plumages, long black legs, long, black, curved bill and white rump distinguish this species from other small sandpipers.

Adults' brick-red breeding plumage is seldom seen in Europe

Juveniles have buff-orange tint on upperparts and chest and pure white underside

95

Little Stint

Calidris minuta

Looks small in flight; shows narrow white wingbar and dark line over white rump, and grey tail

Juvenile

Breeding plumage adult

Note white 'V' mark on juvenile's mantle

THIS tiny wader uses its short bill to pick insects from the surface of mud or plants. It is an active bird when feeding, running and darting in search of prey, which is detected by sight. In winter the little stint is usually found in small backwaters and quieter areas of saltmarshes, entering water less frequently than other larger waders. It often occurs in mixed flocks of other small waders, when its smaller size and more agitated feeding method help distinguish it. There are several similar species of small sandpiper, so accurate identification can be extremely difficult.

Voice: A short 'tip' contact note and 'svee svee svee' display on breeding grounds
Length: 12–14cm
Wingspan: 28–35cm
Weight: 20–40g
Habitat: Breeds on tundra; overwinters on seashores
Nest: In the open, near water; shallow cup, lined with leaves
Eggs: 4; glossy, pale green to buff, with dark chestnut streaks and blotches
Food: Insects on tundra; tiny invertebrates on seashore

Smallest European sandpiper, all ages of which have black legs and short black bill. In summer upperparts are mostly rusty red with dark feather centres; the centre of the crown looks darker. In winter mostly grey-buff above and white below. Larger feathers have dark central shafts, visible at close range. Juvenile resembles summer adult but is paler with a white 'V' on the reddish-brown upperparts and white underparts.

Temminck's Stint

Calidris temminckii

TEMMINCK'S stints prefer slightly richer habitats than little stints during the breeding season, nesting in grassy areas with willow scrub, usually near rivers or pools. They seem to need sites with plenty of look-outs, in the form of rocks or tree stumps, as well as good feeding areas. They often nest near isolated buildings, and appear to be extending their range southwards. They are likely to appear in small groups on migration and may use quite small pools as temporary stop-overs. If startled, Temminck's stints will shoot rapidly upwards following a jerky flight path and move off for quite a distance before settling again.

Juveniles are warm buff above with pale edges to the larger feathers, giving a scaly appearance

Voice: A ringing 'tirrr'
Length: 13–15cm
Wingspan: 30–35cm
Weight: 22–36g
Habitat: Nests in tundra and mountainous Arctic

regions; overwinters on seashores and marshes
Nest: Shallow cup on open ground with plant lining
Eggs: 4; glossy green-grey fading to buff, with brown spots
Food: Small insects, worms

Very small sandpiper with short legs and slightly elongated appearance. Breeding birds look greyish-buff above with some feathers showing dark centres and chestnut fringes. In winter adults have grey-brown plumage above and white underparts; grey colouring extends further down on chest and is more clearly demarcated than in winter plumage little stint. For description of juvenile see caption. Paler clay-coloured legs also separate this species from little stint at all times.

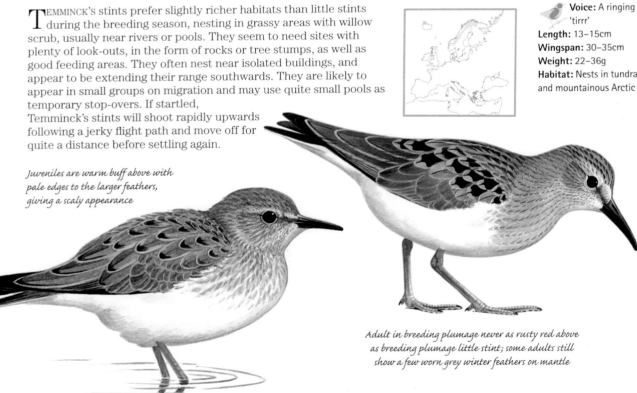

Adult in breeding plumage never as rusty red above as breeding plumage little stint; some adults still show a few worn grey winter feathers on mantle

Sanderling

Calidris alba

Juveniles

Winter adult in flight

Summer bird (above) has rusty-red upperparts and white underparts

THE sanderling has a distinctive method of feeding on sandy shores, running in and out of the surf snatching morsels of food from the sand as a large wave retreats. The hind toe is missing in this species, perhaps as an aid to running along the shore. Only when a large rock or obstruction is reached will the sanderling, usually found in small flocks in winter, take to the air. Sanderlings can be found on almost any stretch of sandy shore around the world during the northern winter, and there is evidence that some use the same over-wintering sites several years in succession.

Voice: A loud 'plitt' flight call; short frog-like trill in display
Length: 20–21cm
Wingspan: 36–42cm
Weight: 48–75g
Habitat: Breeds on high Arctic tundra; overwinters on sandy shores
Nest: On bare ground; small shallow scrape
Eggs: 4; slightly glossy, greenish-olive with darker spots
Food: Insects on breeding grounds; shrimps, kelp flies on winter shores

Small wader with relatively short, straight bill. In breeding plumage, has rusty-red upperparts with black markings on larger feathers giving a mottled appearance. Chest is rusty-red, clearly demarcated from the pure white underside. For description of winter adult, see caption. Juvenile strongly marked above with black and white on upperparts, and with warm-buff tinge to mantle and neck areas. All ages and plumages have black legs and bill, with broad white wingbar seen in flight.

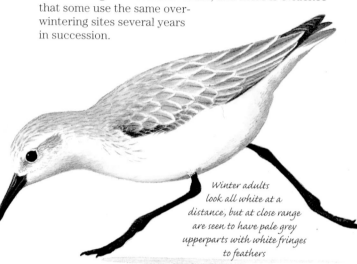

Winter adults look all white at a distance, but at close range are seen to have pale grey upperparts with white fringes to feathers

Knot

Calidris canutus

WHEN breeding on the tundra the knot population is spread out over a vast area, each pair requiring a large territory, but in winter knots gather in large flocks, the bulk of those overwintering in Europe being found around the shores of Britain. When breeding, the knot prefers to be near freshwater, but in winter it is almost exclusively coastal and remains very close to the water's edge. Very high tides force knots to huddle in tightly packed flocks for roosting but they are always the last birds to be pushed off the shore by the rising tide.

In flight all ages and plumages show thin white wingbar and grey rump

Voice: Short, slightly nasal 'kwett' in winter; fluting calls on breeding grounds
Length: 23–25cm
Wingspan: 50–60cm
Weight: 120–190g
Habitat: Breeds on high Arctic tundra; overwinters on coasts
Nest: Shallow scrape in the open, near water; sparse plant lining
Eggs: 3–4; slightly glossy, green with brown markings
Food: Insects and some plant material on tundra; worms, shrimps, etc on seashore

In summer adult has orange-red underside, white undertail coverts and mostly buff upperparts, strongly patterned with chestnut and yellow patches; the largest feathers have black and white markings on them. For description of winter adult, see caption. Juvenile very similar to winter adult, but has warmer brown or pinkish-buff wash with no grey tints. Black and white terminal bands on feathers of upperparts produce scalloped appearance.

summer adult

Stocky wader with medium-sized straight bill

In winter adults lose all the red and brown colours, becoming grey-buff all over apart from mostly white underparts

Purple Sandpiper

Calidris maritima

summer adult

In winter plumage adult is dark grey above and paler grey below with dark streaks on breast

THE purple sandpiper overwinters further north than any other wader. It is usually found in small flocks on rocky headlands and islands where there is some wave action and sufficient tidal range to expose rocks to feed on. Purple sandpipers' favourite food is small molluscs and invertebrates picked from rock crevices on the seashore, but they will also follow behind turnstones and take food left behind after stones or algae have been flipped over. On their breeding sites they can be very tolerant of intrusion, and they are also fairly confiding at overwintering sites where human disturbance is kept to a minimum.

Voice: A short, variable, 'kewitt' call and an agitated call on nest site
Length: 20–22cm
Wingspan: 40–44cm
Weight: 59–80g
Habitat: Breeds on tundra and moors; overwinters on rocky shores
Nest: Small cup on open ground with sparse lining
Eggs: 4; slightly glossy, olive to buff with dark blotches and spots

Food: Insects, spiders and some fruits on tundra; invertebrates on shore

The darkest of all small sandpipers, with only a thin white wingbar showing in flight. Adults in breeding plumage have strongly marked upperparts with black, chestnut and yellow colours on larger feathers, greenish-brown legs and dark bill. For description of winter adult see caption. Juvenile recalls winter adult but has more distinctly patterned appearance than adult.

Turnstone

Arenaria interpres

THE turnstone is a familiar seashore bird in winter. Its name is appropriate as it does indeed find food by turning over stones with its short, strong bill, but it feeds in a variety of other ways as well, foraging among seaweeds and probing into mud. Its short, powerful bill can also be used for breaking into crab and mollusc shells. Rotting kelp on beaches provides a good source of kelp fly larvae, which turnstones relish and from which they very quickly gain weight; their body weight can increase significantly in a few days, enabling them to make long migrations with only short stop-overs.

In breeding plumage male has black and white facial markings, chestnut upperparts with darker bands, pure white underside and orange legs

Voice: Short, nasal alarm calls uttered by feeding birds, and longer urgent-sounding call given in flight
Length: 21–24cm
Wingspan: 49–55cm
Weight: 80–140g
Habitat: Breeds on coastal tundra; overwinters on seashores
Nest: On a slight mound in the open, or in a crevice in rock; shallow scrape with sparse lining
Eggs: 4; slightly glossy, buff or pale olive with heavy blotches and spots
Food: Wide range of marine invertebrates, plus insects on tundra

For description of breeding-plumage male see caption. Breeding-plumage female is duller than male, with darker streaked head and less chestnut on upperparts. In winter, upperparts of both sexes uniform grey-brown and head and neck mottled grey. Juvenile resembles winter adult but dark feathers have buff edges, giving scaly appearance. In flight, wings show bold black, white and chestnut patterning at all ages.

In winter this stocky, short-billed wader can be found on a range of coasts, from exposed rocky shores to sheltered estuaries; its dull-orange legs are distinctive

Ruff

Philomachus pugnax

IN THE breeding season male ruffs gather in leks near their nesting sites and display their colourful plumage. They also perform elaborate dances with much leaping and bowing and occasional moments of freezing so that the plumage can be shown off to best effect. By June most of the male's colourful feathers will be moulted and they will look like larger versions of the females. During the autumn passage, juveniles predominate in ruff flocks, their buff colouring distinguishing them among other, similar waders. On return passage in spring all birds tend to look greyer, but some males will already be showing signs of their display plumage.

Voice: Mostly silent, may make quiet drawn-out squeak
Length: 26–32cm (male); 20–25cm (female)
Wingspan: 54–56cm (male); 45–52cm (female)
Weight: 130–230g (male), 80–130g (female)
Habitat: Sedge-covered swamps, wet meadows, lake margins, muddy pastures
Nest: Shallow scrape with grass lining; concealed by overhanging vegetation
Eggs: 4; slightly glossy, green-olive, with dark brown streaks and spots
Food: Invertebrates caught in shallow water, wet soil or from grasses

Unusual wader with distinctive appearance in breeding season and great variation between the sexes and individuals. For description of breeding male see caption. Smaller female is also variable in appearance, having mostly buff upperparts with varying degrees of darker mottling and streaking. In winter adult male loses 'ruff' and resembles female, both sexes losing warm buff wash to plumage.

In flight shows indistinct wingbars and white oval patches on sides of rump

Juvenile resembles plain female with mostly warm-buff colouring and olive-grey legs

Winter adults

Legs, bill and warty face of male usually orange

Breeding male has elaborate neck and head feathers that may be any colour from black to white with numerous brown shades in between; the 'ruff' may be spotted, barred or plain

Female is significantly smaller than male and much plainer in breeding season

99

Snipe

Gallinago gallinago

Very long-billed wader with distinctively patterned head and back

IN ADDITION to its distinctive long bill, the snipe also has a characteristic feeding action, unlike that of other waders. It probes into soft mud with a very jerky action, vibrating the tip of the bill slightly. The tip is sensitive and food can be sucked up without the bill being withdrawn from the mud. The bird will fly off if disturbed, usually on an erratic flight path, before dropping to safety. In the breeding season males perform aerial displays, making a strange bleating sound with their tail feathers, which stick out as they dive through the air.

Short tail is barred and has buff margin

Legs dull green and bill pale reddish-brown with darker tip in both adults and juveniles

Voice: A sneeze-like call when flushed; rhythmic, repetitive 'tick-a tick-a' on breeding grounds
Length: 25–27cm
Wingspan: 37–45cm
Weight: 90–130g
Habitat: Bogs, wet meadows, upper reaches of saltmarshes
Nest: Small cup hidden by vegetation in damp area
Eggs: 4; slightly glossy, pale green to olive, with red or brown dark blotches
Food: Invertebrates

Sexes similar. Upperparts are brown with pale stripes; larger feathers have dark centres and pale margins, giving scaly appearance. Flanks are barred and underside is greyish-white. Juveniles almost identical to adults but feather margins white, not buff.

Great Snipe

Gallinago media

Great snipe have declined in many areas owing to habitat loss and excessive shooting

THE great snipe is normally only seen when flushed, as it tends to sit tight until approached to within a few metres. Boggy woodland clearings, willow scrub and mountain slopes are usually chosen as nesting areas; plenty of open wet patches and tussocks for display purposes are required. Males congregate in groups and display on tussocks, making strange chirping sounds and a more wooden bill clattering. Sometimes several males perform 'flutter jumps' as well. The females are much more secretive, nesting beneath thick cover and remaining silent.

Has darker belly than snipe and distinctive white outertail feathers; plumage brightest during breeding season

Voice: Mostly silent, but gives short 'itch' call, and has a chirping display call on territory
Length: 27–29cm
Wingspan: 42–46cm
Weight: 185–225g
Habitat: Marshy areas in mountains and lowlands
Nest: Concealed on ground in thick vegetation
Eggs: 4; slightly glossy, buff with dark-brown spots and blotches
Food: Earthworms and other soil invertebrates

Larger and plumper than snipe, with slightly shorter bill, longer legs, stronger barring on the belly and more strongly patterned wing coverts. In flight, white outertail feathers and white wingbars are diagnostic; bird also appears larger than snipe, with more rounded body shape and wings. Flight pattern is more laboured than snipe's and usually straight, not zigzagged; the bird settles rather abruptly by dropping into cover. In winter plumage becomes duller because of wear of buff and cinnamon feather margins. Sexes similar and juveniles essentially indistinguishable from adults in the field, although they are usually less well marked.

Jack Snipe

Lymnocryptes minimus

THE jack snipe is far less sociable than the snipe, normally occurring in low densities and usually only seen when flushed. It prefers to feed in areas where there is some covering vegetation and will freeze until approached to within about 1m before suddenly shooting upwards, turning slightly and dropping again. At the last moment it will open its wings to brake and then vanish into cover. The relatively short bill is a good guide to identification if the bird is seen in flight. Its flight is more direct than the snipe's and looks rather weaker. On the ground the jack snipe moves rather awkwardly with plenty of tail bobbing and crouching. It is usually silent, but its display call has been likened to the sound of distant horses galloping.

Relatively short bill is yellowish with a darker tip

When keeping still among grasses and sedges, pale back gives jack snipe excellent camouflage

Voice: A brief sneezing sound when flushed, otherwise silent except for muffled, whistling display call near nest
Length: 17–19cm
Wingspan: 36–40cm
Weight: 40–70g
Habitat: Breeds on tundra bogs; overwinters on lowland marshes
Nest: Grass-lined cup on ground near water; hidden by vegetation
Eggs: 4; smooth, olive to dark brown with many darker spots and blotches
Food: Insects, worms, molluscs taken from soft mud and from surface

Small, short-billed snipe with conspicuous pale-yellow stripes running along back. Overall impression is of greenish-brown patterned back and boldly marked head. Legs and feet are blue-green. Sexes are similar and it is usually not possible to distinguish juveniles from adults.

Woodcock

Scolopax rusticola

When silhouetted against the sky, plump shape, broad wings, long bill held downwards and bat-like flight distinctive

THE so-called 'roding' flight of the male woodcock is usually all that is seen of this very secretive bird. On spring and summer evenings the male flies around the same area with rather jerky wingbeats, usually at treetop height. If flushed from the woodland floor, which is difficult to do because it sits tight until approached very closely, the woodcock darts off through the trees on a zigzag path and drops quickly when at a safe distance. The female is particularly retiring and rarely leaves the nest. The young are very active soon after hatching and can fly at ten days.

Russet plumage and broad, pale bars on head and wings afford bird excellent camouflage when nesting on leafy woodland floor

Voice: A grunting 'oo-oorrt' call in flight, followed by a shrill squeak
Length: 33–35cm
Wingspan: 55–65cm
Weight: 290–325g
Habitat: Damp woodlands
Nest: On ground in woods, concealed by vegetation; shallow cup with lining of leaves
Eggs: 4; slightly glossy, pale buff with brownish spots and blotches
Food: Earthworms, soil invertebrates

Larger and more rotund bird than snipe, with attractive red-brown plumage, particularly noticeable when seen from behind in flight. Upperparts rufous-brown and marbled with black and white; underside paler and barred with dark grey-brown stripes. Long bill is dark flesh colour, becoming darker at tip. Sexes similar and juvenile very similar to adult except that the forehead is spotted, not plain.

Comparing Immature Small Waders

Many birdwatchers relish the prospect of scanning through flocks of small waders in the autumn. The best advice for any prospective observer of immature waders is to get to know the dunlin, since it is the yardstick by which all others are measured. This species is by far the commonest of its kind to occur around the coasts of Europe; it is also one of the most variable in terms of both overall size and bill length.

TEREK SANDPIPER: Like adult, immature is easily recognised by long, upcurved bill; upperparts greyish with dark lines defining margins of mantle and small, dark patch on carpal joint of wings; bill mainly dark but yellowish at base; yellowish legs proportionately short and set rather far back along body

COMMON SANDPIPER: Shares distinctive 'bobbing' feeding action with adult birds; upperparts grey-brown and rather scalloped on back, contrasting markedly with white underparts; neat division seen between white and dark elements of plumage on chest; legs yellowish and bill mostly dark but dull greenish at base

GREEN SANDPIPER: Very similar to adult, with mostly dark upperparts and white underparts; at close range upperparts can be seen to be covered in small brown spots; legs greenish-yellow and bill mostly dark but dull greenish at base

WOOD SANDPIPER: Looks elegantly proportioned with mainly dark-brown upperparts and greyish-white underparts; good views reveal upperparts to be spangled with off-white to yellowish-buff spots, these being formed by scalloped margins to feathers; legs yellow and proportionately long; bill straight and rather short

DUNLIN: Unique among small European waders in this plumage in having dark streaking on flanks; bill and legs dark; shows warm wash to head and neck; brown feathers on back gradually replaced by by grey feathers during moult during late autumn

CURLEW SANDPIPER: Superficially similar to immature dunlin but appears longer-legged and plumage always looks cleaner, with white underparts and buffish wash to upperparts; pale margins to feathers on back give scaly appearance; feeds in more deliberate manner than dunlin; white rump seen in flight

Comparing Immature Small Waders

BROAD-BILLED SANDPIPER: Recalls miniature snipe or jack snipe with striking black and white stripes on head and back; bill dark and kinked at tip rather than downcurved; legs yellow and proportionately short; set rather far back on body

PURPLE SANDPIPER: Plump-bodied wader with yellowish legs; downcurved bill mostly dark but yellowish at base; underparts whitish and upperparts mostly grey-brown; brown feather margins on back lost by first winter; like adult birds, seldom seen more than a few metres from waves on rocky shores

LITTLE STINT: Tiny wader, often identified by its feeding activity; white underparts contrast with darker upperparts; back shows brown feather margins and white 'V' on edge of mantle; crown looks brown; often shows orange-brown flush on 'shoulders'

TEMMINCK'S STINT: Recalls miniature common sandpiper; bill short and dark and legs yellow; pale underparts contrast with grey-brown upperparts; back appears scaly due to pale feather margins

RUFF: Warm brown tone to plumage is distinctive, as is scaly appearance on back created by pale feather margins; head appears disproportionately small for a wader; legs yellow and relatively long; bill dark and rather short

MARSH SANDPIPER: Even more elegantly proportioned than wood sandpiper with long, yellowish legs and long, needle-like bill; upperparts brown with varying amounts of darker and paler feathering; underparts white

Vagrant Waders from Asia

MANY waders are notorious long-distance migrants. It is not surprising, therefore, that from among those whose breeding range lies in Asia, vagrants should turn up in Europe from time to time. In spring, records usually refer to breeding-plumage birds, many of which possess striking plumage colours or patterns. Autumn and winter records are often immature birds, which can be more of a challenge to identify.

First-autumn bird

Breeds in Siberia and overwinters in Australia; early-autumn vagrant to Europe

Breeds in Siberia and overwinters mainly in southeast Asia; very rare late-summer migrant to Europe

First-autumn bird

SHARP-TAILED SANDPIPER (CALIDRIS ACUMINATA): Adult has brown upperparts, pale underparts, brown cap, brown ear coverts and broad, pale supercilium; in breeding plumage shows streaks on throat and arrow markings on flanks and undertail coverts. Juvenile similar to non-breeding adult, but with buff wash to breast and upperparts

RED-NECKED STINT (CALIDRIS RUFICOLLIS): Bill and legs proportionately shorter than little stint's but wings and tail longer. Adult mainly grey above and white below; head rufous in breeding season and supercilium and base of bill whitish. Juvenile similar to winter adult but reddish-brown on crown and mantle

Autumn vagrant to Europe from deserts of north Africa and Middle East

Adult

Breeds in central Asia and overwinters in northeast Africa; rare vagrant to Europe in late autumn and winter

Winter adult

Breeds in Near East and western central Asia; overwinters in northwest India and northwest Africa; very rare vagrant to Europe as far west as Britain

Adult

CREAM-COLOURED COURSER (CURSORIUS CURSOR): Adult has upright stance, uniformly pinkish-buff plumage, and distinctive head pattern. In flight, note dark underwing, white trailing edge to wing and black and white bands at tip of tail. Juvenile similar but has scaly markings on upperparts and breast, and lacks head pattern

SOCIABLE PLOVER (CHETTUSIA GREGARIA): Breeding adult has grey-buff plumage with striking head pattern and dark patch on belly. Winter adult has white belly; head pattern less distinct. Juvenile recalls winter adult with scaly appearance. In flight, all birds have striking upperwing pattern recalling that of juvenile Sabine's gull

WHITE-TAILED PLOVER (CHETTUSIA LEUCURA): Adult pinkish-buff, palest on face and belly; cap greyish-buff; red eyering; legs yellow; bill dark; black primary tips extend beyond white tail; colours less intense in winter. White rump and tail conspicuous in flight. Juvenile has scaly appearance on mantle

Summer adult

Breeds in central Asia; overwinters in south and east Africa; rare vagrant to Europe, mainly in spring

GREATER SAND PLOVER (CHARADRIUS LESCHENAULTII) Breeds in central Asia; overwinters in Asia and east Africa; recorded annually in eastern Mediterranean, mainly in spring

WINTER ADULT AND JUVENILE: Upperparts sandy brown with narrow chest band, and underparts white

BREEDING ADULT: Generally sandy brown above and white below, with brick-red chest band, white face, dark eye patch and reddish-buff crown. Breeding female similar but with washed-out colours

CASPIAN PLOVER (CHARADRIUS ASIATICUS): Breeding male has dark-grey cap, white face and throat, dark ear coverts, brown back, brick-red chest band and white underparts. Female and winter male duller. Juvenile similar to winter adult

Black-tailed Godwit

Limosa limosa

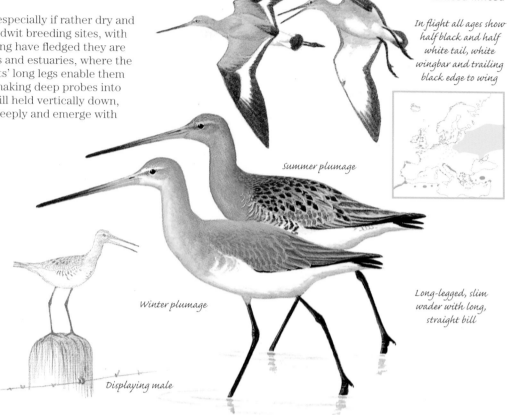

IN THE breeding season, freshwater marshes, especially if rather dry and grazed by cattle, are favoured black-tailed godwit breeding sites, with the birds nesting semi-colonially. Once the young have fledged they are taken away to wetter areas, such as lake shores and estuaries, where the feeding is more productive. Black-tailed godwits' long legs enable them to wade in quite deep water and they feed by making deep probes into the mud. They walk slowly forwards with the bill held vertically down, making short stabs, and then suddenly probe deeply and emerge with the prey, which is swallowed immediately.

In flight all ages show half black and half white tail, white wingbar and trailing black edge to wing

Summer plumage

Winter plumage

Displaying male

Long-legged, slim wader with long, straight bill

Voice: Excited, nasal, 'kee-wee-wee-wee' calls uttered near nest
Length: 36–44cm
Wingspan: 70–80cm
Weight: 230–400g
Habitat: Breeds on damp meadows, boggy areas; overwinters on estuaries, marshes
Nest: Shallow scrape in the open; lining of grass and leaves
Eggs: 3–4; slightly glossy, greenish-olive or brown with dark brown spots
Food: Invertebrates found by probing in soft mud

In breeding plumage head and neck are brick-red and upperparts and chest are mottled with black, chestnut and grey, the colours forming broken bars on upper chest. Underside is mostly grey-white. Amount of red coloration in breeding season is very variable, some adult females being almost grey in summer. Winter birds are pale grey above and grey-white below. Juvenile is warm buff below with brown and buff plumage above.

Bar-tailed Godwit

Limosa lapponica

THE breeding sites of the bar-tailed godwit are restricted to the treeless tundra, but there are many overwintering sites in western Europe and the Mediterranean region. Adults arrive on the breeding sites in late May and return south in July to August. Juveniles follow during August to October and may form mixed flocks with other larger waders on good feeding areas. Feeding methods are similar to the black-tailed godwit's, but the bar-tailed is more energetic. It often walks forwards sweeping its head from side to side with its bill held vertically downwards, the lower mandible vibrating slightly to stimulate prey to move.

Bill is slightly shorter than black-tailed godwit's and has an upwards tilt

Slightly smaller and paler than curlew (top right), with which it sometimes associates

Summer male

In winter both sexes are buff-grey above with white undersides; grey feathers have dark central shafts, giving lightly streaked effect above

Voice: Nasal 'ke-vu' with variations for alarm or flight calls
Length: 33–42cm
Wingspan: 70–80cm
Weight: 240–380g
Habitat: Breeds on tundra; overwinters on muddy shores
Nest: Shallow scrape on dry patch in marshy area; sparse lining
Eggs: 3–4; slightly glossy, green-olive, with brown spots, blotches and speckles
Food: Invertebrates: insects on tundra; worms, shrimps, etc on shore

Superficially similar to black-tailed godwit, but shorter legged and stockier; if seen in flight, lacks that species' distinctive wingbars and tail markings. In summer plumage male has a dark rusty-red underside and mottled chestnut and dark-brown upperparts; larger female has warm-buff underparts and slightly paler upperparts. For description of winter plumage see caption. Juvenile browner above than winter adult, with patterning similar to curlew.

105

Curlew
Numenius arquata

The pale V-shaped area on the curlew's back is clear when seen in flight

THE haunting melodious call of the curlew is a characteristic sound of upland bogs and moors in spring as males establish nesting territories. The 'cour-lee' call can be heard all year round; curlews normally live in large flocks in winter and they are very vocal. The long, curved bill of the curlew is used to good effect when feeding in soft mud, and the tip of the bill can also be used to extract soft-bodied creatures such as molluscs from their shells. Sometimes the curlew can be seen with its head almost horizontal as it seeks insects on grass tussocks.

The long, curved bill of the curlew is a perfect adaptation to feeding in damp ground

Large wader with long downcurved bill. Female larger than male and has longer bill, but both have similar plumage. In summer, fresh plumage has warmer yellowish tinge than in winter. Lower-mandible is pink-flesh coloured in winter. Juvenile plumage very similar to adult; juvenile male has significantly shorter bill than juvenile female.

Voice: A mournful 'cour-lee'; also a tuneful bubbling trill when displaying
Length: 50–60cm
Wingspan: 80–100cm
Weight: 600–1,000g
Habitat: Upland moors and bogs in summer; coasts and marshes in winter
Nest: On ground, sometimes on tussock; large depression with grassy lining
Eggs 4; glossy, green to olive with brownish spots, blotches and speckles
Food: Insects, soil organisms; worms, molluscs, crustaceans on seashore

Whimbrel
Numenius phaeopus

Has more distinctive markings than curlew, with two dark stripes on the crown

In flight looks much smaller than curlew and has more rapid wingbeats

THERE is some overlap in the breeding ranges of the curlew and whimbrel, but the whimbrel extends further north and is also more widespread. In winter whimbrels can be found around the coasts of all the southern continents. They are often seen on estuaries in small groups and when a flock is startled they will all take off, uttering the characteristic seven-note call. Whimbrels seem to be more restless birds than curlews, using estuaries only as stop-overs. They readily take flight and are only really settled when on the breeding grounds.

Length 40–46cm
Wingspan: 75–85cm
Weight: 430–575g
Habitat: Tundra, moors and bogs in summer; seashores in winter
Nest: Shallow depression on open ground; sparse lining
Eggs: 3–4; slightly glossy, olive-green with dark brown spots and blotches
Food: Invertebrates, insects on tundra; marine worms, etc on shore
Voice: A seven-note trill in flight; a brief curlew-like call in display

Smaller than curlew but otherwise superficially similar. Crown has two dark stripes and pale supercilium. Sexes are similar and juvenile resembles adult apart from pale buff spots on crown and wing coverts.

Redshank

Tringa totanus

Adult in summer plumage

THE redshank is both a familiar sight and a familiar sound on coastal marshes and wet meadows across much of Europe. Its readiness to take to the air and give its ringing alarm call has earned it the country name of 'warden of the marshes'. When displaying near the nest site the redshank gives a persistent 'tyoo tyoo tyoo' while rising and falling on rapidly beating wings. When landing, it raises its wings briefly, showing the pure white underside.

Voice: A far-carrying and persistent 'klu-klu-klu' alarm call and a two-syllable 'tu-hu'
Length: 27–29cm
Wingspan: 55–65cm
Weight: 105–165g
Habitat: Wet meadows, coastal marshes in summer; estuaries and shores in winter
Nest: Shallow depression on open ground, with lining
Eggs: 4; slightly glossy, olive or pale green with dark brown spots and blotches

Food: Insect larvae, earthworms, marine invertebrates

At all times adult has orange-red legs and reddish base to bill. Summer plumage grey-brown. Extent of dark markings on grey background varies considerably and birds from more northerly areas have darkest markings. In winter, darker markings fade and bird appears almost uniformly grey-brown above and very pale below. Juvenile has red legs but lacks red base to bill. Shows dark streaks on underside and pale feather margins on mantle, giving slightly mealy appearance. End of tail is barred and outer edges of wings are dark.

Immature bird (above)

The white trailing edge of the wing and white rump are evident in flight on juvenile and adult birds alike

Spotted Redshank

Tringa erythropus

THE spotted redshank breeds in the Arctic. On their breeding sites males help with incubation and the care of the young, remaining long after the females have left. Spotted redshanks often feed in groups, making a distinctive stabbing movement with their long bill. They wade in quite deep water and swim at times, up-ending like ducks. They will also run after small prey items, reaching out and stabbing with their bills. If startled they will shoot upwards, giving a shrill, whistling call and showing the wedge-shaped rump.

Both sexes of this distinctive long-legged, long-billed wader have very pale plumage in winter

The absence of a white wingbar in flight immediately distinguishes the spotted redshank from its cousin

Voice: A shrill 'chu-witt' call, plus a repetitive buzzing 'krruu-ee' uttered in display
Length: 29–32cm
Wingspan: 55–65cm
Weight: 130–200g
Habitat: Bogs and tundra in summer; coasts and estuaries in winter
Nest: Shallow depression on open ground with sparse lining
Eggs: 4; slightly glossy, olive to pale green with brown spots and blotches
Food: Insects in soil and water on tundra; marine invertebrates on shore

Elegant wader with long, red legs, which are darkest during the summer months. Sexes similar. For description of summer adult see caption. Winter adult has essentially pale-grey upperparts and white underparts. Juvenile similar to winter adult but browner overall.

In summer spotted redshank has sooty black plumage relieved by pale margins to the feathers on the upperparts

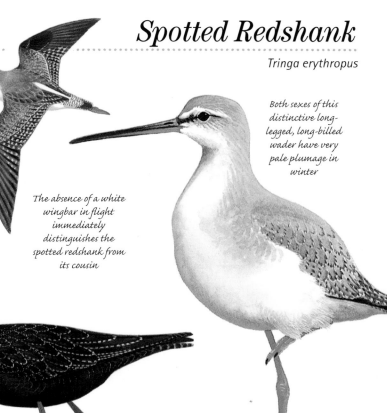

Greenshank

Tringa nebularia

Pale wedge-shaped patch extending along the back is common to adults and juveniles

summer plumage adult (above)

In winter the adult greenshank is pale grey above with darker feather margins bordered with white, and the underside is pure white

THE greenshank is a scarce breeder in Scotland, but more widespread across Scandinavia, Russia and Siberia. It moves south for the winter and is a common passage migrant in autumn. The slightly upturned bill is ideal for catching prey in shallow water, and the greenshank is adept at running after small fish like sticklebacks, with its bill below the surface. When caught, the fish is removed from the water before being swallowed. Greenshanks favour quiet backwaters and shallow creeks, normally avoiding open beaches and areas with strong wave action.

Voice: Clear three-syllable 'chew chew chew' call
Length: 30–35cm
Wingspan: 60–70cm
Weight: 130–240g
Habitat: Breeds on bogs and marshes; overwinters on coasts, lake shores, riversides
Nest: On ground near rock or tussock; shallow scrape with sparse lining
Eggs: 4: slightly glossy, buff, heavily marked with brownish spots and streaks
Food: Invertebrates, fish fry, tadpoles

Mostly grey wader with long green legs and slightly upturned bill; sexes similar. In summer, grey upperparts have darker markings, forming bands along wings; arrow-shaped markings on breast and flanks give streaked effect. For description of winter adult see caption. Juvenile plumage browner than adult's, with neater streaks on neck and breast; bill is slightly shorter and straighter. In flight, tail looks pale and white and wedge-shaped rump patch extends up the back in both adults and juveniles.

Wood Sandpiper

Tringa glareola

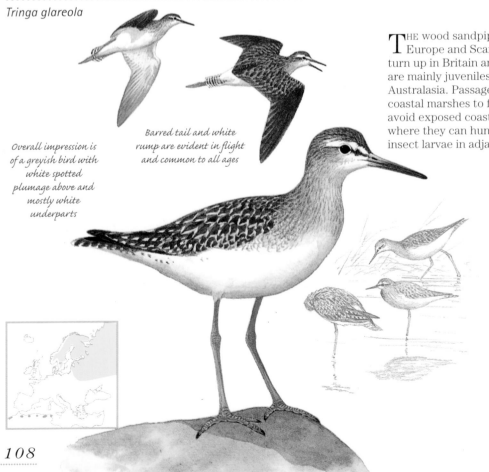

Overall impression is of a greyish bird with white spotted plumage above and mostly white underparts

Barred tail and white rump are evident in flight and common to all ages

THE wood sandpiper is a common breeding wader of the far north of Europe and Scandinavia. From late summer onwards migrants turn up in Britain and western Europe on their way to Africa; these are mainly juveniles. Eastern birds head south for India and Australasia. Passage migrants turn up in a variety of habitats from coastal marshes to flooded meadows and riversides. They usually avoid exposed coasts, preferring shallow, brackish or freshwater areas where they can hunt for small aquatic invertebrates or beetles and insect larvae in adjacent grassy areas.

Voice: Flight call is a whistling 'jiff jiff'; rolling display call uttered on breeding sites
Length: 19–21cm
Wingspan: 50–55cm
Weight: 55–75g
Habitat: Open forests with boggy areas, marshes, riversides
Nest: On ground in dense vegetation, sometimes in old nest in tree
Eggs: 4; slightly glossy, pale green or buff with dark brown spots and blotches
Food: Invertebrates, fish fry, tadpoles, a few seeds and algae

Compared with other small sandpipers, such as common and green, has longer legs and is slimmer. Adults in worn plumage look brownish-grey; sexes similar. Juvenile is browner than adult and has streaked neck, chest and flanks. In flight all ages show pale underwings (those of green sandpiper are dark below), barred tail and white rump.

Green Sandpiper

Tringa ochropus

Very black and white in flight; note the dark underwings

Adult shows white eyering, dull white spots on back and bright white underside

THE green sandpiper is a nervous and agitated bird, taking flight readily if disturbed, when it will give its clear, three-note call. Its usual habit, however, is to sit tight and not take flight until approached very closely. In winter it can be found in places where no other wader is likely to occur. Quite small ditches and enclosed water bodies such as watercress beds are favoured, and although this is usually a solitary bird, several may be found in close proximity to one another in suitable feeding areas.

Voice: A shrill, three-note 'tuEEt-wit-wit' given in flight
Length: 21–24cm
Wingspan: 50–60cm
Weight: 70–90g
Habitat: Boggy areas with open woodland near by; streams, lake margins, watercress beds
Nest: Uses old nest of thrush or pigeon
Eggs: 4; slightly glossy, cream with red-brown blotches and streaks
Food: Invertebrates, fish fry

From a distance, looks almost black and white both when feeding and when in flight; dark wings contrast with white rump and belly. Upperparts of adult dark olive-green, fading to grey-green on head. In winter, white spots seen in summer birds are absent and underparts look gleaming white. Juvenile has buff-brown spots on dark upperparts; neck and chest streaked.

Common Sandpiper

Actitis hypoleucos

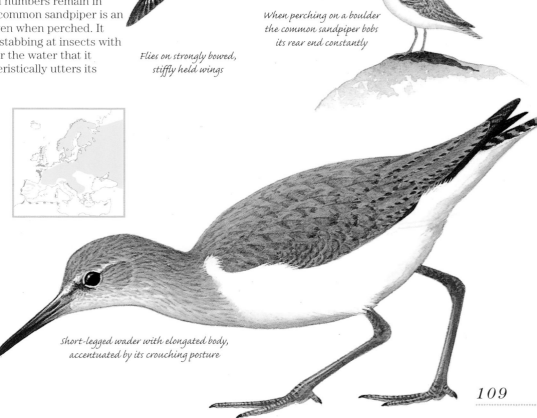

When perching on a boulder the common sandpiper bobs its rear end constantly

Flies on strongly bowed, stiffly held wings

THE common sandpiper is widespread in Europe, its breeding range embracing a huge range of climates and habitat types. In winter there is a migration southwards, although small numbers remain in northwest Europe throughout the winter. The common sandpiper is an active bird, constantly bobbing up and down even when perched. It walks or runs in search of food, and is adept at stabbing at insects with its bill. When flushed, it will fly away so low over the water that it appears to touch it with its wingtips; it characteristically utters its shrill call as it takes to the wing.

Voice: A shrill and penetrating' hee dee dee' call when flushed; song is a more rhythmic and longer version of alarm call
Length: 19–21cm
Wingspan: 35–40cm
Weight: 40–54g
Habitat: Stony rivers and lake shores, sheltered seashores
Nest: On ground, concealed by vegetation; cup-shaped, lined with plant material
Eggs: 4; glossy, buff with red-brown spots and streaks
Food: Insects and other invertebrates

Adult upperparts appear plain grey-buff at a distance, but darker feather centres and pale margins give delicately patterned appearance close up; this patterning is less obvious outside breeding season. Underside pure white with small white patch extending up in front of shoulder. Juvenile very similar to adult but with more scaly appearance owing to pale feather fringes. Legs always grey-green and bill dark brown with dull yellowish base.

Short-legged wader with elongated body, accentuated by its crouching posture

Broad-billed Sandpiper

Limicola falcinellus

THE broad-billed sandpiper is a scarce wader with scattered breeding sites across northern Scandinavia and Siberia; it only turns up in western Europe as a scarce migrant. If mingled with dunlin the bill tip and crown markings are the best features for identification. In summer the broad-billed sandpiper is found on boggy ground between 250 and 1,000m, choosing nesting sites that are almost floating; it prefers areas with plenty of sphagnum moss, cotton grass and sedges. In winter the species seems to like wetter areas, where there is plenty of soft mud to probe.

The broad-billed sandpiper's snipe-like plumage and kink-tipped bill are good identification features

Voice: Rasping 'chrreeeit' and mechanical-sounding 'swirr swirr swirr'
Length: 16–18cm
Wingspan: 34–37cm
Weight: 29–49g
Habitat: Breeds on bogs in sub-Arctic
Nest: Small cup in tussock on boggy ground
Eggs: 4; smooth, pale buff

Marsh Sandpiper

Tringa stagnatilis

THE marsh sandpiper is instantly recognisable by its delicate proportions, especially its long, slender bill and legs. If seen in flight the rapid take-off, agility in the air, wedge-shaped white rump and trailing legs are good identification features. It breeds well inland, preferring freshwater marshes where there is short vegetation for concealment. When feeding on land it adopts a crouching posture to pick up food items. Marsh sandpipers are rare visitors to western Europe, turning up as migrants on their way from their breeding grounds in far eastern Europe and Russia.

straight, thin bill characteristic of species

Breeding-plumage adult

The marsh sandpiper's proportionately long legs give it an elegant appearance

Voice: A clear, whistling 'kiew', repeated frequently
Length: 22–25cm
Wingspan: 50–55cm
Weight: 55–100g
Habitat: Lake margins and marshes in summer; lake shores and sheltered seashores in winter
Nest: Shallow depression in short vegetation; some lining of grasses
Eggs: 4; slightly glossy, cream or buff with dark reddish-brown spots and blotches
Food: Insects, molluscs, crustaceans

Slightly smaller than dunlin, with longer body profile and more sharply downturned bill tip. In breeding and juvenile plumage, head shows pale stripes similar to snipe, and pale supercilium. Upperparts pale in early summer owing to broad, pale feather fringes; these are lost with wear and plumage gradually becomes richer brown. In winter looks similar to winter-plumage dunlin but the pale crown stripes can still be seen in good light and the legs appear muddy grey-green. Juvenile recalls breeding-plumage adult but with pale margins on upperparts.

Sexes similar. Adult in summer has grey to grey-brown upperparts and pale underparts with dark streaks. Adult winter plumage light grey above and almost white below. Dark shoulder patch contrasts with pale grey mantle; at close range dark feather quills and pale margins give slightly scaly appearance. Olive-green legs yellower in spring. Juvenile pure white below with browner upperparts than adult.

Terek Sandpiper

Xenus cinereus

THE Terek sandpiper prefers fairly open terrain during the breeding season, avoiding densely wooded areas, very stony rivers and steep slopes. Outside the breeding season it favours water margins and often consorts with other wader species. The Terek sandpiper is an active feeder, running and darting through shallow water with its head held slightly downwards. It often bobs up and down like the common sandpiper, and distant views of birds where the bill is not visible can lead to confusion with this species. Its varied calls are not often heard from migrating birds but it does produce some melodious-sounding trills.

Voice: A variable, rapid 'chu-du-du' call and other trilling sounds
Length: 22–25cm
Wingspan: 50–55cm
Weight: 70–84g
Habitat: Muddy lake shores, riverbanks
Nest: Shallow cup on open site near water
Eggs: 4; slightly glossy, buff with darker spots and streaks
Food: Invertebrates, seeds

with red-brown speckles
Food: Invertebrates, some seeds and small fruits

Similar to common sandpiper but has distinctive long bill, which is curved upwards, and steeply rising forehead when viewed in profile. Adult has grey-brown upperparts and pale underparts; black 'V' marking seen on back. Juvenile is similar to adult but has dark, anchor-shaped markings on wing feathers. In flight, pale underwing and lack of white rump and wingbars are useful for identification at all ages.

Grey Phalarope

Phalaropus fulicarius

Winter adult

Role reversal occurs in the breeding season with the female (above) having the brighter plumage

AN ALTERNATIVE name for the grey phalarope is the 'whale bird', a name acquired through its habit of feeding on the backs of surfacing whales while overwintering at sea, and gathering in flocks in areas where whales are feeding because of the fish and plankton driven to the surface. Grey phalaropes regularly turn up in small numbers in northwest Europe on autumn migration, usually after storms, and occasionally hundreds are driven inshore. They usually remain for a few days, feeding in the characteristic phalarope way of swimming in shallow water, before continuing on their migration south.

Voice: A sharp 'pik' alarm call; rolling 'prruut' uttered by female in summer
Length: 20–22cm
Wingspan: 37–44cm
Weight: 42–68g
Habitat: Breeds on high Arctic tundra; overwinters at sea in tropical regions
Nest: On ground in low vegetation near water; shallow cup with plant lining
Eggs: 4; slightly glossy, olive with blackish spots and blotches

Food: Insects, molluscs, crustaceans and some plant material on tundra

Has broader, less pointed bill than red-necked phalarope. Breeding female has brick-red underparts, brown back and black and white facial markings. Breeding male similar to breeding female but colours less intense. Winter adults grey above and white below with black 'panda' mask through eye. Juvenile similar to winter adult but with irregular pattern of brown-fringed black feathers on otherwise grey upperparts.

Juvenile

Grey phalaropes stay out at sea for the whole winter

Red-necked Phalarope

Phalaropus lobatus

Winter adult

From the point of fledging, juvenile (below) is as adept at swimming as an adult bird

THE red-necked phalarope is instantly recognised by its habit of swimming in search of food, and often spinning round and round to stir up aquatic insect larvae, which it picks from the water with lightning-quick pecks of its bill. In the breeding season it favours shallow freshwater pools from sea level to altitudes of 1,300m. At this time of year the usual male/female roles are reversed, with the female being the brightest in colour and initiating courtship. The male's more subdued appearance makes him most suitable for sitting on the eggs and he seems to assume all responsibility for the care of the young.

Voice: Calls include short 'kitt' or 'kirrik' sounds
Length: 18–19cm
Wingspan: 34–40cm
Weight: 30–48g
Habitat: Breeds on open tundra; overwinters at sea in tropical regions
Nest: On ground in vegetation; shallow cup lined with leaves
Eggs: 4; slightly glossy, olive with spotting and blotches at blunt end
Food: Invertebrates caught on water while swimming; mostly insects in summer

Bill very thin and pointed. For description of breeding female see caption. Breeding male similar to female but colours subdued. Winter plumage adults of both sexes, rarely seen in Europe, have ashy-grey upperparts and white underparts and look black and white at a distance. Juvenile recalls male with washed-out summer plumage showing paler flanks and undersides, and no red on neck.

Female has striking plumage in summer, with rusty-red neck and upper chest, slate-grey head and white throat

Vagrant Waders from North America

As PREDICTABLY as night follows day, westerly gales in September and October will bring a scattering of rare North American waders to the coasts of western Europe. Some of the species involved are distinctive and easy to identify but others are more of a challenge, especially as they tend to seek the company of superficially similar common European waders. Careful and prolonged observation is often needed by the observer.

Winter adult

KILLDEER (CHARADRIUS VOCIFERUS): Recalls outsized ringed plover but more slender with longer body and legs; has two black chest bands; tail extends well beyond wingtips at rest. Winter adult has pale margins to feathers on upperparts. Juvenile similar to winter adult but washed out

First-autumn bird

AMERICAN GOLDEN PLOVER (PLUVIALIS DOMINICA): Similar to European golden plover; distinguished by longer legs, slimmer body and dark grey (not white) axillaries and underwing coverts. Adult has essentially dark underparts and spangled, golden upperparts. Winter birds and juveniles essentially grey-brown, spangled golden on mantle and back

Summer adult

PACIFIC GOLDEN PLOVER (PLUVIALIS FULVA): Similar to European golden plover but distinguished at all times by pale-grey (not white) axillaries and underwing coverts, more slender body and proportionately longer legs; has longer legs and neck than American golden plover

First-autumn bird

LEAST SANDPIPER (CALIDRIS MINUTILLA): Similar to little stint but with yellow legs. Breeding adult has grey-brown upperparts with chestnut on cap, ear coverts and on back and mantle. Winter adult lacks chestnut. Juvenile has buffish-brown upperparts washed with reddish-brown on back, mantle, crown and ear coverts

First-autumn bird

SEMIPALMATED SANDPIPER (CALIDRIS PUSILLA): Similar to little stint; best identifier is broad-based, blob-tipped bill. Breeding adult has grey-brown upperparts suffused with reddish-brown on back and cap. Winter adult has greyish upperparts. Juvenile similar to winter adult but with reddish-brown feathering on mantle and back

First-autumn bird

PECTORAL SANDPIPER (CALIDRIS MELANOTUS): Neck proportionately longer and head smaller than dunlin's. Adult has mainly grey-brown upperparts; neck and breast heavily streaked and distinctly cut off from white underparts. Juvenile similarly patterned but upperparts, neck and breast warm buffish-brown and well marked

First-autumn bird

WHITE-RUMPED SANDPIPER (CALIDRIS FUSCICOLLIS): Recalls small, winter-plumage dunlin with longer body and longer wings that extend beyond body at rest; medium-length bill dull orange at base of lower mandible; white rump seen in flight. Summer adult has grey-brown upperparts with chestnut and black feathering on back. Non-breeding adult has grey upperparts. Juvenile recalls non-breeding adult but upperparts browner and has pale feather margins on mantle and back

First-autumn bird

BAIRD'S SANDPIPER (CALIDRIS BAIRDII): Similar to dunlin but with shorter bill and elongated rear end. Breeding adult has grey-brown upperparts, suffused on back with chestnut; neck and breast grey-brown; underparts white. Juvenile similar to adult but upperparts, neck and breast essentially grey-buff, pale feather margins on back giving scaly appearance

Vagrant Waders from North America

First-autumn bird

First-autumn bird

First-autumn bird

SPOTTED SANDPIPER (Actitis macularia): Very similar to common sandpiper but with shorter tail. Breeding adult has grey-brown upperparts and white underparts with dark spots. Winter adult uniformly grey-brown above except for well-marked wing coverts. Juvenile similar to juvenile common sandpiper but has boldly marked tips to wing coverts and lacks white markings on tertials

SOLITARY SANDPIPER (Tringa solitaria): Similar to green sandpiper but smaller, with proportionately shorter legs and longer wings; in flight, reveals dark rump, not white. Upperparts dark olive-brown, speckled with white spots in breeding adult and juvenile; outertail shows conspicuous black and white barring

BUFF-BREASTED SANDPIPER (Tryngites subruficollis): Recalls small juvenile ruff but distinguished by uniformly buff throat and underparts (white in ruff), shorter, straighter bill and scaly appearance (especially in juvenile) to mantle and back

First-autumn bird

LESSER YELLOWLEGS (Tringa flavipes): Recalls outsized, long-legged wood sandpiper. Breeding adult has grey-brown head, neck and upperparts; black feathering and white spangling on mantle and back. Winter adult and juvenile plumage more uniform

First-autumn bird

First-autumn bird

GREATER YELLOWLEGS (Tringa melanoleuca): structure and proportions recall greenshank but legs very long and usually bright yellow. Breeding adult has greyish-brown upperparts marked with black feathers and white spotting; head, neck and breast streaked. Winter adult and juvenile have grey back and mantle with pale margins to feathers; juvenile has extensive white spotting on upperparts

Summer adult

LONG-BILLED DOWITCHER (Limnodromus scolopaceus): Recalls outsized, dumpy snipe in silhouette. Breeding adult plumage essentially reddish-brown with dark markings. Winter adult has grey-brown upperparts; juvenile similar but shows chestnut margins to feathers on mantle and back

First-autumn bird

STILT SANDPIPER (Micropalama himantopus): Recalls Tringa waders but has proportionately longer legs and a long bill, downcurved at tip. Breeding adult has black streaking on head and neck and black barring on underparts; chestnut tone on crown and ear coverts. Non-breeding adult and juvenile have essentially grey upperparts; juvenile has buffish wash to neck and breast

UPLAND SANDPIPER (Bartramia longicauda): Recalls miniature, short-billed curlew but has yellowish legs and proportionately very long wings and tail. Adult upperparts mottled brown; head, neck and breast buffish with dark streaks; tail long and barred towards tip. Juvenile similar but mantle and back darker with pale feather margins

113

Great Skua

Stercorarius skua

The great skua will harrass other seabirds into dropping their prey

In flight adult looks broad-winged and short-tailed, sometimes with two slightly projecting central feathers

The white flashes on the dark wings are seen well in flight and during aggressive displays on land when the wings are raised over the head

THE largest of all the skuas is an aggressive bird that allows no intruders, including humans, anywhere near its nest or young. The great skua readily attacks if provoked and shows no fear of any predator. Nesting colonies are normally near colonies of other seabirds, where there are easy meals to be had throughout the breeding season. Great skuas follow other birds at sea and, although they can catch fish for themselves, they invariably attack other birds, catching the fish they drop before it hits the water.

Voice: Utters harsh 'tuk tuk' alarm calls and other fierce contact notes
Length: 53–66cm
Wingspan: 125–140cm
Weight: 1.2–1.8kg
Habitat: Seabird cliffs and islands in summer; overwinters at sea
Nest: Shallow scrape on ground; sparse lining of leaves and feathers
Eggs: 2; smooth, chestnut-brown or paler with variable brown spots and blotches

Food: Takes fish from other seabirds, plus eggs, chicks, fish from sea

Bulky bird, adult reminiscent of juvenile gull but darker and far more heavily built. Juvenile similar to adult but usually darker; may show pale tips to larger feathers on upperparts. When standing on land, short legs and small feet obvious in all birds; when swimming, looks especially bulky and buoyant.

Arctic Skua

Stercorarius parasiticus

Juvenile (below)

Almost falcon-like appearance in flight, with long, slender wings and long tail; has dashing, acrobatic flight when pursuing other birds

Pale phase adult chasing kittiwake

THE Arctic skua is the commonest of the skuas on the coasts of northwest Europe and the Arctic ocean. Arctic skuas are argumentative birds, screaming at each other and fighting over territories in breeding colonies. Defiant birds raise their wings high over their heads to show the white patches and attack any intruders, including humans. The skuas can perform exciting aerial displays to startle a smaller bird into dropping a fish. They will sometimes sit on a rock near a seabird colony and watch for a returning bird with a fish and then attack at the last moment by flying at high speed like a falcon.

Voice: Utters a kittiwake-like 'kee-aah', and short 'kukk' calls
Length: 46–67cm
Wingspan: 97–115cm

Weight: 360–590g
Habitat: Breeds on coasts near other seabirds; overwinters at sea
Nest: Shallow depression on open ground; sparse lining of leaves and feathers
Eggs: 2; smooth, olive or brown, rarely blue, with brownish spots and blotches
Food: Harries other birds to make them drop food

Adult occurs in pale and dark phases, pale being commonest in north and dark commonest in south of range. Dark phase birds have sooty-brown plumage all over with darker cap and yellowish tone to sides of face. Pale phase birds are paler grey on mantle with grey-brown cap; flanks and ventral region light grey-brown and rest of underside, head and neck white. Pale phase birds show some straw yellow around the neck. Legs and bill are black in pale and dark phases, and both have all-dark wings with pale white flashes. Juvenile plumage very variable, pale phase birds having pale heads and light brown plumage with darker markings below, giving scaly appearance; dark birds are almost all dark with a slightly paler head.

Pomarine Skua

Stercorarius pomarinus

THE pomarine skua's principal summer food is lemmings, but it will also take eggs and chicks of other birds and eat carrion; it will even attack and kill smaller birds. It is very agile in the air, so is able to pursue seabirds returning to their young with food and scare them into dropping it. Pomarine skuas can also catch fish for themselves if necessary. In summer they feed mostly on or near to land, but in winter they move far out to sea, following other birds and spending most of their time where there are upwelling currents, which provide rich feeding.

Light phase adult

Juvenile pale brown with darker brown barring; white wing flashes are visible, but tail streamers are absent

Wings long and broad at base, and tail relatively long with twisted streamers in full adult plumage; both light and dark forms have white wing 'flashes' seen on both surfaces and showing very clearly in flight

Voice: Harsh, gull-like 'kowk' or 'geck' anger calls and higher mewing contact calls
Length: 65–78cm
Wingspan: 113–125cm
Weight: 640–770g
Habitat: Breeds on high Arctic tundra, overwinters at sea
Nest: Shallow depression on open ground
Eggs: 2; slightly glossy, olive or brown with dark brown spots and blotches
Food: On tundra breeding grounds, lemmings, eggs, chicks of other birds and fish caught by harrying other seabirds; food-piracy of other seabirds very important in diet outside breeding season

Large, gull-like bird with heavy bill, large head and barrel-shaped body. Adult plumage very variable, with most birds occurring as pale phase and smaller number as dark phase. Pale phase birds are black-brown above and on upper chest and vent; belly white and nape pale yellow. Dark chest markings sometimes form complete band. Dark phase birds have sooty-brown plumage all over; bronze wash to plumage seen only in good light.

Long-tailed Skua

Stercorarius longicaudus

THE breeding success of the long-tailed skua is highly dependent on the populations of lemmings and other small rodents in the tundra and treeless regions of the Scandinavian mountains; in bad rodent years it may fail to breed altogether. The clutch size is also determined by the abundance of small mammals available to the females before breeding. Non-breeding birds live in loose flocks and hunt overland for food, usually away from the nesting areas. Of all the skuas, this is the species most likely to be seen well inland. This is a rare bird in northwest Europe, seen far less frequently on migration than the other species.

Breeding adult

Juvenile's plumage variable, but most birds are very dark with paler feather margins, giving barred appearnce; overall tone greyer than juvenile Arctic skua

Smaller than other skuas, with narrow wings, long tail and slender body; like other skua species, however, powerful chest makes head appear relatively small

Voice: Short 'kreck kreck' calls, and more drawn-out cackling calls for display
Length: 35–58cm
Wingspan: 92–105cm
Weight: 250–380g
Habitat: Breeds on tundra; overwinters at sea
Nest: Shallow depression on open ground with sparse lining
Eggs: 2; slightly glossy, olive-green to buff with brownish spots and blotches
Food: Rodents on tundra, plus fish, insects, carrion, berries; mainly fish-eater at sea

In breeding plumage adult has greyish-brown mantle and flanks, which contrast with darker wingtips and feathers. Cap is black and sides of face and neck are pale yellow; breast is pale, darkening towards ventral region. Bill short but thick.

Black-headed Gull

Larus ridibundus

Underside of wings dark grey with thinner white leading edge

THE black-headed gull is one of the commonest European gulls, breeding over a huge area of central Europe and Scandinavia. In winter, black-headed gulls turn up in most habitats from agricultural land, city parks and coastal marshes to the open sea, where they will follow fishing boats. The black-headed gull is an opportunist feeder, taking a wide range of foods; modern agriculture and waste disposal have provided it with good feeding in winter, so the population has increased. In winter many birds congregate in huge roosts, dispersing during the day to regular feeding areas.

Voice: Utters harsh screaming calls; very vocal near nests and when in feeding flocks
Length: 38–44cm
Wingspan: 94–105cm
Weight: 160–310g
Habitat: Sheltered seashores, lakes, marshes, urban parks, farmland
Nest: Shallow scrape with lining of leaves and feathers; on bare ground or amongst marshy vegetation
Eggs: 2–3; smooth, variable, green, greyish or brown with darker spots and blotches
Food: Insects, earthworms, marine invertebrates, plant matter; some household waste and scraps

In flight all non-juvenile plumages show white leading edge to wing with black border to primaries on upperwing. Summer adult has dark chocolate brown head, colour extending to middle of head but not down back of neck. Bill red with dark tip and legs dark red. Juvenile is buffish white; subsequently, immature birds acquire grey mantle with brown and black wing coverts and black terminal tail band; legs and base of bill in immature birds are dark flesh coloured.

summer adult

1. Juvenile

2. Immature, first winter

White leading edge to upperwing diagnostic in all post-juvenile plumages

3. Immature, first summer

4. Adult, winter

5. Adult, summer

In winter adult's head is white with two blackish smudges around eye and on neck; legs and bill paler than in summer

Mediterranean Gull

Larus melanocephalus

From a distance adult can look all white but close-up view reveals very pale grey mantle

Winter adult

MEDITERRANEAN gulls prefer flat areas such as saltmarshes for nesting, and are most widespread around the Mediterranean and Black Seas. Small numbers also breed in northwest Europe. Adults will fly great distances from the colony each day to feeding areas, and will form large flocks in places where there are hatches of insects such as flying ants. The Mediterranean gull seems to be most at home on the coast, and usually avoids flying far from the sight of land. In winter it frequently joins mixed feeding flocks of gull species in harbours or near refuse tips, where there is scope for scavenging.

Voice: Shrill, nasal calls, mostly heard in spring; generally silent in winter
Length: 36–38cm
Wingspan: 98–105cm
Weight: 250–350g
Habitat: Coasts and lagoons; lake shores mainly in Mediterranean area
Nest: Shallow depression lined with grass and feathers
Eggs: 3; smooth, cream or buff with dark brown spots and speckles
Food: Insects, fish, marine invertebrates

In flight wings of adult appear pure white at the tips. In winter summer adult's black head is lost and bird appears white apart from dark smudges around and behind eye. First-winter bird has black terminal band on tail, black primaries, mostly grey secondaries and brownish-grey wing coverts. Second-winter bird has mainly pale grey mantle but still shows black tips to primaries and partial black head.

In summer plumage adult has black head with incomplete white eyering giving impression of eyelids

Slender-billed Gull

Larus genei

THE long, pointed bill, which is not in fact especially slender, and the pointed forehead and long neck ensure that the slender-billed gull stands out easily from other gulls, such as black-headed gulls, with which it often mixes. It is good at catching fish and can make shallow dives or dip with its bill while in flight. It will also feed on the shore, picking invertebrates from the surface. Birds breeding away from the coast catch insects in flight, and some will visit outfalls to scavenge. In summer, when fish shoals are close to the surface, large excited feeding flocks will form, sometimes in association with other gulls.

Adult similar to adult winter black-headed gull but completely lacking dark markings on head. Slightly larger than that species, however, with longer, broader wings and with slower wingbeats in normal flight. It often flies in 'V' formation like larger gulls. Adult has pale grey mantle with leading white edge to wings and black-tipped primaries; white underside is suffused with pink in summer. Long bill is orange with dark tip, and legs are paler orange than black-headed gull's. Juvenile has pale orange legs and bill, and wings have buff and dark brown coverts; shows tiny smudge of grey behind eye. If seen in mixed flocks with other gulls, appears to have proportionately long bill and small eye at all times.

Voice: Main call a deeper version of black-headed gull's call
Length: 42–44cm
Wingspan: 100–110cm
Weight: 250–350g
Habitat: Lagoons, deltas and large lakes around the Mediterranean, Caspian and Black seas
Nest: Shallow depression with lining of leaves and rim of droppings
Eggs: 2–3; smooth, pale cream or buff with blackish spots and blotches
Food: Fish and marine invertebrates; some insects on land

In the breeding season the adult slender-billed gull shows a pink flush to its underparts

Little Gull

Larus minutus

FROM a distance a little gull in flight appears to flicker as the dark underwing contrasts with the pale mantle. Its energetic and vigorous flight, with frequent dips down to the water to pick up food, distinguishes it from other larger gulls. It can rise vertically for short distances and hover briefly before dipping down again. When at sea, small flocks will follow in the wake of ships or hover over areas of turbulent water. Little gulls breed in colonies in marshy areas, nearly always over fresh water, but occasionally they nest on very sheltered stretches of coast where there is emergent vegetation; they may form mixed colonies with black-headed gulls. In winter they usually remain offshore and are seldom seen in large numbers.

Immature birds in their first autumn and winter have characteristic black 'V' markings on upperwings

summer adult

The bulk of the little gull population is found in northeastern Europe and Russia; in winter many move as far as southwest Europe and southern Britain

Habitat: Breeds on lake shores and marshes; overwinters at sea
Nest: Shallow depression with grass lining; often over water
Eggs: 3; smooth, olive-brown to buff with darker blotches and spots
Food: Mainly insects in summer; marine invertebrates in winter

Voice: Harsh, short, tern-like calls; hoarse mewing calls uttered by juveniles
Length: 25–27cm
Wingspan: 70–77cm
Weight: 90–150g

Smallest gull of the region, with vigorous tern-like flight.

Wings of adult are black on underside with trailing white edge. Mantle is pale blue-grey and rest of plumage is white but suffused with pale pink. In summer head is all black; in winter adult has paler head with dark-grey cap and black spot behind eye. In breeding season legs and bill are red; legs fade to flesh colour and bill becomes black in winter.

Kittiwake

Rissa tridactyla

Kittiwakes build their nests on tiny ledges on sheer cliffs

KITTIWAKES are found in huge colonies around the sheer sea cliffs of Europe's northernmost coasts, where they are very noisy. At important mixed seabird colonies they are often the most numerous species. Breeding birds enjoy access to fresh water for washing, and sometimes take surrounding vegetation back to the nest. Kittiwakes are not truly migratory but they do disperse into the open Atlantic and North Sea during the winter. During autumn gales, flocks of kittiwakes pass the shores in apparently effortless buoyant flight, even in the most stormy seas.

Voice: Utters the musical cawing of its name, 'kit-ee-wak'
Length: 38–40cm
Wingspan: 95–120cm
Weight: 305–525g
Habitat: Breeds on sheer, high sea cliffs; open sea in winter
Nest: Compacted cup of mud, grass and seaweed on cliff ledge
Eggs: 1–3; smooth, pale buff, lightly spotted and blotched dark brown
Food: Marine fish and invertebrates

Slightly larger than black-headed gull but has more compact body and proportionately long wings. Summer adult has bright white head,

neck, underparts, rump and tail. At all times of year bill pale yellow, and legs and feet brownish-black. Juvenile has diagnostic blackish zigzag across grey and white upperwing.

Apart from conspicuous 'W' on wings, immature bird also shows blackish hind collar, black mark on face and dark tip to very slightly forked tail; bill black

Winter adult (right) has variable amounts of grey on nape

Common Gull

Larus canus

THE common gull is not in fact the commonest of the gulls of the region, being confined mainly to breeding colonies in northern Europe. In winter birds disperse to the seas and marshes relatively close to their breeding sites. The common gull can feed at sea like other large gulls but is also adept at feeding on land; it has learnt to exploit foods like cranefly larvae and earthworms, turned up when fields are ploughed. The common gull population seems to have increased in the 20th century, an indication of how this species has adapted to modern fishing and agricultural methods.

Wings show black primaries with white flecks in flight

Juvenile

Voice: Shrill 'keeow' and mewing 'gleeoo' calls
Length: 38–44cm
Wingspan: 110–125cm
Weight: 300–480g
Habitat: Coasts, freshwater lakes, marshes
Nest: Shallow cup of plant material on open ground, sometimes over water
Eggs: 3; smooth, olive or pale blue-green with brown streaks and spots
Food: Fish, marine invertebrates, insects, earthworms

Adult has black wingtips and grey mantle; head and body otherwise pure white and bill plain yellow during summer months. In winter head and neck show grey-brown flecks and bill duller than in summer adult, some individuals showing dark tip. Immature shows extensive brown in wings in first winter and broad, black terminal tail band. In second winter wings almost completely pale grey. Immatures have black bills at first, these becoming dull flesh colour before turning yellower in second winter.

summer adult

Smaller and neater in profile than herring gull, and adult has dark eye

Audouin's Gull

Larus audouinii

Voice: Donkey-like calls and 'mew' calls similar to herring gull
Length: 48–52cm
Wingspan: 127–138cm
Weight: 350–450g
Habitat: Remote Mediterranean headlands and islands
Nest: Shallow scrape on ground with lining of feathers and plants
Eggs: 2–3; slightly glossy, olive-buff with brown spots and blotches
Food: Mainly fish; sometimes insects, invertebrates and plant material

Elegant gull with proportionately slender wings and relatively large bill. In flight, mantle looks pale silvery-grey with trailing white edge and contrasting black tips to primaries; inner primaries have a few white flecks.

Juvenile (left) recalls juvenile lesser black-backed gull

Bill mostly red with black and yellow tip. Legs black. Juvenile has mostly grey-brown plumage, darker mantle and black bill. In second winter juvenile shows dark primaries, mostly grey mantle, and black terminal band to white tail. At this stage bill is red, with black and yellow tip.

AUDOUIN'S gull is a rare breeding bird of the Mediterranean, nesting in colonies that are safe from human interference and usually no more than 50m above sea level. It is a very graceful bird in flight, spending much time wheeling and gliding in search of food; its excellent manoeuvrability enables it to catch fish easily and it stands out among the bulkier yellow-legged gulls. Audouin's gulls can pick food from the surface of the sea without needing to slow down; only in strong winds will they alight on the water to catch prey. During severe storms they will also feed on land, taking insects and worms.

Adult has very pale plumage

Audouin's gulls are rare: the total world population may number no more than 800–1,000 pairs

Lesser Black-backed Gull

Larus fuscus

First-winter bird (above left) has all-dark flight feathers; in second wiuter (above right) acquires grey back and pale bill

Black wingtips clearly darker than dark-grey wings and mantle

Adult birds have more elongated proportions than herring gull; all races show diagnostic yellow legs

Adult bird of race GRAELLSII

THE lesser black-backed gull is a migrant over much of its range, spending its winters at sea but generally staying close to the coast in summer. In recent years more birds have remained inland in winter, where they have learnt to exploit man-made resources such as refuse tips and agricultural land. They often gather in large roosts on reservoirs near cities. Many immature birds remain on the overwintering grounds, south of their breeding grounds, for one or two years, so birds in second- and third-year immature plumage are not often seen in northwest Europe in summer.

Voice: Calls include variations on 'mew' calls; deeper and louder than herring gull;
Length: 52–67cm
Wingspan: 130–148cm
Weight: 700–900g
Habitat: Coasts, marshes, agricultural land
Nest: Large mound of seaweed and plants on open ground; sometimes more concealed in vegetation
Eggs: 3; smooth, olive or brownish with darker spots and blotches
Food: Fish, marine invertebrates, carrion, refuse

Occurs as three races in Europe, all of which have diagnostic yellow legs. Adults of western race, *graellsii*, are slate-grey on mantle and can be confused with dark herring gull; wingtips show less white on black primaries than this species. Birds breeding around Baltic belong to race *fuscus*, and are black above, looking like slim great black-backed gull but with only a single white spot on primaries. Scandinavian birds of race *intermedius* show characteristics of both of others. Juvenile has brown plumage, darker than juvenile herring gull, especially when seen in flight. Adult plumage acquired over subsequent two years. At successive moults, head and body become whiter, and brown on wings replaced by grey.

Yellow-legged Gull

Larus cachinnans

THE yellow-legged gull is able to feed in a variety of ways and has adapted to modern fishing methods, frequently following fishing vessels and scavenging on waste; it is most likely to be seen near harbours or feeding at outfalls and refuse tips. It is now far more common than any other gull in the Mediterranean.

Voice: Utters raucous 'aahhoo' calls and deep chuckling notes
Length: 55–67cm
Wingspan: 130–158cm
Weight: 800–1,000g
Habitat: Mediterranean region, Black Sea
Nest: Large, untidy cup of vegetation on ground
Eggs: 2–3; olive to brown with darker spots and blotches
Food: Wide range of fish and marine invertebrates, plus anything found by scavenging

Very similar to, and formerly considered a race of, herring gull; adult differs in having yellow legs and darker grey mantle when compared to western European herring gulls. In winter, adult lacks dark mottling on head and neck, characteristic of herring gulls. At all times, bill is richer yellow and has larger red spot near tip than herring gull. Three separate races of yellow-legged gull are recognised by experts; these are very similar, and are not considered here. Immature birds are brown as juveniles and in first winter; legs dark. Acquire adult's white head and body plumage, grey mantle and yellow legs through successive moults over subsequent two years.

Herring Gull

Larus argentatus

Herring gulls nest on buildings as well as sea cliffs so can find a home on virtually any stretch of coast

Herring gulls have very expressive calls and behaviour and can show aggression by defiant postures and loud calls

Adult birds

HERRING gulls are able to exploit a wide range of habitats and food sources. They can feed on the seashore and in the open sea, and can also scavenge in refuse tips and feed on agricultural land. They will take small migrating birds over the sea, and frequently prey on other smaller seabirds on nesting colonies. Herring gulls nest colonially, and also feed and roost in large numbers outside the breeding season, but they also may be seen in small numbers on migration after the breeding season. It is suspected that herring gulls pair for life, and pairs are reported to have returned to the same nest site for as long as twenty years.

Voice: Utters long 'aahhoo' calls and deep chuckling notes
Length: 55–67cm
Wingspan: 130–158cm
Weight: 800–1,100g
Habitat: All types of coastline, large lakes, rivers
Nest: Large cup of vegetation; on ground, sometimes on buildings
Eggs: 2–3; smooth, olive to brown, with numerous dark-brown spots and streaks
Food: Diet very varied; will eat almost anything organic that it can swallow

Adult plumage – silvery-grey mantle with black wingtips flecked with white – is acquired in the fourth year. Large bill is yellow with orange spot near tip of lower mandible. Eye is yellow and legs are pink. Immatures are mottled brown in first winter with dark eye and bill, and dirty-pink legs. In second winter, have more grey in mantle, and iris becomes paler. Before attaining full adult plumage, black wingtips may look very pale, potentially causing confusion with Iceland or glaucous gulls.

1. Juvenile

2. Immature, first summer

3. Immature, second winter

4. Immature, third winter

5. Adult, summer

Great Black-backed Gull

Larus marinus

THE great black-backed gull can be solitary but in many areas prefers to breed in loose colonies. It often breeds in the company of other seabirds, which may then become its source of food. The species is not completely migratory, and some great black-backed gulls move offshore in winter; over half the European population uses waters around Britain at this time. Flocks feed around fishing trawlers at sea and in harbours, where they often roost on buildings. Recently developed scavenging habits at rubbish dumps have probably resulted in an increase in the population.

Voice: Utters deep barking 'owk uk-uk-uk'; also various other wailing and squeaking calls
Length: 64–78cm
Wingspan: 150–165cm
Weight: 1–2.2kg
Habitat: Breeds on coastal islands, stacks, beaches and saltmarshes, occasionally inland at freshwater lakes; continental-shelf waters in winter
Nest: Heap of seaweed, vegetation and debris on ground, cliff or roof
Eggs: 2–3; smooth, olive brown, blotched dark-brown and grey
Food: Omnivorous and opportunistic; predator of smaller seabirds and scavenges widely

Great black-backed gulls scavenge at carrion but will also happily bring down adult seabirds returning to colonies with food, either to steal the morsels or kill the birds themselves; auks are particularly vulnerable to these attacks

Much larger and bulkier than herring gull, with large angular head, heavy bill and broad back. Sexes similar. Adult in summer has white head, neck, rump and tail. Back and upperwing slaty-black with white tips to primaries forming row of white spots on closed wingtip. Underparts white. Bill yellow with red spot on lower mandible towards tip. Legs and feet pink. In winter adult head and neck streaked with brownish-grey. Juvenile and immature plumages mottled dark brown and white, with whiter rump and blackish terminal band to tail; bill black.

Juveniles in flight similar to young herring gulls, but head is paler and tail more clearly banded

Unlike with herring gulls, black blotches on wings increase in second and third years

In winter adults stand out in mixed flocks owing to large size and distinctive black and white colouring; young have pale head and chequered upperparts

Iceland Gull

Larus glaucoides

Graceful flight almost tern-like at times

First-winter bird

T HE Iceland gull breeds off the coast of Greenland and northeast Canada, but may be seen in Iceland outside the breeding season, when it also wanders as far as the coasts of Scandinavia and northern Britain. It is more pelagic than other gulls, however, so is not often seen near land. Its usual habit is to follow fishing fleets with other gulls, scavenging for scraps. It has a graceful flight, dipping quickly to the water to pick up food, and sometimes it may submerge completely after a plunge. Sometimes it follows boats into harbour in a mixed flock with other gulls.

First-winter bird (above) is creamy fawn; brown bill has dark tip

Voice: Utters shrill version of herring gull's 'aahhoo' call
Length: 52–60cm
Wingspan: 130–145cm
Weight: 730–870g
Habitat: Breeds on Arctic islands; overwinters at sea
Nest: Does not breed in region
Eggs: Does not breed in region
Food: Mainly fish; will also take carrion, plankton, eggs and chicks of other birds

Smaller than herring gull, with more rounded head and smaller bill. Absence of black on wingtips at all times is good identification feature but may lead to confusion with glaucous gull; Iceland gull is smaller and more graceful in flight. At rest, wingtips project beyond end of tail. Juvenile and first-winter bird very similar to juvenile glaucous gull, with essentially white plumage mottled pale

brown, but bill is brown-grey, not pale pink. Second-winter bird has pale, marbled grey upperparts and pale, streaked head and underparts. Pale grey bill has dark sub-terminal band.

Winter adult

Very pale appearance and rounded head profile immediately separate Iceland gull from all large gulls other than glaucous gulls

Glaucous Gull

Larus hyperboreus

Second-winter bird

T HE glaucous gull prefers coastal breeding sites facing open seas, especially cliffs separated from the sea by a shelf of grassland. It shares its breeding sites with geese and auks, which helps its piratical feeding methods. When found together with the Iceland gull this species requires care with identification: it is almost always larger, and its angular head and heavy bill give it a much fiercer expression than its smaller relative. The glaucous gull is not completely migratory; some individuals disperse only as far south as winter ice forces them to. Storms in early winter move birds further south and west, and at these times they can be found in considerable numbers on west European coasts.

First-winter bird

Voice: Short, high-pitched yapping and wailing calls
Length: 62–68cm
Wingspan: 150–165cm
Weight: 1.2–2.1kg
Habitat: Breeds on small islands on Arctic and sub-Arctic coasts; overwinters on bays and harbours
Nest: Large pile of seaweed and debris
Eggs: 2–3; smooth, buff, blotched and spotted dark brown
Food: Omnivorous; predator and scavenger,

and food-pirate of other seabirds

Larger than Iceland gull but usually smaller than great black-backed gull. Looks pale and white-winged at all times. Summer adult has pale grey back and upperwing, otherwise plumage completely white, including wingtips. In winter, head and neck streaked brown. Pale eye, yellow bill with red spot, and pink legs and feet

seen at all times. Immature plumages white with uniform pale mottled brown gradually lost by moulting until all white by third year; bill pink with black tip.

Winter adult has streaked head and neck

Sabine's Gull

Larus sabini

Winter adult

Sabine's gulls undertake trans-equatorial movements to winter in seas off southern Africa

Juvenile

DESPITE the distance of its summer haunts from northwest European seas, Sabine's gulls are seen regularly from these coasts, mostly in late autumn when storms move the birds from open seas to inshore shelter. This gull is small and dainty, almost tern-like in its erratic and buoyant flight, its forked tail adding to this similarity. Care is needed to distinguish this species from the juvenile kittiwake, which has a superficially similar upperwing pattern with an additional black wingbar across the coverts.

Voice: Various grating cries and whistling calls
Length: 27–32cm
Wingspan: 90–100cm
Weight: 155–210g
Habitat: Arctic coastal lowlands; open seas in winter
Nest: Shallow unlined depression
Eggs: 2; smooth, olive, variably marked, dark brown mostly at broad end
Food: Invertebrates, small fish, occasionally carrion

Smaller than kittiwake, with narrower wings, more deeply forked tail and buoyant tern-like flight action. Summer adult has dusky-grey head with thin black lower border around neck; lower neck and underparts pure white. Mantle is grey, and tail and rump are white; upperwing shows smart and diagnostic triangular pattern of grey coverts, white inner primaries and secondaries, and black outer primaries. In winter, the adult bird loses its dark hood but retains the dusky streaking on the nape of its neck. Bill black with yellow tip at all times; legs and feet blackish-grey. Juvenile has similar upperwing pattern to adult but with grey elements of plumage replaced by warm brown; shows dark tip to tail.

Ivory Gull

Pagophila eburnea

AS A breeding species, the ivory gull's range is confined to the high Arctic. Outside the breeding season, most ivory gulls remain at similar latitudes to those favoured during the brief Arctic summer. Occasionally birds are driven south during the winter months, often seemingly in response to appalling weather conditions; they then reach the shores of northern Europe with northern Scotland, Denmark and Norway being especially favoured. Most sightings occur between late November and February and generally involve immature birds. Fortunately for observers, these birds often stay in the same general location for some days.

Voice: Harsh calls uttered near breeding colonies; otherwise silent
Length: 40–42cm
Wingspan: 110–115cm
Weight: 450–550g
Habitat: Breeds on Arctic cliffs; at other times usually found at edge of pack-ice
Nest: Small mound of vegetation on cliff ledge
Eggs: 1–2; pale buff with darker markings
Food: Small marine invertebrates and fish; also carrion and faeces

A high Arctic gull with a comparatively dainty bill and almost pigeon-like expression. Sexes similar. Adult has pure white plumage although feathers at base of bill sometimes stained from feeding. Bill bluish but grading through yellow towards tip, which is red. Legs and feet black. Black eye outlined by narrow red eyering. Juvenile and first winter birds have essentially white plumage but with variable amounts of black spotting on upperwings and rump, and black tip to tail. Show variable amounts of greyish feathering between base of bill and eye. Bill usually dark and legs and feet black. Black eye surrounded by narrow dark eyering.

First winter

Ross's Gull

Rhodostethia rosea

IN EUROPE, Ross's gull occurs as a rare vagrant, with most records occurring during the winter months in Iceland, north and northeast Britain, Denmark, Norway and Sweden. Although a rare visitor, vagrant Ross's gulls often stay in the same general location for extended periods, especially if they find a reliable source of food. Ross's gull can be difficult to pick out among a distant flock of flying black-headed gulls, but at close range the species should present few problems. The flight action is buoyant, recalling that of little gull or larger tern species.

Voice: Generally silent
Length: 30–32cm
Wingspan: 85–95cm
Weight: 130–150g
Habitat: Breeds on boggy tundra; otherwise found at sea, usually in vicinity of pack-ice edge
Nest: No information available
Eggs: No information available
Food: Insects during breeding season; otherwise marine invertebrates

A small, long-winged gull, all ages of which have a diagnostic wedge-shaped tail and proportionately small bill. Sexes similar. At rest, adult in breeding plumage has pale grey upperparts and underparts essentially white. Pure white head is defined in extent by narrow black necklace. Head, neck and underparts suffused with rosy pink. In flight, shows pale grey upperwings with broad, white trailing edge. Underwings smoky grey with white trailing edge and tail white. Adult in non-breeding plumage loses pink suffusion and black necklace of breeding adult but similar in other respects. Juvenile has distinctive markings on wings best observed in flight: black zigzag across whole of upperwing behind which is white trailing edge. Tail white but black-tipped. Has dark smudging around eye, on nape and on ear coverts. All birds have black bill and red legs, colour most intense in adult.

Winter adult

Comparing Unusual Gulls

G ULL enthusiasts are always on the look-out for a rare vagrant among a flock of more familiar birds, even though they can be a challenge to identify. Some of the unusual but regularly encountered species will have flown all the way from North America.

Central Asian gull; rare vagrant to eastern Mediterranean

First-winter plumage

GREAT BLACK-HEADED GULL: *First-winter bird shows dark-tipped pink bill, dark smudging behind eye and on nape, white underparts and dark-tipped white tail; in flight, recalls outsized immature common gull*

Second-winter bird

GREAT BLACK-HEADED GULL (LARUS ICHTHYAETUS): *Large gull with massive bill and long yellow legs. Breeding adult has black and white on projecting primaries, black hood and orange-tipped bill with black band. Winter adult has black hood replaced by dark smudging*

First-winter plumage

North American gull; very rare vagrant to Europe

FRANKLIN'S GULL: *Head markings on first-winter bird similar to winter adult; bill and legs very dark red. In flight, mantle and back dark grey, wings dark grey-brown with white trailing edge and tail white with black tip*

Winter adult

FRANKLIN'S GULL (LARUS PIPIXCAN): *Breeding adult grey above, white below, with black hood and red bill and legs. In flight, upperwing has broad, white trailing edge. Winter adult has black band on nape; bill and legs can appear almost black*

BONAPARTE'S GULL (LARUS PHILADELPHIA): *Similar in size and habits to little gull. Breeding adult has grey back, black wingtips and blackish-brown hood; bill dark and legs red. In flight, upperwings grey with white leading edge and black trailing edge. Winter adult head white with dark smudges above eye and on ear coverts*

Winter adult

North American gull; very rare vagrant to Europe

LAUGHING GULL (LARUS ATRICILLA): *Similar to Franklin's gull but larger and longer-winged. Breeding adult has dark-grey mantle and upperwings and black wingtips and hood; bill and legs deep red. Winter adult has white head with dark smudging on head; bill and legs blackish*

North American gull; very rare vagrant to Europe

First-winter plumage

BONAPARTE'S GULL: *First-winter bird shows dark diagonal band on inner upperwing and black trailing edge along entire wing; tail white with black tip; plumage otherwise similar to winter adult*

LAUGHING GULL: *First-winter bird has grey back, grey-brown wing coverts and dark flight feathers with white trailing edge; shows dark smudging around eye and on nape, and grey wash to neck; legs and bill dark*

North American gull; rare annual vagrant to Europe

First-winter plumage

RING-BILLED GULL (LARUS DELAWARENSIS): *Very similar to common gull but larger. Breeding adult white with grey back and black wingtips; bill larger than common gull's, with black band; eye has yellow iris. Winter adult has brownish streaking on head and nape*

Winter adult

RING-BILLED GULL: *First-winter bird has variably grey-brown upperparts with pale mantle and pale band on greater coverts and bases of inner primaries; head and neck heavily spotted; tail has dark terminal band; legs pink*

Comparing Immature Gulls

When trying to identify any mystery gull, careful attention should be paid to its overall size relative to nearby birds of known species, its wing pattern and bill and leg colour. Outside the breeding season gulls tend to form single-species flocks. Not surprisingly, therefore, immature gulls are likely to consort with adults of their kind, which often helps to identify them.

First-winter bird

First-winter bird

First-winter bird

COMMON GULL: *Well-marked with dark primaries and trailing edge to innerwing; mantle and rest of innerwing grey except for mottled brown wing coverts; tail white with broad, black terminal band; dark-tipped bill is dull pink*

BLACK-HEADED GULL: *Always shows white leading edge to the wings and black trailing edge to primaries; seen from below the latter are grey except for narrow white leading edge; brown upperwing coverts and black tail bar visible in flight; legs and bill dull pinkish-orange, bill with dark tip*

LITTLE GULL: *Distinctive upperwing pattern, with black angled bars, similar to that of immature kittiwake; recalls tern in size and flight; black on nape and crown striking, as is black tail bar; bill dainty and black*

First-winter bird

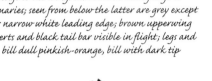

First-winter bird

MEDITERRANEAN GULL (first winter): *Shows striking upperwing pattern comprising marbled brown wing coverts and black on primaries and on trailing edge of innerwing; tail black-tipped, and bill and eye patch look black at a distance*

SLENDER-BILLED GULL: *Superficially similar to first-winter black-headed gull, especially in upperwing pattern, but larger and with more attenuated proportions; in particular, forehead comparatively long, narrowing to join long (but not slender) bill; legs and bill dull pinkish-orange; bill has only small dark tip*

Second-winter bird

First-winter bird

MEDITERRANEAN GULL (second winter): *similar to winter adult with mostly pure white wings except for black spots near tips of primaries; black markings through eye and on nape give menacing appearance; legs red and bill dark red*

AUDOUIN'S GULL: *Recalls first-winter common gull but mantle usually marbled with dark feathers rather than uniformly grey; usually has cleaner-looking plumage than herring gull of similar age; bill looks robust even at a distance and has reddish base*

Comparing Immature Gulls

First-winter bird

Second-winter bird

HERRING GULL (first winter): Seen from above, plumage looks marbled grey-brown, darkest on primaries, trailing edge of innerwing and on terminal band on tail; appears palest on rump and usually shows pale wedge on inner primaries; head looks grubby and bill dark

HERRING GULL (second winter): Compared to first-winter bird mantle is greyer, while inner primaries and rump are paler; bill dull pink and dark-tipped

First-winter bird

Second-winter bird

LESSER BLACK-BACKED GULL (first winter): Similar to first-winter herring gull; seen from above, usually appears more uniformly grey-brown and generally darker overall; in particular, lacks that species' pale wedge on inner primaries

LESSER BLACK-BACKED GULL (second winter): Although marbled with brown feathering, back and upperwings appear dark grey, the tone being much darker than similarly aged herring gulls; bill often appear all dark; legs dull pink

GREAT BLACK-BACKED GULL (first winter): Seen from above in flight, appears mottled dark grey-brown; usually paler than same-age lesser black-backed gull and lacking herring gull's pale wedge on inner primaries; head often looks pale; head and bill always look large

GREAT BLACK-BACKED GULL (second winter): Species can usually be identified by large size and proportionately massive head and bill alone; plumage appears paler overall than herring and lesser black-backed gulls' of similar age, head being particularly pale

First-winter bird

Second-winter bird

127

Sandwich Tern

Sterna sandvicensis

Loses black forehead by late summer and acquires dusky wedge on outerwing through wear

Deep, disyllabic call and bright white plumage allow easy identification

Breeding adult

Juvenile

Most Sandwich terns migrate to west African coasts for the winter; the Black Sea population only moves to the southern Mediterranean

S ANDWICH tern colonies require access to shallow, sheltered waters, usually over sand for fishing, and birds will travel a considerable distance to feeding grounds from where they nest or roost. Nest sites are mostly on offshore islands or calcareous spits with short vegetation in which to place the actual scrape; the birds tend to relocate from one year to the next as the nesting area is often unstable. Sandwich terns are one of northwest Europe's first summer migrants, appearing at the end of March. They are highly sensitive to disturbance when breeding and benefit greatly from artificial protection measures.

Voice: Distinct disyllabic 'keerr-ink'; shorter, sharp alarm note
Length: 36–41cm
Wingspan: 95–105cm
Weight: 225–285g
Habitat: Low-lying coasts with access to shallow, sandy-bottomed waters
Nest: Shallow, unlined scrape on shingle or amongst vegetation
Eggs: 1–2; glossy, creamy-white, variably marked with dark brown
Food: Mainly surface-dwelling marine fish, especially sand-eels

Large and pale tern with long bill and head. Tail short but deeply forked. Wings long and narrow. In breeding season, Sandwich tern has jet black cap with shaggy crest to rear. Back and upperwing very pale grey with silvery flight feathers. Rump and tail white. Underparts bright white. In winter, forehead becomes white and cap is mottled. At all times, adult has black bill with yellow tip, and black legs and feet. Juvenile resembles winter adult, but has shorter all-black bill and blackish flecking on upperwing and back.

sleeping birds show spiky crest on nape

Forster's Tern

Sterna forsteri

Winter adult

F ORSTER's tern is a North American species, but has occurred as a very rare winter vagrant to northwest Europe. The strikingly white plumage with contrasting black eyepatch and bill make identification of non-breeding birds relatively straightforward. There is potential for confusion with the gull-billed tern in non-breeding plumage but since the latter species is entirely absent from the region during the winter this problem should not arise. Forster's tern has not been recorded in the region in the summer months and it would take meticulous observation indeed to attempt to identify a breeding-plumage bird.

Voice: Mainly silent in region
Length: 34–35cm
Wingspan: 75–80cm
Weight: No information available
Habitat: Breeds on marshes; in winter, favours sheltered coastal waters and coastal marshes
Nest: Does not breed in region
Eggs: Does not breed in region
Food: Mainly fish

Forster's tern is most distinctive in non-breeding plumage, that most likely to be seen in vagrants to Europe. Adult in breeding season superficially similar to breeding-plumage common tern but larger and with proportionately longer legs. Has black cap, pale-grey upperwings and otherwise white plumage. Bill orange-red with dark tip and legs orange-red. Non-breeding adult has extremely pale plumage and can look all white in flight and at a distance except for conspicuous dark patch through eye, which gives panda-like appearance. Bill and legs dark. First-winter bird similar to non-breeding adult but upperwings appear less uniformly pale due to contrast between very pale panel on innerwing and darker outer primaries.

Lesser Crested Tern

Sterna bengalensis

summer adult

Although chance observations of lesser crested terns can be obtained during migration times in the eastern Mediterranean, solitary birds also occasionally join nesting colonies of Sandwich terns well outside their normal tropical breeding range. These vagrant birds are usually found paired with Sandwich terns and sometimes have been known to go through the process of nest building and egg laying. Lesser crested terns are elegant birds on the wing with deep, powerful wingbeats and bouyant flight. They will often join with mixed tern flocks, engaging in frenzied diving where the fishing is good.

Voice: Calls include a harsh 'kier-rip'
Length: 34–36cm
Wingspan: 95–100cm
Weight: 200–220g
Habitat: Breeds on coastal dunes and islands; otherwise found in coastal waters
Nest: Shallow scrape on ground
Eggs: 1–2; off-white with dark speckling
Food: Small fish and crustaceans

Lesser crested terns are a similar size to Sandwich terns but have a more robust, orange-yellow bill at all times. Adult in breeding plumage has black cap and grey back and upperwing; plumage otherwise white. Legs dark. Non-breeding adult has black on head confined to patch from eye to nape and on rear of crown; plumage otherwise similar to breeding adult. Juvenile similar to non-breeding adult but back and upperwing mottled grey-brown; first-winter bird similar to juvenile but upperwing appears more uniformly grey.

Little terns' size, narrow wings and bright, white appearance make identification easy

Often plunge-dives into breaking waves right at edge of beach

Little Tern

Sterna albifrons

Looks very small in comparison to Sandwich tern (below), and never has complete black cap

In Britain little terns are exclusively coastal, but elsewhere in Europe they are found along major rivers and around lakes as well as on the seashore. They arrive in Europe in April, when they can be seen fishing just offshore and can be heard courting noisily during their fluttering flight. They leave during September for their overwintering grounds in west Africa, where the first-year birds spend a whole year before joining the northern migrants. Little terns suffer from competition with humans for fine sandy beaches, and their survival here depends on direct protection from disturbance.

Voice: Rasping and churring 'kierr-ink' call; also shorter distinctive 'kik'
Length: 22–24cm
Wingspan: 48–55cm
Weight: 50–60g
Habitat: Coastal or riverine strips of bare shingle, sand with shallow lagoons, inlets
Nest: Shallow, unlined scrape in sand or gravel
Eggs: 1–3; smooth, pale cream with dark spots, blotches and occasional streaks
Food: Small fish, crustaceans, insects

Smallest sea tern with larger head, longer bill and more sharply forked tail than marsh tern of genus *Chlidonias*. Summer adult has black crown, nape and line through eye to bill; forehead white. Back pale grey fading to white uppertail. Underparts pure white. Upperwing grey like back, with blackish outer primaries forming dark leading edge, and whiter trailing edge. Bill long and slender, yellow with black tip. Legs and feet orange-yellow. Non-breeding adult has darker bill and larger white forehead than summer adult. Juvenile has browner-grey feathers on back and upperwing.

Short, yellow legs and yellow bill with small black tip unique

Young birds best identified by small size, dumpy shape and dark bill; beware confusion with immature marsh terns

Juvenile has brown mantle and coverts and dark primaries

Common Tern

Sterna hirundo

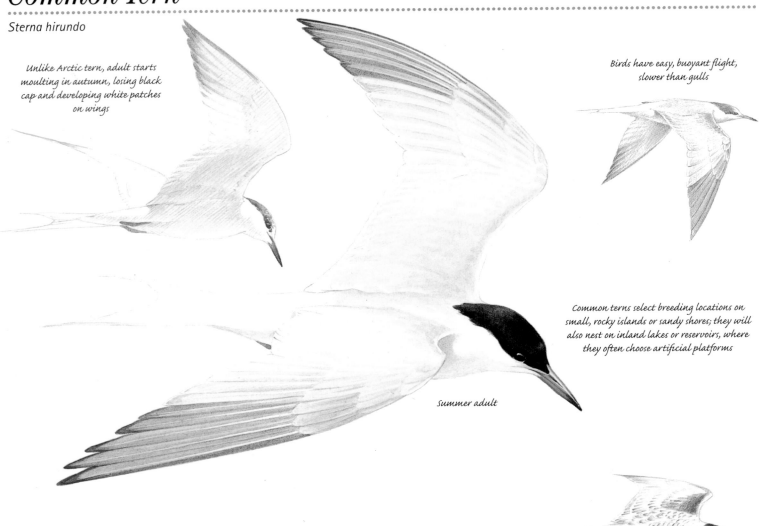

Unlike Arctic tern, adult starts moulting in autumn, losing black cap and developing white patches on wings

Birds have easy, buoyant flight, slower than gulls

Common terns select breeding locations on small, rocky islands or sandy shores; they will also nest on inland lakes or reservoirs, where they often choose artificial platforms

summer adult

COMMON terns are widespread throughout Europe in summer, returning to their nesting colonies in April, and, although tied to water, they are the least exclusively marine of all the sea terns. Nests can be some distance from feeding locations but the birds are well able to cope with any necessary commuting. Like all sea terns, common terns are migratory, with the majority of the European birds overwintering in the tropical seas off west Africa. A useful identification feature to separate them from the Arctic tern on migration is the dark wedge on the outerwing, formed by non-moulted older primary feathers.

Juvenile has ginger-brown tinge to plumage; wing is palest in the centre

Voice: Utters harsh rasping and emphatic 'keey-yah' call; also short, sharp alarm
Length: 31–35cm
Wingspan: 77–98cm
Weight: 90–150g
Habitat: Along coasts and on inland fresh waters, sometimes on artificial platforms
Nest: Shallow depression lined with available material
Eggs: 1–3; buff, variably tinted with green or blue, spotted and lined with black-brown
Food: Fish, crustaceans

Often seen with black-headed gulls, but are fractionally shorter, with narrower, more pointed wings and long forked tail. Very similar to Arctic tern, but with larger bill and head, stouter body and shorter tail; legs longer than Arctic tern's. Summer adult has jet-black cap, pearl-grey upperparts with darker grey outer primaries and white rump and tail. Underparts white. In winter, adult has white forehead and mottled black cap. At all times

adult has red, black-tipped bill, and red legs and feet. Juvenile is like winter adult but with ginger-brown mottling to back and forewing, and pale orange bill with black tip.

Legs very short but longer than Arctic tern's; dark outer primaries visible when bird is standing

Arctic Tern

Sterna paradisaea

ARCTIC tern colonies are mainly confined to coasts, where grassy islands are favoured, but in Norway and Russia birds will move inland along rivers to find ice-free nesting grounds. Arctic terns return to their colonies in early May in the south of their range but arrive later further north. They often share nesting islands with other sea terns and eiders. A visit to an Arctic tern colony is a noisy and exciting experience as the birds defend their territories by dive-bombing intruders. Arctic terns perform the longest migration of any bird, spending the winter on the margins of the Antarctic pack-ice.

Voice: Utters shrill, nasal, grating notes and short, sharp alarm call; colonies very noisy
Length: 33–35cm
Wingspan: 75–85cm
Weight: 87–119g
Habitat: Inshore and offshore waters with grass covered islets; sometimes inland along rivers
Nest: Shallow, unlined scrape

Eggs: 1–3; pale buff, variously spotted and scrawled dark brown
Food: Marine fish, crustaceans, insects

Summer adult

Difficult to separate from the common tern, but has shorter bill and head, longer tail and much shorter legs. Summer adult pale blue-grey above, white below but with dusky grey wash on breast and belly. Rump and tail bright white. Jet-black cap, white cheeks and blood-red bill. White flight feathers, translucent from below, lack dark markings of common tern. Winter birds, not seen in region, have crown speckled white. Legs and feet coral-red in summer, darker in winter. Juvenile has white forehead, marked black cap and is pale grey above, lacking brown tints of other juvenile sea terns.

Pure white forehead and rump and black bill help distinguish juvenile from juvenile common tern

Shorter head and bill and longer tail give Arctic tern subtly different flight shape from common tern

Roseate Tern

Sterna dougallii

BRITAIN and Ireland are the most important areas in Europe for roseate terns and they breed there in small colonies on offshore islands close to shallow, sheltered bays where they can fish. There a few pairs in northwest France and a healthy population on the Azores, but they are very rare throughout Europe as a whole. Roseate terns are the most marine of the European sea terns and their autumn migration takes them swiftly down to the tropical coasts of west Africa; they are very rarely seen inland. They can be identified at migration points by their very white appearance and long tail.

Voice: Calls include distinct rasping 'aakh' and whistled 'chewit'
Length: 33–38cm
Wingspan: 72–80cm
Weight: 100–130g
Habitat: Maritime coasts with low rocky islets, sand dunes
Nest: Shallow, unlined scrape under vegetation or in shelter of rock
Eggs: 1–2; smooth, pale cream with black-brown spots and scrawls at broad end
Food: Mainly small marine fish

Similar to the common tern but has shorter wings and longer tail, giving slimmer appearance. In breeding season, adult has narrow, jet-black cap on crown and nape. Lower face, rump and tail white. Upperparts have blue-grey wash, paler than in common tern. Underparts washed with strong pink. Flight feathers pale silvery grey and translucent from below. Winter adult loses rosy wash and forehead becomes white. Long, narrow, black bill with red base seen at all times in adults. Legs and feet coral red in summer, dull red in winter. Juvenile has heavy brown spotting on upperparts, reminiscent of young Sandwich tern.

Juvenile

Medium-sized, pale sea tern with long, flowing tail streamers; elegant in summer plumage

Gull-billed Tern

Gelochelidon nilotica

THE gull-billed tern is more catholic in its choice of colony sites than other terns and is less dependent on close proximity to water. From its overwintering grounds south of the region it returns north in spring, arriving at European breeding sites in late April; it is during this period of spring migration that individuals very occasionally arrive as vagrants in northwest Europe. The gull-billed tern will forage over damp agricultural land, but it can also be seen fishing in coastal lagoons. It can survive in a wide range of man-managed habitats.

summer adult

Great care is needed to distinguish this species from Sandwich tern; thick bill and harsh, grating call are best identification features

Voice: Loud, deep, trisyllabic grating call
Length: 35–38cm
Wingspan: 100–115cm
Weight: 190–280g
Habitat: Lowland coasts and deltas; inland to lakes rivers and marshes
Nest: Shallow depression in soil, close to grassy tuft or other object; lined with vegetation
Eggs: 1–4; smooth, pale yellow-buff, speckled black-brown
Food: Wide range of small mammals, bird chicks, amphibians, fish and insects

Comparable in size to Sandwich tern but has bulkier outline with heavier, more direct flight. In breeding season, has black crown reaching low down nape; white hindneck, face and underparts. Back, rump and tail ash grey. Upperwing pearl-grey with duskier primaries towards tip. Underwing white except for dusky wedge near tip. Winter adult loses black cap but retains black mask. At all times in adult, bill black, thick and blunt, and legs and feet black. Juvenile darker than winter adult, with grey feathers of back and shoulders smudged brown; legs and feet red-brown.

Caspian Tern

Sterna caspia

THE impressive-looking Caspian tern is not common in Europe, being mainly restricted to the Baltic coasts. Breeding birds arrive in late April and forage for fish on large, sheltered waters, travelling some distance from the nest in order to do so. The Caspian tern is a strong flier, often seen at higher altitudes than other terns, and looks very gull-like in flight. Like all sea terns, Caspian terns are migratory, moving south for the winter. Migration begins in late summer and it is often in August that wandering individuals turn up on western European coasts. However, the Caspian tern seldom stays long and its unpredictability makes it a difficult bird to see.

Breeding adult

The Caspian tern is shy at its breeding grounds and tends to choose more isolated locations in Europe to avoid disturbance

Voice: Utters loud, deep, barking notes with short, sharp alarm call
Length: 47–54cm
Wingspan: 130–145cm
Weight: 600–750g
Habitat: Sheltered continental coasts with rocky islets, sand dunes, spits
Nest: Shallow unlined depression on ground, in the open
Eggs: 1–3; smooth, cream, speckled dark brown-black
Food: Mainly fish; occasionally invertebrates

Huge gull-sized tern with massive bill, round body, blunt wings and short tail. In breeding season, crown and shaggy nape black, and hindneck, face and underparts white. Back and upperwing silvery grey, darker towards wingtip. Underwing has large dusky patch at tip. Rump and tail whitish, sometimes with grey cast. In winter, cap more mottled with black speckling extending on to face; wings become darker with wear. Massive dagger bill is bright coral red in summer, more orange in winter with dark tip. Legs and feet black at all times. Juvenile has mottled black cap extending on to face, and irregular brown flecking on back.

Black Tern

Chlidonias niger

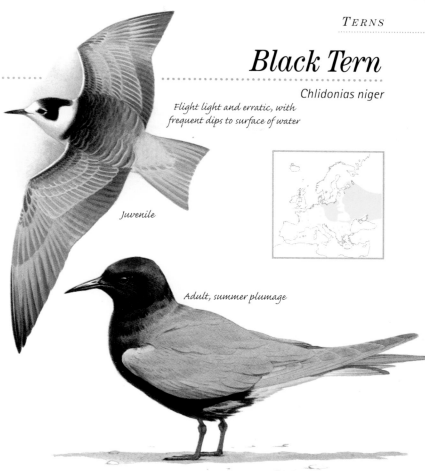

Flight light and erratic, with frequent dips to surface of water

Juvenile

Adult, summer plumage

THE black tern is a breeding bird of eastern Europe with many scattered colonies to the west, especially round the swampy meadows and pools of the Netherlands. Birds return in May to breeding waters, where they are loosely colonial. Foraging adults fly buoyantly over water, dipping to the surface to take invertebrate prey. Black terns are migratory, overwintering in tropical west Africa. During migration periods large numbers can sometimes be seen in northwest Europe. The spring movement is most impressive: in favourable conditions, many thousands pass through reservoirs and lakes, and along coasts, often on the same day.

Voice: Squeaky harsh 'kik-keek' call; growling 'krrr' when on nest
Length: 22–24cm
Wingspan: 64–68cm
Weight: 60–85g
Habitat: Continental, fresh or brackish waters, rich in floating and emergent vegetation
Nest: Low heap of waterweed or shallow scrape lined with water weed

Eggs: 2–4; oval, glossy, cream, spotted and blotched dark brown
Food: Insects and aquatic invertebrates; some small fish and amphibians

Smaller than all sea terns, with shorter, less forked tail. Summer adult dark slate-grey, with head almost black and upperwing ash-grey. Rump and uppertail grey. Underwing very pale grey, vent and undertail coverts white. In winter, grey upperparts and white underparts reminiscent of sea terns, but upperparts darker and with black smudge at shoulder. Moult between summer and winter plumages can give very blotchy appearance. Juvenile plumage as winter adult. At all times bill black, long and fine, and legs and feet red-brown.

Whiskered Tern

Chlidonias hybridus

Juvenile

Breeding adult

THE whiskered tern has a more southerly distribution in Europe than the black tern, requiring a warmer climate than that species. The Camargue, in southern France, is a typical habitat. Here the terns nest semi-colonially, building floating nests from vegetation stirred up by wild horses, and often foraging on adjacent flooded rice paddies. The species overwinters in tropical Africa and Asia.

Voice: Loud croaking and cawing 'krrerch'; sharper alarm call
Length: 23–25cm
Wingspan: 74–78cm
Weight: 80–90g
Habitat: Clear water, lakes and marshes with floating vegetation
Nest: Cone-shaped raft of vegetation, anchored to submerged plant
Eggs: 2–3; oval, glossy, pale-blue or grey, spotted and blotched brown
Food: Insects and their larvae; some small fish, amphibians

Relatively bulky size invites confusion with sea tern, but has shorter, less forked tail. Summer adult has jet-black crown and nape, contrasting with white lower face. Neck and rest of upperparts uniform dark grey, including rump and uppertail. Below white face underparts become dark slate grey, darkest on flanks. Vent and undertail coverts white. Upperwing grey, underwing coverts white. In winter much more like sea tern, with grey upperparts and white underparts. Bill dark crimson-red in summer adult but black in winter and juvenile. Legs and feet red at all times. Juvenile resembles winter adult, with dark brown back and pale grey upperwing, giving saddle effect.

White-winged Black Tern

Chlidonias leucopterus

Breeding adult

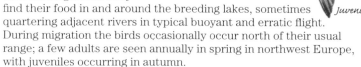

Juvenile

THE natural marshes and alkaline pools among the vast grasslands of Poland and Hungary are the white-winged black tern's favoured breeding areas. Birds arrive in mid-May from wintering grounds in Africa to begin building their floating nests. They find their food in and around the breeding lakes, sometimes quartering adjacent rivers in typical buoyant and erratic flight. During migration the birds occasionally occur north of their usual range; a few adults are seen annually in spring in northwest Europe, with juveniles occurring in autumn.

Voice: Call is a sharp churring 'keer'; shorter alarm notes
Length: 20–23cm
Wingspan: 63–67cm
Weight: 56–80g
Habitat: Natural flooded grasslands and swamps
Nest: Heap of floating, partly submerged waterweed with shallow depression
Eggs: 2–3; oval, glossy, cream with large blackish blotches
Food: Mainly aquatic or terrestrial invertebrates; some fish and amphibians

Breeding plumage bird has black head, neck and body, upperwings greyer and show bright silver-white wing coverts. Underwing shows black coverts and pale-grey flight feathers. Rump, vent and tail white. In winter, grey above and white below, with white collar and white rump contrasting with grey tail. Bill short and pointed, crimson when breeding, otherwise black. Legs and feet bright red in summer, darker in winter. Juvenile similar to winter adult but with darker, mottled brown back forming saddle.

Guillemot

Uria aalge

The bridled form shows white spectacle round eye

Britain and Ireland are guillemot strongholds; the more northern birds tend to have darker summer plumage

GUILLEMOTS are found around the coasts of northwestern Europe in densely packed cliff-ledge colonies, often numbering tens of thousands of birds. Winter attendance at the breeding cliffs is not uncommon, but it is March when the masses start to assemble on ledges. Guillemots are strong fliers but lack agility, so precision landing at the nest site often requires more than one attempt, and cliff bays can be alive with circling birds. Guillemots catch fish by diving underwater in pursuit of their quarry, sometimes crashing through the surface into shoals spotted from the air.

Voice: Growling and guttural crowing calls
Length: 38–41cm
Wingspan: 64–70cm
Weight: 650–1,100g
Habitat: Breeds on rocky sea cliffs and stacks; overwinters in marine offshore and inshore waters
Nest: None; eggs laid in gravelly crevice or on ledge
Eggs: 1; pointed, oval, roughened, blue-green to white heavily blotched with dark scribbles
Food: Mainly fish; some invertebrates

Longer-bodied and shorter-tailed than razorbill. In summer, head, neck and upperparts dark brown, underparts mainly white. Flanks streaked with brown. White line across closed wing formed by white tips to secondaries. Dark furrow behind eye; this feature is white and extends around eye in so-called bridled form, giving spectacled appearance. In winter, cheeks and neck white, upperparts greyer. At all times in adult birds, bill black, long and tapering, and legs and feet dark blue-grey. Juvenile has plumage like winter adult but smaller bill.

The single egg is laid directly on to the cliff ledge and is sometimes incubated on the bird's feet; its distinctive shape may have evolved to stop it from rolling off

The young are ready to jump from the cliff ledge into the sea at about 20 days; they follow the male parent

Winter adult; note dark line running back from eye

Most adults spend the winter in seas close to colonies but first-year birds wander more widely

The cliff-ledge colonies are often so tightly packed that neighbours are actually touching

Distinguished from razorbill in flight by dagger-like bill and longer neck

Brünnich's Guillemot

Uria lomvia

Colonies of Brünnich's guillemot are confined to high Arctic islands and coastal sea cliffs, with concentrations in Svalbard, Jan Mayen Island and Iceland. The birds avoid areas of permanent pack-ice, preferring circulating, cold, open water, which supports an abundance of plankton. Brünnich's guillemots return to their colony sites, which they often share with guillemots, in April. Nesting ledges face the open sea so that the fledgelings can glide safely down to the water. Winter ice formation forces Brünnich's guillemots to be migratory, though dispersal is confined mainly to northern Arctic waters.

Voice: Utters growling and hoarse crowing calls
Length: 39–43cm
Wingspan: 65–73cm
Weight: 750–1,080g
Habitat: Breeds on Arctic sea cliffs and steep boulder slopes; open Arctic waters in winter
Nest: None; egg laid on cliff ledge or rested on feet
Eggs: 1; pointed, oval, roughened, grey with dark blotches and scribbles
Food: Mainly fish; some invertebrates

Slightly larger and bulkier than guillemot, with heavier bill and thicker head and neck. Plumage very similar to guillemot. In summer adult has darker brown-black upperparts than guillemot and white underparts; lacks brown flank streaks, and white breast meets brown-black throat in a sharp point. In winter upperparts retain blackish cast; white from throat extends on to face only below eye, not above as well, as seen in guillemot. At all times adult has

black, deep and strong bill, with white lower edge to upper mandible extending from base to mid-point. Legs and feet are brown to front, black to rear. Juvenile is smaller than winter adult, which it resembles in plumage except for mottled throat.

Summer adult has distinctive white gape streak

Winter adult

Black Guillemot

Cepphus grylle

Not as intensely colonial as the other auks, black guillemots select nesting sites in natural rock holes or crevices, often among boulders at the base of sea cliffs. They return to their breeding areas in May, when small groups can easily be seen sitting on the sea below the cliffs making their thin whistling calls. Black guillemots are bottom feeders and so require shallow waters all year round. Winter dispersal is undertaken only where necessary to avoid sea ice. Around Britain birds stay on inshore waters and can often be seen either singly or in small groups around harbours and estuaries during the winter months.

Voice: Utters a thin, shrill whistle
Length: 30–32cm
Wingspan: 52–58cm
Weight: 340–450g
Habitat: Breeds on sea cliffs and maritime boulder slopes; overwinters in shallow coastal seas
Nest: Natural holes and crevices in boulder scree
Eggs: 1–2; oval, matt white-buff, spotted or blotched red-brown
Food: Marine fish and crustaceans

Medium-sized auk with round body, smallish head and oval-shaped wings. Strikingly different plumage patterns in summer and winter. Summer adult uniform dark chocolate brown except for large, white, oval patch on both upperwing and underwing coverts. In winter appears much whiter with back speckled grey and white; head, neck and underparts dirty white. Wing retains summer pattern. At all times, adult has sharply pointed black

bill with vivid orange gape, and bright red legs and feet. Juvenile resembles winter adult but with upperparts and flanks more darkly mottled.

Bright white wing patches clearly visible in flight; flies fast and low over water

The bright gape is usually only seen during courtship displays

Nesting among boulders has made black guillemots vulnerable to predation by introduced North American mink

Summer adult (right)

Winter bird pale; retains white wing patches

Razorbill

Alca torda

The distinctive square-ended bill gives the razorbill its name

Summer adult

RAZORBILLS nest on sea cliffs and among boulders on the coasts of northern Europe, where they are sometimes found in mixed colonies with their commoner relative, the guillemot. Britain and Ireland are very important for this species, holding half the world population. Returning from the winter in the open sea, razorbills occupy their cliff ledges in April. They are noisy and quarrelsome at nesting colonies and their lack of manoeuvrability in the air causes many territorial disputes on landing. Razorbills are most at home in the sea, diving and swimming underwater, using feet and open wings for propulsion when chasing fish.

The chick loses its white down by 15 days, and leaves for the sea two days later; at this stage it cannot fly

Winter bird much paler

Voice: Utters various growling calls
Length: 37–39cm
Wingspan: 63–68cm
Weight: 600–800g
Habitat: Breeds on sea cliffs and boulders of undercliff; overwinters inshore or on open sea
Nest: In cliff crevice, among boulders or in burrow entrance; rarely on open ledge
Eggs: 1; pale brown or greenish; spotted and scribbled with dark brown
Food: Mainly fish; some invertebrates

Size of guillemot, with head, neck, back, upperwings and tail jet black in summer; underparts bright white. In winter throat and upper breast become dirty white and upperparts greyer. At all times adult has deep, heavy black bill with neat white line across middle, and a white line connecting base of bill to eye. Legs and feet black. Juvenile smaller than adult, browner and with bulbous bill.

Little Auk

Alle alle

Flies with very fast wingbeats; underwing paler than puffin's

Summer bird (left) has black head and upperparts; winter bird (below) has white throat and breast

On the water the short, plump neck and almost bill-less profile are striking

LITTLE auks are the most northerly distributed of the auk family, breeding in colonies numbering millions of individuals on high Arctic islands. In spring, little auks congregate on melting pack-ice just offshore from their breeding cliffs. They can endure severe weather, with nesting sites sometimes still snow-covered at the time of egg laying in late June or July. After breeding, little auks stay in cold northern waters until forced south by midwinter storms. When the storms are particularly severe birds can be driven inland and tired individuals may be seen almost anywhere.

Voice: Twittering trills uttered at breeding colonies; whinnying alarm call in flight
Length: 18cm
Wingspan: 40–48cm
Weight: 140–170g

Habitat: Breeds on Arctic mountain and cliff scree slopes; cold open sea in winter
Nest: Shallow layer of pebbles, hidden in rock crevices
Eggs: 1; pale greenish-blue
Food: Mainly planktonic crustaceans

Size of starling, with smart black and white plumage showing narrow white lines on shoulder and white tips to secondaries, visible when wings closed. Bill very small and black. Body short and stubby with neckless appearance. Summer adult has black head, neck and breast. In winter throat and breast white. Rest of upperparts black, underparts white. Juvenile similar to adult but browner.

Puffin

Fratercula arctica

The large, powerful bill is slightly hooked to help the bird hold slippery prey; the bright colouring is lost in the winter

Summer adult

Newly hatched chick

Four-week-old chick

Six-week-old-chick

Immature, first winter

Adult, winter

Adult, summer

THE puffin is a locally abundant north Atlantic seabird breeding in large colonies on offshore islands and isolated mainland cliffs. Puffins return to their clifftop colonies in March in the south of their range, but not until May in the north. They prefer to excavate nesting burrows on sloping terraces of peaty turf above coastal cliffs, where colonies become very large. Displaying pairs make their strange growling and creaking calls as they stand bill to bill at the burrow entrance. Puffins swim and dive expertly to catch fish. In the open sea they are less vulnerable to oiling than some species, but their breeding success can be affected by human fishing activities.

Voice: Least vocal of the auks; creaking, growling and grunting calls heard in breeding season only
Length: 27cm
Wingspan: 47–63cm
Weight: 370–400g
Habitat: Breeding colonies on sloping sea cliffs; open sea outside breeding season
Nest: Shallow burrow under boulder or in natural crevice
Eggs: 1; dull white, sometimes with purplish-brown markings
Food: Marine fish; some crustaceans

Smaller than guillemot and razorbill, with obvious deep, colourful bill making head appear large. Has black upperparts and white underparts in all plumages, smartest in breeding adult, duller in juvenile. Summer adult has grey face and triangular bill, coloured bright red, blue-grey and yellow. Brightness of bill much reduced in winter. Red eye has surround of blue-grey horny appendages. Back, upperwing, rump and tail black. Underwing grey, rest of underparts white. Legs and feet bright orange. Juvenile has flesh-coloured feet and small, blackish bill, thinner than adult's.

Pair performing 'billing' display

Woodpigeon

Columba palumbus

THE woodpigeon is a powerful flier able to employ fast jinks and swerves to avoid predators, and its undulating, wing-clapping display is well known. When alighting it invariably raises and lowers its tail, a characteristic that aids long-distance identification. Woodpigeons are catholic in their choice of habitats and are adaptable to change, which has allowed them to colonise most of Europe. The presence of woodland is one of their major requirements and often woodland edges bordering agricultural land are favoured; they are also common in urban areas, where they inhabit parks and tree-lined streets. In western Europe the population is mainly resident.

Voice:
Multisyllabic cooing, with emphasis on second note
Length: 40–42cm
Wingspan: 75–80cm
Weight: 460–570g
Habitat: Woodland and scrub; agricultural fields next to woods in winter
Nest: Flimsy platform of twigs, usually high in tree
Eggs: 1–2; glossy, white
Food: Mainly plant material including roots; occasionally insects

Largest pigeon in Europe. Adult easily identified by blue-grey plumage with white neck patch, white wing crescents and black terminal band to longish, full tail. Sides and back of neck glossy green with purple sheen. Breast warm mauve-pink. In flight adult's white wing crescents very obvious; also shows blackish primaries with white outer webs sometimes showing as pale panel. Bill is reddish with yellow tip and off-white patch at base. Pale yellowish eye. Legs mauve-pink. Juvenile much duller than adult; lacks white neck patch.

White crescent on wing and adult's neck patches diagnostic

The display flight consists of a high, steep climb followed by one or two wing claps and a downward glide on stiffly held wings with fanned tail

From a distance overall impression is of a grey bird, but at closer range browner back and pink breast discernible

Take-off is quick and agile with noisy, clattering wings; the very high upstroke and deep downbeat give instant power

Juvenile bird has adult wing markings but lacks white neck patches

Feeding birds look long-bodied and short-legged; often forage regularly in fields in morning and evening

Over the last hundred years or so woodpigeons have expanded their range northwards through Britain and Scandinavia; this is linked to the increase in agricultural production and the easy availability of winter food

Rock Dove

Columba livia

THE rock dove must be the best-known European bird because of the abundant populations of so-called feral pigeons that inhabit our towns and cities. As a naturally wild species it is much harder to see because its choice of habitat takes it into wilderness areas where the lack of trees discourages competitive species. Feral populations became established following a long history of domestication by humans, and it is difficult now to distinguish between wholly wild populations and those augmented by town birds that have returned to their ancestral haunts. Truly wild rock doves are shy, fast-flying birds, and are very wary of predators.

The continual encrocachment of the feral form is the greatest threat to the rock dove's survival

Black wingbars obvious in flight

Voice: Various moaning, cooing calls
Length: 31–34cm
Wingspan: 63–70cm
Weight: 238–370g
Habitat: Oceanic coasts and rocky areas; inland amongst open country; feral in towns
Nest: Loose cup of roots, stems and other vegetation, on ledge
Eggs: 2; smooth and glossy, white
Food: Cereal and weed seeds; green leaves and buds; insects

Much smaller than woodpigeon. Adult is medium-sized, blue-grey pigeon with two obvious black bars across rear half of innerwing; plumage relieved on nape, neck and upper breast by green-purple gloss. Back, scapulars and innerwing paler ash-grey, tail with broad brownish-black terminal band. Bright white underwing coverts and lower back seen in flight. Bill lead-coloured, off-white at base. Legs and feet dull to bright red. Juvenile like adult but duller, except for sharing bright white on lower back.

As its name suggests, the rock dove prefers rocky habitats – in northwestern Europe this often means exposed sea cliffs and offshore islands

Stock Dove

Columba oenas

STOCK doves are found mostly in the lowlands, although they will venture into the uplands where suitable habitats occur. Their nests are usually sited in tree-holes, often the old cavities once used by black woodpeckers, and breeding birds are unobtrusive and would be easily overlooked were it not for the male's distinctive call. In western Europe and Scandinavia stock doves are migratory, spending the winter months in warmer countries such as Turkey. They are resident particularly in Britain, where feeding flocks in winter fields are easily seen.

Flight action faster than woodpigeon's

Upperwings have darker edges; two small bars visible close to body

Medium-sized, blue-grey pigeon, slightly smaller than rock dove, which it resembles except that it never has any white in its plumage at any age

Voice: Disyllabic, warm, cooing 'oo-look'; also growling calls at nest
Length: 32–34cm
Wingspan: 63–69cm
Weight: 263–335g

Habitat: Border of woodland and open country
Nest: Hole in tree, cliff or building; slight lining of twigs and grass
Eggs: 2; glossy, creamy-white
Food: Seeds, green leaves, buds and flowers; occasionally invertebrates

Adult plumage basically grey. Head and underbody bluer and sides of neck have glossy green sheen. Upper breast has warm pink wash. Grey tail has broad black terminal band. Bill grey-buff, off-white at base. In flight upperwing shows paler grey central panel and twin black bars on tertials. Eye brown with grey orbital ring. Legs bright pinkish-red. Juvenile browner and duller than adult, lacking any green sheen.

Collared Dove

Streptopelia decaocto

Flight action is fast, with clipped wingbeats

When alarmed birds can suddenly spring into the air with clapping wings

COLLARED doves expanded north and west into Europe very quickly from 1930 onwards, reaching Britain in the 1950s and Norway in the 1960s. This spread is continuing with movements to Russia in the northeast. The speed of colonisation has relied on the ready availability of food, which collared doves find on arable farms and processing plants where there is an abundant supply of grain. In winter, birds congregate in very large feeding flocks, and they will readily enter buildings in search of grain. Despite such new-found abundance collared doves are not as yet seriously threatened by predators or persecution from farming interests.

Larger than turtle dove, with longer tail and uniform pale, sandy-grey plumage. Adult has pale-grey crown. Face, neck and breast pinkish-buff, fading to cream on belly and undertail coverts. Narrow, white-edged black half-collar. Back, scapulars and smaller wing coverts sandy grey-brown. Greater coverts and secondaries show grey panel next to darker, dusky primaries. Underwing coverts white. Uppertail brown with whitish tips to outer feathers. Broad, white terminal band to undertail. Bill black. Eye dark red with pale orbital ring. Legs and feet mauve-red. Juvenile duller than adult, lacking black half-collar.

In western Europe collared doves favour mixed habitats such as gardens, orchards and parks, where they readily use buildings and wires for perching

Voice: Repeated, penetrating, unmusical cooing
Length: 31–33cm
Wingspan: 47–55cm
Weight: 150–200g
Habitat: Mixed habitats of gardens, farms, orchards and town avenues
Nest: Rough platform of twigs and roots, in tree
Eggs: 1–2; glossy, white
Food: Cereal grain and other seeds; fruits

Juvenile (below) is pale and dull, and lacks adult's collar

Collared doves regularly come to gardens or anywhere they can pick up spilled grain or scraps

Turtle Dove

Streptopelia turtur

THE turtle dove with its deep, purring, cooing song is a quintessential summer bird of Europe. The species is distributed widely across Europe but its dislike of cold, wet weather keeps it away from the most northern latitudes and from mountain ranges. As with most pigeons, the turtle dove is a woodland edge species preferring open country with mature vegetation; its liking for concealment within dense vegetation can make it hard to see. It requires the close proximity of croplands and scrub where it can find a good supply of food. Turtle doves are migratory and spend the winter in Africa, south of the Sahara.

Voice: Lazy, deep, purring 'coo'
Length: 26–28cm
Wingspan: 47–53cm
Weight: 100–170g
Habitat: Warm woodlands, open scrub, orchards and parks
Nest: Flimsy platform of small twigs, in hedge or small tree
Eggs: 1–2; glossy white
Food: Seeds and fruits of weeds and cereals

Smaller and slighter than collared dove. Adult has blue-grey crown with face, neck and breast warm pink. Patch of narrow black and white lines on neck. Back and rump brown with indistinct dark flecking. Closed wing has dappled pattern with black-centred, rich brown feathers. In flight shows blue-grey greater coverts and dusky flight feathers. Complicated tail pattern of white-tipped black feathers, except for central pair, which are wholly brown. Undertail black, rimmed white, contrasting with cream underparts. Dark bill with pale tip. Yellow eye with crimson orbital ring. Legs reddish. Juvenile duller, lacking neck patch.

Characteristic flight action consists of flickering, jerky wingbeats interspersed with irregular short glides; flight quieter than woodpigeon's but some wing clatter still audible

Turtle doves can sometimes be seen perching on telephone wires, but usually they stay out of sight in hedges and thickets

When seen with woodpigeon (above) turtle doves' smaller size is immediately apparent

Small, slim dove with thin neck, protruding round head and deep chest; has comparatively long, wedge-tipped tail and swept-back wings

Complicated rump and tail pattern clearly visible when tail is fanned out on landing

Although it tolerates human presence, the turtle dove does not breed in and around towns like the collared dove, and its liking for concealment within dense vegetation can make it hard to spot

141

Cuckoo

Cuculus canorus

Adult male keeps his bill closed when calling and waves his tail from side to side

Juvenile (above) has a squeaking hunger call; it is fed by its 'parent' even when it is already quite well grown

Neat transverse barring on underparts

Unlike falcon or hawk, cuckoo has weak flight action with rapid wingbeats not raised above the horizontal; wings are pointed

Juvenile is rufous with pale nape patch

Like hawks, which they superficially resemble, cuckoos are vulnerable to mobbing by passerines

Each female cuckoo concentrates on one host species (usually the one that reared her); her eggs will closely resemble that species' eggs and so be recognised as the host's own

THE cuckoo's silhouette in flight can resemble a small falcon or hawk; however, a prolonged view will reveal that the cuckoo has a different flight action. The cuckoo is most often seen in open scrub and woodland, though the abundance of its host species in upland grasslands and reedbeds will attract it to these habitats too. It has many host species and will commonly lay a single egg in each nest of the dunnock, reed warbler or meadow pipit. The cuckoo is migratory, with European adults flying off to Africa in July; mysteriously, juveniles, which follow several weeks later, know without any contact with parents where to go for the winter.

Voice: Familiar male call 'cu-coo'; female makes repeated bubbling notes
Length: 32–34cm
Wingspan: 55–60cm
Weight: 100–130g
Habitat: Woodland, scrub, parkland and open uplands
Nest: Eggs laid in host species' nests, mainly meadow pipit, dunnock and reed warbler
Eggs: Average 9; smooth, glossy, very variable, resembling host species' eggs
Food: Insects, mainly hairy caterpillars and beetles

Similar in size to collared dove but with longer tail. Adult male has slate-grey head, breast and upperparts. Underparts, from lower breast to undertail coverts, white with close, narrow blackish barring forming pattern of transverse lines across underbody. Upperwing darker grey-black, underwing paler. Darker tail feathers tipped and spotted white. Female similar to male but browner with buff breast band; occasional form has grey replaced with rufous, barred black. Decurved bill has yellow base with darker tip. Legs and feet yellow. Juvenile similar to rufous female but differs in having barred throat, white nape and white edges and tips to dark feathers.

Yellow-billed Cuckoo

Coccyzus americanus

YELLOW-BILLED cuckoos are recorded almost annually in Europe, invariably in the autumn. In common with their European cousins, hairy caterpillars are their preferred food; as a consequence of this rather specialised diet, autumn vagrants to Europe usually have to struggle to find enough food. Rather sadly, many of these birds eventually die from starvation. Vagrant yellow-billed cuckoos are often lethargic, this behaviour contrasting markedly with that observed in America. Unlike its European cousin, the yellow-billed cuckoo generally constructs a flimsy nest of its own and incubates the eggs itself.

Voice: Vagrants to Europe silent
Length: 28–30cm
Wingspan: 40–45cm
Weight: 40–60g
Habitat: Open woodland and scrub
Nest: Does not breed in region
Eggs: Does not breed in region
Food: Insects, particularly caterpillars

Distinctive North American cuckoo. Sexes similar. Adult has essentially grey-brown upperparts with chestnut on flight feathers; this feature particularly striking in flight. Underparts whitish. Shows narrow yellow eyering. Underside of long tail is black with large white spots at tips of tail feathers producing striking pattern. Bill dark but base of lower mandible yellow. Legs greyish. Juvenile similar to adult but pattern on underside of tail more subdued and extent of yellow on bill much reduced.

Great Spotted Cuckoo

Clamator glandarius

Adult

THE great spotted cuckoo feeds mainly on caterpillars, which it searches for by hopping along the ground with its tail raised. The prey is taken to a nearby perch, where the irritant hairs are removed by wiping on a branch before the caterpillar is eaten. This parasitic species lays single eggs in each of up to 18 host nests. The European population is migratory, leaving breeding areas in July for overwintering grounds in Africa. In early spring birds returning north sometimes overshoot, so vagrant individuals can appear in northern Europe.

This impressive bird is strikingly patterned, has a long tail and perches prominently

Voice: Loud harsh rasping calls and double 'kioc-kioc'
Length: 38–40cm
Wingspan: 58–61cm
Weight: 140–190g
Habitat: Warm Mediterranean scrub; open woodland
Nest: Eggs laid in host nest, usually crows
Eggs: Up to 18; smooth, pale green-blue, spotted red-brown mimicking host
Food: Hairy caterpillars and other insects

Much larger than cuckoo, with crest, broader wings and tail. Adult has blue-grey crested crown; upper face and neck blackish-brown. Rest of upperparts dusky brown with prominent white tips to scapulars, underwing coverts and long graduated tail. Chin, throat, foreneck and breast have warm orange-buff wash; rest of underparts off-white. Underwing coverts cream. Longish, stout, grey-black bill. Red eyering. Brown-grey legs and feet. Juvenile recalls bright adult but lacks crest; whole of crown dark brown. Light tips to feathers are cream not white, and bright chestnut primaries conspicuous in flight.

Juvenile unmistakable in flight, with black cap, chestnut primaries and adult's disproportionately long tail

Black-bellied Sandgrouse

Pterocles orientalis

THE black-bellied sandgrouse is the larger of the two European species of sandgrouse and is found only in Spain and Turkey. Nesting birds are well camouflaged and usually very wary of humans, so the species is most often seen flying in pairs or small parties. It flies great distances to water at dusk and dawn, when larger flocks are on the move, and its evocative bubbling calls echo across the plains. This wary bird will circle a watering hole many times before landing to drink.

Voice: Musical cluckings and low bubbling notes, heard mostly in flight
Length: 33–35cm
Wingspan: 70–73cm
Weight: 350–550g
Habitat: Flat plains on sandy soils, grassland steppes
Nest: Unlined depression on gravelly ground, sometimes with pebble surround
Eggs: 2–3; glossy, buff or greenish-grey, heavily marked with brown and purple
Food: Mainly seeds

Large, heavy-bodied, pigeon-like bird with short, pointed tail and broad, pointed, swept-back wings. Male head, neck and breast grey with chestnut and black half-collar on foreneck. Grey breast separated from black belly by narrow black and white bands. Back and upperwing ochre-yellow with blackish flecking. Flight feathers darker grey-black. Underwing distinctive with black flight feathers and white coverts. Pointed tail barred yellow and black. Female is similar to male but upperparts buff and spotted with black; breast buff with black spots. Juvenile similar to female. Bill and feet dark in both adult and juvenile.

Adult male

Pin-tailed Sandgrouse

Pterocles alchata

IN EUROPE the pin-tailed sandgrouse is confined to the warm, arid steppes of Spain, with a northerly outlying population on the stony Crau plain, adjacent to the Camargue in southern France. Like all sandgrouse it often flies in large flocks, when its rapidly beating whistling wings draw attention, and the distinctive chattering flight call can be heard. Access to fresh water is essential in such arid conditions and the pin-tailed sandgrouse also collects water in its belly feathers to take back to young chicks at the nest. It is a shy bird and is most likely to be seen when flushed accidentally.

Voice: Noisy and distinctive repeated 'chata-chata' flight call
Length: 31–39cm
Wingspan: 54–65cm
Weight: 230–290g
Habitat: Warm arid Mediterranean steppes, dried-out marshes
Nest: Shallow unlined depression on ground
Eggs: 2–3; glossy, buff with brown and grey blotches and speckles
Food: Seeds, shoots, green leaves

underwings white. Back and upperwing have greenish marbling, white-edged maroon wing coverts and black-barred yellow rump. Dark tail streamers. Female similar to male but with crown and nape streaked black, more yellow, less chestnut and more fine black barring on upperparts. Juvenile resembles female but less bright and with short tail.

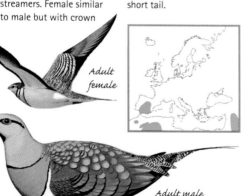

Adult female

Both sexes have brown bill, white feathered legs and grey feet. Male has chestnut face, black throat, black margins to chestnut breast band; underbody and

Adult male

Barn Owl

Tyto alba

Barn owls lay their eggs staggered over several days, so the first owlet in a family is usually about a week older than the fifth

Bᴀʀɴ owls are found in many countries around the world, preferring mild, middle latitudes without extreme weather conditions. A hunting barn owl is a beautiful sight, with its slow, buoyant flight, wavering direction, hovering and swift plunges into the undergrowth for prey. Not strictly nocturnal, this owl can be seen in the half-light of winter afternoons, patrolling silently along hedgerows next to country lanes. The European population is in decline and factors known to be affecting numbers are the reduction in traditional farming systems and the increasing use of pesticides.

Voice: Screeching, whistling and snoring notes in breeding season
Length: 33–35cm
Wingspan: 85–93cm
Weight: 240–360g

Habitat: Open lowlands with small woods, hedges and fields; upland grasslands and heaths
Nest: In hole of tree or building; on bare wood or artificial platform
Eggs: 4–7; smooth, not glossy, white
Food: Small mammals; fewer small birds and amphibians

Smaller than tawny owl but with longer, narrower wings. Adult from south and west European race has warm, vermiculated yellowish-brown upperparts contrasting with clear silver-white underparts. Crown, nape, back and rump warm yellowish-brown with soft grey mottling and rows of tiny blackish spots. Coverts on closed wing similar; in flight shows warm-buff flight and tail feathers with dark-brown barring. Face has complete heart-shaped white facial disc with dark rusty eye pits and black eyes. Underparts, including feathered legs, silky white. Feet grey-brown. Bill pinkish. Adult from central European race has buff body underparts and underwing coverts. Similar in other respects to white-breasted race. Juvenile resembles adult as soon as down is lost.

Barn owls have an affinity with farm buildings and will site their nests in barns, old churches and farmhouses; artificial nest platforms are also used, though barn owls are sensitive to disturbance at the nest

South and west European adult

The powerful toes are equipped with long, sharp talons; the outer toe is reversible to give a better grip on prey

Pellets contain the undigested remains of prey

Adult of central European race

Eagle Owl

Bubo bubo

The eagle owl is a truly impressive bird when seen standing on a cliff ledge or when flying down prey in a fast glide

THE eagle owl's direct and purposeful flight action is similar to that of a buzzard, so care is needed to identify it when it is flying away from the observer; it is the only large owl with ear tufts. The eagle owl is a bird of wilderness areas, uncluttered by human impact and free from disturbance; it is thus absent from most of the industrialised northwest. It nests where it can have an unobscured view of approaching danger. Most of the day is spent perched motionless, but active hunting begins at sunset, or earlier when there is a chick to feed.

Voice: Deep, booming, far-carrying disyllabic hoot with sharp, croaking alarm call
Length: 60–75cm
Wingspan: 160–188cm
Weight: 1.6–2.5kg
Habitat: Wilderness with rocky crags and mosaic of woods and open country
Nest: On cliff ledge, crevice or in cave; occasionally in old tree nest of other species
Eggs: 2–4; smooth but finely pitted, slightly glossy, white
Food: Mainly mammals up to size of adult hare; birds up to size of adult mallard

Largest European owl; barrel-shaped with prominent ear tufts. Adult plumage usually warm brown, heavily marked on upperparts with thick, black streaks and spots. Flight feathers barred black. Paler brown underparts have black droplets on breast; narrower streaks and fine dark bars on belly and flanks. Head has laterally flattened blackish ear tufts and well-marked pale-grey facial disc with bright orange eyes. Chin and throat show furry, whitish ruff. In flight the dark leading edge to wing

contrasts with yellowish flight feathers, barred blackish. Feathered legs and feet. Bill black. Juvenile paler and fluffier than adult, lacking ear tufts, and has more completely barred underparts.

Scops Owl

Otus scops

Grey phase bird

THE scops owl is a nocturnal, arboreal species, which hunts in the open and thus requires secluded perches for daytime roosting and plenty of open varied habitats in which to find prey. Where mixed open woodland is unavailable, this owl will select managed orchards, olive groves, parks and farmland landscapes. It can also be found in many southern European towns, where it frequents tree-lined boulevards and city squares. The scops owl advertises its presence at night with its penetrating and repetitive whistling call, but actually sighting the bird is difficult. European scops owls are migratory, moving south of the Sahara for the winter.

Voice: Repeated, short, human-like whistle reminiscent of slow time signal pips
Length: 19–20cm
Wingspan: 53–63cm
Weight: 80–120g
Habitat: Warm, dry lowlands in open mixed woodland; parks with old hollow trees
Nest: In hole of tree, building or nest box; occasionally in old nest of crow
Eggs: 4–5; smooth and glossy white
Food: Mainly insects; a

few small birds, reptiles and mammals

Small, large-headed owl with slender body and fairly long wings. Adult seen with either brown-grey or rufous upperparts; both have blackish streaks, bars and delicate pattern of vermiculations. Scapulars show as prominent line of black-tipped white feathers. Facial disc with incomplete blackish-brown border, mainly on sides. Shape accentuated by

prominent streaked ear tufts, which are often flattened sideways. Paler brown to buffish-white underparts with dark-brown streaks and vermiculations. Outer flight feathers broadly barred buff. Underwing paler buff. Bill blue-black. Eye yellow. Legs feathered, buff; feet grey. Juvenile inseparable from adult.

With its excellent camouflage and habit of roosting during the day in mature trees and bushes, the scops owl is very hard to see

145

Snowy Owl

Nyctea scandiaca

Adult female

Very large, essentially white owl, exceeded in size among European owls only by eagle owl

Adult male

THE snowy owl requires huge expanses of tundra in which to select its nest site, usually on a low hummock with good visibility all around. In Europe it is a rare breeding bird, with fluctuating numbers in Scandinavia and a more stable population in northern Russia. The adult does not tolerate disturbance from humans and spends long periods watching over the nest or scanning for intruders. In flight it is an active hunter and is surprisingly swift in its chase and falcon-like capture of prey. Snowy owls are irruptive: when lemming populations are low, large numbers are forced to move from the normal range in search of food, especially in winter.

Voice: Loud, booming double hoot and barking alarm; silent outside breeding season
Length: 53–66cm
Wingspan: 142–166cm
Weight: 800–2,500g
Habitat: Arctic tundra, from sea level into uplands
Nest: Slight, unlined scrape on ground
Eggs: 3–9; smooth, glossy white
Food: Small mammals and birds; often exclusively lemmings

Mainly white owl with relatively small, round head and long, rounded wings. Golden-yellow eyes sunk in dusky pits. Bill black. Legs and feet densely feathered, white with black claws. Adult male almost entirely creamy white. Occasional small, dark-brown spots on underwing coverts hardly noticeable. Adult female ground colour is white but heavily spotted and chevronned dark brown over whole of upperparts and most of underbody.

Pure white face and centre of breast stand out. Juvenile has dark-grey head and body; rest of plumage like adult female.

Little Owl

Athene noctua

An upright posture is adopted when the bird is alarmed

Little owls are fairly easy to see because of their willingness to perch in the open; they are most active around dawn and dusk

THE little owl is widely distributed across Europe, and is a bird of open country. A common requirement of the species in all its diverse habitats is the abundance of perches from which the birds can hunt prey and watch for danger. The little owl's flight action is distinctive, with woodpecker-like bounding undulations, but it can be difficult to follow as it flies close to the ground before swooping up to perch. The species usually nests in tree-holes, and it is usual to see one parent perched on guard near the nest. When alarmed it will bob up and down, giving hissing and barking calls.

Voice: Hollow, rising whistle sometimes repeated in crescendo; chattering warning call

Length: 21–23cm
Wingspan: 54–58cm
Weight: 140–225g
Habitat: Lowland agricultural habitats in west; more arid rocky gorges and plains in east
Nest: Hole in tree or building, or crevice in cliff
Eggs: 2–5; smooth, matt white
Food: Mainly insects; some small mammals and birds

Small, dark owl with longish legs. Adult upperparts dark brown-grey, spotted and flecked with white. Crown and nape closely spotted white. Back more uniform dark brown with whitish fringes to lower neck feathers, scapulars and coverts, creating pale lines. Tail has four pale-brown bars. Facial disc buff-grey, more rectangular than round, with prominent pale eyebrows and yellow eyes. Underparts paler buff-grey with gorget of heavy streaks on upper breast, finely streaked on belly and flanks. Bill grey-brown. Legs feathered buff-white; feet brown. Juvenile similar to adult but paler; plumage is more uniform with less streaking and spotting.

Long-eared Owl

Asio otus

The ear tufts are erect when the owl is alarmed

THE long-eared owl is distributed widely throughout Europe wherever there are trees. It is less dependent on forests than some other owls and is often found in mixed agricultural areas where there are small woodland copses or riverine trees. It can also colonise the conifer plantations of uplands in northwest Europe. Adults usually hunt at night, spending the day in dense vegetation, where they are difficult to detect. This is a migratory species in the north of its range, moving to southern Europe in the winter. Long-eared owls roost communally in winter, often in thick scrub; if found, the birds are hard to disturb.

Voice: Quiet, but far-carrying, repeated 'oo' notes; young like squeaking gate
Length: 35–37cm
Wingspan: 90–100cm
Weight: 200–400g
Habitat: Woodland copses and scrub with open habitats for hunting
Nest: In old tree nest, usually of crows
Eggs: 3–5; smooth, slightly glossy, white
Nest: Usually small rodents; some birds, larger mammals and shrews

Smaller than tawny owl, though appears tall and thin when alarmed. Adult plumage ground colour is rufous-brown on upperparts, only slightly paler on underparts. Most feathers fringed pale buff. Crown, neck and back streaked and barred with black. Closed wing shows white shoulder and white covert spots. Flight feathers are rich orange, barred blackish. Facial disc warm orange-buff divided by point of grey crown and white eyebrows. Prominent, blackish, pale-fringed ear tufts. Eye bright orange. Bill grey. Underparts buff-brown with heavy, blackish arrowhead streaks. Belly and undertail unstreaked. Legs and feet feathered, buff; claws grey. Juvenile similar to adult but greyer, with more barring.

The tufts are lowered and the facial expression is quite different when the bird is relaxed

Immatures adopt threat posture when alarmed

Short-eared Owl

Asio flammeus

THE short-eared owl can be identified by its long, narrow wings, buoyant flight and horizontal posture when perched. It will feed both by day and at night, and, unusually for an owl, it does not require the presence of trees. However, in Britain it takes advantage of the early growth conifer plantations, which are replacing traditional moorland habitats. Northern populations are migratory, mostly overwintering in the southern part of the breeding range. Coastal marshes are favoured in winter, when it is possible to see several birds at the same place quartering the marsh in typical buoyant, floating flight.

Ear tufts are very small and seldom seen

Voice: Low-pitched hollow 'hoo-hoo-hoo' series of notes; hissing and rasping calls at nest
Length: 37–39cm
Wingspan: 95–110cm
Weight: 260–425g
Habitat: Open country moorlands, rough grazing, sand dunes, marshes
Nest: Shallow scrape on ground, roughly lined with vegetation
Eggs: 4–8; smooth, white
Food: Mainly small voles but will also take birds and other mammals

Long-winged owl with fairly small head, often confused with long-eared owl. Adult plumage yellowish-buff, heavily streaked with black. Head and neck buff with bold, dark streaks. Back so heavily streaked it appears mostly blackish. Rump paler with fewer streaks. Tail yellowish-buff, broadly barred dark brown. Striking facial disc surrounded by heavy black spotting. Pale-buff cheeks and reversed white brackets between yellow eyes sunk in blackish pits. Underbody clearer, warm buff with lighter streaks. In flight wing shows dark carpal patch and dark tip. Bill grey. Legs and feet feathered, buff. Juvenile similar to adult but with greyer head and less heavily marked underparts.

Always nests on ground in thick cover

Hawk Owl

Surnia ulula

The hawk owl has a fierce expression that reflects its voracity as a predator of small mammals and birds; it is also an aggressive defender of its nest, repeatedly attacking intruders

Russia contains huge areas of suitable habitat for hawk owls, but they also breed in Scandinavia, where they move into more southerly habitats in periodic population irruptions. In tundra forest this species chooses clearings surrounded by trees, often using broken-topped stumps from which to watch for prey. The hawk owl could easily be mistaken for a sparrowhawk in flight. However, it intersperses direct flight with bursts of undulating, bounding flaps and glides, and it usually approaches a perch with a fast upward sweep. Hawk owls are nomadic, following fluctuating small mammal populations.

Voice: Trilling, hooting notes and screeching alarm call
Length: 36–39cm
Wingspan: 75–80cm
Weight: 250–370g
Habitat: Arboreal; pine and birch forest in tundra with clearings
Nest: In tree-hole or old crow nest; no material added
Eggs: 6–10; smooth, glossy white
Food: Mostly small voles; a few birds and larger mammals in winter

Similar in size and shape to sparrowhawk, with proportionately smaller head, slimmer body and longer tail than other owls

Adult has strongly patterned blackish and pale-grey plumage. Crown, nape and back blackish-brown, spotted white. Large whitish shoulder patch. Closed wing dark brown with few white spots. Flight feathers dark with whitish bars. Rump pale, barred blackish. Long, dark-brown tail narrowly barred pale grey. Face whitish with broad, blackish, curved borders to facial disc. Breast and belly very pale grey, narrowly barred blackish. Wings short and pointed. Eyes striking pale yellow. Bill yellow-horn. Legs and feet feathered white. Juvenile paler and fluffier than adult, with more barring; other characteristics similar to adult.

Pygmy Owl

Glaucidium passerinum

THE pygmy owl's fast, undulating, almost urgent flight is reminiscent of a small woodpecker, and when perching it often waves its tail up and down or sits with it cocked like a flycatcher. It is the prey of larger raptors and owls, and so chooses the deep forest interior with large, old trees to provide nest holes. It favours open areas for hunting, such as clearings and woodland meadows. The preferred diet of the pygmy owl is small birds, which it pursues actively and relentlessly mostly during the day. It also hunts small mammals at dusk and dawn.

Voice:
Monotonous, fluty, repeated whistle; various hissing notes
Length: 16–17cm
Wingspan: 34–35cm
Weight: 50–70g
Habitat: Taiga and montane coniferous forest
Nest: In tree-hole, often old nest of woodpecker; will use nest box
Eggs: 4–7; smooth, slightly glossy, white
Food: Small mammals and small birds

Tiny, small-headed owl, roughly size of hawfinch. No real facial disc but curved rows of brown and buff spotting and white eyebrows and white sides to chin neatly frame face. Adult has dark-brown upperparts, spotted and barred with whitish-buff. Shows two whitish curves back to back on nape, and buff-spotted brown crown. Throat and sides of breast brown, barred black. Rest of underparts white, streaked blackish, extending up

centre of breast. Relatively long narrow tail, brown with white barring. White bars on brown flight feathers. Eyes yellow. Legs and toes feathered, white. Juvenile similar to adult but duskier, with less pale spotting and barring.

Tengmalm's Owl

Aegolius funereus

IN THE north Tengmalm's owl has a preference for spruce and birch forests where these border open moorlands, but in central Europe montane mixed forests of fir and beech are preferred. In these woodlands it uses old black woodpecker nesting holes to raise its young. Tengmalm's owl can be difficult to observe and it can be confused with other small owls. It is a voracious hunter of mammals and small birds, and can be very manoeuvrable in pursuit amongst the dense stands of trees. Tengmalm's owl is resident in central Europe, though wandering juveniles may make short movements out of the main habitat range.

Voice: Soft, far-carrying, repeated short whistles; short, smacking yelp
Length: 24–26cm
Wingspan: 55–62cm
Weight: 100–200g
Habitat: Taiga lowlands; montane coniferous forests with rides and clearings
Nest: Hole in tree; often old nest of black woodpecker
Eggs: 3–7; smooth, fairly glossy, white
Food: Mainly small voles, mice and shrews; some small birds

Smallish, dark owl with large, square head and longish tail. Adult upperparts dark brown with copious white spotting on crown, and fewer, larger spots on nape and back. Broad white edges to scapulars show as pale braces. Wing coverts and flight feathers dark brown, finely spotted with white. Tail dark brown with rows of tiny white spots. Squarish grey facial disc outlined in black. Yellow eyes set in dark pits. Underparts pale greyish-

white, spotted with light brown. Bill yellowish-grey. Legs and feet feathered, white. Juvenile dark chocolate brown with white eyebrows and moustache; white spotting on wings. Similar to adult in other respects.

Tawny Owl

Strix aluco

The tawny owl's quavering hoot is one of the best-known bird songs in Europe

In daylight the tawny owl's neat, rounded appearance and pale spots on the closed wing make identification straightforward

Juvenile

Looks bulky in flight, with big head, short tail and broad wings

Undigested parts of prey are regurgitated as pellets, which accumulate under perches

Tawny owls may be mobbed by smaller birds, giving its presence away

IN NORTHWEST Europe the tawny owl is the most likely owl to be encountered by the casual observer, as the adaptability of the species makes it tolerant of humans. The tawny owl is a nocturnal species and night-time viewing can lead to difficulties with identification. In car headlights it often appears paler than it really is and care is needed to note the large-headed, round-bodied appearance and its flapping and gliding flight. This owl is resident throughout much of its range, taking advantage of good conditions for breeding as early in the year as February, even quite far north in its range.

Voice: Classic melodious hoot 'huit-houuu'; common call 'ke-wick'
Length: 37–39cm
Wingspan: 95–100cm
Weight: 350–500g
Habitat: Deciduous or mixed woodlands, forest and parks in towns
Nest: Hole in tree or building, occasionally in old nest of magpie or squirrel
Eggs: 2–5; smooth, glossy white
Food: Wide range of small mammals; birds, amphibians, earthworms and insects

Medium-sized, broad-winged owl with large, rounded head and no ear tufts. Mottled, barred and streaked plumage varies from rufous-brown to grey-brown. Greyish facial disc bordered blackish with white eyebrows, lores and sides to chin. Eyes large and black. Crown, neck and back brown, boldy streaked with black. Prominent line of white-spotted scapulars. Flight feathers softly barred dark brown. Underwing buff-brown. Underparts greyer and usually paler with uniform blackish streaks. Bill yellowish-grey. Legs and feet buff, feathered; claws grey. Juvenile similar to adult, but with shaggier feathers and finer barring.

Great Grey Owl

Strix nebulosa

T HE great grey owl is a diurnal hunter, using forest glades, bogs and adjacent open moorlands. Mature forests of pine and fir provide it with nesting sites, although recently in Finland great grey owls have used artificial nesting platforms. Great grey owls are easily capable of catching prey in snow, listening for small mammals moving underneath before plunging with open talons through the surface on to the prey beneath. Although usually a sedentary species, the great grey owl can become nomadic in response to fluctuating populations of prey mammals. Its survival depends also on the availability of tall, mature forest habitat.

This huge owl could be mistaken for an eagle owl or Ural owl; it is proportionately longer-winged than either species, slimmer-bodied than eagle owl and shows less barring on wings than Ural owl

Voice: Deep, muffled, pumping hoots with squealing and growling alarm notes
Length: 65–70cm
Wingspan: 135–160cm
Weight: 500–1,000g
Habitat: Dense, mature boreal pine, fir forests and adjacent moorland
Nest: In old tree nest of other raptor; occasionally on ground
Eggs: 3–6; smooth, slightly glossy white
Food: Mainly small voles, shrews and birds

Large, round head, long wings and tail. Adult plumage dark brown-black and white, appearing grey at distance. Head, back, rump and tail are pale grey, profusely streaked and barred dark brown. Dark blotching on back. Indistinct rows of pale spots on scapulars and coverts. Closed wing is brown, heavily streaked and barred blackish. Facial disc striking, with concentric fine black and grey barring, bright white eyebrows, lores, moustache and chin.

Bright-yellow eye and bill. Underbody pale grey, heavily streaked dark brown. Juvenile like adult but fluffier and more heavily barred, not streaked.

Ural Owl

Strix uralensis

I N SUMMER the Ural owl hunts along forest fringes and in glades, either from tree-stump perches or in searching flight. In winter it moves towards villages or farms, where more open habitats and cultivation can provide an easier source of food. The Ural owl can be mistaken for a short-eared owl or even a goshawk when its long tail is evident in flight. However, it is heavier and more purposeful than the short-eared owl, with broader wings and greyer plumage.

The survival of this sedentary species is dependent on the availability of a year-round feeding territory and, in central Europe, undisturbed woodland habitat

Voice: Deep hoot of three di- or trisyllabic notes; also harsh croaks
Length: 60–62cm
Wingspan: 125–135cm
Weight: 500–1,000g
Habitat: Temperate forests of Europe with glades; also overwinters in parks and around villages
Nest: Hole in tree, top of stump or old nest of raptor or crow; rarely on rocky ground
Eggs: 2–4; smooth, white
Food: Mainly mammals and birds up to size of woodpigeon

Larger than tawny owl, with longer tail. Adult plumage pale grey. Head, neck, back and underbody pale grey with uniform pattern of dark brown streaks. Circular, pale brownish-grey facial disc neatly outlined in dark brown. Eyes blackish-brown. Edges of scapulars white, forming distinct rows of pale spots down back. Wings grey with warmer brown tones to broadly barred flight feathers. Underwing contrastingly marked with whitish, black-tipped

coverts and dark-brown barred flight feathers. Tail grey with broad, dark-brown bands. Bill yellow. Legs and feet feathered, buff-grey. Juvenile similar to adult but has whiter head and softly barred underparts.

Comparing Owls

BARN OWL: Pure white underparts and pale upperparts; flight buoyant and leisurely

GREAT GREY OWL: At least partly diurnal; plumage mostly grey-brown except for orange-brown flash near wingtips

EAGLE OWL: Massive with extremely broad, rounded wings; wingbeats surprisingly rapid and shallow; strictly nocturnal

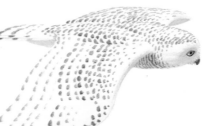

TAWNY OWL: In car headlights underparts and underwing can look surprisingly pale; when flushed from daytime roost upperparts look rich brown; wings broad and rounded

SHORT-EARED OWL: The most diurnal owl; underwings pale except for dark trailing edge and narrow barring near tips; upperwings tawny brown with dark carpal patches

SCOPS OWL: Entirely nocturnal; recalls little owl in flight but plumage more uniform and head shape rather angular

PYGMY OWL: At least partly diurnal; undulating flight; plumage rich brown above and pale but streaked below

SNOWY OWL: Large size and essentially white plumage distinctive; active in daytime and after dark

URAL OWL: Mainly nocturnal; in daylight recalls buzzard with long, broad, rounded wings and relatively long tail, but size and head shape diagnostic

LITTLE OWL: At least partly diurnal and relatively easy to observe; round-headed and dumpy in flight; undulating, woodpecker-like flight

LONG-EARED OWL: strictly nocturnal; darker brown than short-eared; head and body uniformly dark brown; upperwings show dark carpal patch; underwings pale

TENGMALM'S OWL: Entirely nocturnal; dumpy and large-headed in flight with broad, rounded wings; seen in fleeting glimpses

HAWK OWL: At least partly diurnal; in direct flight recalls sparrowhawk with broad, pointed wings and long tail

Common Nighthawk

Chordeiles minor

THE common nighthawk is a very rare vagrant to Europe, with records invariably occurring in September and October. These are presumably birds caught up in strong westerly airflows while on migration. In their native North America, common nighthawks not only feed throughout the night like most nightjars but often become active in late afternoon; vagrant birds in Europe have been observed doing the same. The flight pattern is swift and active, birds wheeling and diving to catch fast-flying insects. Because of their superbly camouflaged plumage, roosting birds can be extremely difficult to locate.

Voice: Vagrants to Europe silent
Length: 24–25cm
Wingspan: 60–65cm
Weight: 70–80g
Habitat: Forest clearings, open hillsides, grassland
Nest: Does not breed in region
Eggs: Does not breed in region
Food: Insects, caught on the wing

Superficially similar to European nightjar but with proportionately shorter, forked (not rounded) tail and longer wings. Adult male has essentially grey-brown plumage but with pattern of barring and fine markings giving excellent camouflage when resting on tree bark or among fallen leaves. Distinctive white throat, white transverse patch across primaries and white sub-terminal band on tail appear most striking in flight. Adult female similar to adult male but lacks white on tail; throat patch is buff not white. Juvenile similar to adult female but buff patch on throat less distinctive and plumage overall greyer.

THE nightjar is nocturnal and more likely to be heard than seen. The song is distinctive, far-carrying but difficult to locate exactly. When not hunting moths at night the birds spend most of their time sitting on the ground, where their plumage renders them almost completely invisible when motionless. At dusk on warm summer evenings it is possible to see the dimly lit shapes of flying nightjars in courting displays, when males use spectacular wing-clapping to advertise themselves.

Voice: Monotonous whirring 'churr'; disyllabic 'kwa-eek' note
Length: 26–28cm
Wingspan: 57–64cm
Weight: 65–100g
Habitat: Dry, open conifer woods, scrub, sandy heaths and semi-deserts
Nest: Shallow, unlined scrape on ground
Eggs: 2; glossy, cream, spotted and blotched with yellow or dark brown
Food: Insects, mainly moths and beetles, taken aerially

Shape similar to small falcon or cuckoo. Adult plumage dark grey and rufous-brown with heavy black barring and delicate pattern of vermiculations. Head, nape, back and rump

grey, lightly streaked with black. Long, grey tail, barred black outer feathers tipped white in male, buff in female. Scapulars and coverts edged silvery white, showing as pale lines. In flight, rufous-brown flight feathers heavily barred black, showing white patch near wingtip in male, buff patch in female. Underparts brown, finely barred black, becoming rufous towards undertail. White moustache. Bill very short; black with wide gape. Juvenile resembles pale adult female, but lacks wing and tail spots.

Nightjar

Caprimulgus europaeus

The nightjar is a summer visitor to Europe; it is thought the entire population overwinters in sub-Saharan Africa

Red-necked Nightjar

Caprimulgus ruficollis

THE red-necked nightjar prefers open habitats with bare patches of dry, sandy soil and scattered trees to use as song-posts. The stone pine woods of the Coto Donaña in Spain are typical of the preferred habitat, but the birds will also use arid hillsides with dwarf vegetation. The red-necked nightjar is mainly nocturnal and its song, which is repeated continuously for long periods, can be the best clue to its presence. The species is migratory, breeding between May and August and overwintering in west Africa.

Larger than nightjar, with longer wings and tail and large head

Voice: Repetitive, low-pitched, double knocking 'cut-oc, cut-oc'
Length: 30–32cm
Wingspan: 65–68cm
Weight: 65–70g
Habitat: Stone pine woods; plantations with open, sandy ground
Nest: Shallow, unlined scrape on ground
Eggs: 2; fairly glossy, grey-white, marbled and blotched yellow-brown
Food: Insects, mainly moths

Adult has mostly rufous-brown plumage with complex variegated markings. Greyish crown, brown back, rump and tail variously streaked black. Pale-buff tips to scapulars and coverts create pale lines across closed wing. Warm rufous-pink collar and throat relieved by narrow, white moustache and broad, white spots to side of chin. Underparts pale rufous-brown with narrow, black bars and greyish band across breast. In flight, both male and female show white wing spots and long white patches on outertail feathers. Juvenile resembles dull adult with more buff plumage.

Swift

Apus apus

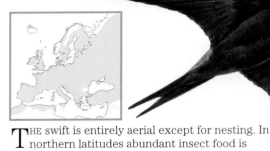

Parties make screaming calls as they fly together

The swift's familiar crescent shape is ideal for rapid sustained flight

Juvenile

THE swift is entirely aerial except for nesting. In northern latitudes abundant insect food is available only in the short summer months, so swifts are migratory, overwintering in sub-Saharan Africa; they arrive in Europe in early May and are gone again by late August, raising young quickly on a rich protein diet of airborne insects. Nestlings are able to enter torpor to endure fluctuations in food supply when wet conditions reduce the adults' ability to catch prey. When a fledgeling takes flight for the first time it is likely to remain on the wing for the next couple of years, feeding and sleeping in flight.

Voice: Shrill screaming whistle in breeding season
Length: 16–17cm
Wingspan: 42–48cm
Weight: 35–50g
Habitat: Aerial; usually in and around towns and villages
Nest: Shallow cup of vegetation and feathers, cemented with saliva, in roof space or under eaves

Eggs: 2–3; smooth, matt white
Food: Flying insects; airborne spiders

Medium-sized, all-brown swift, with small white throat patch. Very similar in size and shape to pallid swift, but wings slightly narrower and tail more noticeably forked. Greyish forehead visible at extremely close range. In bright sunlight pale upper surface to flight feathers. Powerful rapid flight with winnowing wings. Juvenile bird essentially indistinguishable from adult, showing long crescent-shaped wings, short, forked tail and all-dark plumage.

White-rumped Swift

Apus caffer

THE white-rumped swift has only recently been found in Europe, where it is confined to the southern tip of Spain. This Iberian population is remarkable in its behaviour as a nest-parasite, using the nests of the red-rumped swallow in which to lay its eggs. These sites are usually under rocky outcrops in the midst of farmland, over which the birds forage. The white-rumped swift consorts with swallows and martins more than other swifts. It is believed to be migratory, but very little is known about its movements and individuals have been recorded as present in December.

Eggs: 2; smooth, matt white
Food: Airborne insects and spiders

Has very fluttery flight, lacking power of larger relatives

Voice: Whistle beginning as chatter, merging into trill
Length: 14cm
Wingspan: 34–36cm
Weight: 20–28g
Habitat: Rocky habitats; in vicinity of coastal towns in southern Spain
Nest: In Spain, in nests of red-rumped swallow

Smallish, slim-bodied swift with long, deeply forked tail and dark plumage. Adult has mainly blue-black colour to body and wings, with noticeable narrow, bright white band across upper rump. Greyish crown and line over eye, small whitish chin and silvery sheen to underwing flight feathers, visible at close range. Long, narrow wings give distinctive silhouette. Juvenile shows more whitish tips to body feathers than adult and less blue-black sheen to dull, dark plumage.

Little Swift

Apus affinis

Adult

Voice: High-pitched screaming call uttered in flight
Length: 12cm
Wingspan: 34–35cm
Weight: 25–30g
Habitat: Nests in buildings and on cliffs; otherwise entirely aerial
Nest: Almost spherical construction of plant material held together with saliva; may also use old nest of house martin or red-rumped swallow
Eggs: 2–3; white
Food: aerial insects

THE little swift is sometimes suspected of breeding in southern Spain and is observed on a scarce but regular basis feeding over coastal marshes in the southern Iberian peninsula. Elsewhere in Europe, little swifts occur as rare vagrants, mostly in late autumn, and have been reported as far away as Britain and Sweden. The small size, square-ended tail and conspicuous white rump of the little swift allow it to be readily identified. It hawks for insects like other swifts and often glides on stiffly held wings, but unlike its relatives it intersperses this flight pattern with bouts of fluttering flight that can appear almost bat-like.

Small compact swift. Recalls house martin in plumage details but easily recognised as a swift species by silhouette. Sexes similar. Adult has dark sooty-brown plumage except for square, white rump and white throat; forehead greyish. Tail relatively short and square-ended. Juvenile similar to adult but plumage not as dark.

Pallid Swift

Apus pallidus

THE warm, sunny, coastal Mediterranean towns are where pallid swifts look most at home. Bright sunlight and a dark background assist in definite identification, allowing the pale sandy colour to be seen well. Pallid swifts are migratory, though the more reliable climate in southern Europe allows them to have two broods of young before departing as late as September for African overwintering areas. They return north again in April and it is at this time that individuals may get caught up with flocks of common swifts and arrive as very rare vagrants in northern Europe.

Voice: Screaming whistle in breeding season, deeper than swift
Length: 16–17cm
Wingspan: 42–46cm
Weight: 35–45g
Habitat: Mediterranean zone, around towns, villages and coasts
Nest: Shallow cup of vegetation and feathers, cemented with saliva, in dry, rocky area, building or cliff crevice
Eggs: 2–3; smooth, matt white
Food: Flying insects

Similar in size to swift but subtle differences in shape and colouring are important for identification. A slightly bulkier bird than the swift overall, particularly noticeable in broader wings and shorter, more rounded tail forks. Adult and juvenile essentially indistinguishable. Plumage brown with pale margins to feathers creating sandy effect in good light. Forehead greyish-white. Slightly darker brown saddle on back contrasts with paler rump and upper surface to wings. Prominent white throat patch. Underbody very pale sandy brown caused by pale margins to most feathers.

Can be confused with swift; note the blunter, broader wings, which do not seem to beat as quickly

Pallid swifts prefer dry, rocky areas, and will nest in old town churches and other large traditional buildings; alternatively they will select sea cliffs, where the nest can be sited in a natural crevice

Alpine Swift

Apus melba

THE Alpine swift is common and well distributed across all of southern Europe. The underlying habitat is not of great significance, but it does use air currents generated by landscape features and so prefers hilly areas. It is an impressive bird to watch, with its powerful, fast flight, easy glides and chattering call. At first glance, distant birds can appear like small falcons. The Alpine swift is migratory and in winter can be seen in many African countries. Its return north in the spring regularly results in individuals being seen much further north in Europe than the breeding range.

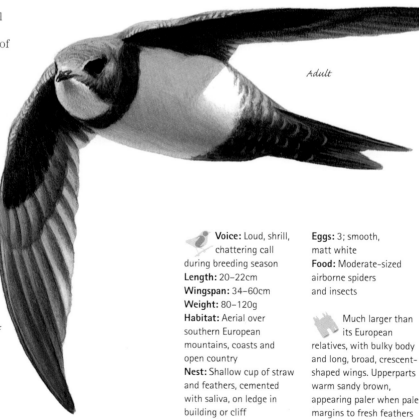

Adult

Close views of Alpine swifts can be obtained by watching from the tops of sea cliffs or rocky gorges; as the birds pass by their wings make an audible swishing sound

Voice: Loud, shrill, chattering call during breeding season
Length: 20–22cm
Wingspan: 34–60cm
Weight: 80–120g
Habitat: Aerial over southern European mountains, coasts and open country
Nest: Shallow cup of straw and feathers, cemented with saliva, on ledge in building or cliff

Eggs: 3; smooth, matt white
Food: Moderate-sized airborne spiders and insects

Much larger than its European relatives, with bulky body and long, broad, crescent-shaped wings. Upperparts warm sandy brown, appearing paler when pale margins to fresh feathers

are evident. Black patch in front of eye noticeable at close range. Chin and throat white. Broad, sandy-brown breast band. Lower breast, belly and flanks are white. Underwing brown with darker brown flight feathers showing above and below wing. White chin hard to see but large white belly patch obvious. Juvenile shows more prominent white tips to brown feathers than adult.

Kingfisher

Alcedo atthis

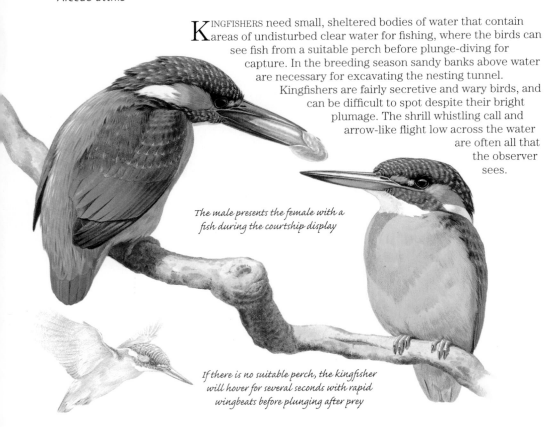

KINGFISHERS need small, sheltered bodies of water that contain areas of undisturbed clear water for fishing, where the birds can see fish from a suitable perch before plunge-diving for capture. In the breeding season sandy banks above water are necessary for excavating the nesting tunnel. Kingfishers are fairly secretive and wary birds, and can be difficult to spot despite their bright plumage. The shrill whistling call and arrow-like flight low across the water are often all that the observer sees.

The male presents the female with a fish during the courtship display

If there is no suitable perch, the kingfisher will hover for several seconds with rapid wingbeats before plunging after prey

Voice: Song comprises starling-like bubbling whistles; also plaintive chattering whistle calls
Length: 16–17cm
Wingspan: 24–26cm
Weight: 35–45g
Habitat: Streams, rivers and lakes with surrounding vegetation
Nest: Tunnel in clay or gravel bank of stream; pit usually above water
Eggs: 6–7; almost round, smooth, glossy white
Food: Mainly small freshwater fish; some aquatic insects and crustaceans

Small kingfisher with long bill and relatively large head. Adult has crown, nape, moustache and all upperparts bright blue, tone varying with light and viewing angle. Pale sheen on back. Crown and wing coverts have pale blue spotting. Scapulars, flight feathers and tip of tail darker blackish-blue. Face, underbody and underwing coverts rich orange-chestnut, paler on throat and centre of belly. White spots in front of eye, on side of neck and under chin. Long dagger-shaped bill, all black in male, with reddish base in female. Legs and feet coral red. Juvenile lacks brilliance of adult, and has greener upperparts and bluish-grey breast. Legs dull orange.

White-breasted Kingfisher

Halcyon smyrnensis

THE white-breasted kingfisher's main range extends across the Indian subcontinent and southeast Asia. Its distribution continues westwards into the Middle East and the species occurs sparingly in southern Turkey. White-breasted kingfishers favour perches that are 1–3m above water. Extended periods of time are spent simply watching for fishing opportunities, but the birds will also take terrestrial prey such as insects and lizards from river banks and dry land. Nesting burrows are usually sited close to areas of good feeding and can be more than a metre long.

Adult's bright colouring is distinctive

Voice: Utters loud rattling calls and shrill whistles
Length: 26–29cm
Wingspan: 40–42cm
Weight: 80–85g
Habitat: Wetlands of all types; also occasionally hunts over dry land
Nest: Sited at end of tunnel, excavated in bank
Eggs: 5–6; white

Food: Mainly fish but also amphibians, crustaceans and insects

A beautifully marked and distinctive kingfisher. Sexes similar. Adult has striking white throat and chest, and chestnut head, neck, breast and underparts. Back, tail and wings iridescent blue except for black tips to primaries and black and chestnut wing coverts. Bill proportionately massive and bright red; legs and feet bright red. Juvenile similar to adult but colours duller.

Pied Kingfisher

Ceryle rudis

Adult male

Voice: Loud, high-pitched screaming call
Length: 25–26cm
Wingspan: 45–46cm
Weight: 80–100g
Habitat: Always found close to water; generally fresh water but sometimes also coastal
Nest: At end of tunnel

excavated in bank
Eggs: 4–5; white
Food: Mainly fish but occasionally crustaceans, frogs and aquatic insects

Distinctive and well-marked kingfisher. Adult male has striking black and white marbled upperparts. Underparts essentially white except for two black breast bands. Adult female similar to adult male but has one, not two, black breast bands. Juvenile similar to adult female but has chest band grey not black. All birds have black bill and feet.

THE pied kingfisher is a widespread tropical species; in Europe, it is restricted to the southern coasts of Turkey. It is essentially resident throughout its range, but it is a rare, regular winter visitor to Cyprus. Pied kingfishers are entirely dependent on water for feeding and can be found along almost any fish-rich stretch of water. Like other kingfishers, they spend long periods of time perched on overhanging branches, scanning the water below. Prior to actually diving after fish, they habitually hover in mid-air before plunging down.

Blue-cheeked Bee-eater

Merops superciliosus

THE blue-cheeked bee-eater occurs as a breeding species in northwest Africa and locally from the Middle East to northwest India; small numbers also breed in southeast Turkey. It is a very rare vagrant to Europe, mainly appearing in late spring. Although superficially similar in outline to European bee-eater, this species should present few identification problems when seen well. Like other bee-eaters, blue-cheeked bee-eaters spend considerable periods of time perched on prominent branches from which passing flying insects can easily be spotted.

Voice: Bubbling, ringing disyllabic 'prr-ipp'
Length: 28–30cm
Wingspan: 46–48cm
Weight: 45–50g
Habitat: Open, arid terrain, usually close to water
Nest: At end of tunnel excavated in bank
Eggs: 5–7; white
Food: Exclusively flying insects

Attractively marked and aerobatic bee-eater. Sexes similar. Adult plumage essentially green although appears bluish on rump and lower back. Head markings distinctive. Has black eyestripe and white forehead grading to sky blue supercilium. Cheeks sky blue and throat yellow, grading to orange-red. Tail streamers extremely long, at least twice length of those of bee-eater. Juvenile similar to adult but plumage duller and tail streamers much shorter.

Bee-eater

Merops apiaster

Hot, sheltered valleys with clumps of trees are the bee-eater's favoured habitat, but it will inhabit treeless grassy plains if there are places to use as perches

The bee-eater prefers to be in close proximity to water, which ensures an abundant supply of large insects such as dragonflies; it goes after them with a typical slow glide

THE bee-eater breeds in warm, sunny open landscapes in the drier parts of Europe. Sandy or clay banks are required for colonial nesting tunnels. Bee-eaters are migratory, returning to Europe from their African overwintering areas in April and May. During the spring rush to reach breeding areas they regularly overshoot their normal range and can often be seen in northwest Europe. In such circumstances they occasionally stay to breed, accounting for the historical expansion and contraction of the species' range.

Voice: Liquid bubbling 'pruupp'
Length: 27–29cm
Wingspan: 44–49cm
Weight: 45–75g
Habitat: Warm open habitats with mixed agriculture; clumps of trees, often near rivers
Nest: Colonial tunnels in vertical or sloping sandy bank

Eggs: 6–7; smooth, glossy, pinkish-white
Food: Flying insects, preferably bees and wasps

Longer than blackbird, with much slimmer, delicate appearance and multicoloured plumage. Adult has chestnut crown, nape and back shading to yellowish-brown on scapulars and rump. Uppertail dark shiny green, duller below with central two feathers darker and elongated. Wing coverts chestnut, surrounded with bluish-green. Flight feathers shiny blue, dark-tipped. Whitish forehead and narrow pale blue supercilium. Black eye-mask and black border to bright yellow throat. Underparts pale turquoise-blue. Underwing orange with darker tipped flight feathers. Long, slim, black decurved bill. Eyes reddish. Legs and feet brownish-black. Juvenile resembles dull adult but bluer on back and wings.

Roller

Coracias garrulus

In the breeding season the male performs an acrobatic mating dance, where he dives rapidly towards the ground with half-rolls, like a lapwing

Flight action is direct and strong, and a good view reveals the phenomenal blues displayed by the bird's spread wings

The roller selects mainly large insects such as mole crickets, characteristic of dry, warm lowlands, but will also steal nestling birds and catch small reptiles

THE roller is a spectacular bird of warm, dry southern and central European lowland habitats. Its favoured habitat is open old forest with healthy clearings and adjacent grasslands. Stands of riverine poplars are chosen in large areas of otherwise treeless grasslands, such as in the pusztas of Hungary and Poland. The species migrates to Africa for the winter and it is at migration times that wanderers can be encountered well north of the usual range. The roller uses the old nest holes of other species, particularly woodpeckers, to nest in. It also perches in trees to locate and drop down on to prey from. It is an easy bird to find within its range as it habitually perches prominently along roadside wires.

Voice: Rasping, accelerating rattle; harsh, short contact call
Length: 30–32cm
Wingspan: 66–73cm
Weight: 110–160g
Habitat: Warm continental lowlands, old open forest, heaths and grasslands
Nest: Hole in tree; less often in building or amongst rocks
Eggs: 3–5; smooth, glossy white
Food: Mainly large insects; also small mammals, nestling birds, amphibians and reptiles

Large crow-like bird, with very brightly coloured plumage. In flight upperwing shows two-tone blue coverts and blackish flight feathers. Underwing shows pale blue coverts and blue black-tipped flight feathers. Adult has head, neck and underbody pale green-blue. Forehead and chin whitish, with narrow black eye-mask. Back chestnut, rump purple-blue. Shoulder iridescent cobalt blue with pale green-blue coverts and blue-black flight feathers. Tail blue-black with pale greenish outer webs and dark tips to feathers. Strong, decurved and slightly hook-tipped black bill. Legs and feet black. Juvenile has similar pattern to adult, but all colours duller.

Hoopoe
Upupa epops

Disproportionately large, rounded wings show well in flight; hoopoe has erratic, bounding flight action, reminiscent of a giant butterfly

In flight looks strikingly black and white; on the ground, however, it can be surprisingly difficult to spot, especially on broken terrain

T HE hoopoe spends a lot of time on the ground catching insects, walking with a rather short, pigeon-like gait. The hoopoe chooses dry, warm, open landscapes with some bare sandy ground and trees or other surfaces for perching. It requires a good supply of large insects and their pupae for food, sometimes using its long bill to probe into the ground. The young are usually raised in a tree-hole nest, often in an orchard, but the bird will use nest boxes. European hoopoes are migratory, overwintering in Africa; on returning to Europe early in the spring, some birds overshoot the normal range to reach more northern and western countries.

Voice: Song low, far-carrying mellow 'oo-oo-oo'; cawing contact calls
Length: 26–28cm
Wingspan: 42–46cm
Weight: 50–80g
Habitat: Warm, dry, open, varied landscapes with some trees and bare ground
Nest: In hole, usually in tree, though buildings and walls are also used; sometimes lined with grass
Eggs: 7–8; greyish-olive, marked with pores
Food: Large insects, including larvae and pupae; also reptiles and amphibians

Adult has head, neck, back and underbody pale brownish-pink, with warmer pinkish shade on breast. Long erectile crest of pink feathers, tipped with white and black. White crescent on rump. At rest, transverse black and creamy-white barring crosses wings and shoulders, the foremost bar being pale orange. Tail black with wavy white band near base. Undertail coverts whitish. In flight, primaries are black with single white crescent near tips. Long, slender, decurved bill, black with pinkish base. Legs and feet black. Juvenile duller than adult, with dingy cream barring and shorter bill.

Similar to jay in size and colour but slimmer when perched; crest is only raised when bird is alarmed

When disturbed hoopoe freezes and will not rise until approached very closely

Wryneck

Jynx torquilla

similar in size to nightingale but longer and slimmer, with plumage recalling nightjar

The nest hole is usually situated in a tree branch rather than on the main trunk

THE wryneck needs open, warm, sunny habitats, often with bare sandy ground where it can easily find ants on which to feed. It nests in trees, but does not drum or excavate a nest hole, instead using the old site of another species. It is unobtrusive during the breeding season, when the only clue to its presence may be its quiet, ringing call. The wryneck flies with a low, direct flight and its camouflaged plumage makes it difficult to detect. Some wrynecks are migratory, the northern birds overwintering in Africa. Populations in southern Europe are only partially migratory, with birds present in Spain all year.

Voice: High-pitched, ringing 'pee-pee-pee', like small falcon
Length: 16–17cm
Wingspan: 25–27cm
Weight: 30–40g
Habitat: Lowland woodland fringes, orchards, parks and large gardens
Nest: Natural or artificial hole in tree, wall or bank
Eggs: 7–10; smooth, matt white
Food: Principally ants, with some other insects; includes berries on migration

At a distance, adult appears mottled grey and brown; at close range very finely marked. Grey crown, sides to mantle and back bordered by black scapular stripe, which connects on side of neck with elongated black eyestripe. Wings brown with heavy dark barring and vermiculation. Long, grey full tail has transverse black bars. Throat and upper breast yellowish with short black bars. Lower breast and belly creamy white with dark spots. Bill, legs and feet pale brown. Juvenile slightly paler than adult, with less barring.

Grey-headed Woodpecker

Picus canus

Adult male

Smaller than green woodpecker with less robust bill

THE grey-headed woodpecker is found across the middle latitudes of Europe wherever woodland is plentiful. It reaches higher altitudes in the mountains than its close relative, the green woodpecker, and selects coniferous forests, mainly of larch. Nest holes are excavated in mature trees. Both species are predominantly ant-feeders and spend much of their time on the ground; however, the grey-headed woodpecker is a less specialised feeder, eating other insects gleaned from tree trunks or walls, and in winter it will visit garden birdtables. Like most woodpeckers this species is resident in Europe, although there is some evidence of irruptive behaviour when individuals can be seen outside the normal range.

Like the green woodpecker, the grey-headed woodpecker uses only the trunks of trees, not the canopy

Voice: Short drumming; repeated fluty whistles slowing and descending in pitch
Length: 25–26cm
Wingspan: 38–40cm
Weight: 100–150g
Habitat: Open deciduous woods and riverine carr; montane larch woods in central Europe
Nest: Excavated tree-hole; lined with wood chips
Eggs: 7–9; smooth, glossy white
Food: Mainly ants and other insects; some seeds and fruit

Adult male has grey head marked only with red forecrown and narrow black moustache above whitish throat. Back, scapulars and wing coverts pale but intense green. Rump yellow. Breast and underbody pale grey. Tail greenish. Folded flight feathers brownish-black, barred with white. In flight upperwing shows an even green colour, except for dark brown-grey primaries conspicuously barred white. Underwing dark grey, barred white. Bill dark grey, yellowish towards base. Female has no red on crown and is similar to but duller than male. Legs and feet of both sexes grey. Juvenile browner and scruffier than adult.

Green Woodpecker

Picus viridis

A LTHOUGH it is traditionally a forest species, the green woodpecker has adapted to the loss of this type of habitat and is now also found in more open terrain with trees. Its preferred food is ants, and where they are abundant in old pastures and sandy heaths the green woodpecker feeds exclusively on the ground. It uses its strong bill to dig into the ants' nest and its long sticky tongue picks up adults, larvae and pupae alike. The green woodpecker is difficult to observe because of its shy nature, particularly at the nest, where the only clue to its presence may be an occasional glimpse of the adult silently slipping away with its heavy undulating flight. More generally heard than seen, this bird has a ringing, laughing call, which is responsible for its local name, the yaffle.

Voice: Ringing laugh known as a yaffle; alarm call is a short 'kyack'
Length: 31–33cm
Wingspan: 40–42cm
Weight: 180–220g
Habitat: Open, broad-leaved, lowland forest with clearings; parks, gardens and heaths
Nest: Excavated hole in tree
Eggs: 5–7; smooth, glossy white
Food: Almost exclusively adult and pupal ants; occasional seeds and fruit

A large, bulky woodpecker. Adult male has red crown extending on to nape; he has black face patch with red moustachial stripe set in black. Upperparts bright green with bright yellow rump and brown-black primaries, barred cream. Tail dark greenish-grey with faint cream spotting. Rear of face, sides of neck and underparts pale, clear yellow except for darker barring on flanks. Bill grey with yellowish lower mandible. Legs and feet grey. Adult female similar to male but has smaller black face patch and lacks red moustache. Juvenile plumage pattern similar to adult but colours dulled by white spotting and barring on upperparts; dark bars on underparts.

Red centre of the male's moustachial streak hard to see in poor light

Adult male

Adult female

Signs of green woodpecker attacks can often be seen on forest anthills

Black Woodpecker

Dryocopus martius

T HE black woodpecker's noisy and showy behaviour makes it easy to track down. When foraging on trees it climbs with very pronounced bounds, using its massive bill to chisel rapidly into even healthy wood. Its flight is irregular, with periods of closed wings causing non-rhythmical bounds, but the overall impression is of a fast-flying crow dodging through the tall trees. The black woodpecker does not readily tolerate the close proximity of humans and its reliance on mature old-growth forest makes it vulnerable to habitat destruction by commercial forestry activities.

Voice: Loud, far-carrying drumming; loud, melodious, repeated notes – often in flight
Length: 45–47cm
Wingspan: 64–68cm
Weight: 260–360g
Habitat: Mature northern taiga; southern montane deciduous forests with mature tall trees
Nest: Excavated hole in tree or telegraph post
Eggs: 4–6; smooth, glossy white

Food: All life cycle stages of ants and wood-boring beetles; occasional fruit and birds' eggs

Largest European woodpecker, half the size again of the green woodpecker. Adult male glossy black with scarlet forehead and long crown. Adult female browner and lacking plumage gloss, with red on crown restricted to small patch above nape. Massive, grey-brown, chisel-like bill with darkish tip. Legs and feet dark grey. Juvenile resembles adult, but with grey chin and red on crown less extensive or sometimes absent.

Large trees are required for nest sites, and the black woodpecker's ability to excavate living wood creates many opportunities for other hole-nesting species

Adult female

Adult male

161

Great Spotted Woodpecker

Dendrocopos major

Male

Female

The loud drumming made by the repetitive striking of the great spotted woodpecker's bill on hollow trees can be heard in European woods from early March

THIS is the commonest woodpecker in the region, and the most adaptable with regard to habitat. This species exhibits racial differences across the continent: the British race is smaller, with less clean plumage than its mainland Europe counterparts; it is also generally sedentary. Races in northern coniferous forests show irruptive behaviour. The great spotted woodpecker gleans food from cracks and holes in the timber and excavates rotten wood to search for beetles. It is largely resident in Europe and begins breeding activity quite early in the year. A new nest hole is excavated each year.

Voice: Loud drumming; call is a sharp 'tchicc' and short rattle of similar notes
Length: 22–23cm
Wingspan: 34–39cm
Weight: 70–100g
Habitat: Adaptable to various habitats with trees; prefers open, mature, deciduous woods
Nest: Excavated hole in tree
Eggs: 4–7; smooth, glossy white
Food: Mainly insects; some seeds; occasional birds' eggs and nestlings

Blackbird-sized, strong-billed pied woodpecker. Upperparts almost wholly black, relieved by large white scapular patches, lines of white spots across flight feathers and white barring on outertail feathers. Adult male has crimson nape patch, absent in female. Face, including eyering, mainly white with black moustache connecting with black nape and with black extension bar on to sides of breast. Enclosed white patch on sides of neck. Underparts creamy white with pinkish-red vent area and 'trousers'. Bill, legs and feet dark grey. Juvenile has red crown, dirty-white underparts and less distinct white barring on wings than adult.

Syrian Woodpecker

Dendrocopos syriacus

The close similarity of this species to the great spotted woodpecker hinders identification in newly colonised areas

Adult female

Adult male

THE Syrian woodpecker has spread northwestwards into central Europe this century; it replaces its close relative, the great spotted woodpecker, in the warmer, drier, open lowland habitats of the Balkans. It is less attracted to large stands of forest and can be found mainly in orchards, parks, avenues and riverine woods. The Syrian woodpecker is one of three pied species in Europe with white shoulder patches, so care is needed with identification. Its unmarked face is often difficult to be sure of, but it has a soft contact call and a very long drumming bout.

Similar to great spotted woodpecker. Adult has generally black upperparts and white underparts. On face black moustachial line turns up and back, but stops before joining with back of neck, giving more open-looking white face than great spotted woodpecker's. Male has red nape. Bolder white barring on wings but tail completely black – lacking white bars as on outer feathers of great spotted woodpecker; vent paler pink than that species. Bill, legs and feet dark grey. Juvenile similar to adult but has red crown and flank streaks.

Voice: Long, loud drumming; call soft, short 'chjuck'
Length: 22–23cm
Wingspan: 34–39cm
Weight: 70–80g
Habitat: Warm, open landscapes with scattered trees; orchards and parks
Nest: Excavated hole in tree
Eggs: 4–7; smooth, glossy white
Food: Mainly insects; also fruit and nuts

Middle Spotted Woodpecker

Dendrocopos medius

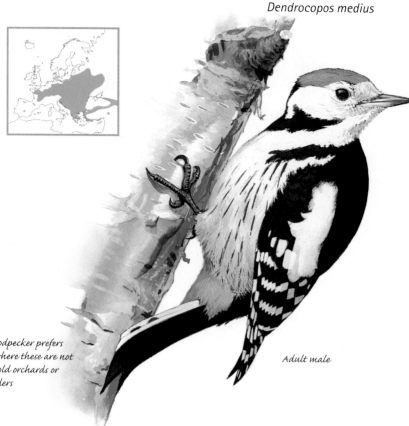

THE stronghold of the middle spotted woodpecker is the hornbeam-oak forests of mainland central Europe. It prefers old stands of forest, particularly where traditional woodland management has resulted in a mosaic of coppiced undershrubs and large standard trees. Plenty of dying timber is important for excavating nest sites and food. It is significantly smaller than the great spotted woodpecker, and its more delicate bill cannot exert the same power in excavating healthy hardwoods, so the two species can coexist in similar habitats, utilising different parts of the woodland.

Voice: Drumming rare; far-carrying jay-like 'quahh'; contact call soft and short
Length: 20–22cm
Wingspan: 33–34cm
Weight: 55–80g
Habitat: Mixed deciduous woods of hornbeam and oak, parkland elms and riverine alder
Nest: Excavated hole in decayed tree
Eggs: 4–7; smooth, glossy white
Food: Almost exclusively insects; occasional seeds

Smaller, less cleanly marked version of great spotted woodpecker. Adult male has red crown, which is shorter and duller in female. Remainder of upperparts black with white scapular patches (smaller than on great spotted woodpecker), white barring across flight feathers and white outertail feathers, barred black. Face white with black moustachial border not connecting with black on nape. Downward extension of moustache onto sides of throat gives way to black streaking, extending down flanks. White chin and throat shading to dirty yellowish breast. Belly and vent pinkish. Bill, legs and feet grey. Juvenile similar to adult but duller, with less contrast and fewer flank streaks.

The middle spotted woodpecker prefers broad-leaved forests but where these are not available will occupy old orchards or riverine alders

Adult male

White-backed Woodpecker

Dendrocopos leucotos

Adult male

THE white-backed woodpecker is the largest pied woodpecker in Europe. It requires large tracts of relatively undisturbed old-growth forest with a high proportion of dead and decaying timber. In the north it can find these conditions in swampy coniferous forest, but further south the steep montane beech and fir forests are favoured, such as those in the mountain national parks of Hungary and Slovakia. Identification of this species should be straightforward, especially if seen in flight, when the white back and wingbarring is obvious. Clues to its presence are the long and accelerating bouts of loud drumming.

Voice: Long, loud accelerating drumming. Low, quiet 'kjuck' and other hoarse squeaks
Length: 24–26cm
Wingspan: 38–40cm
Weight: 100–120g
Habitat: Extensive deciduous or mixed forests
Nest: Excavated hole, usually in rotten tree
Eggs: 3–5; smooth, glossy white
Food: Mainly insects, particularly beetle larvae; nuts and berries

Large pied woodpecker. Adult upperparts predominantly black with heavy white barring across wings, and white lower back and rump. Black tail has barred white outer feathers. Male crown red, extending slightly on to nape; female crown black. White face with black moustachial stripe turning up, but not connecting with, black nape, and extending down to break into heavy black streaks covering sides of breast and flanks. Chin and throat white. Breast pale-buff, lower belly and vent bright pink-red. Bill, legs and feet grey. Juvenile similar to adult but has black streaks intermixed with red crown, greyish flanks and less red around vent.

The white back, which gives this species its name, is not obvious until the bird is in flight

163

Lesser Spotted Woodpecker

Dendrocopos minor

Distinguished from great spotted woodpecker by small size and absence of white patches on wings

Adult males

This tiny woodpecker avoids dense stands of mature forest, particularly conifers

THE lesser spotted woodpecker does not need large trees, as foraging and nesting usually take place in smaller side branches and along twigs in the canopy. The bird's behaviour, small size and unobtrusiveness make it difficult to spot. With its fluttery, buoyant flight, the lesser spotted woodpecker is more like a passerine than its larger relatives, and is often found up among the highest branches. When feeding it creeps along thin twigs and investigates dead wood with a barely audible tapping. The best clues to its presence are the weak, but ringing, repeated whistles and, in early spring, quiet but fairly long drumming bouts.

Voice: Quiet, high-pitched drumming; soft whistling 'pee-pee-pee', repeated up to 20 times
Length: 14–15cm
Wingspan: 25–27cm
Weight: 20–30g
Habitat: Open, broad-leaved woodland; riverine alders, parks, orchards and tree-lined avenues
Nest: Excavated hole, often underside branch of tree
Eggs: 4–6; smooth, glossy white
Food: Almost exclusively insects and their larvae

Smallest pied woodpecker, about size of nuthatch. Adult upperparts predominantly black with heavy white barring across back and wings; black tail with outer feathers barred white. Male has short red crown; white in female. Rear of crown black. Buff-white face above black moustache curving upwards around ear coverts, with downward-extending bar. Underparts buffish-white, streaked black on flanks, with black spots on undertail coverts. No red around vent. Bill, legs and feet grey. Juvenile similar to adult, but with browner and more streaked and spotted underparts.

Three-toed Woodpecker

Picoides tridactylus

Adult male of northern race

Medium-sized woodpecker with black and white plumage, differently patterned from other pied woodpeckers and lacking red

THERE are two geographically separate races of three-toed woodpecker in Europe; the majority belong to a northern boreal and Arctic subspecies, with a less common Alpine race in the mountains of central Europe. The northern race of three-toed woodpeckers is the only true Arctic European woodpecker and is also a more exclusively conifer forest dweller than other species. This woodpecker is a tame species, but is unobtrusive in its habits, being less flighty and not as energetic a feeder as some species. Although insect larvae are important in its diet, three-toed woodpeckers regularly ring spruce trees with holes to extract sap. The bird's calls and drummings can be quite soft. This species is mainly a sedentary European resident but northern populations can be irruptive. In the central European mountains it is sedentary and stays put even during harsh winters.

Voice: Long, rattling drumming; contact call soft, longish 'gjug'
Length: 21–22cm
Wingspan: 32–35cm
Weight: 60–75g
Habitat: Northern, dense, moist, coniferous forests; central montane steep-slope spruce forests
Nest: Excavated hole in dead or dying conifer
Eggs: 3–5; smooth, glossy white

Food: Insects, mainly adult and larvae of wood boring beetles; also drinks sap

Adult of northern race has black nape, face and moustache with white rear supercilium and white stripe under ear coverts. Back and rump white with ragged black border. Wings and tail black with narrow, white barring on flight feathers and outertail feathers. Underparts buff-white with grey barring on sides of breast and flanks and black-spotted undertail coverts. Male has yellow crown; this black with white flecks in female. Alpine race darker, with less white on back and heavier markings on underparts. Bill, legs and feet grey. Crown mottled yellow. Juveniles of both races greyer on underparts than respective adults.

Comparing Woodpeckers in Flight

M OST European species of woodpecker are, on the whole, rather retiring birds and often the best views are had of birds in flight. Such observations are generally brief and so it is important that observers familiarise themselves with key aspects of plumage and behaviour to make positive identification possible. All the woodpeckers shown here are in adult male plumage.

BLACK WOODPECKER: Unmistakable when seen well. Recalls crow in flight with exaggerated and slow wingbeats; flight direct, not undulating

GREEN WOODPECKER: Low, undulating flight invariably accompanied by loud yaffling alarm calls. In good light rump looks strikingly yellow, and red on cap and nape often visible; plumage otherwise greenish on upperparts and grubby grey on underparts

GREY-HEADED WOODPECKER: Superficially similar to green woodpecker with essentially greenish upperparts and yellow rump; smaller than that species, however, and proportionately less bulky. Head looks paler than that of green woodpecker due to absence of mask-like dark markings

MIDDLE SPOTTED WOODPECKER: Upperwing pattern similar to great spotted and Syrian woodpeckers: largely black with interrupted white barring on flight feathers and white shoulder patches. Note the mainly pale head with red on nape

GREAT SPOTTED WOODPECKER: Seen in flight, superficially similar to Syrian woodpecker. Look closely at facial markings to see whether black moustache links to black on nape and shoulders

SYRIAN WOODPECKER: Similar to great spotted woodpecker with mainly black upperwings showing interrupted white barring on flight feathers and white shoulder patches. Close scrutiny of facial markings will reveal that black moustachial stripe does not link to black on nape or shoulder

WHITE-BACKED WOODPECKER: Upperwings largely black with interrupted white barring on flight feathers; white shoulder patches absent. Shows conspicuous and diagnostic white rump and lower back

THREE-TOED WOODPECKER: Upperwings look more uniformly black than other medium-sized woodpeckers'. Extensive white band along entire length of back is diagnostic

LESSER SPOTTED WOODPECKER: Easily recognised by small size and extensive interrupted white barring on otherwise black upperwings

165

Skylark

Alauda arvensis

TRADITIONALLY a species of steppe grassland, the skylark has adapted to a variety of habitats; it does not require trees as it feeds and nests exclusively on the ground. The skylark's familiar song is delivered while the bird maintains a fluttering position high in the sky. In the northeast of its European range the skylark is migratory, increasing the resident populations of western Europe in winter. Large flocks can often be seen moving ahead of winter snows. Skylark numbers are declining, probably as a result of pesticide use and intensive cereal production.

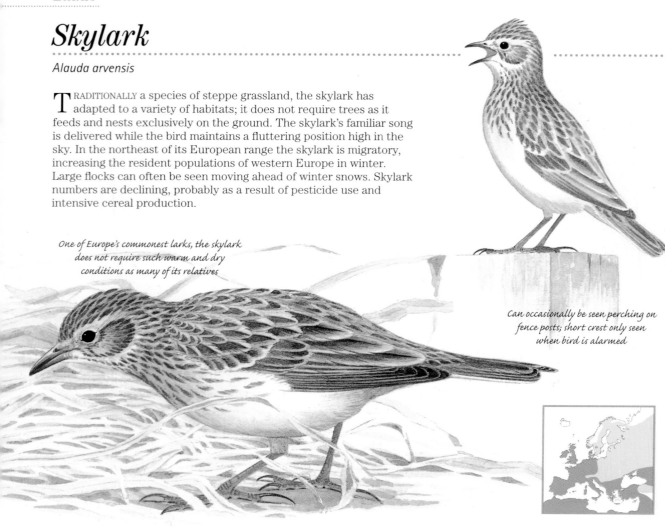

One of Europe's commonest larks, the skylark does not require such warm and dry conditions as many of its relatives

Can occasionally be seen perching on fence posts; short crest only seen when bird is alarmed

Voice: Loud melodious warbling flight-song; call is a liquid rippling 'chirropp'
Length: 18–19cm
Wingspan: 30–36cm
Weight: 30–50g
Habitat: Grasslands in lowlands and uplands; cultivated fields
Nest: Shallow depression amongst growing grass; lined with vegetation
Eggs: 3–5; smooth, glossy greyish-white, spotted brown
Food: Insects in summer; at other times mixed with seeds, grains, flowers and roots

Smaller than song thrush, with a stout bill that distinguishes it from pipits. Sexes similar. Adult upperparts buff, streaked blackish-brown. Crown well streaked, with short crest prominent only when erect. Pale buff supercilium and surround to dull buff cheeks. Closed wing shows blackish buff-edged coverts forming wingbars. Tail blackish-brown with white edges. In flight wings show clear white trailing edge. Underparts buff-white with heavy streaking across breast and flanks. Bill grey-brown. Legs and feet pale brown. Juvenile recalls adult but has heavily speckled white on upperparts with black drop-shaped markings on breast.

short-distance flight is fluttery; over longer distances flight action is strong and undulating

In winter skylarks from northern Europe move south and gather in feeding flocks that may number several hundred birds; local resident flocks remain separate

---

Dupont's Lark

Chersophilus duponti

ALTHOUGH Dupont's lark is not rare in Spain, it has limiting habitat requirements that restrict it to certain very distinct areas. Since the species is remarkably reluctant to fly, open stony ground is required for it to run. Clumps of vegetation are used both for nesting and concealment. It is one of the most difficult species to see in Europe, and finding the right habitat is the first challenge for the observer. Dupont's lark's beautiful, mournful flight song is performed after dark and especially just before dawn.

Voice: Song beautiful mixture of fluty notes and finch-like twittering
Length: 18cm
Wingspan: 26–31cm
Weight: 35–45g
Habitat: Dry, open, Mediterranean steppes with sparse vegetation; cereal fields in winter
Nest: Scrape on ground, hidden under bush or rock; sparsely lined with vegetation
Eggs: 3–4; smooth, glossy pinkish-white, densely spotted red-brown
Food: Mainly insects and seeds

Smaller than skylark but with long bill and no crest. Adult upperparts brown, heavily streaked with blackish-brown. Face well marked with long buff-white supercilium and eyering forming spectacle; pale grey half-collar surrounding brown cheeks. Mantle, scapular and wing feathers neatly edged with buff, giving scaly effect. Brown tail, edged with white. Underparts white with heavy black spotting across chest and streaking down flanks. Long, decurved grey-brown bill. Long, brownish-white legs. Juvenile similar to adult but upperparts less streaked and more scaly with white feather edgings.

Woodlark

Lullula arborea

In flight shows very short tail and more rounded wings than skylark

On the ground the bright face and black and white wing markings are good features to look for

THE woodlark prefers habitats often found where heathland meets woodland edge. Here the ground is usually well drained, with low vegetation cover for nesting and trees for perching. In winter birds will often move onto adjacent fallow farmland. Overall the woodlark resembles the skylark; however, the short tail and blunt wings make the woodlark look quite different in flight, with a hesitant fluttering action. It has a beautiful fluty song, which can be heard in the early spring. In central Europe woodlarks are migratory, but the maritime populations, such as in southern England, are mainly resident.

Voice: Flight-song is a beautiful descending series of rich, mellow, fluty whistles
Length: 15cm
Wingspan: 27–30cm
Weight: 25–35g
Habitat: Warm, dry, sandy lowlands with heathland vegetation and scattered trees
Nest: Deep depression in the ground in sheltered position under bush; lined with vegetation
Eggs: 3–5; smooth, fairly glossy, olive-white spotted and blotched brown at broad end

Food: Insects in breeding season; mainly seeds at other times

Smaller and slighter than skylark, though plumage superficially similar with buff upperparts, heavily streaked blackish. Adult has face well marked with bold white supercilia meeting on nape, and dark brown surround to warm buff cheeks. Hindneck and rump pale whitish buff. Head has small crest at rear of crown. Closed wing shows black and white bar at wing bend. Tail short and dark. Underparts buff-white with necklace of prominent black streaks. Fine bill, dark grey-brown with paler base. Legs and feet pink. Juvenile similar to adult but has less well-marked face and white spotting on upperparts.

Shore Lark

Eremophila alpestris

IN SWEDEN and Finland the shore lark breeds in the driest stony areas of tundra, where the dominant sparse vegetation is lichen. In the southern mountains it chooses similar habitats on the bare upland plateaux. It is often difficult to spot on the ground, using stones and vegetation to hide its progress when feeding. Its thin song is mostly delivered from the ground. The most northern shore larks are migratory, and in winter are found among sand dunes and salt marshes along the North Sea coasts of western Europe. With its distinctive appearance and habitat preferences, the shore lark is unlikely to be confused with any other species in Europe.

Flight appears strong and powerful, with bounding action between flaps

smaller and slimmer than skylark, with crouched appearance when seen on ground

Voice: Subdued twittering song of thin musical notes
Length: 14–17cm
Wingspan: 30–35cm
Weight: 30–45g
Habitat: Sub-Arctic or Arctic lowland tundra or montane plains; on coasts in winter
Nest: Unlined depression on ground; usually sheltered under stone or tussock
Eggs: 2–4; smooth, greenish-white spotted with pale brown
Food: Insects and seeds in summer; seeds in winter

Adult male has pale yellow face and throat with black forecrown and black mask curving down below eye. Black gorget across upper-breast. Reddish-brown rear crown and nape with tufted black feathers on sides of crown forming 'horns'. Facial markings made more striking by abrasion through winter into spring. Rest of upperparts warm brown, heavily mottled with black. Tail black with brown centre and white outer feathers. Lower breast and belly white with pinkish-brown wash and faint black streaking on flanks. Adult female is duller and more heavily streaked than male. In both sexes bill grey, and legs and feet black. Juvenile recalls adult but is speckled and lacks face pattern.

Winter adult

summer adult

167

Crested Lark

Galerida cristata

Important field characteristics to aid identification are orangey underwing, spiky crest at rear of crown and long bill; similar in size and appearance to thekla lark

One of the commonest larks in the region, the crested lark is scattered widely across central Europe

THE crested lark prefers warm, open plains with low vegetation and is most at home in grassland or cultivated areas with some bare ground. It is able to take advantage of human-modified habitats and can be found on urban waste ground, airfields and gravel pits. In Spain it occupies traditional low-intensity cereal fields. The crested lark has a shorter, weaker song than the thekla lark, and is a ground-dwelling bird, rarely perching on shrubs or walls. This species is largely resident in Europe, but it is possible that juvenile crested larks wander at migration times.

Voice: Song from ground or in flight is loud with fluty whistles and mimicry
Length: 17cm
Wingspan: 29–38cm
Weight: 40–50g
Habitat: Open, dry plains with low vegetation; artificial habitats such as waste ground
Nest: Shallow depression on ground; roughly lined with grass
Eggs: 3–5; off-white, smooth and glossy with fine buff-brown speckles
Food: Seeds, leaves, shoots and roots; some insects

Bulky, skylark-sized bird with long bill, spiky crest, deep chest and upright stance. In flight it looks compact with broad wings and short tail. Adult plumage ground-coloured, sandy-buff on upperparts and underparts. Blackish streaking most obvious on crown, including crest and back, and on chest and flanks. Face strikingly marked with cream supercilium and eyering forming spectacle; also neat black moustachial and malar stripes. Dark tail with buff outer feathers.

Underwing coverts bright orange-buff. Longish dark grey-brown bill. Legs and feet flesh coloured. Juvenile has shorter crest than adult, darker upperparts with white speckling and whiter underparts.

Thekla Lark

Galerida theklae

The thekla lark is difficult to separate from the crested lark where the ranges overlap, but the practised observer will learn to associate it with different habitats

Song is longer and louder than crested lark's, with rich, fluty whistles, but do not rely solely on this for identification

IN EUROPE thekla larks are closely associated with Mediterranean habitats and there is considerable overlap in Spain with their close relatives, crested larks. The thekla lark prefers complex habitats with open soil, trees and bushes, walls, cereal fields and river valleys. It enjoys hilly and rocky locations, especially where habitats have been over-grazed or where farmland has been abandoned. On the Mediterranean islands it is found along the coasts and favours sand dunes. Close attention to plumage details is needed to separate this species from the crested lark.

Voice: Loud, fluty song with whistled notes and mimicry, alarm-call is a repeated fluting whistle
Length: 17cm
Wingspan: 28–32cm
Weight: 25–40g
Habitat: Mediterranean mixed habitats of forest edge, scrub and cultivated plains
Nest: Shallow depression on ground; roughly lined with vegetation
Eggs: 3–4; smooth, glossy, off-white with brown speckling
Food: Insects and seeds

Same size as crested lark but slighter build, shorter bill and fuller fan-shaped crest are all useful identification features. Adult upperparts greyish-brown; underparts show greyer chest and whiter belly. Distinct blackish streaks on crown, whole of neck and back. Rump rufous. Finely streaked throat. Heavy black spotting on greyish-brown chest extends on to flanks. In flight underwing appears dull grey-brown. Bill grey-brown with paler base. Legs and feet flesh-

coloured. Juvenile similar to adult but has shorter crest and upperparts speckled with white; almost inseparable from juvenile crested lark.

Lesser Short-toed Lark

Calandrella rufescens

THE lesser short-toed lark favours much more open, sandy ground than the short-toed lark, but both species breed in the Coto Donaña in southern Spain. They are very similar so identification is tricky. Note the lesser short-toed's prominent wing point, the streaking across the breast and the pale forehead. In spring the jerky, jangling song is an important feature, and the song flight is always low and circular. The species is sedentary.

Voice: Long, continuous and melodious song in flight; quite loud, rippling alarm call
Length: 13–14cm
Wingspan: 24–32cm
Weight: 20–25g
Habitat: Continental steppes and semi-deserts, especially sandy ground with low shrubs
Nest: Shallow scrape on ground, sheltered by tussock and lined with vegetation
Eggs: 3–5; smooth, glossy, variable whitish, yellowish or buff, spotted with brown
Food: Mainly insects in summer; seeds at other times

Very similar to short-toed lark but with more heavily streaked upperparts and chest, long wing point and tiny bill. Adult upperparts rufous-brown with strongly marked blackish feather centres, particularly on crown and mantle. Pale cream supercilia frame brown face and meet across pale forehead. Underparts buff-white with brown wash across chest, and gorget of black streaks, which extend on to flanks. Wings brown with pale feather edgings; three primaries project into point when at rest. Bill pale grey-brown with darker tip. Legs and feet yellowish. Juvenile similar to adult but more speckled.

Short-toed Lark

Calandrella brachydactyla

Regularly encountered in northern Europe as rare passage migrant

Compared to those of the skylark, underparts look clean and unmarked

THE short-toed lark feeds unobtrusively on the ground, often making use of ruts and vegetation to obscure its presence. It can be confused with its close relative, the lesser short-toed lark, but has long tertials that cover the wing point at rest and a cleaner-looking breast. The short-toed lark's song is a plaintive, persistent series of mellow whistles. This species is migratory, overwintering in Africa. During the autumn passage, juvenile birds sometimes exhibit reverse migration and head north instead of south.

Nest: Shallow depression on ground; lined with vegetation, soft seeds and down
Eggs: 3–5; smooth, glossy, whitish, spotted and blotched brown and purple
Food: Insects and seeds in summer; seeds only in winter

Voice: Song from ground or in flight is shrill, jingling and melodious with swallow-like twittering
Length: 13–14cm
Wingspan: 25–30cm
Weight: 20–30g
Habitat: Dry, open steppes on plains and undulating landscapes; often in fields in winter

Smaller and paler than skylark, with compact body, neat finch-like bill and no crest. Adult upperparts sandy-buff, lightly streaked dull brown.

Crown warm rufous-brown. Off-white supercilium contrasts with brown cheeks. Closed wing shows line of blackish-centred coverts with pale buff margins. Pale buff rump contrasts with blackish tail with white edges. Underparts clear white with faint sandy wash across breast and darker brown patches on breast sides. Bill grey-brown with yellow base. Legs and feet brown. Juvenile similar to adult but more obviously speckled on upperparts and has gorget of dark streaks across upper breast.

Calandra Lark

Melanocorypha calandra

THE calandra lark's heavy bill, long legs and bulky body are all helpful in identification. The wings are broad and give the bird a powerful and direct flight action; they are very dark underneath, which is another useful pointer for identification. It sings in flight, whether hovering at a great height like a skylark or simply undertaking a low-level, flapping sortie. This lark is mainly resident in Europe, though the large winter flocks may wander nomadically in search of food, gathering on cultivated land to feed on winter-sown grain.

Voice: Loud, rich fluty song interspersed with grating notes; shrill buzzing contact call
Length: 18–19cm
Wingspan: 34–42cm
Weight: 50–70g
Habitat: Grassland steppes of lowland plains and upland plateaux; in cultivated fields
Nest: Shallow depression on ground under tussock; lined with grass and softer vegetation

Eggs: 4–5; slightly glossy, white, spotted and blotched dark brown and purple
Food: Mainly insects in summer; seeds and shoots in winter

Larger than skylark with broader wings, short tail and heavy bill. Adult has crown, nape, back and wings buff-brown with blackish feather centres forming streaks.

Can run strongly on the ground and will perch prominently on bushes in the open

Warm brown face with creamy supercilium and narrow eyering. Dark brown tail with white outer feathers. Underparts creamy white with blackish patches on sides of breast and warm yellowish wash, spotted black extending down on to flanks. In flight shows white trailing edge to wings and black underwing. Bill grey-brown with dark tip. Legs and feet pale brown. Juvenile similar to adult but more speckled on upperparts and throat and lacking clear blackish patches on breast.

169

Swallow

Hirundo rustica

Juvenile

In September and October swallows gather in their hundreds in preparation for their long migration

Adult male

The mud and straw nest is usually built in recesses inside buildings or under bridges

Long tail streamers and steady, gliding flight make this species easy to identify

T HE swallow is found throughout nearly the whole of Europe, and is absent only from Arctic latitudes, desert regions and the highest mountain areas. It prefers to hawk for insects over old pasture, agricultural crops, along hedges, woodland edge and over water, and is often found in the vicinity of villages, which provide nesting sites in old buildings and wires and roofs on which to perch. The swallow is migratory, overwintering in the southern half of Africa. It is the traditional harbinger of summer, returning by the middle of April and advertising its presence with its pleasant, warbling song.

Voice: Song is a pleasant warble with some rattling notes; alarm call is a loud, short 'chit'
Length: 17–19cm
Wingspan: 32–35cm
Weight: 16–24g
Habitat: Aerial above pasture, open water, villages and farms
Nest: Cup of mud attached to ledge against building; lined with feathers
Eggs: 4–5; elongated, oval, smooth glossy white, lightly speckled with red-brown
Food: Flying insects, particularly flies

Classic swallow shape with small bill and long, forked tail streamers. Adult upperparts and breast band shiny blue-black. Forehead, chin and most of throat above breast band rich rufous-red. Underparts, including underwing coverts and long undertail coverts, buff-white, with black under surfaces of flight feathers and black underside to tail. When spread, tail shows white spots towards the tips of all but outermost feathers, which are elongated into streamers. Female has shorter streamers than male. Bill and feet black. Juvenile similar to adult but has less shiny plumage, paler head, mottled breast band and no real tail streamers.

Red-rumped Swallow

Hirundo daurica

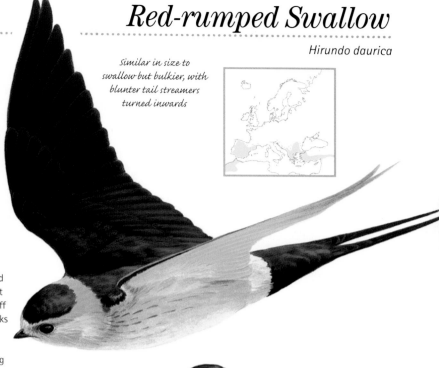

similar in size to swallow but bulkier, with blunter tail streamers turned inwards

THE red-rumped swallow is a very attractive member of the swallow family, but care is required to identify it when seen from a distance. It is structurally similar to the swallow and shares some plumage characteristics and flight behaviour with the house martin. Identification is further complicated by the occurrence of hybrids involving all three species. It enjoys rocky upland habitats, particularly warm gorges where it can hawk for insects above a river in hot, sheltered conditions. It nests in natural crevices and rocky hollows and occasionally on artificial constructions, particularly underneath old stone bridges. The red-rumped swallow is migratory, and overshooting birds are sometimes seen in northwest Europe during spring migration.

Voice: Quiet, twittering, chattering song; short, descending, whistling alarm note
Length: 16–17cm
Wingspan: 32–34cm
Weight: 20–28g
Habitat: Aerial over meadows and pasture, open water and villages; in warm latitudes
Nest: Mud pellets in bowl shape with extended entrance tunnel attached under overhang

Eggs: 4–5; long, smooth, glossy white with some delicate red-brown speckling
Food: Aerial insects; may take prey from ground in bad weather

Sexes similar. Adult has crown, mantle, scapulars and upperwing coverts blue-black, not as shiny as swallow. Wings and tail brown-black, including undertail coverts, which gives effect of whole tail having been dipped in black paint. Broad, pale chestnut band across nape, and chestnut lower back shading to buff rump. Forehead and cheeks speckled rufous-buff. Underparts buff, faintly streaked black. Underwing coverts buff, contrasting with blackish flight feathers. Bill black. Legs and feet brown-black. Juvenile duller than adult, with much shorter tail streamers.

Note rich buff band on nape and mostly rufous face with neat blue-black cap

Crag Martin

Ptyonoprogne rupestris

THE crag martin prefers sheltered valleys, warmed by the southern summer sun. As for most aerial feeders the underlying habitat is not especially important, but the crag martin does hunt low down over fast-flowing water. It has a graceful, slow flight, repeatedly quartering along the same sheltered crag or cliff. This is not a wholly migratory species, which is unusual for a European hirundine. There is altitudinal movement in the winter and some birds stay in southern Europe, particularly in the west. Northern birds generally migrate to north Africa for the winter.

Voice: Quiet, but persistent, guttural twittering song. Short, single-note contact call
Length: 14cm
Wingspan: 32–34cm
Weight: 20–25g
Habitat: Mountainous regions and river valleys and gorges with exposed rock faces; coasts in winter
Nest: Half-cup of mud under overhang or in short tunnel on cliff; lined with feathers
Eggs: 3–5; long, slightly glossy white, delicately

spotted reddish at broad end
Food: Small aerial insects

Heavier and more bulky than sand martin, with broad wings, almost unforked tail and uniform dusky plumage. Adult upperparts dusky brown-grey. Underparts dark buff with smoky tone. Underwing coverts blackish. At close range buff throat is speckled with dark brown. Lateral tail coverts show pale

chevrons. In flight white spots are visible towards tips of tail feathers. Bill black. Legs and feet dark brown. Juvenile similar to adult but has warmer plumage tones, with paler throat.

Unlikely to be confused with any other species in Europe, but at first glance may look like a small swift, especially as it tends to glide in flight; lacks sand martin's brown chest band

House Martin

Delichon urbica

THE house martin's association with human habitats has made its range extensive throughout Europe. It takes its prey of insects aerially, usually at higher altitudes than its relatives, and its habit of foraging high in the sky means that birds go unnoticed except where they actually nest, although in bad weather foraging birds are often forced lower and can be seen hawking for insects over water. House martins nest in loose colonies and, once a building is chosen, many nests are built in the eaves and walls sheltered by the roof. The species is migratory, overwintering in the southern half of Africa.

Summer adult

Flight is a mixture of long gliding bouts and rapidly fluttering wingbeats with sudden swoops and changes of direction

Voice: Soft, sweet twittering song; long, trill alarm call
Length: 12.5cm
Wingspan: 26–29cm
Weight: 16–23g
Habitat: Usually in high air-space above towns, villages and occasionally coastal cliffs
Nest: Half-cup of mud pellets and feathers, attached to vertical surface, usually a building
Eggs: 3–5; smooth, glossy white, occasionally finely marked red-brown
Food: Flying insects

Short and stubby hirundine with large head and noticeably forked short tail. Summer adult has dark blue-black upperparts, except for prominent white rump. Underbody from chin to vent clear white in male, slightly dirty white in female. Dull grey underwing coverts and dusky grey under surfaces to flight and tail feathers. Winter adult has white underparts mottled or smudged with brownish-black, and is less smart. Bill black. Legs feathered white, and feet flesh-pink. Juvenile is duller greyish-black on upperparts than adult, with some white mottling on nape.

Sand Martin

Riparia riparia

THE sand martin is a common bird around bodies of water, particularly if there are nearby sandy banks for its colonial nest tunnels. It will also use artificial nest holes, such as drain pipes in walls, so colonies can be found along city rivers and around coastal harbours. Sand martins are wholly migratory, with the European population overwintering in Africa south of the Sahara. Before departure for the winter quarters large flocks gather over lakes and reservoirs. In early spring the sand martin is often one of the first migrants to return, sometimes being seen in March.

Has rather fluttery flight action

Plumage distinctive when seen well: pattern of clear white underparts separated by brown breast band is diagnostic

Voice: Harsh, twittering, quiet song; harsh, grating, single-syllable contact call
Length: 12cm
Wingspan: 27–29cm
Weight: 10–17g
Habitat: Aerial, in vicinity of sandy banks and near to water
Nest: Excavated hole in river bank or sand-cliff; cup of feathers and grass
Eggs: 4–6; fairly glossy, smooth, white
Food: Small airborne insects and spiders

with light brown smudges on flanks. Rest of underparts white. Underwing dusky brown. Throat often speckled or shaded with brown. Black bill, legs and feet. Juvenile similar to adult but upperparts less uniform with pale fringes to feathers.

Smallest hirundine in Europe, with short, slightly forked tail. Adult has whole of upperparts, including flight and tail feathers, dark greyish-brown, often with sandy tone. Brown extends down onto cheeks and broad band across breast,

Birds are hard to detect against a sandy background, but can often be seen perching on wires, branches or even the ground

Olive-backed Pipit

Anthus hodgsoni

THE olive-backed pipit is an Asiatic species, and it is a rare vagrant to Europe, mostly during late autumn. Although superficially very similar to tree and meadow pipits, identification is easy given reasonably good and prolonged views. The colour of the upperparts and markings and colours on the supercilium and ear coverts are diagnostic. The olive-backed habitually pumps its tail up and down, and will feed in the branches of trees, both of which traits are almost unique to this species. Vagrants to Europe are usually found in grassy areas, often near woodland.

Voice: Call a thin 'tseep'
Length: 14–15cm
Wingspan: 25–26cm
Weight: 20–25g
Habitat: Breeds in taiga forest and boggy woodland; otherwise favours damp, grassy areas
Nest: Does not breed in region
Eggs: Does not breed in region
Food: Mainly insects but also seeds in winter

Small, well-marked bird, superficially similar to tree pipit. Sexes similar. Adult has dull olive-green upperparts with little streaking on mantle and back compared to other pipits; rump unstreaked. Underparts are marked with lines of black spots on breast and flanks; belly and undertail white. Head has broad supercilium, buff in front of eye and white behind eye. Distinctive black and white marks on ear coverts. Legs pink and bill buffish-pink. Juvenile similar to adult but upperparts browner.

ALTHOUGH clearly a pipit, specific identification of this species can be difficult, but its numbers and voice are a help to the observer. Its most usual call is a thin repeated 'tsip' note uttered as the bird escapes in a bounding flight from any disturbance. In the mountains of southern Europe it does not extend to the high altitudes occupied by its relative the water pipit, but in Britain it is an abundant bird on the highest moorlands. Northern and eastern populations are migratory and augment those further west in Europe. Meadow pipits can be seen in winter in southern Europe, when flocks congregate on inland pasture or coastal salt-marshes.

Voice: Flight-song comprises thin whistling calls ending in descending scale; thin quiet 'tsip' call
Length: 14.5cm
Wingspan: 22–25cm
Weight: 14–24g
Habitat: Open, completely vegetated landscapes, particularly grasslands, bogs and tundra
Nest: Cup of grasses, lined with hair concealed under vegetation

Eggs: 3–5; smooth, glossy, variable grey to reddish; spotted, mottled or streaked blackish
Food: Mainly invertebrates; some plant seeds in winter

Adult head, nape, back and wings have variable ground colour of greenish-olive to dark buff-brown, with blackish streaks prominent on crown and back. Mantle sometimes shows pair of indistinct buffish braces. Face shows thin, off-white supercilium. Rump brighter, usually olive-brown, unstreaked. Underparts greyish-white to olive with chest band of narrow blackish spots and streaks extending on to flanks. Bill grey-brown. Legs pinkish-buff. Juvenile has heavier streaking on upperparts than adult, and cleaner, brighter, pale margins to wing feathers; underparts warmer yellowish-olive.

Meadow Pipit

Anthus pratensis

sings in flight and parachutes to earth while delivering a fluty, descending flourish to end the song

Tail dark brown with white edges

THE tree pipit feeds and nests on the ground but requires trees for look-outs and song-posts. It also likes parkland and heathland in the early stages of woodland colonisation and will use young conifer plantations. The tree pipit can be difficult to identify because of its similarity to other pipits; however, its flight song is distinctive – a finch-like chatter as it ascends from its tree-top perch and a series of decelerating piping notes while descending. Tree pipits are wholly migratory, and it is likely that all but the most eastern of Europe's birds move to Africa for the winter; Russian populations probably winter in Asia.

Voice: Loud, rich song starting with rattle, ending in descending piping notes; Loud 'tseeep' call
Length: 15cm
Wingspan: 25–27cm
Weight: 18–28g
Habitat: Mosaic of open grassland or heath and woodland edge or forestry plantations
Nest: On ground; shallow cup of grass, leaves and moss with lining of fine grass and hair
Eggs: 2–6; smooth, glossy, very variable in colour and markings
Food: Insects; some plant material in winter

Smart pipit with clear markings. Adult head, nape, back and wings warm buff-brown with black streaks on back. Face well marked with yellowish supercilium and eyering, and brown eyestripe. Cream margins and tips to blackish-brown wing feathers give closed wing a striking pattern. Rump unstreaked. Tail dark brown with white edges. Chin and throat buffish-white, warmer yellowish on breast and flanks with bold brown-black spotting. Belly and undertail coverts buff-white. Bill dark grey-brown with pale flesh-coloured base. Legs and feet flesh-pink. Juvenile very similar to adult, with buffer ground colour and more streaking.

Tree Pipit

Anthus trivialis

Very clean-looking bird with warm buffish-yellow tones and upright stance

Rock Pipit

Anthus petrosus

Overall dark plumage creates rather dull appearance

Underparts sometimes so heavily streaked that they look as dark as upperparts

THE rock pipit is now treated as the specific coastal replacement of the water pipit; formerly, both were regarded as races of a single species. It is not strikingly patterned, but draws attention to itself by its very bold and noisy behaviour, and can often be seen in open habitats along the shore. Most rock pipits are sedentary, particularly where they breed along ice-free coasts, but some northern populations do move considerable distances. During the breeding season, rock pipits favour cliffs and slopes within sight of the sea, nesting in rock crevices. Outside the breeding season, they favour beaches where small groups hunt for insects and sandhoppers.

Voice: Song is an accelerating series of loud, full, rattling notes; alarm call is a loud, metallic 'tsup'

Length: 16–17cm
Wingspan: 22–27cm
Weight: 22–26g
Habitat: Rocky sea cliffs and also coasts; salt-marshes in winter
Nest: Cup of grasses and seaweed; hidden under overhanging bank in vegetation
Eggs: 4–6; smooth, glossy grey-white, heavily spotted olive-brown
Food: Mainly insects; occasional seeds

Larger and darker than meadow pipit, with strong bill and legs. Adult upperparts dark olive-grey with blackish mottled streaking. Pale-buff supercilium and pale-grey wingbars and tertial edgings relieve rather drab appearance. Tail dark brown with dirty-buff edges. Underparts creamy buff to darkish olive, with variable amounts of streaking across breast and on flanks. Northwestern races so heavily streaked on underbody as to appear fairly uniform on upperparts and underparts. In winter paler birds become much darker with more blackish streaking. Bill dark grey-brown. Legs dull brown-grey. Juvenile similar to adult but appears more mottled.

Water Pipit

Anthus spinoletta

THE water pipit was for long considered the same species as the rock pipit, but recently it has been given its own specific status. It is common in the Pyrenees, the Alps, the Apennines and the higher mountain ranges of central and eastern Europe. In winter it moves altitudinally, occupying lower slopes and valleys, usually in wet and boggy areas. The more eastern breeding birds migrate further, and it is probably these individuals that occasionally overwinter on the coasts and estuaries of western Europe close to rock pipits. Both have strong flight and loud calls, which should aid identification.

In winter, plumage paler and cleaner-looking than rock pipit's; habitat preferences of the two species are generally entirely different

With smart, clean plumage and limited habitat choice, the water pipit is easy to identify in summer

Voice: Melodious, abandoned, twinkling song; contact call is a full, almost grating 'tseep'
Length: 17–18cm
Wingspan: 23–28cm
Weight: 20–28g

Habitat: Montane short grasslands and heaths; lowland wetlands in winter
Nest: Cup of grass and leaves; hidden under overhanging vegetation or bank
Eggs: 4–6; smooth, glossy grey-white, heavily marked brown-grey
Food: Mainly insects; some seeds and other plant material, including algae

Medium-sized pipit, less streaked in summer than other pipits. Summer adult has grey-brown upperparts, brownest on back and closed wing. Prominent double wingbar formed by pale grey margins and tips to wing coverts, and panel caused by pale edgings to tertials gives strong pattern to closed wing. Tail brown-black with outer edges white. Underbody dull white with pinkish wash on breast. Winter adult loses grey cast to upperparts, and pink wash from breast becomes browner with streaked underparts. Bill dark grey-brown. Legs and feet dark brown-grey. Juvenile similar to winter adult but with cleaner appearance.

Red-throated Pipit

Anthus cervinus

THE red-throated pipit chooses open habitats north of the forest belt, preferring willow and birch swamps, where trees are widely spaced. It often creeps slowly through low vegetation, keeping very close to the ground, and can be hard to flush. Probably the best opportunity for seeing it in Europe is during the autumn or spring passage when vagrants appear along coastal migration watch-points south and west of their normal range. They often migrate with flocks of meadow pipits, which provide a useful comparison.

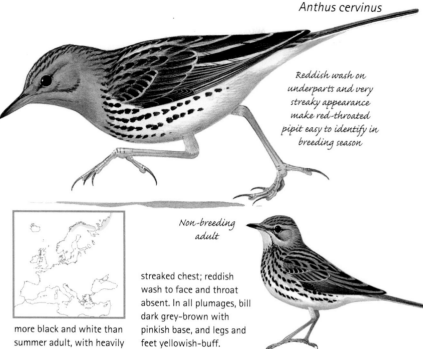

Reddish wash on underparts and very streaky appearance make red-throated pipit easy to identify in breeding season

Voice: Loud twittering and whistling song with bubbling trill; call is a loud, thin, buzzing note
Length: 15cm
Wingspan: 25–27cm
Weight: 17–24g
Habitat: Arctic and sub-Arctic mossy tundra and swamps; muddy grazed pastures in winter
Nest: Mossy hollow under shrub; lined with grass, hair and feathers

Eggs: 5–6; smooth, glossy, variable grey to pinkish-olive with red-brown speckling or blotching
Food: Insects; small water snails; some seeds

Smallish, short-tailed, stripy pipit with markedly different summer and winter plumage. Breeding adult has dark-brown upperparts, heavily streaked with black.

Mantle often shows pale-buff braces. Yellowish-buff margins to blackish wing coverts show as double wingbars. Buff margins to tertials are distinct, contrasting with dark, heavily streaked rump. Tail dark with white edges. Face and chin plain pinkish-buff. Breast and flanks warm reddish-buff; flanks streaked black. Rest of underbody paler buff. Winter adult and juvenile

Non-breeding adult

more black and white than summer adult, with heavily streaked chest; reddish wash to face and throat absent. In all plumages, bill dark grey-brown with pinkish base, and legs and feet yellowish-buff.

Tawny Pipit

Anthus campestris

THE tawny pipit is a bird of warm, dry lowlands, selecting sandy habitats, where it is well camouflaged. It prefers scant vegetation with bare ground in between clumps, so it can run easily when searching for its prey or when avoiding danger. Adult tawny pipits are usually distinctive, with their unstreaked appearance and horizontal running gait reminiscent of a wagtail, but juveniles are more problematic and their streaked appearance allows confusion with some of the rarer members of the family.

Voice: Monotonous song of metallic repeated phrases; alarm call like house sparrow 'cherrup'
Length: 16.5cm
Wingspan: 25–28cm
Weight: 22–28g
Habitat: Sunny, dry, sandy ground with scant vegetation; grasslands and coastal dunes
Nest: On ground, under tussock; cup of grasses and leaves lined with finer material and hair
Eggs: 4–5; smooth, glossy, whitish, heavily marked with purplish-brown blotches
Food: Mainly insects; some seeds in winter

Long, slim pipit, size of yellow wagtail. Adult has crown, mantle, scapulars and rump sandy ochre, mottled

with dark brown on all but rump. Closed wing darker sandy brown with noticeable line of dark spots formed by blackish coverts with pale tips. Tail brown with pale-cream edges. Face pale with long, cream supercilium and narrow, black lores and moustachial stripe. Chest and flanks sandy buff, usually unstreaked; rest of underbody whiter. Longish fine bill, brown with buff-pink base. Spindly legs and feet yellowish with long hind-claw. Juvenile much more streaked than adult, with some streaking on breast.

The largest pipit breeding in Europe, the tawny pipit is found in sandy habitats

Richard's Pipit

Anthus novaeseelandiae

RICHARD'S pipit is recorded as a rare but annual vagrant in most European countries. In Europe, the vagrants invariably favour lush grassland where the height of the vegetation often conceals their presence for much of the time. If alarmed, a bird will sometimes stand upright with head and neck craned upwards and just occasionally it may venture into the open. When seen well, Richard's pipits are comparatively easy to identify. Size alone is a useful pointer, but the birds are similar to juvenile tawny pipits. Choice of habitat, call and hind-claw length are other useful pointers.

Voice: Flight call a loud, sparrow-like 'chrreep'
Length: 18cm
Wingspan: 30–32cm
Weight: 30–35g
Habitat: Grassland
Nest: Does not breed in region
Eggs: Does not breed in region
Food: Insects and other invertebrates

Large pipit with diagnostic long hind-claw. Sexes similar. Adult has brown upperparts well marked with dark streaks. Underparts very pale buff with warm wash and dark streaks on breast. Head has streaked crown, buff lores and broad supercilium,

palest behind eye. Bill proprotionately long and stout; upper mandible dark, lower mandible pink. Legs and feet pink. Juvenile similar to adult

but feathers on back darker but with paler margins giving scaly appearance. Dark streaks on breast extremely prominent. First-autumn birds (those most likely to be seen in Europe) have plumage intermediate between juvenile and adult.

Large, long-legged, long-tailed pipit with extremely long hind-claw

Pied Wagtail

Motacilla alba yarrellii

THE pied wagtail is the British and Irish race of the white wagtail, and the striking plumage, active habits and bounding flight with loud calls all draw attention to it. Separating pied wagtails from other races of white wagtail in anything but adult male plumage can be difficult, and juveniles could be confused with juvenile yellow wagtails of some races. Pied wagtails prefer open areas, except for roosting, when reedbeds are often used. The easy availability of insects around human habitation has enabled this species to live close to people.

Voice: Song is a hurried warbling twitter; main contact call loud 'chissik'
Length: 18cm
Wingspan: 25–30cm
Weight: 17–26g
Habitat: Mainly waterside habitats and bare areas created by human activity
Nest: Cup of twigs and grass lined with moss and hair; in natural or artificial crevice

Eggs: 5–6; smooth, glossy bluish-white, finely speckled grey-brown
Food: Small invertebrates

Adult male in summer has black on crown, nape, chin and upper breast. Back, wings and tail black except for white fringes and tips to wings and white outertail feathers. Adult female in summer similar to male but with greyer back. Black throat absent in non-breeding adults, leaving narrow black breast band. Juvenile recalls non-breeding female but has dusky brown tinge to plumage, and buff fringes to wing feathers.

Differs from white wagtail in having black, not grey, mantle and rump

Resembles slim black and white pipit with fast running action and wagging tail

Adult male in summer

White Wagtail

Motacilla alba alba

AS A BREEDING species, the white wagtail is the most common and widespread wagtail in Europe. In western and southern Europe the species is generally a year-round resident, while in the north and east of its breeding range it is a migrant. Like other wagtails, the white wagtail is constantly active in its search for invertebrate prey. In some plumages, notably juvenile, white wagtails are very difficult to distinguish from pied wagtails. A close look at the lower back and rump, which are always grey in the white wagtail and black in the pied wagtail, is needed for certain identification.

Voice: Song is a twittering warble; call is a shrill 'tchissick'
Length: 18cm
Wingspan: 25–30cm
Weight: 19–27g
Habitat: Farmland, wetlands, open country
Nest: Grass and moss construction placed in holes in walls, ivy-covered banks, buildings, etc
Eggs: 5–6; pale grey with speckles
Food: Invertebrates and seeds

Breeding male has black cap and nape and black throat and upper breast. Back and rump grey, not black as on pied wagtail. Underparts white. Blackish wings show two white wingbars. Tail long and black with white outer feathers; constantly pumped up and down. On non-breeding male black on underparts is confined to upper breast band; plumage somewhat grubby but otherwise similar to breeding male's. Breeding female similar to male, but markings less well defined. In winter loses black cap, and face grubby. Juvenile similar to non-breeding female.

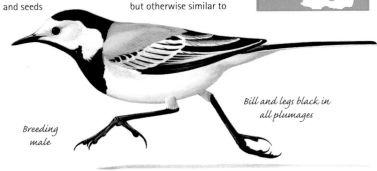

Breeding male

Bill and legs black in all plumages

Grey Wagtail

Motacilla cinerea

THE grey wagtail prefers fast-flowing rivers and streams and is found in upland regions of Europe, where it swoops and darts above streams in short sallies for insects, or stands on a rock in the water with the rear of the body appearing to move up and down with the wagging tail. Grey wagtails usually nest in a waterside crevice, and a dislodged brick under a bridge is a common site; they will also sometimes use other man-made structures. The grey wagtail is partially migratory, with some birds staying throughout the winter, and others moving to more southerly parts of the European range. Northern birds overwinter mostly in Africa.

Long, slim wagtail with a very long black tail with white outer feathers

Voice: Song is a series of shrill elements, getting louder; usual contact call is a shrill 'tchee'
Length: 18–19cm
Wingspan: 25–27cm
Weight: 15–22g
Habitat: Running fresh water, particularly upland streams with rocky margins
Nest: In hole or crevice, usually above water; cup of grass, roots and twigs lined with moss
Eggs: 4–6; smooth, glossy creamy-buff, faintly marked grey
Food: Mainly insects and spiders; some small fish and tadpoles

Adult male has grey upperparts with olive-yellow rump. White supercilium connects white surround to cheek, contrasting with black bib. Closed wing shows yellowish-white fringes to tertials and inner secondaries; main flight feathers blackish. Underbody lemon yellow with greyish flanks. Female and non-breeding male lack summer male's black bib; underparts buffer. Legs and feet flesh-coloured in all birds and bill greyish-black. Juvenile resembles non-breeding adult but with buff fringes to wing feathers.

Adult male in summer

In flight upperwing shows white bar; underwing greyish with white centre

Citrine Wagtail

Motacilla citreola

Adult male

Juvenile

CITRINE wagtails breed sporadically in eastern Finland and occur as rare vagrants to northwest Europe, mainly in September and October as juvenile or first-winter birds. These are similar to white and yellow wagtails: attention should be paid to the broad, pale supercilium, the pale forehead, the absence of dark markings on the chest and the two white wingbars.

Voice: Flight call a sharp 'srreep'
Length: 17–18cm
Wingspan: 24–25cm
Weight: 19–22g
Habitat: Damp grassland and freshwater margins; inundated ground in winter
Nest: Cup-shaped nest constructed on ground and hidden by vegetation
Eggs: 4–6; pale greyish-buff with dark speckling
Food: Mainly insects and other invertebrates

Breeding-plumage male has lemon-yellow head and underparts and black collar. Back grey and wings dark, with two prominent white wingbars. Tail black with white outer feathers. Non-breeding adult male and breeding female have dull yellow face and underparts and grey-brown crown, nape and back; white wingbars less conspicuous than on breeding male. First-winter birds have pale grey upperparts with white supercilium and border to ear coverts and two white wingbars; underparts white. Bill and legs dark in all birds.

Voice: Song is a rhythmic series of twittering notes; usual call is shrill 'pseeep'
Length: 17cm
Wingspan: 23–27cm
Weight: 15–20g
Habitat: Lowland wetlands, particularly water meadows, salt-marshes and dune slacks
Nest: Cup of grass leaves and stems; in shallow scrape on ground
Eggs: 4–6; smooth, glossy buff-white, densely spotted with brown
Food: Small invertebrates

Adult males of the various geographical races separable in breeding plumage (see illustrations below). Females and juveniles duller yellow than males, with more uniform olive-buff plumage tones; geographical races essentially inseparable in field.

Yellow Wagtail

Motacilla flava

THE yellow wagtail is widely distributed across lowland Europe. The species is represented in Europe by a spectrum of different geographical races which are mainly separable in adult male plumages, and are distinct enough to have earned them separate colloquial names. In the breeding season it favours wet meadows with grazing animals and can be found in large numbers where this traditional agricultural management is still practised. Yellow wagtails are migratory and often one of the first species to arrive in Europe in spring. Their distinctive flight call often announces their arrival on coastal marshes in late March or early April.

Adult female

Juveniles are brown above with blackish bib

Adult males of all races have greenish-yellow mantle, greyish-green wings with whitish-yellow fringes to coverts and tertials, and dark greyish tail with outer feathers

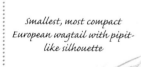

Smallest, most compact European wagtail with pipit-like silhouette

Adult males of race FLAVISSIMA; breeding range confined mainly to Britain

Above: adult male of race FLAVA (so-called blue-headed wagtail) shows blue-grey head, white supercilium and moustache, dark cheeks and yellowish throat; breeds across Central Europe and Scandinavia

Below: adult male of race FELDEGG (so-called black-headed wagtail) shows entirely black head and yellow throat; breeds in south-east Europe and the Balkans

Above: adult male of race THUNBERGI (so-called grey-headed wagtail) shows slate-grey head, dark cheeks, white moustache and yellow throat; breeds in north-east Europe and Russia

Above: adult male of race IBERIAE (so-called Spanish wagtail) shows blue-grey head, white supercilium and throat and black cheeks; breeds on Iberian peninsula

Below: adult male of race CINEREOCAPILLA (so-called ashy-headed wagtail) shows blue-grey head, black cheeks and white throat; breeds in Italy

Waxwing

Bombycilla garrulus

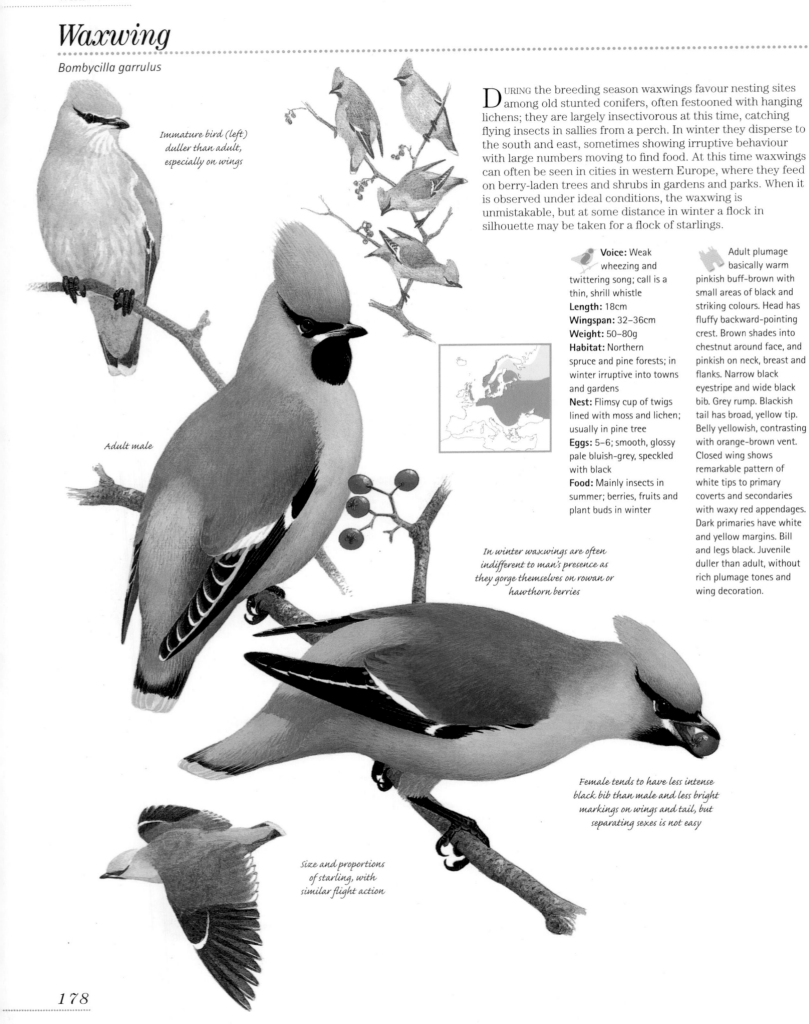

Immature bird (left) duller than adult, especially on wings

Adult male

DURING the breeding season waxwings favour nesting sites among old stunted conifers, often festooned with hanging lichens; they are largely insectivorous at this time, catching flying insects in sallies from a perch. In winter they disperse to the south and east, sometimes showing irruptive behaviour with large numbers moving to find food. At this time waxwings can often be seen in cities in western Europe, where they feed on berry-laden trees and shrubs in gardens and parks. When it is observed under ideal conditions, the waxwing is unmistakable, but at some distance in winter a flock in silhouette may be taken for a flock of starlings.

Voice: Weak wheezing and twittering song; call is a thin, shrill whistle
Length: 18cm
Wingspan: 32–36cm
Weight: 50–80g
Habitat: Northern spruce and pine forests; in winter irruptive into towns and gardens
Nest: Flimsy cup of twigs lined with moss and lichen; usually in pine tree
Eggs: 5–6; smooth, glossy pale bluish-grey, speckled with black
Food: Mainly insects in summer; berries, fruits and plant buds in winter

Adult plumage basically warm pinkish buff-brown with small areas of black and striking colours. Head has fluffy backward-pointing crest. Brown shades into chestnut around face, and pinkish on neck, breast and flanks. Narrow black eyestripe and wide black bib. Grey rump. Blackish tail has broad, yellow tip. Belly yellowish, contrasting with orange-brown vent. Closed wing shows remarkable pattern of white tips to primary coverts and secondaries with waxy red appendages. Dark primaries have white and yellow margins. Bill and legs black. Juvenile duller than adult, without rich plumage tones and wing decoration.

In winter waxwings are often indifferent to man's presence as they gorge themselves on rowan or hawthorn berries

Female tends to have less intense black bib than male and less bright markings on wings and tail, but separating sexes is not easy

Size and proportions of starling, with similar flight action

Dipper
Cinclus cinclus

THE dipper is found erratically throughout the continent, breeding exclusively along fast-flowing streams and rivers. Dippers rear their young in a concealed nest, usually under a river bank. They are often seen perching on rocks in mid-stream, bobbing in characteristic fashion, then suddenly disappearing underwater. They swim and walk along the bottom of the river against the current, foraging and identifying prey by touch. Most European populations are resident, moving to lower valleys in winter, but some northern birds are partial migrants. Eggs are laid at any time between March and June.

Voice: Song is a pleasing rippling warble of mellow whistles; sharp 'tzit' call
Length: 18cm
Wingspan: 26–30cm
Weight: 50–70g
Habitat: Fast-flowing, rocky streams and rivers, usually in mountains; lower altitude in winter
Nest: Dome of moss and grass; in hole or crevice in stream bank
Eggs: 4–5; smooth, glossy white
Food: Large, mainly aquatic invertebrates; some worms and small fish

Adult has dark-brown head and neck. Rest of upperparts, wings and tail very dark slate with blackish feather margins, giving mottled effect. Chin, throat and breast bright white. Rear underparts blackish-brown. Underwing black-brown. Juvenile has all dark-slate upperparts, mottled by black feather margins. Underparts white, heavily mottled, spotted and barred with dusky feather tips. All ages show white eyelid when blinking and black-brown bill and legs.

Continental race

Recalls a small, rotund thrush with short, rounded wings and cocked tail; British race has chestnut patch on anterior margin of dark underparts

Wren
Troglodytes troglodytes

THE wren is usually found in scrub or rank herbage, close to ground level where it forages for insects and spiders, creeping and flitting among the stems. It is often very difficult to locate, as it stays in thick cover, but on occasions it advertises its presence by engaging aggressively with neighbours or even birds of other species. Male birds build a series of nests with which to tempt the female. Once she has chosen the best, the others are left unused. In winter wrens often survive extremely cold nights by roosting communally in tightly packed clumps, either in substantial cracks in tree bark or in nest boxes.

Voice: Powerful, shrill, trilling song; ticking alarm call
Length: 9–10cm
Wingspan: 13–17cm
Weight: 7–12g
Habitat: Wide variety of habitats which offer some cover
Nest: Dome of leaves, grass and moss lined with hair; in crevice usually near ground
Eggs: 5–8; smooth, glossy white, occasionally speckled blackish at broad end
Food: Mainly insects and spiders; occasional fruits and seeds

Adult has rufous-brown upperparts with paler buff-brown underparts, barred all over. Supercilium narrow and creamy, and throat pale buff. Closed wing shows lines of white barring on short, dark primaries. Undertail coverts and flanks also show some buffy-white barring. Bill long, thin and slightly decurved, dark grey-brown with yellowish lower mandible. Legs light brown. Juvenile like adult, but with even warmer brown tones to plumage.

Probably shortest bird in Europe when holding short tail erect

In flight whole appearance is of warm-brown, round, whirring, bee-like bird

Dunnock

Prunella modularis

The lively, warbling song is often delivered from an exposed perch

Can be difficult to identify as it resembles a sparrow but has a warbler's bill

Most accentors are mountain birds, and the dunnock's habitat preferences were probably originally similar – in the Alps it chooses cool, damp coniferous forest with plenty of glades surrounded by scrub. In western Europe it is less fussy and has colonised a wide variety of lowland habitats, including parks and gardens. The dunnock is unobtrusive for much of the year, creeping along close to the ground, twitching its wings and tail nervously. It has a complicated breeding strategy, with a varying number of males and females coming together for mating.

Voice: Song is a weak, truncated warble; call is a sharp 'tzchik'
Length: 14.5cm
Wingspan: 19–21cm
Weight: 15–25g
Habitat: Natural scrub in northern and upland coniferous forest; secondary scrub in western Europe
Nest: Substantial cup of plant material lined with wool, hair and feathers, in bush or hedge
Eggs: 4–6; smooth, glossy blue with reddish spotting
Food: Mainly insects; seeds in winter

Size of house sparrow but slimmer. Adult head, neck, throat and breast slate grey with brown streaks on crown and greyish-white streaks on face. Mantle, scapulars and wing coverts rich brown, streaked with black. Closed wing dark with buff fringes forming wingbar. Rump unstreaked dull brown, tail blackish-brown. Slate-grey of breast shades into brown on flanks, and to whitish-grey on belly. Eye noticeably red-brown. Short, fine bill blackish with pale-brown base. Legs pinkish-brown.

Juvenile like adult but browner, with more streaks on underparts and striking wingbar

Alpine Accentor

Prunella collaris

Bulky passerine recalling small lark

The Alpine accentor is restricted in Europe to the highest mountain ranges of the central continent, preferring exposed but sunny short Alpine grasslands and boulder fields. It feeds and nests on the ground and chooses habitats without any tall vegetation. Alpine accentors often sing from the top of boulders and rocks. In winter they sometimes descend to valleys and lower slopes, often around villages or ski installations, where they can become very tame. In southern Europe birds regularly choose lower, arid habitats in winter.

Voice: Musical chattering warble; ventriloquial rippling call
Length: 18cm
Wingspan: 30–33cm
Weight: 33–43g
Habitat: Montane habitats above tree-line
Nest: In crevice amongst rocks; inner cup of moss and feathers surrounded by grass and stems
Eggs: 3–4; smooth, glossy pale blue
Food: Mainly insects with some spiders, earthworms, snails and plant seeds

Adult head, breast and belly ash-grey with brownish tinge in some lights. Chin whitish with neat black speckling. Mantle grey-brown with heavy black-brown streaking. Rump grey and uppertail coverts rufous, streaked black. Tail dark brown, tipped white. Closed wing patterned with black, white-tipped coverts forming noticeable panel against rufous-edged secondaries and dark primaries. Underwing mottled rufous and grey. Flanks boldly streaked and blotched chestnut. Undertail coverts have black and white arrowhead barring. Bill black with yellow base. Legs red-brown. Juvenile like adult but duller and scaly.

Rufous Bush Robin

Cercotrichas galactotes

THE rufous bush robin is likely to be first seen in flight, when it appears dashing and fluttering like a large warbler. However, when it is seen perched its similarities with chats are obvious; it cocks its long tail over its body, droops its wings and bobs its head. It looks odd in silhouette, with its long legs completing the picture, and is often visible perched on top of a bush delivering its song. On the ground the bird takes large hops, jerking its tail each time. European rufous bush robins are migratory, overwintering in Africa south of the Sahara, and only return to their breeding areas in late May.

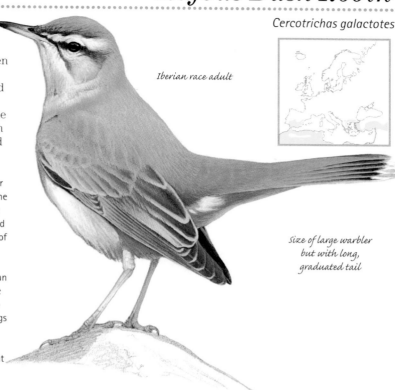

Iberian race adult

Size of large warbler but with long, graduated tail

Voice: Song is a jerky robin-like warble; contact and alarm calls are short 'tsip' notes
Length: 15cm
Wingspan: 22–27cm
Weight: 21–26g
Habitat: Southern steppes with planted scrub; also trees, parks, orange groves and gardens
Nest: In low, thick bush; untidy collection of twigs and grasses lined with hair and feathers

Eggs: 4–5; pale grey, tinged bluish, heavily marked with purplish-brown spots and streaks
Food: Large insects and earthworms; some fruit

Adult Iberian race has rufous-brown upperparts and wings with brighter rump and bright reddish-chestnut tail, tipped black and white. Head shows long, cream supercilium and eyering, brown eyestripe and paler cheeks. On closed wing the pale-tipped coverts show as two wingbars. Chin and throat whitish, with rest of underbody sandy pink, brightest on breast and flanks; southeast European race greyer. All birds have strong bill, which is grey-brown with pale base. Legs and feet brown. Juvenile very similar to adult but has lightly speckled throat and breast.

Robin

Erithacus rubecula

ROBINS choose shady habitats, usually with moist ground in which they can easily forage; they tend to stay away from open, dry and sunny locations. In Britain, in particular, they have become popular because they have adapted to living close to humans in gardens and parks. Robins feed on insects, worms and other invertebrates, and will often accompany gardeners in search of creatures disturbed by their activities. Both adult males and females use song to defend exclusive territories from each other during autumn and winter; the autumn song can sound very melancholy. Juveniles are not so easily identified and care should be taken not to confuse them with other young chats. This species is a partial migrant, with northern populations moving into the southern breeding range for the winter.

The male sings loudly in spring to proclaim his territory and attract a mate; the female chases the male until she is accepted, after which the male feeds her

Juvenile

In the north of their range robins favour coniferous forests, while further south they prefer broad-leaved woodlands or even gardens and parks

Voice: Both sexes sing series of mellow whistled warbles; call is a sharp 'tic'
Length: 14cm
Wingspan: 20–22cm
Weight: 13–23g
Habitat: Shady, undisturbed coniferous and broad-leaved woodland; also gardens and town parks
Nest: In natural or artificial hollow; base of dead leaves, cup of moss, grass and leaves
Eggs: 4–6; white with reddish speckling and spotting giving rusty appearance
Food: Invertebrates, especially beetles; some

fruit and seeds in autumn and winter

Small, round chat with large head. Sexes similar. Adult has olive-brown upperparts. Rump grey-brown with warmer brown uppertail coverts and tail. Often shows short, narrow wingbar formed by buff tips to greater coverts. Orange-red forehead, surround to eye, forecheeks, chin, throat and breast. Brown upperparts separated from orange face and chest by band of soft blue-grey. Flanks warm buff, belly and undertail coverts white. Bill dark brown and legs brown. Juvenile very different from adult, with brown upperparts and buff underparts all copiously spotted with pale buff.

181

Nightingale

Luscinia megarhynchos

IN EUROPE the nightingale is the more westerly counterpart of the thrush nightingale, but prefers warmer climates and is less restricted to lowland valleys near water, often inhabiting dry, sunny hillsides on sandy soils. Woodland scrub is its preferred habitat. Traditional woodland management, where oak standards and hazel coppice are encouraged, has provided one suitable habitat in parts of Europe. It also chooses invasive scrub on chalky hillsides and Alpine meadows, and it is these more open habitats that allow the species to live around the Mediterranean. The nightingale probably has the best-known song of any European bird.

Voice: Beautiful, mellow, musical and varied song, with pure whistles and rattles
Length: 16.5cm
Wingspan: 23–26cm
Weight: 20–28g
Habitat: Scrub in woodland, along rivers or on dry, sunny hillsides

Nest: On or near ground; bulky loose cup of plant material, lined with fine grasses and feathers
Eggs: 4–5; pale blue, finely speckled and mottled red-brown

Food: Mainly terrestrial insects, spiders, woodlice, snails and earthworms; berries in autumn

Adult has fairly uniform russet-brown upperparts with warmer tone to rump and uppertail coverts, and bright chestnut-brown tail with dark central feathers. Head has uniform brown face with buff eyering. Closed wing shows darker-brown centred flight feathers. Underparts are dull cream-white with brownish suffusion across breast and down flanks. Vent and undertail coverts brighter cream-buff. Bill dark grey-brown with pale base. Legs pale brown or flesh. Juvenile is very speckled, but when this plumage is lost, looks like adult with buff tips to wing coverts and tertials.

Juvenile

Confusion with the thrush nightingale is easy when trying to identify this species by sight, but the more russet-toned plumage, brighter tail and cleaner underparts are all useful features

The long, broad tail with its bright chestnut colouring is the most obvious feature as the bird disappears into cover

Thrush Nightingale

Luscinia luscinia

The rich and varied song with solemn, pealing bell-like notes, clipped phrases and rasping notes lacks only the crescendo elements of nightingale's song

The thrush nightingale is wholly migratory in Europe, overwintering in east Africa

THE thrush nightingale and the nightingale are very similar species in Europe and great care is needed in their identification. The thrush nightingale is more definitely a lowland plains species and likes proximity to water. Nesting occurs in deep shade and cover. Identification by sight depends on prolonged views in good light, when plumage tone, the contrast between the warm brown tail and the rest of the upperparts, and the mottled chest are all important features. The songs of the two species are different but care is needed to detect the differences.

Voice: Beautiful, long and varied warble with deep 'tchock' notes and rattles
Length: 16.5cm
Wingspan: 24–27cm
Weight: 25–32g
Habitat: Open woodland and thicket scrub, often along rivers; also orchards and parks
Nest: On ground; loose cup of grass and leaves, lined with hair

Eggs: 4–5; variable buff, olive or greenish-blue with reddish and white marks
Food: Woodland floor invertebrates; fruits and seeds in autumn

Resembles a small thrush. Very difficult to separate from nightingale on sight alone. Adult has dark olivaceous-brown upperparts with warmer brown uppertail coverts and dull rufous-brown tail. Underparts dull whitish-grey with clean throat bordered by brown malar stripe and breast. Chest and flanks mottled dusky brown. Bill dark grey-brown with pale base to lower mandible. Legs brown. Juvenile appears darker, with contrasting pale spots on tips of tertials and wing coverts. Legs pale flesh.

Like nightingale, prefers thick woodland scrub habitat

Bluethroat

Luscinia svecica

I N THE north of its range the bluethroat prefers wooded tundra with marshy glades, often among spruce, willow or juniper for nesting; further south it usually selects thick scrub by water, though in Mediterranean latitudes it lives in broom scrub on open, sunny hillsides. The red-spotted form is the southwestern type from the central continent and Spain, while the white-spotted form extends east. Birds from some mountain ranges in central Spain are unspotted. In autumn, when non-breeding birds can be seen on passage, the skulking behaviour and chestnut patch on the tail usually give away the bird's presence. The majority of European bluethroats overwinter in the African and Asian tropics, but some birds overwinter on the Mediterranean. The northward passage in spring allows observers in Europe to see occasional bluethroats further north and west of their breeding range.

Voice: Song mimics other species in loud, short, warbling phrases; contact call 'chuck'
Length: 14cm
Wingspan: 20–23cm
Weight: 15–25g
Habitat: Moist, wooded tundra with glades and scrub near water
Nest: Concealed amongst thick ground vegetation; cup of plant material lined with hair
Eggs: 5–6; smooth, slightly glossy pale bluish-green, finely marked red-brown, looking rusty
Food: Mainly insects; some seeds and fruits

Adults of both sexes have buffish supercilium bordered by black above and brownish cheeks below. Tail dark brown with orange-chestnut base to outer feathers. Breeding male has metallic blue throat and upper breast with either a reddish or white central spot, depending on race; the spot is sometimes absent in some races. Blue throat is bordered below by narrow black, white and chestnut bands. Underbody off-white with greyish flanks. Non-breeding adult has pale throat and otherwise more subdued colours than breeding male. For description of adult female see caption. Grey-brown bill and ochre-brown legs seen in both sexes. Juvenile spotted with pale buff, assuming female-like plumage in autumn.

Adult male is easily identified in breeding plumage, when male shows distinctive blue throat, mostly with either a red or a white spot

Adult female usually lacks male's throat pattern but has black moustache joining brown-black necklace

Siberian Rubythroat

Luscinia calliope

T HE Siberian rubythroat breeds across northern Siberia between May and August. It occurs as a very rare vagrant to northwest Europe; these records occur mostly in autumn and refer mainly to first-autumn birds. The Siberian rubythroat is generally shy and skulking, in winter as well as summer. It has a remarkable song, however: the rich, tuneful phrasing often includes elements of mimicry of local species. First-autumn birds look superficially similar to thrush nightingales but the striking facial markings on the Siberian rubythroat are diagnostic.

Voice: Calls include a loud whistle and a harsh 'tchak'; song is rich and melodious
Length: 14cm
Wingspan: 23–25cm
Weight: 22–25g
Habitat: Open taiga forest and damp woodland
Nest: Constructed of plant fibres and sited on ground
Eggs: 4–6; pale blue with dark speckling
Food: Mainly insects

Size and shape similar to that of bluethroat; male unmistakable. Adult male has essentially grey-brown plumage, palest on underparts. Head is well marked with pale supercilium, dark lores, white sub-moustachial stripe and ruby-red throat narrowly outlined in black. Adult female lacks male's red throat but plumage otherwise similar. Juvenile plumage mostly brown but with pale spots on upperparts and dark spots on underparts. First-year birds have similar plumage to adult (male and female differences apparent) but usually retain juvenile's pale tips to greater wing coverts. Bill dark and legs pinkish in all birds.

Adult male's plumage is brightest in late spring

Redstart

Phoenicurus phoenicurus

THE redstart requires fairly shady, wooded habitats with old trees, walls or banks to provide nest holes. Regular perches are often used as starting points for fly-catching or ground foraging sorties. The redstart's behaviour accentuates the smart plumage, with prominent perching and shivering of the reddish tail. Migrants are often quite shy and skulking, dashing away into cover, displaying the bright tail as they swoop up to a hidden perch. Females and young birds may be difficult to separate from the black redstart, but the redstart is paler fawn and has a neat, pale eyering. Redstarts migrate to tropical Africa for the winter.

Female (right) duller than male (far right) but retains chestnut tail coloration

Voice: Melancholy song with sweet and rattling phrases; contact call is a soft 'tchuk'
Length: 14cm
Wingspan: 20–24cm
Weight: 11–20g
Habitat: Open, broad-leaved woodland and parkland or heaths, but requires shade
Nest: In tree-hole or nest box; cup of grasses and moss, lined with hair and feathers
Eggs: 5–7; smooth glossy pale blue
Food: Mainly insects; fruit in autumn

Slimmer than robin, with longer wings and tail. Adult male has white forehead and supercilium. Crown and back blue-grey. Wings blackish-brown with buffish fringes and tips to feathers. Rump, uppertail coverts and tail bright chestnut with dark-brown central feathers. Face, throat and upper breast black, contrasting with orange-buff lower breast and flanks. Belly white and undertail coverts orange. Underwing coverts pale chestnut. Female plumage greyish-brown, darker on upperparts than underbody. White throat and eyering; chestnut tail. Bill and legs black in both sexes. Juvenile has tail like adult but rest of plumage speckled buff and brown.

Black Redstart

Phoenicurus ochruros

Female has dull, grey-brown body plumage with orange areas less bright than on male, and buff wing panel

THE black redstart is a common bird throughout much of Europe. Its preferred habitat is open, rocky and craggy terrain, often in mountain regions. However, it has adapted to nesting in holes and crevices on buildings, and so has evolved into more of a village and city bird in some regions of Europe. Females and juveniles require careful separation from common redstarts but always look much more uniformly dusky. The flight silhouette is compact and resembles the robin's. Black redstarts overwinter mainly in the southern part of the breeding range, around the Mediterranean.

Male is blackest on head, back and breast

Voice: Song is a quick, scratchy warble; contact call 'sit'
Length: 14.5cm
Wingspan: 23–26cm
Weight: 14–20g
Habitat: Open, rocky and stony habitats in mountains; also wasteland and buildings in cities
Nest: On ledge or in crevice; loose cup of plant material, lined with hair and feathers
Eggs: 4–6; smooth, glossy, pale blue to white
Food: Invertebrates and fruit

In spring adult male has dusky slate head, back, wing coverts and underparts. Wings brown-black with off-white panel. Centre of belly greyish-white, vent and undertail coverts orange. Rump and tail are chestnut with central tail feathers and tips dark brown. After fresh moult in autumn, plumage colours are muted by pale feather edgings, and wing panel is brighter white. For description of female see caption. Bill and legs black in both sexes. Juvenile resembles speckled female.

Red-Flanked Bluetail

Tarsiger cyanurus

Adult male

THE breeding range of the red-flanked bluetail extends across northern Eurasia, reaching into Finland in the west. First-autumn birds also occur as rare vagrants to northwest Europe. An adult male is unmistakable but all birds can be recognised easily by the combination of orange-red flanks, blue tail and white throat. The birds stand with an upright posture on the ground but will happily forage among leaves and branches too. Birds tend to bob up and down while spreading or flicking the tail.

Voice: Calls include a soft 'hueet'; male has high-pitched, whistling song, recalling that of redstart
Length: 14cm
Wingspan: 22–24cm
Weight: 12–14g
Habitat: Breeds in northern taiga forest and upland coniferous and mixed forests; wooded areas in winter
Nest: Mossy, cup-shaped nest constructed on ground or among tree roots
Eggs: 5–7; white
Food: Mainly insects and other invertebrates but also some fruit in autumn and winter

Adult male has dark-blue upperparts including tail and pale underparts, pure white only on throat; flanks are washed with orange-red. Adult female has blue tail but otherwise brown upperparts. Underparts pale; whitest on throat and with orange-red wash to flanks. Eye has white eyering. Juvenile similar to adult female but with pale spots on upperparts and dark bars on underparts. First-autumn male and female similar to adult female. Legs dark and bill dark and stubby in all birds.

Siberian Stonechat

Saxicola maura
(formerly comprised
Saxicola torquata maura,
S. t. variegata and
S. t. armenica)

*Adult
male*

FROM a distance an adult male Siberian stonechat can look entirely black and white, especially in flight. Female and immature birds are very similar to corresponding plumages of stonechat but much paler overall. Siberian stonechats occur as rare but regular vagrants to Europe, mostly in late autumn after stormy weather; there are also a few spring records of adult males.

Voice: Calls include a harsh 'tchack'; male's song comprises a rapid warbling
Length: 12.5cm
Wingspan: 18–20cm
Weight: 13–15g
Habitat: Breeds on marshes and wetlands; vagrants usually on rough ground
Nest: Does not breed in region
Eggs: Does not breed in region
Food: Mainly insects and other invertebrates

Male's underparts white, extending as half-collar on to sides of neck (collar more extensive than in stonechat); shows orange-red flush to breast. Very similar to stonechat and still considered by some authorities to be a race of this species. Adult male has black head and upperparts except for pure white, unstreaked rump and white wing panel. Adult female and immature birds have buffish-brown upperparts, darkest on cap and back. Throat white and underparts pale with dull-orange wash to breast and flanks. Rump appears very pale, and has pale supercilium, white wingbar and white panel on secondaries.

Whinchat

Saxicola rubetra

THE whinchat occurs most widely to the north and east of its close family relative, the stonechat. A bird of the open country, it is found in tall grass, bracken or annual herbs, often on dry, stony ground. Confusion with identification can arise between the juveniles of this species and the stonechat, because young whinchats do not display a lot of the adult plumage characteristics. The buff supercilium, usually present behind the eye, buff fringes to upperparts and pale underparts are useful pointers. Whinchats migrate to Africa, south of the Sahara, for the winter.

Both sexes show distinctive white supercilium, but female (left) lacks black face mask of male (right)

Voice: Song is a long series of short units, varied with fluty and scratchy phrases; call is a harsh 'tzec'
Length: 12.5cm
Wingspan: 21–24cm
Weight: 14–22g
Habitat: Open grassland and scrub, particularly hay meadows; bracken on hills
Nest: On ground; cup of leaves and grasses, lined with fine stems, hair and moss
Eggs: 4–7; smooth, glossy pale blue, finely speckled red-brown
Food: Mainly invertebrates; some seeds

Smaller than robin. Adult male has black-brown head with long, broad, white supercilium reaching nape, and similar white border to cheek, upturned at rear. Back dark brown with heavy blackish streaking. Rump paler with rufous tinge. Wing coverts black with bold, white bar extending on to tertials. Flight feathers brown-black with white bases to outer primaries. Tail black with white sides to base. Underbody uniform warm orange. Adult female similarly patterned to male but duller. Bill and legs black in both sexes. Juvenile recalls female but not as distinct; has buff underparts and no clear pattern to face.

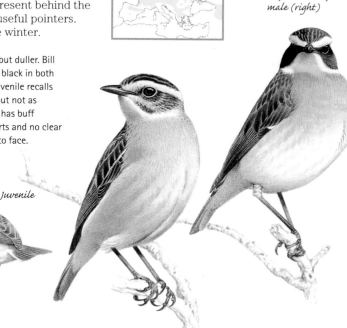

Juvenile

Stonechat

Saxicola torquata

THE stonechat requires substantial vegetation cover, so shuns bare areas and steppes that have only extensive grass cover. Where it does occur the stonechat will tolerate many different habitats, often on the edge of agriculture where there are scattered scrub, fences and walls. Stonechats are resident over much of their European range, but the most northern and eastern populations escape the cold by moving south within Europe.

smaller than robin, with shorter, more rounded wings than whinchat

Voice: Shrill and fairly monotonous series of short, scratchy and whistled phrases; call is a harsh 'tchack'
Length: 12.5cm
Wingspan: 18–21cm
Weight: 13–18g
Habitat: Dry, scrubby areas, particularly heaths and sand dunes; also young conifer plantations
Nest: Loose cup of dry stems and leaves lined with hair, feathers and wool; hidden near ground
Eggs: 4–6; smooth, glossy pale blue to greenish-blue, variably marked reddish
Food: Mainly invertebrates but can take tiny lizards; seeds in autumn and winter

Adult male has dark-brown head and throat, with isolated white patches on sides of neck. Mantle and scapulars evenly dark brown. White rump streaked blackish. Closed wing shows white panel on coverts. Breast and flanks orange, shading to greyish-white on centre of belly and undertail coverts. Underwing dark. Adult female upperparts mottled brownish, and white areas replaced by buff. Juvenile greyer and heavily spotted, resembling bright but uniform buffish female by first autumn.

Bill and legs of both sexes dark grey-brown

Female

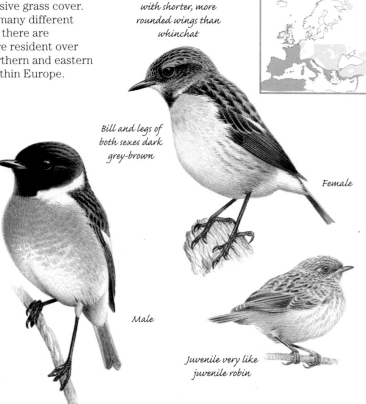

Male

Juvenile very like juvenile robin

Northern Wheatear

Oenanthe oenanthe

Male (right) easily identified; female (far right) and first-winter birds similar to other wheatears

Autumn male (below left) loses his striking spring markings; juvenile (below right) resembles female

THE northern wheatear is the most widespread and best-known species of wheatear. This bouncy, ground-loving bird is found in a variety of open habitats from the Arctic to the Mediterranean, from sea level to over 3,000m. It overwinters in Africa, and is often the first song-bird to arrive in northwest Europe in spring, commonly appearing in March. Autumn migration is protracted, from August to October. In its breeding territory the male northern wheatear is a conspicuous bird on lowland grassland, but is well camouflaged among the rocks of hillsides. The northern wheatear is solitary on its breeding grounds but forms small flocks at coastal stop-overs on migration. It is a wary bird; when disturbed it bobs its whole body, and if pressed dashes away low, showing its striking tail pattern.

Voice: Song is an energetic, short warble; call is 'chak'; alarm call is 'weet-chak, chak'
Length: 14.5–15.5cm
Wingspan: 26–32cm
Weight: 22–28g
Habitat: Open, very diverse habitats; Arctic tundra, sand dunes, cliff-tops, moors, mountains
Nest: In hole in rock or wall, or rabbit burrow; loose cup of grass and moss, lined with grass and wool
Eggs: 5–6; very pale blue, unmarked

Food: Mainly insects; also spiders, snails and earthworms; berries in autumn

Adult male has diagnostic grey crown and back, white supercilium, black mask through eye widening over cheek, and black wings; chin to breast pink-buff, rest of underparts white. Rump, uppertail coverts and tail white, the last with tip marked by broad, black upside-down 'T'. Adult female similarly patterned but wings, crown, cheek patch and back all brown-toned. Underparts usually buffer. Juvenile has dark upperparts with scaly appearance, and pale underparts with darker crescent-shaped markings. In many plumages similar to other wheatears; identification is best done by noting tail pattern and length, face pattern and colour tones of body plumage. This is the only wheatear breeding in north and northwest Europe.

Isabelline Wheatear

Oenanthe isabellina

The isabelline wheatear's stance is more upright than that of other wheatears, its long legs making it look as if it is on stilts

IDENTIFICATION of this pale wheatear, which lacks a clear plumage pattern, is difficult. These subtle differences from other wheatear species should be noted: longer bill; rather shorter, broader tail with wider black tail band and shorter vertical bar; limited face pattern; larger wing and tail area with a more powerful and less flitting flight action; and it glides well. The male's territorial song differs from all other wheatears'; it is loud and amazingly rich in mimicry of other birds and sounds, so the bird has been called 'the nightingale of the desert'. It feeds by making quick dashes along the ground after its prey.

Voice: Song is loud and mimetic, unlike other wheatears; call is 'tchok', 'click' and 'dweet'
Length: 16.5cm
Wingspan: 27–31cm
Weight: 25–32g
Habitat: Bare hillsides and dry plains, all with sparse vegetation
Nest: Among stones, in holes or burrows; cup of plant materials, with softer lining

Eggs: 4–5; pale blue, with reddish-brown speckles mostly at larger end
Food: Invertebrates, especially ants and beetles

Largest and palest wheatear in the region. Sexes similar. Less contrast between upperparts and underparts than in other wheatears. Generally pale sandy brown above and buffish-white below, with brown wings showing broad creamy fringes to coverts and secondaries. Dirty-white supercilium, black lores and eyes. Tail white with broad, black terminal band and less noticeable vertical bar. Bill and legs long and black. Hard to distinguish from some female wheatears. Juvenile paler than adult but otherwise similar.

Desert Wheatear

Oenanthe deserti

DESERT wheatears breed in a narrow band through North Africa, locally in the Middle East and more extensively in western central Asia. They occur as rare but regular vagrants to Europe, perhaps most regularly in southeast Europe but appearing almost annually in the northwest. Most birds have been recorded in late autumn or early winter. The desert wheatear is an active feeder, generally using low perches such as rocks or bushes, to scan for insects.

Voice: Alarm call a sharp 'chek'
Length: 14–15cm
Wingspan: 25–27cm
Weight: 20–22g
Habitat: Arid steppe and semi-desert
Nest: Does not breed in region
Eggs: Does not breed in region
Food: Mainly insects and other invertebrates

All-black tail is diagnostic in all birds. Male is superficially similar to male black-throated race of black-eared wheatear. Adult male has striking black face and throat continuous with black wings. Other elements of plumage pale sandy brown except for white rump and hint of pale supercilium. First-winter male has plumage pattern similar to that of adult male but pale feather margins make contrast between pale and dark elements of plumage far less striking. Adult female has essentially sandy-brown plumage, palest on throat and belly and warmest on breast. Rump white and tail black as in male. Juvenile birds and immature females resemble adult female. Bill and legs black in all birds.

Pied Wheatear
Oenanthe pleschanka

Cyprus Pied Wheatear
Oenanthe cypriaca

A T THE western edge of its range, the pied wheatear has a toe-hold in Europe, having bred in Turkey and the former Yugoslavia and nesting on a regular, if local, basis in Bulgaria. It occurs in small numbers on migration in the eastern Mediterranean, and as a rare vagrant further north and west. Unfortunately most of these extralimital records refer to first-autumn birds, which are easily confused with immature northern wheatears. The species overwinters in east Africa.

Voice: Calls include a sharp 'tchek'; song includes rattling, buzzing and warbling phrases
Length: 14–15cm
Wingspan: 26–27cm
Weight: 18–20g
Habitat: Stony hillsides and broken ground
Nest: Grassy nest constucted in hole or under boulder
Eggs: 4–5; pale blue
Food: Mainly insects and other invertebrates

Adult male has black face and throat linked by black feathering to black wings. Crown, nape and underparts essentially white. Superficially similar to black-throated form of black-eared wheatear. Tail pattern also similar to that of black-eared wheatear: white with black central feathers and trailing edge. Males in autumn and winter have pale-brown feather edges and so white elements of plumage look buff and black elements look greyish. Adult female has dark grey-brown head, throat and upperparts; underparts grubby white. During winter months pale feather margins reduce contrast in plumage. Bill and legs dark in all birds.

S OME authorities believe the Cyprus pied wheatear to be a race of the widespread Asian species, known simply as the pied wheatear. Because it occurs on an island where the only other wheatears are migrants or overwintering species, identification of the species in summer should present few problems, especially as it is so numerous. This species is migratory, with birds overwintering in northeast Africa, and returning to Cyprus from late March.

Voice: Song is a continuous series of buzzing, sawing notes; various clicking calls
Length: 14cm
Wingspan: 23–25cm
Weight: 15–20g
Habitat: Open, stony, arid areas and fallow fields
Nest: In hole in bank or under rock; grass cup lined with wool or hair
Eggs: 4–6; smooth, glossy pale bluish-green, spotted and speckled red-brown
Food: Mainly insects, with some worms and snails; berries in autumn

Adult male has white crown and nape. Face, chin to upper breast, neck, back and wings black. Rump and uppertail coverts white. Tail white with black central feathers; all feathers black-tipped. Underparts from lower breast to undertail coverts black and flight feathers dusky. After autumn moult, plumage is browner with little contrast; breeding plumage acquired by wear. Female resembles dull male with dark olive-brown crown contrasting with pale-buff supercilium and nape. Juvenile dark with pale-spotted upperparts.

Black-eared Wheatear
Oenanthe hispanica

Male of black-throated race (left); both races have black face and wings and white rump

T HE adult male black-eared wheatear is one of the smartest passerines in Europe; females and juveniles are not so easy to identify and can resemble other wheatears. The pale-throated race, *O. h. hispanica*, occurs in the west of the range while the black-throated race, *O. h. melanoleuca*, is found in the eastern Mediterranean. The whole European population overwinters across northern tropical Africa.

Voice: Song is a rich warble interspersed with scratchy, buzzing phrases
Length: 14.5cm
Wingspan: 25–27cm
Weight: 15–20g
Habitat: Warm Mediterranean and steppe open habitats with dry stony ground
Nest: Cup of grass and moss, lined with hair; on ground under rock or bush
Eggs: 4–5; smooth, glossy pale blue, finely marked red-brown at broad end
Food: Mainly insects; some snails and berries, particularly in autumn

Males of both black- and pale-throated forms have sandy-buff crown, nape, mantle and underbody. Tail white with black inverted 'T' caused by black central feathers and narrow black tips. Forehead and supercilium creamy white. Throat either black or sandy as underbody. Underwing coverts black, contrasting with grey flight feathers. In autumn fresh buff feather margins reduce contrast between black and sandy plumage. Females of both races recall male but lack strong head pattern. Bill and legs black in both sexes. Juvenile resembles female but has buff spotted underparts and scaly, brown breast.

Pale-throated male

Black Wheatear
Oenanthe leucura

T HE black wheatear is generally a sedentary bird. It is less solitary than most other wheatears, and three to five commonly feed together. They are territorial, probably pair for life and, although shy and wary, are actually more approachable in the breeding season, from mid-March in southern Spain. The black wheatear's nest is a remarkable construction: it has to be in a hole big enough to contain a foundation of stones built by both male and female. Favourite sites are used for several years; one was recorded to contain around 9,300 stones and covered 2sq m of a cave floor.

Voice: Call is a distinctive 'pee-pee-pee'; song is a quiet mixture of warbles and chatter
Length: 18cm
Wingspan: 26–29cm
Weight: 38–42g
Habitat: Gorges and rock-strewn places, quarries and screes
Nest: In a hole; bulky cup of grass and leaves, lined with wool and feathers
Eggs: 3–6; very pale blue, sparsely spotted reddish-brown at larger end
Food: Mainly insects, up to size of beetles as long as itself

Male black except for white rump and tail coverts, white tail with end marked by upside-down 'T', the end bar being narrower than the northern wheatear's. Black underwings contrast with greyish-white in fringes of flight feathers. Female separable at close range; more sooty brown than black, especially on face and underparts when feathers are worn. Bill and legs black in both sexes. Juvenile similar to female.

The males are easily spotted from February onwards, when they perform the song-flight, rising up like a pipit and singing a more melodious song than most wheatears before gliding to a perch

Comparing Immature Wheatears

WHILE adult wheatears in spring usually present few problems to the observer, the identification of immature wheatears in autumn is fraught with difficulties. Migrant birds are often seen out of range and normal habitat and so close attention must be paid to subtle plumage differences and the pattern of markings on the tail and rump.

First-autumn bird

NORTHERN WHEATEAR (Adult female for comparison): similar to juvenile but plumage generally greyer on upperparts; shows more striking eyestripe and supercilium

Adult female

First-winter male

NORTHERN WHEATEAR (first autumn): Plumage generally sandy brown, palest on underparts and showing orange-buff flush to throat and upper breast; tail and rump markings as adult – white rump and upper tail with black terminal band and central feathers forming inverted 'T'

BLACK-EARED WHEATEAR: Overall plumage colour is sandy brown but shows facial mask, and wings always appear dark and well-defined; pattern on rump and tail as adult – dark terminal band on tail much narrower than on northern wheatear

First-winter bird

ISABELLINE WHEATEAR: Always difficult to distinguish from immature northern wheatear but is larger and longer-legged with more upright posture, and contrast between sandy body plumage and darker wings never as striking; lacks that species' warm-toned flush to throat and upper breast; broader black terminal band on tail

First-winter bird

First-winter bird

DESERT WHEATEAR: Plumage looks rather sandy grey except for suggestion of adult male's black plumage pattern on throat and pale supercilium; despite pale feather tips wings appear dark; pattern of white rump and entirely black tail diagnostic and identical to that of adult

PIED WHEATEAR: Upperparts and throat look dark olive-brown while underparts are warm orange-buff; shows buffish supercilium and tail and rump pattern as adult – 'T'-shaped black marking on otherwise white tail, but terminal band not as broad as on northern wheatear

Rock Thrush

Monticola saxatilis

Breeding male

Voice: Song is a mellow, flute-like warble; call is 'chack, chack'
Length: 18.5cm
Wingspan: 33–37cm
Weight: 48–58g
Habitat: Sunny, dry, stony terraces with scattered trees
Nest: In a hole under rocks or in wall; cup of plant material, lined with finer grass
Eggs: 4–5; pale blue, usually unmarked
Food: Mostly large insects, especially beetles, grasshoppers and caterpillars

THE rock thrush is a very shy and solitary bird in its breeding grounds, seeking cover among the rocks when disturbed – it is more likely to be heard than seen. The male's fluting, melodious song is often given in flight; he sings as he ascends, then suddenly plummets and rises again singing, finally coming to perch using a 'parachute-descent' with wings and tail outspread. All males are mimics and song-flights always include an imitation of the chaffinch's song. The rock thrush ranges widely in search of food in the breeding season, often coming down to hayfields and farmland. The species overwinters in sub-Saharan Africa.

Adult summer male unmistakable, with slate-blue head and throat, white back, blue rump and brownish-black wings. Uppertail coverts, tail, underparts and underwing orange; striking in flight. In winter male appears more scaly owing to pale feather fringes. Adult female resembles non-breeding male but lacks blue in plumage. Head, throat and back mottled brown and buff. Lacks male's white patch on back. Underparts buff with brown, crescent-shaped markings. Tail orange. Bill and legs of both sexes dark brown. Juvenile similar to female but even more strongly marked.

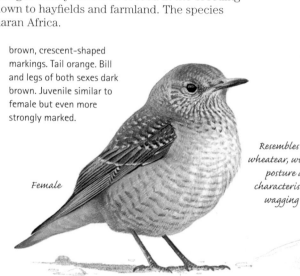

Female

Resembles large wheatear, with erect posture and characteristically wagging tail

Blue Rock Thrush

Monticola solitarius

Larger than any wheatear and nearly as big as a redwing, but stockily built

Adult male

Adult female

Voice: Call and alarm deep 'tak, tak'; song loud and melodious, of simple phrases
Length: 20cm
Wingspan: 33–37cm
Weight: 50–60g
Habitat: Rocky coastlines, rocky mountain valleys, big buildings
Nest: Loosely made cup of grass and moss, lined with finer material in a hollow in rocks
Eggs: 4–5; very pale blue, usually unmarked
Food: Mainly invertebrates; also lizards, small snakes, seeds and fruits in autumn

SOME European blue rock thrushes are resident; most are migrants, or at least disperse from their breeding grounds in winter. They are territorial and shy, and may be best observed when the male is singing. The usual song period is from March to May, but some song may be heard through the summer. The male sings mostly in the mornings and evenings; he characteristically performs in flight with spread wings and tail, moving from one exposed perch to another in the morning, and from a solitary perch in the evenings. On the perch he flicks his wings as he sings, in the manner of a starling.

Adult male is the only all-blue songbird in the region. Plumage mostly dull slate-blue but with black tone on wings and tail. Whole bird looks black in poor light. Female dark grey-brown, with no blue tone; sides of head and throat spotted brown, rest of underparts covered with scaly, buff markings. Bill dark grey-brown and legs black in both sexes. Juveniles similar to female.

Blackbird

Turdus merula

Female is much darker than song thrush

Male's song is delivered from exposed perch

Juvenile more spotted than female

Adult male unlikely to be confused with any other bird

T HE blackbird is basically a woodland bird but inhabits many places, from wooded mountain sides to city centres. Northern populations are migrants, moving to the south and west of the breeding range; others are resident. The blackbird does not suffer as badly in cold winters as other thrushes. It hunts in leaf litter, flicking material aside with its bill or scratching like a hen to seek invertebrates. It also forages in meadows and lawns for worms, which it can find at the rate of one or two a minute. It can even dig through 5 to 7cm of snow. The blackbird commonly rears two to three broods a year.

but also on moors and in towns
Nest: Stoutly built cup of grass and leaves, lined with mud, then with finer grass
Eggs: 4–5; light blue, usually profusely speckled and mottled reddish-brown
Food: Insects, earthworms; wild fruits in autumn and winter

Voice: Call sounds like 'see'; alarm is a shrill chatter; song is a variety of flute-like, musical phrases
Length: 24–25cm
Wingspan: 34–38.5cm
Weight: 95–110g
Habitat: In most places where trees are present,

Male is only small all-black bird in Europe with bright golden-yellow bill and long, broad tail. Black is glossy but not iridescent. Orange-yellow eyelids form an eyering. Legs dark brown. Immature male's bill is dark grey-brown, turning golden through the first winter, and plumage is dull black. Female head and body dark brown. Underparts often have rufous tone and dark thrush-like mottling on breast; some birds more marked than others. Legs dark brown and in parts of northwest bill dark but yellow at base of lower mandible. Juvenile like female, but more rufous and more spotted below.

Ring Ouzel

Turdus torquatus

T HE ring ouzel has a somewhat restricted breeding range in Europe, preferring wild and remote upland areas for nesting. Ring ouzels arrive on breeding territory early in the season, and are often present by mid-April. They leave again by August and September, most European birds overwintering around the Mediterranean region, with a few crossing to north Africa. During the winter months they favour open, stony slopes, reminiscent of their breeding habitat. Ring ouzels can be difficult to see. If undisturbed, males will sit out on rocks and sing, but if alarmed they skulk.

Female

Voice: Song rich and fluty; chattering alarm call
Length: 24cm
Wingspan: 38–42cm
Weight: 95–130g
Habitat: Mountains and moorland; winters on Mediterranean slopes
Nest: Woven grass and leaves among boulders
Eggs: 4–5; dark speckled on bluish-green background
Food: Mainly invertebrates; berries and fruit in autumn

Male has blackish plumage with pale fringes to feathers on wings and underparts. Conspicuous white crescent on breast is diagnostic. Legs dark flesh in colour, and bill yellow with black tip. Female has brownish plumage, with more noticeable pale fringes to feathering giving scaly appearance. Pale crescent of female has dark feather edging. Juvenile is similar to female but crescent band is usually faint. In flight wings of both sexes show pale upperwing panel.

Bright white breast crescent and yellow bill obvious on adult male

Flight pattern recalls that of other thrushes, although it is noticeably deep-winged and powerful

Song Thrush

Turdus philomelos

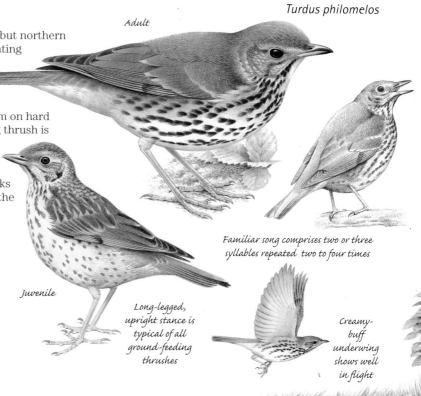

Adult

Voice: Call 'tsip'; alarm rattle 'tic-tic-tic'; song loud, repetitive, musical
Length: 23cm
Wingspan: 33–36cm
Weight: 65–85g
Habitat: Parks, woods, hedges, even in towns and cities
Nest: Well-shaped cup of grass, with unique, smooth inner lining of wood pulp or mud
Eggs: 4–6; bright, light blue, sparingly spotted with black
Food: Wide variety of invertebrates; snails; fruit in autumn and winter

MANY song thrush populations are resident, but northern birds are migratory, with more birds migrating in bad weather. The song thrush is found wherever grassland and nearby trees and bushes provide a plentiful supply of invertebrate food. It has a characteristic way of eating snails, beating them on hard ground or a stone to break the shells. The song thrush is more solitary and shy than other thrushes. Its song is a succession of musical phrases, each phrase repeated from two to four times; the song period often begins in November, but peaks in March and April. Most song is performed in the early morning and late evening.

Sexes similar. Adults have warm-brown upperparts. Rump and uppertail coverts more olive, crown and tail with a rufous tone. Indistinctly marked face has whitish eyering, pale-cream moustachial stripe and blackish-brown streak from base of bill, which contrasts with white throat. Underparts white with golden-brown wash on sides of breast and flanks, breast marked with blackish-brown spots that fade out on belly; spots arranged more in streaks than random spots of mistle thrush. Underwing coverts and axillaries golden-buff. Bill blackish-brown; legs pale flesh. Juvenile similar to adult but with pale streaks on back.

Familiar song comprises two or three syllables repeated two to four times

Juvenile

Long-legged, upright stance is typical of all ground-feeding thrushes

Creamy-buff underwing shows well in flight

Mistle Thrush

Turdus viscivorus

Gleaming white underwing obvious in flight

Voice: Call harsh, distinctive rattle; song loud, short, fluty phrases
Length: 27cm
Wingspan: 42–47.5cm
Weight: 100–130g
Habitat: Orchards, woods, farmland, parks and gardens
Nest: Bulky cup of plant materials, lined with fine grass, in a tree-fork
Eggs: 4–5; pale blue or pale greenish, with reddish and purplish blotches
Food: Wide variety of invertebrates; berries in autumn and winter

Sexes similar. Adult recalls song thrush but is larger, with whitish underparts covered with large, wedge-shaped black spots; flanks and breast marked with buff. Upperparts and wings greyish-brown with conspicuous greyish-white fringes to tertials and wing coverts. Tail grey-brown with diagnostic white tips to outer feathers noticeable when bird flies away. White underwing striking in distinctive, powerful flight; it closes its wings after each burst of wingbeats but the flight path is still direct, not undulating. Upright stance on ground emphasised by long tail. Juvenile similar to adult but spotted white on head, mantle and wing coverts.

THE mistle thrush breeds widely across the region, but is comparatively scarce in Norway and southeast Europe. Birds in the south of the range are mostly sedentary but northern and eastern populations move south and west in the winter months. They form small flocks in late summer, prior to dispersal, many becoming nomadic rather than migratory. The mistle thrush tends to sing from a high, bare bough even in wild weather in December or January. The song is a wilder version of the blackbird's, and distinct from the song thrush's. Mistle thrushes vigorously defend large breeding territories.

Juvenile shows white spotting on back and wings

Overall appearance very grey when compared to song thrush

Fieldfare

Turdus pilaris

THE fieldfare breeds widely and commonly across northern Europe. Northern and eastern populations are migratory, although birds reach southern Europe only in the hardest winters. Research has shown that emigration from Scandinavia is linked to the success or failure of the rowan crop. In winter large, roving flocks feed on open ground or in fruiting hedgerows and trees, and many hundreds roost together. The fieldfare breeds most commonly in colonies of up to 40 to 50 pairs; all feeding by the colony is done on neutral ground away from the nest site. It is a noisy, aggressive bird at nest sites and in defence of a winter food source.

Combination of white underwing, grey rump and black tail diagnostic

Large thrush with unmistakable plumage pattern

On ground shows upright stance and hopping run typical of all thrushes

Voice: Call 'tchak, tchak'; song weak warble with some wheezes and chuckles
Length: 25.5cm
Wingspan: 39–42cm
Weight: 90–110g
Habitat: Open woodland, and beyond tree-line, gardens and parks
Nest: Bulky cup of plant materials, lined with mud, then grass, in a tree or on the ground; open ground or hedgerows in winter
Eggs: 5–6, very variable; basically light blue with brown markings

Food: Wide variety of invertebrates; fruits in autumn and winter

Adults of both sexes have slate-grey head, nape and rump contrasting with chestnut back and black tail. Throat and breast golden-brown, streaked black. Bill yellow on breeding male; has dusky tip and culmen in winter male, females in all plumages and juveniles. Juvenile plumage recalls mistle thrush but shows pale streaks on back.

Redwing

Turdus iliacus

THE redwing is the smallest of the common European thrushes. The species is mostly migratory, many millions of birds moving to western and southern Europe for the winter. In hard weather it gets driven into city parks and gardens, and may suffer mass mortality. Redwings are usually first noticed in northwest Europe in early October. They migrate at night in loose flocks, often with other thrushes, their quiet but penetrating calls keeping the flock together. In winter, redwings roost together in flocks of several hundred in shrubberies and evergreens. When disturbed a flock will fly to the tops of the nearest trees.

Adult upperparts uniformly dark warm brown, darkest on flight feathers

In flight, tawny-red underwing is best identifier

Voice: Call far-carrying 'see-ip'; song variable, 4–6 fluty notes plus warbling
Length: 21cm
Wingspan: 33–34.5cm
Weight: 60–65g
Habitat: Open woods, thickets, birch scrub; winters on grassland, stubble, rooftops, and open woodland
Nest: Thick cup of grass and moss, then mud, lined with grass; up to 3m above ground

Eggs: 4–5; light blue or greenish, profusely speckled reddish-brown
Food: Wide variety of invertebrates; berries in autumn and winter

Plumage recalls song thrush but adult recognisable by red flanks and long, creamy supercilium contrasting with dark-brown cheeks and brown crown. Sexes alike. Dark-brown streak runs from base of bill. Breast yellowish-buff on sides, dark-brown streaks spreading out to form a gorget. Undertail coverts white. Belly white, streaked with lighter brown on side. Underwing chestnut-red. Bill blackish-brown. Legs yellowish or flesh-brown. Juvenile recalls adult but shows darker streaking and spotting with buffish wash to face and flanks.

Vagrant Thrushes

Aᴜᴛᴜᴍɴ and winter are the seasons to look for rare vagrant thrushes. From North America come the tiny *Catharus* thrushes, all of which have proportionately large heads for their bodies. They are generally solitary and retiring in their habits; vagrant *Turdus* thrushes, on the other hand, invariably consort with migrant winter flocks of redwings and fieldfares.

North American thrush; very rare vagrant to Europe, usually in September/October

First-winter bird

SWAINSON'S THRUSH (Cᴀᴛʜᴀʀᴜs ᴜsᴛᴜʟᴀᴛᴜs): *All birds have conspicuous buffish-yellow eyering. Adult generally olive-brown above and greyish-white below; shows black spots on neck. Juvenile similar but overall tone of upperparts warmer brown, sometimes showing pale spots*

North American thrush; rare autumn vagrant to Europe

First-winter bird

GRAY-CHEEKED THRUSH (Cᴀᴛʜᴀʀᴜs ᴍɪɴɪᴍᴜs): *Similar to Swainson's thrush but lacks buffish eyering. Adult grey-brown above and greyish-white below, with dark spots on breast. Juvenile similar but often has buffish margins to wing coverts and tertial feathers*

North American thrush; very rare autumn vagrant to Europe

First-winter bird

VEERY (Cᴀᴛʜᴀʀᴜs ғᴜsᴄᴇsᴄᴇɴs): *Plumage recalls nightingale. All birds have warm-brown upperparts and tail; underparts mostly greyish-white; throat, sides of neck and upper breast have pale buffish wash and faint grey-brown spotting*

North American thrush; very rare vagrant to Europe

First-winter bird

HERMIT THRUSH (Cᴀᴛʜᴀʀᴜs ɢᴜᴛᴛᴀᴛᴜs): *Recalls thrush nightingale. Has olive-brown head and back, reddish-brown lower rump and tail, and greyish-white underparts; shows dark spots on throat and upper breast; margins of primaries reddish-brown*

American thrush; very rare autumn and winter vagrant to Europe

Adult

AMERICAN ROBIN (Tᴜʀᴅᴜs ᴍɪɢʀᴀᴛᴏʀɪᴜs): *Adult male has sooty-grey upperparts, white 'eyelid' and dark streaking on throat; breast and belly red. Adult female similar but red much less intense. Juvenile similar to female but even duller, appearing browner on upperparts*

Central Asian thrush; very rare autumn and winter vagrant to Europe; most records are of race ᴀᴛʀᴏɢᴜʟᴀʀɪs

BLACK-THROATED THRUSH (Tᴜʀᴅᴜs ʀᴜғɪᴄᴏʟʟɪs): *Occurs as two distinct races. Adult male of both races pale grey-brown above and white below; race* ᴀᴛʀᴏɢᴜʟᴀʀɪs *has black breast and race* ʀᴜғɪᴄᴏʟʟɪs *(red-throated thrush) red breast and outertail. Females and juveniles of both races similar to adult males but colours more mottled*

A Siberian thrush; very rare autumn and winter vagrant to northwest Europe

Adult

WHITE'S THRUSH (Zᴏᴏᴛʜᴇʀᴀ ᴅᴀᴜᴍᴀ): *Recalls immature mistle thrush but markings much bolder and more contrasting, and overall appearance scaly. Adult covered with black crescent markings everywhere except wings and tail; wings buff-brown with pale feather margins. Juvenile similar but dark markings more rounded than crescent-shaped*

A Siberian thrush; very rare autumn vagrant to Europe

Adult male

EYE-BROWED THRUSH (Tᴜʀᴅᴜs ᴏʙsᴄᴜʀᴜs): *Adult male has dark-grey head with white supercilium, brown back and wings and orange-red breast and flanks. Female and juvenile male similar but colours less intense*

A Siberian thrush; very rare autumn vagrant to northwest Europe, usually among migrating redwings and fieldfares

Adult male

SIBERIAN THRUSH (Zᴏᴏᴛʜᴇʀᴀ sɪʙɪʀɪᴄᴀ): *Adult male blue-black with prominent white supercilium; flanks paler than upperparts and show dark crescent-shaped markings; belly white. Juvenile male similar but dark colours less intense. Female similar to juvenile male but dark elements of plumage warm brown*

Cetti's Warbler

Cettia cetti

Song has been described as loudest song among small European birds

Cetti's warbler is unusual for several reasons: most passerines have 12 tail feathers but Cetti's has only 10; it lays red eggs; the males are often polygynous, mating with two to four females, and they take little part in rearing the young. However, it is the song that is the most distinctive feature: a sudden explosion of sound, usually 2.5 to 5 seconds long, composed of clear-cut, rhythmic phrases, which may be rendered as 'CHE–che-weechoo-weechoo-wechoo-wee'. Each male has an individual song pattern that birdwatchers can learn to recognise.

Medium-sized warbler with short, rounded wings and relatively long, broad, graduated tail

There has been a marked increase in Cetti's warbler numbers this century, with the species spreading its range west

Voice: Call is a sharp 'chip'; song is very distinctive, loud and abrupt
Length: 13.5cm
Wingspan: 15–19cm
Weight: 9.9–15.9g
Habitat: Bushy places giving shelter by swamps, watersides, marshes
Nest: Untidy outer shell of dead leaves and grass; deep inner cup with fine lining
Eggs: 4; bright chestnut or deep brick red
Food: Chiefly insects, adults and larvae; also spiders and worms

Sexes similar but male larger and heavier than female. Adult upperparts and wings uniform chestnut brown. Face broken only by off-white eyering and short, grey supercilium. Chin and central underparts off-white, rest grey-brown or darker brown, especially on flanks and undertail coverts; dull-white tips of undertail coverts usually obvious when birds cocks its tail in excitement. Bill short and fine, dark brown. Legs strong, brown-flesh. Juvenile similar to adult.

Fan-tailed Warbler

Cisticola juncidis

The fan-tailed warbler is a skulking bird, but inquisitive, and may be seen perching on grass stems, sometimes with its feet on separate stems, or in flight. The male's song-flight is long and undulating, each bounce synchronised with the song-note 'zit'. The songster covers 300–400m or more and utters over 100 song-notes. The male is polygynous, often mating with four females. He builds on average six nests in a season lasting from April to September. He builds the outer shell while the female lines the nest, lays the eggs and rears the young with no help from her mate.

May be seen flitting across the grass with whirring wings and short, spread tail like a big, buff bee; most conspicuous on male's song-flight

Chin, throat, belly and undertail coverts white

Voice: Call is persistent 'zip'. Song is high-pitched, sharp 'tsip-tsip- ...' or 'zit-zit- ...'
Length: 10cm
Wingspan: 12–14.5cm
Weight: 8–11g
Habitat: Rough, grassy plains, grain fields, marshes, rice fields
Nest: Deep and pear-shaped, with opening at top; made of fine grass bound with cobweb
Eggs: 4–6, variable; white or pale blue, with or without coloured specks
Food: Small insects and larvae, some as large as grasshoppers

Adult has warm buff upperparts streaked blackish-brown on crown, mantle and wings. Nape, rump and uppertail coverts almost unstreaked. Paler face has short, creamy supercilium and pale circle around eye. Breast and flanks buff. Tail brown with underside marked with black sub-terminal band and white tip. Bill brown above and grey below, with dark tip on breeding male and flesh-pink tip on other males and females. Juvenile similar to adult female.

Grasshopper Warbler

Locustella naevia

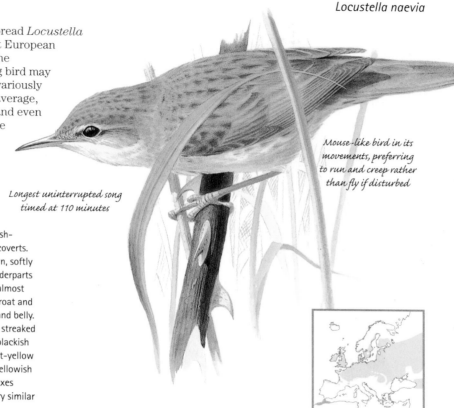

Mouse-like bird in its movements, preferring to run and creep rather than fly if disturbed

Longest uninterrupted song timed at 110 minutes

THE grasshopper warbler is the commonest and most widespread *Locustella* in Europe. Its winter quarters are not well known, but most European birds return to their breeding grounds in late April. Although the grasshopper warbler is retiring it is not especially shy; a singing bird may be approached to within a metre or so. Its far-carrying song is variously described as like a fisherman's reel or trilling insects, with, on average, 26 notes per second. It is far-carrying, commonly up to 250m, and even up to 1km in still conditions. The high pitch is inaudible to some people. Like Savi's warbler's song, it is difficult to pinpoint, with a peculiar waxing and waning of volume, apparently as the bird turns its head. The male sings from mid-April to July, by day and night, but mainly at dusk and dawn.

Voice: Short quiet 'pitt' call; song is a high-pitched, monotonous trill
Length: 12.5cm
Wingspan: 15–19cm
Weight: 13–16g
Habitat: Undergrowth in marshes, thick hedges, heathland, new plantations
Nest: Low down in thick vegetation; dead leaves and grass, lined with hair and fine grasses; often approached through a little tunnel

Eggs: 6; white, finely, often densely, speckled purplish
Food: Mostly insects, to size of grasshopper and dragonfly

Small, uniformly coloured warbler. Adult upperparts olive-brown, spotted and streaked with dark brown from crown to rump. Wings darker brown with buff to reddish fringes to feathers, visible at close range. Streaks on rump fade out on reddish-brown uppertail coverts. Tail reddish-brown, softly barred darker. Underparts mostly buff, but almost white on chin, throat and centre of breast and belly. Undertail coverts streaked with brown. Bill blackish brown with bright-yellow base. Legs pale, yellowish brown to pink. Sexes alike. Juvenile very similar to adult.

River Warbler

Locustella fluviatilis

Combination of unstreaked upperparts and faint mottling on chest is best distinguishing feature

THE river warbler is a bird of central and eastern Europe, though it has spread westwards since the 1950s; it favours areas of very dense vegetation up to 2m tall among trees, such as bogs, carr, damp forest clearings and abandoned orchards. It is a summer visitor to Europe. Breeding starts in late May and the birds leave for Africa early, in late July or August. The river warbler is a skulking bird, feeding in dense cover, so it is difficult to observe. Unusually for a warbler, it obtains its food as it runs about in the thick grass, nettles and fallen leaves. Its calls are confusingly like those of several other species, so the best chance of a sighting is to watch a male singing from its exposed perch. The slow, throbbing song consists of clearly separated disyllabic notes, 'chuff-chuff, chuff-chuff', delivered at a rate of about seven pairs a second, sounding like a distant steam engine, bush-cricket or cicada. A distant bird is hard to locate.

Voice: Sharp 'tsick' call; song is a curious, rhythmic 'chuffing' sound
Length: 13cm
Wingspan: 19–22cm
Weight: 16–19g
Habitat: Dense vegetation in backwaters, bogs, carr, flooded woods
Nest: On the ground, in thick herbage; loose structure of grass and leaves, lined with finer material

Eggs: 5–6; white, densely speckled all over purplish and brown
Food: Arthropods, especially small beetles, spiders and bugs

Unstreaked small- to medium-sized warbler. Upperparts, wings and tail olive-brown, darker on uppertail coverts and tail, slightly greyer on head and back. Underparts dull white with olive-brown wash on flanks and sides of breast. Undertail coverts long, to tip of tail, buff-brown with broad, white tips. Bill dark brown with pale base. Legs flesh to brown. Sexes similar but female greyer above. Juvenile similar to adult.

Generally prefers a higher song-post than grasshopper warbler, often selecting a perch a few metres up in a bush or tree

Savi's Warbler

Locustella luscinioides

Bird turns its head as it sings, making its position very difficult to pinpoint

Medium-sized warbler, resembling large reed warbler

Savi's warbler is a bird of unbroken swamps and reedbeds, and the nest site can usually only be approached by wading. Its preference for this type of habitat gives the species a very fragmented distribution from Spain across central and eastern Europe. In the past 40 years it has expanded its range north and west on the continent, recolonising England in 1960; it is now one of Britain's rarest breeding birds. Males return to the reedbeds from Africa in mid-April and set up territories about 12 days before the females arrive. Their reeling songs can, with practice, be recognised as different from those of other *Locustella* warblers, but they are remarkably like that of Roesel's bush-cricket! Savi's warbler is less shy than other *Locustella* warblers with reeling songs, and regularly climbs to a prominent perch to sing. It often sings through the night.

Habitat: Reedy swamps and fens, overgrown fringes of lakes
Nest: Loose outer cup of waterside plants; firm inner cup, lined with finer fibres
Eggs: 4–5; white, densely speckled with shades of brown, mostly at larger end
Food: Adult and larval flies, butterflies and moths, bugs, spiders and beetles

Voice: Call 'pit'; alarm sharper rattle; song accelerating ticking sound
Length: 14cm
Wingspan: 18–21cm
Weight: 13–17g

Similar to other plain warblers. Sexes similar. Adult distinguished by dark, unstreaked, reddish-brown head and upperparts, with faint, buff supercilium fading out behind the eye. Underparts brownish-white with rufous-brown along sides of breast and flanks to undertail coverts. Wings and tail uniform reddish-brown like upperparts. Tail broad and graduated towards the tip. Bill dark grey-brown. Legs pale brown. Juvenile similar to adult.

Moustached Warbler

Acrocephalus melanopogon

The moustached warbler occurs widely but discontinuously across its southern European range, being dependent on finding suitable wetland habitats, such as in the Camargue, along the River Danube and Albufera Marsh on Mallorca. It is mostly sedentary but more northerly populations migrate to overwinter further south along the northern and eastern fringes of the Mediterranean. This warbler is noted for skulking, but it can be approached closely on occasions. The song is richly varied and is notably different from the sedge warbler's. It includes a diagnostic, introductory series of low, pure notes, 'tu-tu-tu-tu', with a crescendo reminiscent of the nightingale's; this is followed immediately by a scratchy warble.

Voice: Call is a soft 't-rrrt'; alarm is 'churr'; song is a distinctive musical medley
Length: 12–13cm
Wingspan: 15–16.5cm
Weight: 10–12g
Habitat: Swamps of sedges, reeds and reedmace
Nest: Deep cup, loosely made of plant material, lined with reed flowers and feathers
Eggs: 3–4; white, with light-olive mottling all over
Food: Almost wholly arthropods, especially small beetles

Similar to aquatic and sedge warblers, but clearly separable with care; note especially the head pattern, upperparts, duller wings, behaviour and diagnostic song. Sexes similar. Adult has nape and mantle rufous brown, nape unmarked but mantle streaked black. Unstreaked rump almost same colour as dark-brown tail. Wings olive-brown with paler feathers. Underparts whitish with rusty flanks, vent and sides to breast. Head has distinctive pattern of black crown and broad, white supercilium – square-ended behind eye – highlighted by dusky lore and eyestripe. Juvenile similar to adult.

When nervous moustached warbler has been reported to have a habit of cocking its tail like a wren

The southerly counterpart of the sedge warbler, the moustached warbler prefers emergent vegtation over water, where its large feet and claws enable it to move easily among the reed stems when searching for food

Aquatic Warbler

Acrocephalus paludicola

THE aquatic warbler is a summer visitor to lowland marshes, mostly in eastern Europe. Its distribution has probably always been broken because of its preferred habitat and it is now one of Europe's rarest passerines. The aquatic warbler is a difficult bird to watch because of its love of low, dense cover. However, it can be drawn into the open by imitating its call, and the male can be watched on his breeding territory during his song-flights between mid-May and mid-July. He rises between 3 and 30m, fluttering up silently, and then with fanned and raised tail he sings on the way down. Peak song periods are before sunrise and at dusk.

Aquatic warblers are rare but regular passage migrants to northwest Europe in the autumn

Very similar to sedge and moustached warblers but clearly distinguishable with care

Voice: Call is a harsh 'churr'; song incorporates short rattles, with some fluty notes
Length: 13cm
Wingspan: 16.5–19.5cm
Weight: 9–15g
Habitat: Marshes of sedge and iris, with low vegetation
Nest: Well-shaped cup of grasses and cobwebs, lined with feathers; low down
Eggs: 5–6; pale buff with darker mottling
Food: Mostly insects, from small dragonflies to small flies

Sexes similar. Adult upperparts more sandy than sedge warbler's, with long, dark-brown streaks highlighted by paler stripes. Rump rusty, streaked with brown. Underparts creamy buff, becoming whiter with wear, with fine, brown streaks on side of breast and on flanks. Head pattern diagnostic: long, pale-buff crown stripe and supercilium, separated by dark-brown stripe at side of crown; supercilium highlighted by brown

eyestripe from behind eye. Tail distinctive: dull black with tawny fringes and pointed feathers. Bill dark brown and legs orange-yellow. Juvenile has brighter colours than adult and looks like many juvenile sedge warblers.

Sedge Warbler

Acrocephalus schoenobaenus

THE sedge warbler is the most common and widespread *Acrocephalus* warbler in Europe; it is also the easiest to observe. The species favours low vegetation in moist habitats from the high Arctic to the edge of the Mediterranean zone. It is a summer visitor to the region and is common from May to August. In Britain, and in many other parts of its range, the sedge warbler has undergone a decline in breeding numbers; this is thought to be because of poor survival in drought conditions on its overwintering grounds in Africa.

Sedge warblers are territorial in winter and summer, defending feeding and breeding areas

Inquisitive birds often sidle up vertical stems to investigate an intruder or noise

Voice: Call 'tuc'; alarm 'churr'; song is a loud and varied mix of harsh and musical notes
Length: 13cm
Wingspan: 17–21cm
Weight: 9.5–13.6g
Habitat: Reedbeds and other lush vegetation near water
Nest: Low in herbage; loose outer shell of grass, sedge etc, lined with soft materials
Eggs: 5–6; pale greenish, profusely speckled olive or buff, often covering the egg
Food: Chiefly insects, from aphids to dragonflies; also spiders

Adult upperparts and head strongly marked. Shows olive-brown nape, mantle and scapulars with dark streaks. Rump tawny and unstreaked, tail dark brown. Wings buff-brown with lighter edges to tertials and greater coverts. Underparts off-white, washed whitest on throat and belly, more rufous on flanks. Head has black-streaked crown and long, creamy-white supercilium above dusky-olive lores. Bill blackish, paler at base; legs greyish. Juvenile separable from adult by creamier

supercilium, yellower underparts and distinct brown spots across breast.

Marsh Warbler

Acrocephalus palustris

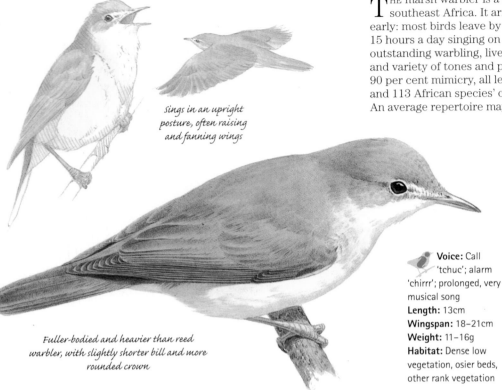

sings in an upright posture, often raising and fanning wings

Fuller-bodied and heavier than reed warbler, with slightly shorter bill and more rounded crown

THE marsh warbler is a summer visitor to Europe, overwintering in southeast Africa. It arrives in northwest Europe in late May and leaves early: most birds leave by the end of August. The marsh warbler spends 12 to 15 hours a day singing on arrival at a breeding site. The song is an outstanding warbling, lively chatter, with a remarkable amount of mimicry and variety of tones and pitches, sung by day and night. Some songs may be 90 per cent mimicry, all learned in the bird's first year. At least 99 European and 113 African species' calls have been recognised in marsh warbler songs. An average repertoire may contain 76 species, 45 African and 31 European.

Nest: Untidy nest of plant fibres, fixed by 'handles' to plant stems
Eggs: 4–5; very pale blue or green, bold spots of olive-green and grey
Food: Chiefly insects and spiders; some snails and berries

Voice: Call 'tchuc'; alarm 'chirrr'; prolonged, very musical song
Length: 13cm
Wingspan: 18–21cm
Weight: 11–16g
Habitat: Dense low vegetation, osier beds, other rank vegetation

Medium-sized warbler, very hard to separate from reed and Blyth's reed warblers (latter breeds from Baltic eastwards). Sexes similar. Adult usually has more olive-brown upperparts than reed warbler and lacks rufous rump. Has short, wide-based bill, round head, long wings showing eight to nine primary tips, pear-shaped or pot-bellied appearance and long undertail coverts. Less agile than reed warbler. Juvenile similar to adult.

Reed Warbler

Acrocephalus scirpaceus

Warm reddish hues on rump visible in flight

This very agile bird clings to reed stems with both feet, or to adjacent stems; moves up and down in jerks, or hops from one plant to another

Shows indistinct dull-cream supercilium

THE reed warbler is a skulking but not especially shy bird of reedbeds. It is common and widespread throughout much of Europe, wherever suitable habitats occur. A summer visitor to the region, the entire population overwinters in Africa. The reed warbler is closely, but not exclusively, associated with reedbeds; it will also breed in other vegetation such as willowherb, and recently in crops of rape. Its large footspan is an adaptation allowing it to move easily through a forest of vertical plant stems. This species is at risk because its habitat is in constant danger of being drained for development.

Voice: Call 'churr-churr'; alarm harsher; song low, guttural churring, with long phrases
Length: 13cm
Wingspan: 18–21cm
Weight: 10–13g
Habitat: Edges of reedbeds with strong stems, and nearby vegetation
Nest: Deep cup of grass and flower heads woven round several reed stems
Eggs: 4; pale green, blotched and speckled olive, usually at larger end
Food: Chiefly insects, especially flies; also spiders, small snails

Medium-sized warbler. Sexes similar. Adult upperparts uniform olive-brown, with often noticeably more rufous rump and uppertail coverts, and darker-brown primaries and tertials. Underparts white with buff undertail coverts and sides of breast. Bill dark grey or greyish-brown with pale base. Legs sturdy, variable, but usually greyish. Juvenile brighter and rustier than adult, but face pattern less distinct. Similar to juvenile marsh warbler.

Olive-tree Warbler

Hippolais olivetorum

THE olive-tree warbler is an arboreal species, favouring oak woods, orchards and olive groves; in Greece and Bulgaria it is found in bushier places on hillsides and in vineyards. It overwinters in Africa and arrives back in its breeding areas in early May. Though it is not a numerous species, it forms neighbourhood groups and so is locally common. The olive-tree warbler is a more skulking, secretive species than other *Hippolais* warblers, feeding mostly in the canopy of the trees.

Voice: Call 'tuc'; song distinctly lower-pitched and slower than its relatives'
Length: 15cm
Wingspan: 24–26cm
Weight: 15–20g
Habitat: Coastal, insular, open-canopy woods, groves and orchards
Nest: Deep, well-made cup of plant materials and cobwebs, up to 3m from ground
Eggs: Usually 4; very pale pink, with sparse black markings
Food: Presumably insects and their larvae; some fruit

Large greyish warbler, with long wings and dagger-like bill. Sexes similar. Adult upperparts and wings brownish-grey, with whitish edges to greater coverts, secondaries and tertials, forming striking wing panel. Has buff-white supercilium and whitish eyering. Bill's large size accentuated by long, flat crown. Tail grey with white edges. Underparts dirty white with grey wash on breast, flanks and neck. Feather wear by late summer makes bird look even duller and wing panel obscured. Juvenile as adult but upperparts more olive and wing panel more extensive than autumn adult.

THE great reed warbler breeds widely across Europe from Iberia to Russia, mostly in the lowlands. It is a summer visitor, arriving from mid-April onwards; European birds overwinter in Africa south of the Sahara. Great reed warblers are territorial; good habitats often have high populations with contiguous territories. Many of the clusters are known to be formed by polygynous males with as many as three females; these males do not help with nest building or incubation. The male great reed warbler sings more or less throughout the day, from arrival until a mate is found, and thereafter again if he attempts to attract another female. The song is well known for its remarkable volume and great variety of pitch and tone; it may carry as far as 1km.

Voice: Call 'chak'; alarm harsh chatter; song very loud, harsh 'churrs' and rattles
Length: 19–20cm
Wingspan: 25–29cm
Weight: 25–33g
Habitat: Mostly lowland in aquatic vegetation, especially dense reedbeds
Nest: Mostly in thick reeds; deep cup of plant material, attached to six or so stems of common reed
Eggs: Usually 4–5; pale green or blue, spotted dark brown, olive
Food: Mainly insects, but also spiders, snails and small frogs

Similar in appearance to reed warbler but clearly larger with longer, stouter bill. Adult upperparts warm olive-brown, crown darker, rump fawnier, wing coverts edged rufous. Shows creamy supercilium, dusky eyestripe and pale-cream eyering. Underparts mainly creamy buff but more buff on flanks, and chin and throat off-white. Bill grey-brown, with bright pinkish base to lower mandible. Legs pale brown. Singing bird reveals bright orange-yellow mouth. Female tends to be brighter above and less white below than male. Sexes otherwise similar. Juvenile similar to adult.

Great Reed Warbler

Acrocephalus arundinaceus

Colouring similar to reed warbler, but has heavier bill and rather greyish face

Large warbler, nearly as big as a small thrush

Olivaceous Warbler

Hippolais pallida

WARBLERS of the genus *Hippolais* can be extremely difficult to identify; the olivaceous warbler, being the least marked of the genus, generally causes the most problems, resembling in many respects reed and marsh warblers. It is a summer visitor to the Mediterranean basin, breeding from May onwards; it overwinters in Africa. Olivaceous warblers are quite common in a variety of habitats and are not particularly shy, but their dull appearance and preference for shrubby places can make observation difficult. The males are very vocal during the breeding season and are territorial, but show a strong tendency to form neighbourhood groups.

Voice: Call 'tack'; alarm repeated ticking; song high-pitched, rapid, scratchy warble
Length: 12–13.5cm
Wingspan: 18–21cm
Weight: 8–16g
Habitat: Shrubs, orchards, gardens, palm groves, lowlands and bushy hills
Nest: Well-built cup of twigs and grass, lined with finer materials, in tree or bush
Eggs: 3–4; pale grey-white, sparingly spotted with black
Food: Chiefly insects, to size of grasshoppers and dragonflies; some fruit

Medium- to large-sized warbler. Sexes are similar, and adults and juveniles are similar. Plumage recalls garden warbler; dull brown above, creamy white below with pale-buff wash on sides of breast and flanks; yellowish wash in spring. Shows dull-white supercilium. Face dominated by flat crown, rather long, prominent bill and dark eye with whitish eyering. Rump washed buff, faintly distinct from tail. Wings short relative to body size. Legs very variable, brownish to bluish-grey.

Nondescript bird sings its simple, repetitive song from thick cover

Icterine Warbler

Hippolais icterina

Adult

The icterine warbler's song may include mimicry and can last for up to 40 seconds and carry 500m on a still evening

Careful attention to structure is needed to separate icterine warbler from other HIPPOLAIS warblers, in particular melodious warbler

Juvenile

Rare but annual visitor to northwest Europe on migration

THE icterine warbler is a robust bird with a dramatic song, and is the eastern counterpart of the melodious warbler. This warbler is a summer visitor; the entire population overwinters in Africa, arriving back in Europe in from late April to June. The male defends his territory passionately at the start of the season, driving rivals and other species away with song, bill-snapping and even fights. The icterine warbler does not sing much after pairing, but until then its vigorous, varied, musical song is a splendid feature of central and eastern European countryside. The nest is said to be the best built by any warbler. The species is generally shy and retiring on passage.

Voice: Call 'tec' and, in spring, diagnostic 'deeteroo', song loud with remarkably long warble
Length: 13.5cm
Wingspan: 20.5–24cm
Weight: 11–16g
Habitat: Mainly sunny wooded lowlands, cultivated lands and gardens, even in towns
Nest: Deep, well-made cup in fork, 1–4m up; made of plant fibres, lined with hair, fur and feathers
Eggs: 4–5; pale purplish-pink, sparingly spotted with black
Food: Chiefly adult and larval insects; butterflies, grasshoppers, beetles; various fruits

Medium-sized warbler, with long bill accentuated by rather flat crown and long wings reaching at least to end of uppertail coverts. Sexes similar. Adult basically green above and yellow below. Area between bill and below eye yellow, giving a pale-faced effect. Wings have distinct pale panel formed by yellow edges to dark-olive tertials and secondaries. Legs bright blue-grey. Late-summer adults in worn plumage are browner above and whiter below. Juveniles usually flushed with yellow.

Melodious Warbler

Hippolais polyglotta

Melodious warblers are found in a variety of habitats: tree-lined roads, thickets with scattered trees, coppices and thick hedges around cultivation

Difficult to separate from icterine warbler, but smaller, with shorter rounded wings that do not reach tips of uppertail coverts

THE melodious warbler is the western counterpart of the icterine warbler, and like its relative is a summer visitor to Europe, overwintering in west Africa. It is a very vocal bird at the start of the breeding season in late April, and several pairs may nest close together. The male's song, a prolonged warble, may last from 7 to 13 seconds, and carries for up to 70m. The melodious warbler feeds restlessly in shrubs and trees using a round-winged, fluttering action, often moving abruptly, or stretching its neck to reach an insect. When moving through foliage in search of insects it can appear clumsy.

Voice: Call 'hooeet'; alarm harsh 'tchurrrr'; song sustained, varied and musical
Length: 13cm
Wingspan: 17.5–20cm
Weight: 10–13g
Habitat: Principally on wooded lowlands, often near water
Nest: Deep cup in a fork 1–2m above ground; of plant fibres, lined with roots, hair and feathers

Eggs: 3–5, usually 4; light purplish-pink, sparsely spotted and streaked black
Food: Adult and larval insects; fruit in autumn

Medium-sized, long-billed warbler. Sexes similar. Adult upperparts brownish-green (less bright than icterine), underparts rich yellow. Wings and tail olive-brown; wings without pale wing panel (*cf* icterine). Head round-crowned, brownish-green with yellow supercilium from bill to just behind eye, which has yellow eyering. Late-summer adults in worn plumage are bleached and appear dun-coloured above and whitish below. Juvenile in fresh plumage sometimes bright yellow or yellowish-green.

Dartford Warbler

Sylvia undata

In poor light all ages and sexes look uniformly dark

Breeding male

THE Dartford warbler is easy to separate from all other warblers except Marmora's. It is a skulking bird and patience is needed to see it well. Its flight is weak; damp, windy days drive it out of sight until the weather changes. Fine, sunny mornings are the best times to see a male clearly, perched with tail cocked on a bush, and singing his scratchy song. In the south, this is a common bird of the maquis, but in the northwest of its range it is typical of lowland heath. It is mostly sedentary, although some juveniles disperse southwards in winter.

Voice: Call 'tuc' and grating alarm 'tchirrr'; song musical chatter, some liquid notes
Length: 12.5cm
Wingspan: 13–18.5cm
Weight: 8.5–10g
Habitat: Low, dense cover on coastal scrub, heathland or maquis
Nest: Low down; cup of grass, wool, plant down with soft, fine lining
Eggs: 4; usually white, tinged green or grey, finely speckled brown
Food: Exclusively invertebrates in Britain; occasionally autumn fruits elsewhere

Adult male is dark slaty brown above with greyer head, and wine red below. Wings almost uniformly brownish-black. Tail grey-black with narrow, white edges. Throat white-spotted in fresh plumage but spots wear off by June or July. Bill dark brown. Legs brownish-yellow. Eye and eyering orange to red. Female and juvenile resemble male but are browner on upperparts and paler below.

Marmora's Warbler

Sylvia sarda

MARMORA'S warbler is confined in the breeding season to the western Mediterranean islands between Ibiza and Pantelleria (southwest of Sicily). In the Balearics it is sedentary, but other birds migrate to northwest Africa in winter. Marmora's warbler is found in the lowest vegetation layer, and, unusually for a warbler, it spends up to one-third of its time on the ground. Although often very skulking, it has been recorded as very tame on the Balearic island of Formentera, allowing observation from only a metre away. It often sings from the top of bushes or in a song-flight, which is a steady ascent to between 4 and 7m, followed by a dive to cover.

Voice: Call explosive 'crrip' or 'tsig'; song weak, high-pitched warble
Length: 12cm
Wingspan: 13–17.5cm
Weight: 9–12g
Habitat: Heath and low scrub on dry hillsides and coastal slopes
Nest: Cup of dry plant pieces, cobwebs and wool, with finer lining
Eggs: 3–5; white or greyish-white, spotted grey and reddish-brown
Food: Chiefly small insects

plumage drabber and browner than male's. Juvenile even browner than female with dull-yellow eyes.

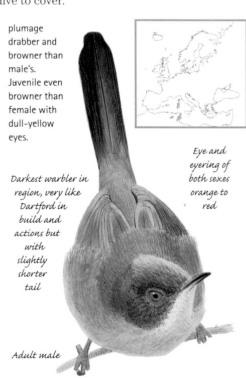

Darkest warbler in region, very like Dartford in build and actions but with slightly shorter tail

Eye and eyering of both sexes orange to red

Adult male dull blue-grey above and below. Wings and tail dull black, latter with dusky-white edges, often not noticeable. Legs yellow-brown. Female's

Adult male

Spectacled Warbler

Sylvia conspicillata

SPECTACLED warblers are summer visitors to most of their southern European breeding range, overwintering in northwest Africa; eastern birds are mostly resident, however, with some moving south to the Nile and Eilat. The spectacled warbler is typically shy and skulking but, like a whitethroat, it scolds intruders from a prominent perch, cocking its tail and showing off its white outertail feathers. Once alarmed it dives for cover and stays there. Good views are best had by watching a singing male, either on a perch or in his song-flight.

Voice: Call high 'tseet'; song short, sweet, rapid, variable warble
Length: 12.5cm
Wingspan: 13.5–17cm
Weight: 8–11g
Habitat: In low scrub and rough ground beside cultivation; also in glasswort in wet lowlands with salt-laden soils
Nest: Neat cup of grass, leaves and roots, lined with wool, hair and fine roots
Eggs: 4–5; very pale greenish- or buffish-white, finely spotted olive or greenish
Food: Mainly invertebrates, including grasshoppers, flies and spiders; some autumn fruit

Adult male

Recalls small whitethroat or subalpine warbler without moustache but with striking white eyering

Adult male grey to sandy brown above with striking orange edges to wing feathers forming glowing patch. Black tail clearly edged white. Underparts pink except for white chin, grey throat and buffish-grey head, which in some lights appears black between bill and below eye. Female browner on head and upperparts than male with no black on face; underparts less pink, more buff. Chin white. Female looks more like whitethroat than male. Juvenile similar to female but with buffish suffusion to plumage.

Sardinian Warbler

Sylvia melanocephala

THE Sardinian warbler breeds throughout much of the Mediterranean basin, occurring mainly in coastal regions; it is more widespread inland in Iberia and Italy. Mainland and northern populations migrate to north Africa and the eastern Mediterranean; island and coastal populations are mostly sedentary. The Sardinian warbler spends much of its time in thick cover but appears frequently in the open. Its song is more tuneful than the whitethroat's, but uttered similarly from a perch or in flight. The male is quarrelsome, noisily chasing rivals.

Adult male (above left) distinctive but needs some care at first to separate from other black-headed warblers

Like male, female (right) has red eye and eyering; dark-brown tail has same white edges as male's

Voice: Harsh alarm rattle; 'treek, treek' call; song rapid medley, harsh and musical
Length: 13.5cm
Wingspan: 15–18cm
Weight: 11–14g
Habitat: From scanty undergrowth, scattered shrubs and thickets to open woodland
Nest: Low down; cup-shaped, of grass, cobwebs and plant down, lined with grass and hair
Eggs: 3–4, variable; whitish or tinted background, finely speckled with buffs and greys
Food: Chiefly insects; fruit in autumn and winter; fruit all year in south

Adult male has black hood extending well below eyes to lores and ear coverts; sharp division between cap and pure white chin and upper throat. Steep forehead helps to accentuate red eye and eyering. Rest of upperparts grey; rest of underparts off-white, fading to grey on flanks. Bill buffish-brown with black tip. Legs reddish. Wings blackish with feathers edged grey. Tail black, edged white. Female has same pattern on head as adult male but black replaced by dusky grey. Upperparts dirty brown; underparts and breast pinkish-brown, flanks dull brown; otherwise white. Juvenile similar to female.

Cyprus Warbler

Sylvia melanothorax

As a breeding bird, the Cyprus warbler is enirely restricted to Cyprus; it is, however, widespread and common in a suitable habitat, especially in coastal maquis, although it tends to be shy and skulking. Most birds seem to be resident, but some migrate (to Egypt and Sinai), so the bird is less common in winter. Breeding grounds above 1,000m are vacated outside the breeding season. Resident birds are believed to hold territories all year, and overwintering birds at Eilat have been observed defending territories too.

Food: Mainly invertebrates; little is known in detail

Adult male easily separated from other *Sylvia* warblers by black and white mottled underparts, from chin to undertail coverts, and pale fringes to innerwing feathers. Pronounced white moustache. Black tail with white edges contrasts with grey mantle, back and rump. Yellow to chestnut eye in yellowish to red eyering.

Female similar to male but much duller and browner; moustachial stripe dull white. Eye and eyering duller than male's. Juvenile similar to female but markings on throat less pronounced; difficult to distinguish from juvenile Sardinian warbler.

Voice: Call grating 'tchek'; song vigorous rattle of high and low notes
Length: 13.5cm
Wingspan: 15–18cm
Weight: 10–15g
Habitat: Maquis scrub, especially among cistus; also scrub forest edge
Nest: In low scrub; cup of leaves, grass, juniper bark, lined with grass and hair
Eggs: 4–5; very pale green, spotted with olive-brown and violet-grey

Bill buffish-yellow and legs vary from flesh-yellow to reddish-brown

Adult male

Subalpine Warbler

Sylvia cantillans

THE subalpine warbler is a summer visitor to the region, overwintering in Africa; it is a rare but almost annual visitor to northwest Europe, most often in spring. This warbler is most often seen in garigue where broom, cistus and fragrant shrubs bloom, and in thorny maquis; it also occurs among holm oaks, on sunny hillsides and in bushy ravines. The male usually sings from cover but is conspicuous when he sings from a perch or in flight.

Voice: Call 'tec'; alarm oft-repeated 'tec'; song like whitethroat's, but more musical
Length: 12cm
Wingspan: 15–19cm
Weight: 9.2–13g
Habitat: Woodland glades, thickets, stream banks
Nest: In low shrub; cup of dry grass and plant down, with finer lining
Eggs: 3–5; white or palely tinted, variably speckled and mottled
Food: Adult and larval insects; fruit in late summer and autumn

Adult male has pale blue-grey upperparts, dark pink-chestnut breast and unmarked throat, and conspicuous white 'moustache'. Rest of underparts and belly white, undertail coverts buff. Wings and tail dark grey-brown with pale-grey fringes to wing feathers and white outertail feathers. Bill blackish-brown, legs yellowish-brown. Rich red eye in red eyering. Adult female is pale grey-brown above, with clear but duller moustache. Underparts pinkish-buff; white area more extensive than on male and wings browner. Juvenile has washed-out colours but usually a hint of a white 'moustache'. Often hard to separate this species from spectacled warbler in autumn.

Male

Female

Rüppell's Warbler

Sylvia rueppellii

Wings mainly black with striking whitish fringes and tips to tertials

Voice: Hard 'tak, tak;. song rapid, chattering, with some call notes and pure tones
Length: 14cm
Wingspan: 18–21cm
Weight: 12–16g
Habitat: Thorny scrub, maquis, on rocky slopes and in gullies; also undergrowth in old woods
Nest: A neat cup of grasses, lined with plant fibres, in a bush
Eggs: 4–5; white tinged with green, profusely speckled, sometimes appearing olive all over
Food: Adult and larval insects; autumn fruits

RÜPPELL'S warbler is a summer visitor to its eastern Mediterranean breeding range, overwintering in northeast Africa. There is a marked passage in spring and autumn through Egypt, and it is quite common in Cyprus in spring. Rüppell's warbler has a splendid song-flight, with the bird rising to a height of 10 to 20m on a zigzag path with fully extended, slowly flapping wings, followed by a parachute descent on outspread wings like a pipit. Males arrive before the females and half-build several speculative nests to attract the female.

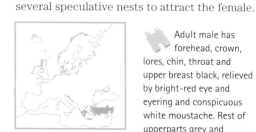

Adult male has forehead, crown, lores, chin, throat and upper breast black, relieved by bright-red eye and eyering and conspicuous white moustache. Rest of upperparts grey and underparts greyish-white, greyer on flanks and whiter on belly. Tail black with white outer feathers. Bill quite long, blackish with paler, yellowish base to lower mandible. Female and juvenile duller and browner than adult male, with most showing faint impression of male's head markings.

Adult male

Legs reddish-brown

Orphean Warbler

Sylvia hortensis

BASICALLY a Mediterranean bird, the Orphean warbler is a summer visitor to the region, occurring from May to August and overwintering in sub-Saharan Africa. It is a vagrant to northwest Europe, including Britain. Although not a shy bird, it is not necessarily easily observed because it spends much of its time searching the upper foliage of thickets for food. The Orphean warbler prefers trees and larger bushes to lower vegetation, and the male sings from the cover of bushes and small trees rather than on song-flights. In defence of its young the Orphean warbler has been seen to lure an intruder away by pretending to be disabled.

Voice: Call 'tac, tac' or 'trrrr' alarm; song pleasant, thrush-like warble
Length: 15cm
Wingspan: 20–25cm
Weight: 20–27g
Habitat: Stunted open forest and scrub on hillsides; also orange and olive groves, and gardens
Nest: Loosely made; thin twigs, grass and cobwebs, lined with finer roots, grass and hair
Eggs: 4–5; white or faint bluish-white, sparingly marked with spots of several colours
Food: Chiefly

invertebrates, as big as grasshoppers and stick insects; autumn fruits

Robust warbler resembling a large blackcap but easily distinguished by white outertail feathers and adult's pale yellow-white eyes. Adult male has dark cap extending to lores and ear coverts. Nape and upperparts grey-brown; wings and tail dusky

brown. Pale-grey fringes to tertials and larger coverts. Underparts basically white but with pinkish flush on breast in breeding season. Bill long, blackish. Female closely resembles male but duller with more grey on upperparts. Juvenile even browner than female and lacks adults' dark head.

Adult male

Legs grey or grey-brown

Barred Warbler

Sylvia nisoria

THE barred warbler is a summer visitor to Europe, overwintering chiefly in Kenya; it appears annually in northwest Europe in late summer. This is the largest and among the most secretive of the *Sylvia* warblers. The males are best observed when displaying. They perch conspicuously, jerking and fanning their tails, and then sing in flight for 5 to 10 seconds, in an erratic loop above a bush. The song is often preceded by audible wing-clapping. During the breeding season, the barred warbler often nests close to the red-backed shrike.

Voice: Call harsh 'charr'; song short, rich warble with harsh call notes mixed in
Length: 15.5cm
Wingspan: 23–27cm
Weight: 23–26g
Habitat: Often thorn thickets, riverine woodland or orchards
Nest: In fork of twigs; loosely built of dead grass, lined with fine roots and hair
Eggs: Usually 5; pale whitish- or greenish-grey, finely speckled with darker greys
Food: Insectivorous; fruits and berries in autumn

coverts, less clear bar on median coverts and pale, bright-grey edges and tips to tertials. Undeparts dull white from chin to undertail coverts, liberally barred with dark grey-brown crescents, emphasised by white tips. Tail long and broad, dark brown with white edges.

Adult female like male but duller and browner above with barring less clear below and paler eye. Juvenile recalls garden warbler, being unbarred and dark-eyed.

Juvenile

Robust warbler, all plumages of which show pale wingbars, pale-edged tertials and white-tipped tail. Adult male's head, face and upperparts grey. Pale-yellow eye. Wings dark brown-grey with pale bar on greater

Bill grey-brown with pale base; proportionately large legs greyish or brownish at all times

Adult male

Whitethroat

Sylvia communis

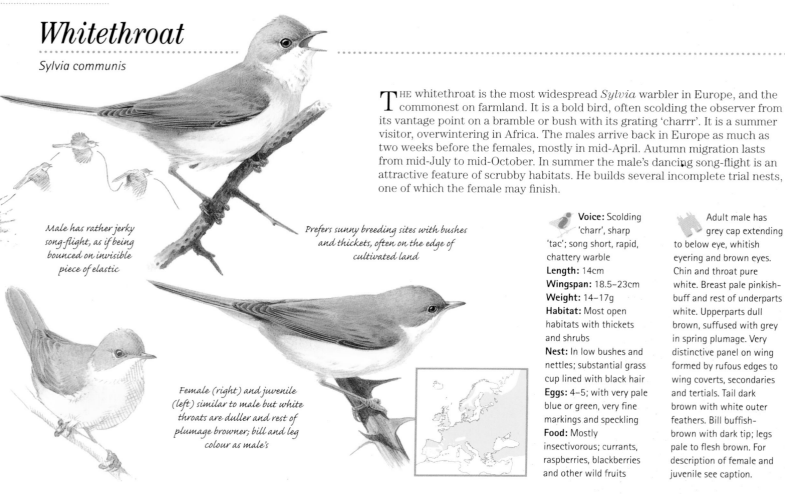

THE whitethroat is the most widespread *Sylvia* warbler in Europe, and the commonest on farmland. It is a bold bird, often scolding the observer from its vantage point on a bramble or bush with its grating 'charrr'. It is a summer visitor, overwintering in Africa. The males arrive back in Europe as much as two weeks before the females, mostly in mid-April. Autumn migration lasts from mid-July to mid-October. In summer the male's dancing song-flight is an attractive feature of scrubby habitats. He builds several incomplete trial nests, one of which the female may finish.

Male has rather jerky song-flight, as if being bounced on invisible piece of elastic

Prefers sunny breeding sites with bushes and thickets, often on the edge of cultivated land

Female (right) and juvenile (left) similar to male but white throats are duller and rest of plumage browner; bill and leg colour as male's

Voice: Scolding 'charr', sharp 'tac'; song short, rapid, chattery warble
Length: 14cm
Wingspan: 18.5–23cm
Weight: 14–17g
Habitat: Most open habitats with thickets and shrubs
Nest: In low bushes and nettles; substantial grass cup lined with black hair
Eggs: 4–5; with very pale blue or green, very fine markings and speckling
Food: Mostly insectivorous; currants, raspberries, blackberries and other wild fruits

Adult male has grey cap extending to below eye, whitish eyering and brown eyes. Chin and throat pure white. Breast pale pinkish-buff and rest of underparts white. Upperparts dull brown, suffused with grey in spring plumage. Very distinctive panel on wing formed by rufous edges to wing coverts, secondaries and tertials. Tail dark brown with white outer feathers. Bill buffish-brown with dark tip; legs pale to flesh brown. For description of female and juvenile see caption.

Lesser Whitethroat

Sylvia curruca

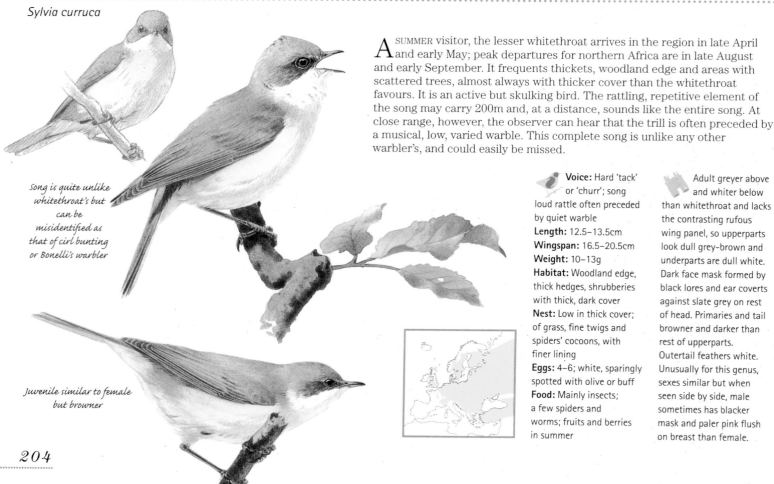

A SUMMER visitor, the lesser whitethroat arrives in the region in late April and early May; peak departures for northern Africa are in late August and early September. It frequents thickets, woodland edge and areas with scattered trees, almost always with thicker cover than the whitethroat favours. It is an active but skulking bird. The rattling, repetitive element of the song may carry 200m and, at a distance, sounds like the entire song. At close range, however, the observer can hear that the trill is often preceded by a musical, low, varied warble. This complete song is unlike any other warbler's, and could easily be missed.

Song is quite unlike whitethroat's but can be misidentified as that of cirl bunting or Bonelli's warbler

Juvenile similar to female but browner

Voice: Hard 'tack' or 'churr'; song loud rattle often preceded by quiet warble
Length: 12.5–13.5cm
Wingspan: 16.5–20.5cm
Weight: 10–13g
Habitat: Woodland edge, thick hedges, shrubberies with thick, dark cover
Nest: Low in thick cover; of grass, fine twigs and spiders' cocoons, with finer lining
Eggs: 4–6; white, sparingly spotted with olive or buff
Food: Mainly insects; a few spiders and worms; fruits and berries in summer

Adult greyer above and whiter below than whitethroat and lacks the contrasting rufous wing panel, so upperparts look dull grey-brown and underparts are dull white. Dark face mask formed by black lores and ear coverts against slate grey on rest of head. Primaries and tail browner and darker than rest of upperparts. Outertail feathers white. Unusually for this genus, sexes similar but when seen side by side, male sometimes has blacker mask and paler pink flush on breast than female.

Blackcap

Sylvia atricapilla

To most of Europe the blackcap is a summer visitor from Africa. Birds from the Mediterranean region are generally resident, however, and small numbers are increasingly overwintering in northwest Europe. The blackcap is essentially a woodland bird, but it will also nest and overwinter in parks and gardens in towns if there are sufficient trees and undergrowth. Although the cap is diagnostic, the blackcap could be confused with the marsh or willow tit, or in the south with Orphean or Sardinian warblers. The song is easily confused with that of the garden warbler.

Voice: Call loud repeated 'tac'; song loud, rich warble, rising in pitch
Length: 13cm
Wingspan: 20–23cm
Weight: 15–22g
Habitat: Open woodland and copses with thick undergrowth; in towns
Nest: Low down, in bush, briar, nettles; thin, well-made cup of grass, rootlets and cobweb
Eggs: Usually 5, variable; mainly white or buff with dark spots
Food: Many types of insect; fruit and berries especially in autumn

Adult male has diagnostic black forehead and crown (cap) above ash-grey nape and face. Upperparts ashy brown, darker on tail and primaries (although wing coverts and tertials edged paler). Chin, breast and flanks grey, the first two silvery when plumage is fresh; belly and undertail coverts white. Bill dull black, legs slate. Adult female similar to male but cap bright red-brown and upperparts browner. Juvenile very like female but cap much duller brown.

Adult female

Adult male

Largish warbler, easily identified if seen clearly

Unlike marsh tit's cap, male's black crown only extends as far as eye, not below; red-capped female unmistakable

Garden Warbler

Sylvia borin

The garden warbler is a bird of broad-leaved woodland with thick undergrowth. It is a summer visitor to Europe, overwintering in Africa. Its skulking habits and the similarity of its song to the blackcap's mean that it may be a long time before an observer sees one and confirms its identity. Its song is distinguishable from the blackcap's by its lower, contralto pitch and longer phases. The garden warbler avoids competition with the blackcap, even in overlapping territories, by arriving later, in or about the third week of April; by vertical separation in the habitat (the blackcap generally feeds higher); and by feeding on different prey.

Voice: Call loud, hard 'tac, tac'; song rich, sustained, flowing warble
Length: 14cm
Wingspan: 20–24.5cm
Weight: 19–22g
Habitat: Open deciduous or mixed woodland with thick undergrowth
Nest: Substantial, loose cup in low shrub, of dry grass, lined with grass and hair
Eggs: 4–5; usually whitish ground colour; markings very variable, like blackcap's
Food: Mostly insects

and spiders; some fruit and berries

Sexes similar. Adult has plain, brown plumage on upperparts, darker brown wings and pale-buff underparts (latter feature separating it from *Phylloscopus* warblers); belly and undertail coverts white. Eyering pale. Rounded head and stubby bill help distinguish it from *Hippolais* warblers. Juvenile more strongly marked buff below and tawny above.

Song lacks blackcap's flourish and wider range of pitch but this is compensated for by greater persistence and richness of sound

Plainest of the SYLVIA warblers and medium- to large-sized

On migration may be seen in hedgerows, eating berries

205

Greenish Warbler

Phylloscopus trochiloides

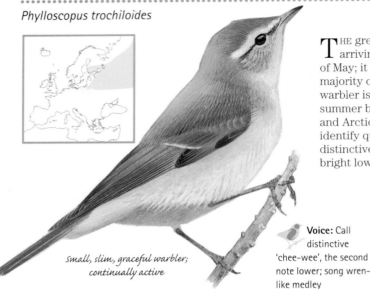

small, slim, graceful warbler; continually active

THE greenish warbler is a summer visitor to the region, arriving from the Indian sub-continent in the second half of May; it is a vagrant to northwestern Europe, with the majority of records coming in early autumn. The greenish warbler is always on the move, usually in the forest canopy in summer but lower down in winter. Because it is so like willow and Arctic warblers and the chiffchaff it is very difficult to identify quickly. Careful observation will confirm its distinctive call and song, shape and behaviour, clear wingbar, bright lower mandible, head pattern and dusky legs.

Voice: Call distinctive 'chee-wee', the second note lower; song wren-like medley

Length: 10cm
Wingspan: 15–21cm
Weight: 6–8g
Habitat: Open woodland (coniferous or broad-leaved) copses, overgrown orchards
Nest: On the ground in tall herbage; domed, of moss, grass and dead leaves
Eggs: 4–6; white
Food: Almost wholly insects; some, unusually for this genus, picked off the ground

Small and superficially similar to willow warbler. Plumage pale greyish-olive above, dull white below. Shows long, yellowish-white supercilium reaching nearly to the nape (often upturned at the end), dark eyestripe and pale wingbar (in fresh plumage). Bill has pale lower mandible; legs variable shade of brown, distinguishing bird from Arctic warbler. Juvenile in first-winter plumage similar to adult but sometimes shows faint second wingbar.

Arctic Warbler

Phylloscopus borealis

THE Arctic warbler is a common breeding bird within its range; it overwinters in southeast Asia. It is also a vagrant to western Europe, with a handful of sightings a year coming after strong easterly winds. Despite its English name, the Arctic warbler might better be called the sub-Arctic warbler since it does not breed beyond the tree-line. At the start of the breeding season, the male's display includes a remarkable wing-rattling as he flies between song-posts. The nest on the ground is usually built into the herbage or under a rotting stump so that only the entrance shows.

Voice: Calls 'tzic' and 'tseep'; song loud, energetic but monotonous trill
Length: 10.5–11.5cm
Wingspan: 16.5–22cm
Weight: 8.5–11g
Habitat: Taiga forest, willow and birch forest, often near water or damp ground
Nest: On the ground; domed, of moss, dry grass and dead leaves, lined with finer grasses
Eggs: 5–6; white, finely and sparsely spotted with light reddish-brown
Food: Almost wholly insectivorous, especially mosquitoes, ants and insect larvae

Superficially similar to several other members of the genus *Phylloscopus* (especially willow and greenish warblers, and chiffchaff) but bulkier in the body. Adult largely greenish above and off-white below. Best features are obvious creamy wingbar and yellowish-white supercilium from bill to nape, often upturned at hind end. Shows dark eyestripe, noticeably pointed brown bill and pale yellowish-brown legs. Juvenile similar to adult but with brighter colours.

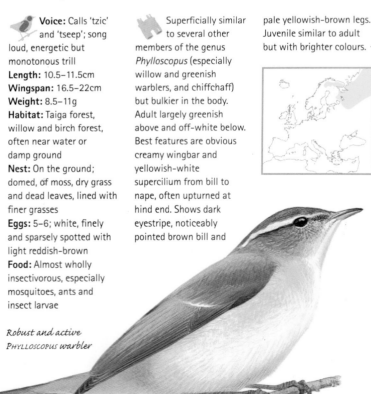

Robust and active PHYLLOSCOPUS warbler

Bonelli's Warbler

Phylloscopus bonelli

BONELLI's warbler is a summer visitor to the region, overwintering in Africa. The main autumn migration is in August; at this time vagrants are recorded annually in northwest Europe. Bonelli's warbler is an unobtrusive bird of the upper leaf canopy of woodlands. Its song often attracts attention; it is reminiscent of the wood warbler's but is lower pitched, slower and lacks the final acceleration. Care must also be taken that it is not confused with the songs of the lesser whitethroat and cirl bunting.

Voice: Call 'hu-eet' (western race), 'chirp' (eastern race); song trill on one note
Length: 11.5cm
Wingspan: 16–20cm
Weight: 7–8g
Habitat: Woods, very often cork oak or pine, usually 700–2,000m above sea level
Nest: On the ground; domed, of grasses, lined with finer grass, roots, hair; camouflaged
Eggs: Usually 4–6; white, finely and profusely spotted with dark red and purplish-brown
Food: Insects and a few other invertebrates; young also feed on insects

Adult generally pale, with light grey-brown upperparts, washed with pale olive-green. Sexes similar. Head and nape often appear particularly pale. Silky white underparts and pale yellowish rump (often seen only when it hovers). Upper mandible of bill brown, lower mandible flesh-coloured. Legs dull brown. Juvenile similar to adult but duller.

small, highly active warbler

Most birds arrive at the breeding grounds by mid-April and the eggs are laid by mid-May

Chiffchaff

Phylloscopus collybita

Very like willow warbler but appears less streamlined and a little smaller

THE chiffchaff is a summer visitor and usually the first warbler to arrive; migrants first appear at the beginning of March, later further east and north. Autumn migration begins in August and peaks in September. Most chiffchaffs overwinter around the Mediterranean and across sub-Saharan Africa, although a few overwinter in the British Isles. The chiffchaff is an active bird, flitting among the foliage and twigs, flicking its wings and tail with a distinctive sideways movement. The male defends his territory vigorously. In courtship he follows the female with quivering wings, calling, or flies towards her in the so-called 'moth flight'.

Voice: Call monosyllabic 'hweet, hweet'; song diagnostic 'chiff-chaff-chiff'
Length: 10–11cm
Wingspan: 15–21cm
Weight: 7–8g
Habitat: Woodland, but not deep forest or coniferous plantations; also copses, hedgerows
Nest: A few centimetres above ground in thick herbage; domed, of grass, lined with feathers
Eggs: 4–9, but usually 5–6; white, sparingly spotted with purple or purplish-brown

Food: Almost exclusively insects

Adult is dull brownish-olive above and dull, pale yellow below, shading to buff flanks. Browner above and more buff below than willow warbler, with much less yellow tint (although this is more noticeable on autumn juveniles). Eastern forms noticeably greyer above and whiter below than western forms, with whitish wingbar not normally found on western and southern races. Otherwise all forms lack distinctive features except for pale-yellow supercilium, pale eyering, contrasting dark eyes and dark legs (distinguishing it from willow warbler). Juveniles and first-winter migrants have warm-brown upperparts and underparts suffused with yellow.

Late-summer plumage adult

Wood Warbler

Phylloscopus sibilatrix

THE wood warbler arrives on its breeding grounds in early May, appreciably later than most of its relatives; it also leaves earlier at the end of the summer. It overwinters in equatorial Africa. On arrival the male wood warbler vigorously defends a territory, and on his courtship flight dodges in and out of the trees like a big dragonfly, until he lands by the female with quivering wings and fanned tail. The male has two strikingly different songs: the first is a repeated note, starting slowly but developing into a passionate trill; the second comprises a series of notes like the call note. He sings as many as 10 or 12 of the first sort to one of the second.

Start of the first song form often delivered in flight, but trill invariably comes from a perch

Voice: Usual call plaintive 'pew, pew'; song in two phases, mainly a trill
Length: 12cm
Wingspan: 19.5–24cm
Weight: 8–11g
Habitat: Prefers hilly terrain, and woodland with good canopy (beech and oak especially)
Nest: On the ground, with little or no ground cover; domed, of grass and dead leaves
Eggs: 6–7; white, heavily marked with reddish- or purplish-brown and greyish spots
Food: Insects and other invertebrates; some berries occasionally in autumn

The most distinctive *Phylloscopus* warbler; larger than others, with relatively longer wings and shorter tail. Sexes alike. Adult appears to be a three-colour bird: yellowish-green upperparts; bright-yellow supercilium, throat and breast; pure white belly and undertail coverts. Tail, flight feathers and tertials brown, outer edges of first two edged yellowish-green, but tertials edged white or yellowish-white. Bill has dark-brown upper mandible, pale-flesh lower mandible. Legs pale yellowish-brown. Juvenile similar to brightly coloured adult.

Long wings are not flicked; they droop either side of shortish tail

Willow Warbler

Phylloscopus trochilus

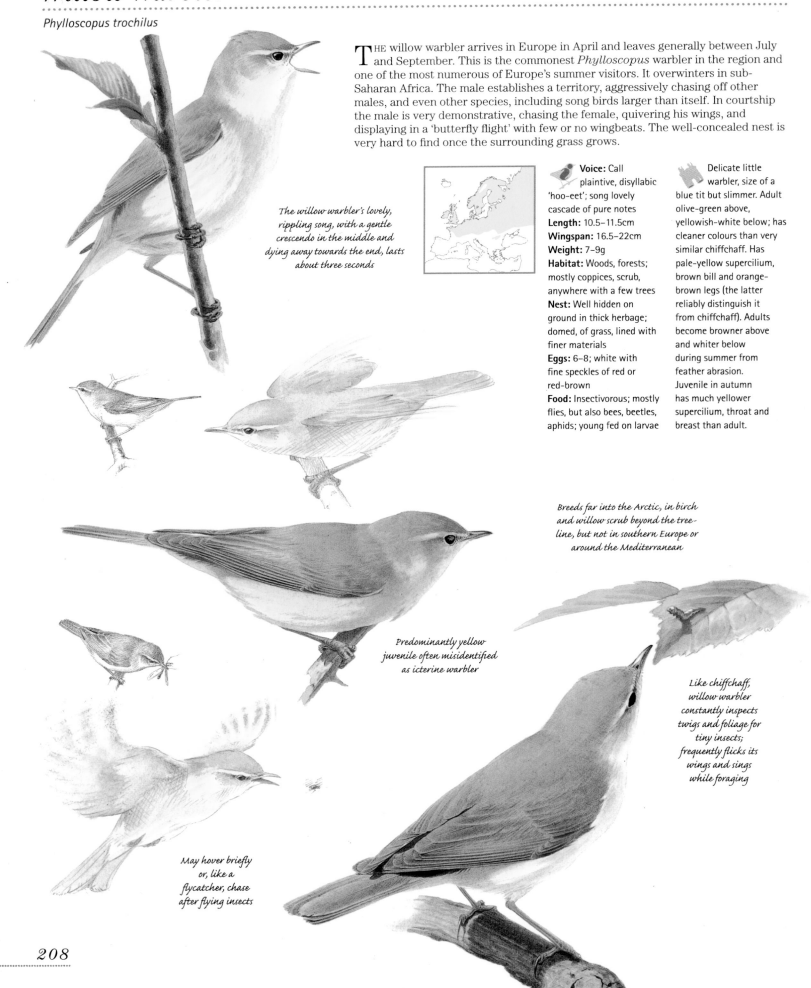

THE willow warbler arrives in Europe in April and leaves generally between July and September. This is the commonest *Phylloscopus* warbler in the region and one of the most numerous of Europe's summer visitors. It overwinters in sub-Saharan Africa. The male establishes a territory, aggressively chasing off other males, and even other species, including song birds larger than itself. In courtship the male is very demonstrative, chasing the female, quivering his wings, and displaying in a 'butterfly flight' with few or no wingbeats. The well-concealed nest is very hard to find once the surrounding grass grows.

The willow warbler's lovely, rippling song, with a gentle crescendo in the middle and dying away towards the end, lasts about three seconds

Voice: Call plaintive, disyllabic 'hoo-eet'; song lovely cascade of pure notes
Length: 10.5–11.5cm
Wingspan: 16.5–22cm
Weight: 7–9g
Habitat: Woods, forests; mostly coppices, scrub, anywhere with a few trees
Nest: Well hidden on ground in thick herbage; domed, of grass, lined with finer materials
Eggs: 6–8; white with fine speckles of red or red-brown
Food: Insectivorous; mostly flies, but also bees, beetles, aphids; young fed on larvae

Delicate little warbler, size of a blue tit but slimmer. Adult olive-green above, yellowish-white below; has cleaner colours than very similar chiffchaff. Has pale-yellow supercilium, brown bill and orange-brown legs (the latter reliably distinguish it from chiffchaff). Adults become browner above and whiter below during summer from feather abrasion. Juvenile in autumn has much yellower supercilium, throat and breast than adult.

Breeds far into the Arctic, in birch and willow scrub beyond the tree-line, but not in southern Europe or around the Mediterranean

Predominantly yellow juvenile often misidentified as icterine warbler

Like chiffchaff, willow warbler constantly inspects twigs and foliage for tiny insects; frequently flicks its wings and sings while foraging

May hover briefly or, like a flycatcher, chase after flying insects

Goldcrest

Regulus regulus

Adult

THE goldcrest is resident in much of its range, migrating in winter only from the harshest weather in the far north and east; in winter, numbers in northwest Europe are noticeably increased by immigrants from northern Europe. In the breeding season goldcrests will inhabit deciduous woods, gardens, cemeteries and parks if there are some suitable conifers, especially when populations are high. In winter small groups often move with tits and treecreepers and are found in pine stands of deciduous woodland as well as conifer forests. Feeding flocks keep up a continuous stream of contact notes (like the song, too high-pitched for some people to hear).

When foraging for food goldcrests are often seemingly indifferent to human observers

Voice: Calls frequently; song repeated double note and trill; all very high pitched
Length: 9cm
Wingspan: 13.5–15.5cm
Weight: 4.5–7.5g
Habitat: Coniferous woods for breeding; wanders widely in winter
Nest: Hammock of moss, lichens and cobwebs near end of conifer twig
Eggs: 7–10; white or pale buff, finely speckled with buff-brown
Food: Insectivorous; especially springtails, aphids, leafbugs and lepidoptera larvae

Tiny: Europe's smallest bird. Adults have dull, greenish upperparts, pale olive-green underparts, darker on the flanks. Wing coverts greenish with two white wingbars. Appears to be large-eyed, black on a whitish face. Forehead whitish; crown of male orange-yellow, lined each side with black, often not noticeable in the field; in display male raises crest to reveal startling orange centre. Crown centre of female yellow. For description of juvenile see caption.

To maintain body weight goldcrests need to feed almost continually during daylight hours

Juvenile similar to adult but lacks crown colours and markings

Firecrest

Regulus ignicapillus

THE firecrest is much less widespread than the goldcrest, breeding only in more temperate and warmer parts of central and southern Europe. Northern and eastern populations are migratory, moving in winter to the Mediterranean basin and the far southwest. In display the male points his bill towards the bird he is displaying at, thus showing the crest and the startling face pattern of black and white stripes. The firecrest spends more time in broad-leaved trees than the goldcrest; in conifers it feeds in less dense branches, moves about more and prefers larger prey. The male holds a larger territory and defends it with a louder, more penetrating song.

Male

Greener above and whiter below than goldcrest, and shows bright-orange shoulder patches

Voice: Very high-pitched; 'zit, zit,' call lower than goldcrest; song rapid string of calls
Length: 9cm
Wingspan: 13–16cm
Weight: 4.5–6.5g
Habitat: Less restricted to conifers than goldcrest; gardens, scrub, tree heath
Nest: Deep cup slung under a twig near end of branch; of moss, lichen and cobwebs
Eggs: Usually 7–11, sometimes 12; pinkish buff colour with very fine red dots

Food: Arthropods, especially springtails, aphids, spiders; insect larvae

Adult is more brightly coloured than goldcrest. Most striking feature is striped head: male has golden-orange crown stripe, lined each side with black; crown stripe of female yellow. Adults of both sexes have similar plumages to goldcrest, but more brightly coloured. Both show white supercilium underlined by

black eyestripe. Mantle to uppertail coverts bright olive-green, tail darker and browner; all underparts white. Striking bronze patch on side of neck. Bill black, legs brown. Juvenile plumage colour similar to adult, but lacks yellow or orange crown. Immature birds on autumn migration have invariably acquired adult-like plumage.

Often feeds closer to the ground than goldcrest does; on migration favours bracken and brambles

Female

209

Comparing Immature Phylloscopus *Warblers*

ADULT *Phylloscopus* warblers in spring are comparatively easy to identify, not least because males often sing distinctive and diagnostic songs. In autumn, however, it is a diffferent matter. Birds are generally silent, apart form uttering the occasional call, and the plumages of immature birds often differs in subtle ways from that which characterises the adult of the same species.

CHIFFCHAFF: Plumage generally warmer-toned than adult's with upperparts olive-brown and underparts paler and flushed with yellow; never as yellow as immature willow warbler and legs always black

BONELLI'S WARBLER: Considerably duller than adult but still degree of contrast between greyish head and neck, white underparts and greenish-yellow upperparts; yellowish rump and flash on wings usually visible; frenetic feeding activity often useful clue

WOOD WARBLER: Plumage duller than spring adult but still shows contrast between greenish-brown upperparts and white underparts; yellowish wash to face and to broad, conspicuous pale supercilium

WILLOW WARBLER: Immatures often look strikingly yellow; palest and brightest on underparts; leg colour always flesh-toned

GREENISH WARBLER: Small, active warbler with olive-green upperparts and pale olive-grey underparts; always shows long, narrow supercilium and two faint wingbars

ARCTIC WARBLER: Dull olive-brown upperparts and pale-grey underparts, long, narrow supercilium; often shows two pale wingbars (adult has one) like greenish warbler; note Arctic's bulkier size, larger head and bill and paler pink legs

Vagrant Old World Warblers

BLYTH'S REED WARBLER (*ACROCEPHALUS DUMETORUM*): Medium-sized, slim warbler; superficially very similar to both reed and marsh warblers. Sexes similar; juvenile similar to adult but upperparts warmer brown

Breeds in north central Russia and just into Sweden and Finland; very rare autumn vagrant to northwest Europe

YELLOW-BROWED WARBLER (*PHYLLOSCOPUS INORNATUS*): Tiny, active warbler, intermediate in size between goldcrest and chiffchaff. Sexes similar; most striking features are long, pale-yellow supercilium and double pale-yellow wingbar. Juvenile similar to adult but browner and duller

Breeds in Siberia; scarce late-autumn vagrant to Europe, often in good numbers

PALLAS'S WARBLER (*PHYLLOSCOPUS PROREGULUS*): tiny, extremely active warbler; superficially similar to yellow-browed warbler but smaller and more strikingly marked. Sexes similar; juvenile similar to adult but upperparts browner

DESERT WARBLER (*SYLVIA NANA*): Small, extremely pale warbler. Generally skulking but sometimes perches on top of bush like Dartford warbler. Sexes similar; juvenile similar to adult

Resident in north Africa and breeds in central Asia; very rare, mostly late-autumn migrant to northwest Europe

Breeds in Siberia; rare but regular autumn vagrant to Europe, mainly to northwest

Breeds locally in Bulgaria and Romania; very rare vagrant to northwest Europe

PADDYFIELD WARBLER (*ACROCEPHALUS AGRICOLA*): medium-sized, skulking warbler; similar to reed warbler but with more contrast in plumage. Sexes similar; juvenile similar to adult but plumage shows less contrast

DUSKY WARBLER (*PHYLLOSCOPUS FUSCATUS*): small, active warbler; superficially similar to chiffchaff but legs pink, not blackish, and plumage darker (similar to Radde's warbler's). Sexes similar; juvenile similar to adult

Breeds in Siberia; rare autumn vagrant to northwest Europe

Breeds in eastern central Asia; rare autumn vagrant to northwest Europe

Breeds in Siberia; rare autumn vagrant to northwest Europe

RADDE'S WARBLER (*PHYLLOSCOPUS SCHWARZI*): large, plump warbler with short, thick bill and proportionately large head; movements slower than other warblers'; sexes similar; juvenile similar to adult but with yellowish upperparts

BOOTED WARBLER (*HIPPOLAIS CALIGATA*): small and pale, superficially similar to *PHYLLOSCOPUS* warbler, but more stocky with more robust bill and pale lores; sexes similar; juvenile similar to adult but with darker upperparts and flanks

Spotted Flycatcher

Muscicapa striata

Juvenile

Adult

Members of the first brood are known to feed the second brood, which helps to ensure that both broods are able to migrate

Tᴴɪꜱ drably coloured flycatcher is the most widespread flycatcher in the region, breeding throughout lowland Europe except where tree cover is absent or where the forest is dense. It is often the last summer visitor to arrive on its breeding territory from Africa, in early May, yet many manage to rear two broods before leaving, usually in August and September. The spotted flycatcher obtains most of its food in flight. It uses an open perch from which it sallies forth, sometimes with several twists and turns, before it catches an insect. It often returns to the same branch, where it perches with its characteristic upright stance, legs and feet hardly showing.

Voice: Call 'tzee-zuk-zuk'; song quiet, short, squeaky
Length: 14.5cm
Wingspan: 23–25.5cm
Weight: 14–18g
Habitat: Woodland edge, glades, parks, orchards, gardens
Nest: In a tree-fork, crevice or creeper; plant material and twigs, lined with feathers and hair
Eggs: 4–5; very pale blue, mottled and blotched reddish and purplish
Food: Mainly flying insects, especially flies and bees

Largest flycatcher in the region and the only one with streaked underparts. Adult has all upperparts, wings and tail grey-brown, appearing unmarked at long range. Sexes similar. Forehead and crown streaked black, outlined in white. Underparts white, washed with brown on side of breast and flanks. At close range throat, side of breast and flanks show dull-brown streaks. Bill dull grey-brown. Legs brown or black. Juvenile superficially similar to adult but upperparts buffer than adult's; feathers of head, back, rump, lesser and median coverts have pale, round, buff-white spots; underparts not streaked like those of adult but spotted dark brown.

Pied Flycatcher

Ficedula hypoleuca

Tᴴᴇ pied flycatcher is a summer visitor, overwintering in Africa in the forests bordering the Gulf of Guinea. Pied flycatchers arrive in Europe between mid-April and late May; the males arrive first and choose the nest hole, and sing until they have attracted mates. These visitors leave in August and September, stopping over in Portugal before their trans-Saharan flight. Many males successively take two or three mates, each in different territories, but will help to feed only the first brood. After the breeding season, pied flycatchers become remarkably secretive as they prepare for migration.

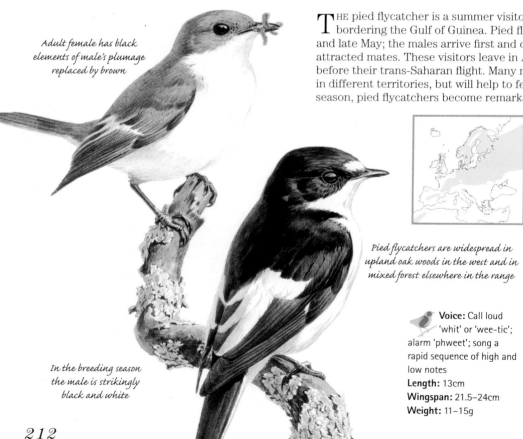

Adult female has black elements of male's plumage replaced by brown

Pied flycatchers are widespread in upland oak woods in the west and in mixed forest elsewhere in the range

In the breeding season the male is strikingly black and white

Habitat: Deciduous and mixed open woodland; has spread to orchards, gardens
Nest: In a tree-hole; loose cup of leaves, grass and bark, lined with finer materials
Eggs: 6–7; pale blue, rarely with fine reddish-brown speckles
Food: Flying and non-flying arthropods, especially bees, flies and beetles

Voice: Call loud 'whit' or 'wee-tic'; alarm 'phweet'; song a rapid sequence of high and low notes
Length: 13cm
Wingspan: 21.5–24cm
Weight: 11–15g

Very similar to collared and semi-collared flycatchers. Breeding male black above and unmarked white below, but black is relieved by white forehead (often divided into two spots), white-edged tertials, which meet white bar on greater wing coverts and white basal half of outertail feathers. From central Europe eastwards males are increasingly grey-brown, not black. After breeding, male moults and black elements of plumage replaced by brown or grey, so white wing panel not so striking. Female resembles non-breeding male but tail and rump not as black. Bill and legs black in all plumages. Juvenile looks like non-breeding adult with buff-spotted crown, mantle and breast.

Red-breasted Flycatcher

Ficedula parva

THE red-breasted flycatcher is a forest bird, preferring tall trees, especially beech in the west of its range. It is a summer visitor, overwintering in Asia, and usually arrives in Europe in early May. It is a rare but annual passage migrant to northwest Europe, first-winter birds being recorded mainly in September and October. The red-breasted flycatcher is very agile on the wing, flicking and cocking its tail more than its relatives do. Although it is secretive and unobtrusive for most of the breeding season, the male is more noticeable in May, when he sings in flight, fluttering from perch to perch.

Voice: Call short, harsh 'zit'; song cadence, descending in pitch
Length: 11.5cm
Wingspan: 18.5–21cm
Weight: 9–13g
Habitat: Mixed and deciduous forest with much undergrowth
Nest: In tree hollow or hole; small cup of moss, leaves and lichen, lined with hair

Eggs: 5–6; whitish, very finely speckled with reddish-brown
Food: Insects and other invertebrates, mostly in the tree canopy

Adults of both sexes ashy brown above; flanks washed with buff; wings and tail dark brown. Tail has diagnostic long, white patches each side at the base, noticeable in flight and when bird flicks its tail. Male has orange-red chin, throat and upper breast, and looks like diminutive robin, but female has buff throat and breast. Juvenile is spotted, but retains the white tail patches. First-winter plumage similar to female. In all plumages, dark eye is highlighted by white eyering, more noticeable in the male.

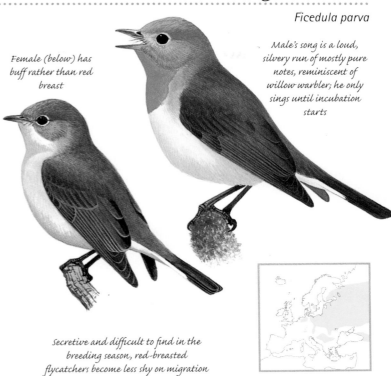

Female (below) has buff rather than red breast

Male's song is a loud, silvery run of mostly pure notes, reminiscent of willow warbler; he only sings until incubation starts

Secretive and difficult to find in the breeding season, red-breasted flycatchers become less shy on migration

Collared Flycatcher

Ficedula albicollis

THE collared flycatcher overwinters south of the Equator in eastern Africa. It returns to southern Europe to breed in late April, but does not reach the north of its range until mid-May. It is a vagrant to northwest Europe. Collared flycatchers are more shy than pied and semi-collared flycatchers and forage more in tree canopies. The best chance of finding one in a wood would be to recognise either the wistful song or the far-carrying, distinctive 'seep' alarm note; or better still be introduced to a nest box-using population.

Voice: Call 'seep'; song like pied flycatcher's, a series of high and low notes and whistles
Length: 13cm
Wingspan: 22.5–24.5cm
Weight: 12–16g
Habitat: Sunny, deciduous woodland and forest, well-timbered parks, orchards
Nest: Cup of leaves and grass, lined with fine grass, in a hole in a tree or wall, or a nest box
Eggs: 5–7; very pale blue, unmarked

Food: Flying and non-flying arthropods and their larvae

Very like pied and semi-collared flycatchers; breeding male unmistakable but other plumages probably not separable from these two species. Breeding male white below and black above relieved by white forehead and diagnostic features: broad white collar round neck separating cap from mantle; white wing panel from tertials to flight feathers; whitish patch on lower back and rump; black (or mottled white) outertail feathers. Female, immature and winter male have black elements of male's plumage replaced by brown, and lack white collar.

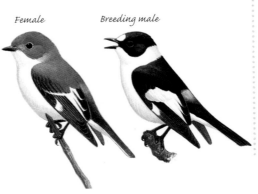

Female   *Breeding male*

Semi-collared Flycatcher

Ficedula semitorquata

THE semi-collared flycatcher is the rarest flycatcher in the region; its distribution is limited by its preference for oak or hornbeam forest in its main breeding area, and ancient beech forest in Greece. The males arrive at their breeding grounds several days before the females and select suitable nest holes. When the females arrive, the males advertise their holes by singing and displaying close by, particularly a 'dancing-display'. In this the male silently flies in a bouncing line to a female at the nest hole, hovers, then dances back to his perch. The song is similar to the collared flycatcher's but faster.

Voice: Calls include a loud 'whit'; song a rapid sequence of high and low notes; hard to distinguish from related flycatchers'
Length: 13cm
Wingspan: 23.5–24cm
Weight: 13–15g
Habitat: Deciduous forest on mountain slopes up to 2,000m above sea level, and riverine forest
Nest: In a tree-hole; cup of dead leaves, grass and moss, lined with finer grass
Eggs: 5–6; pale blue, unmarked
Food: Mainly flying insects

Breeding male basically black above and white below; black broken by white patch on forehead. White on side of neck extends into half-collar up to side of nape. Large wing panel formed by white outer halves to tertials meeting white-tipped greater coverts and bases to flight feathers. Short white bar on median coverts not found on pied or collared flycatchers. Greyish band across lower back and rump. White outertail feathers, with more white throughout than pied or collared flycatchers. Male moults before autumn migration, then looks like female. Female has black elements of male's plumage replaced by grey-brown; positive identification only possible if second wingbar is clear. Bill and legs black in all plumages. Juvenile similar to female.

Breeding male

Willow Tit

Parus montanus

Adult of British race very similar to marsh tit; has plumper appearance, duller black cap and buffish flanks

The nest hole is excavated by both male and female but only the female builds the nest

THE willow tit favours three different habitats in different parts of its range. Conifers are preferred on the slopes of southern mountains while lowland river valleys and overgrown stands of trees on damp ground are chosen at lower altitudes. Northern birch and conifer woodlands are the species' haunt at northern latitudes. The willow tit excavates its own nest hole, low in a very soft, rotten stump, generally alder, birch, willow or elder. Willow tits pair for life, live in the same territory all year round, and in winter are gregarious and will forage with other tits.

Nest: In hole in rotten tree stump; cup of plant materials, rarely moss, lined with hair
Eggs: 6–9; white, variably speckled with red-brown
Food: Mainly invertebrates in breeding season; seeds and berries at other times

Voice: Calls 'eez-eez-eez' and characteristic, nasal 'tchay, tchay'; warbling song
Length: 11.5cm
Wingspan: 17–20.5cm
Weight: 10–13g
Habitat: Montane, coniferous forest; trees on damp ground; mixed woodland

Very similar in size and appearance to marsh tit, but looks less smart than that species. Adult has black cap extending down to mantle. Black bib quite extensive, with poorly defined borders. Tail is slightly round-ended, not square or slightly forked. Best plumage difference is this species' light patch on secondaries in closed wing (not always conspicuous, however). Scandinavian and central European birds much greyer on back and whiter on face than British birds, which are closest in appearance to marsh tit. Juvenile very similar to adult of any given race. Always note call notes as well as plumage details to separate this species from marsh tit.

Marsh Tit

Parus palustris

The nest is in a hole, often low down in an old or decaying tree, so the marsh tit avoids unsympathetically managed woodland

Neck is slimmer and bib neater than on willow tit

Marsh tits hold tough seeds like beech-mast under one foot and hammer at them with their strong bills

Ringing has shown that marsh tits rarely move more than 20km from where they were ringed

THE marsh tit is separable from the willow tit only with difficulty, by noting its glossy black cap, which does not extend as far down the nape, its small bib with well-defined edges, its paler underparts, its lack of a pale wing panel and its quite distinct calls and song. It does not visit birdtables as frequently as other tits, nor does it readily take to a nest box. Marsh tits pair for life and spend the whole year in the same territory. They sometimes join other tits but rarely stray out of their own territory, even in hard weather.

Voice: Calls 'pitchoo' and nasal 'ter-char-char-char'; song repetition on one note
Length: 11.5cm
Wingspan: 18–19.5cm
Weight: 9–12g
Habitat: Deciduous woodland, especially oak and beech, not marshes
Nest: Low, in hole in tree or stump; cup of moss, lined with hair and feathers

Eggs: 7–10; white, usually with fine reddish-brown spots at larger end
Food: Mostly insects and spiders in spring and summer; seeds and nuts in winter

In Europe, one of four dark-capped tits with similar plumage pattern (see also willow, Siberian and sombre tits), though each each has clear size and colour differences. Sexes similar. Adult has glossy black cap from bill to nape. Small black chin and centre of throat, rest of face white. Wings, tail and upperparts greyish-brown, with dark-brown centres to tail feathers. Underparts dull white, with pale-buff tinge on flanks and undertail coverts. Bill short and black. Legs dark blue-grey. Juvenile very similar to adult but cap not glossy. Acquires adult plumage by September.

Coal Tit

Parus ater

THE coal tit is often considered the most typical tit of coniferous woods, but in southern and western Europe it is more often found in mixed and deciduous forest, as well as almost anywhere where there are a few conifers. It readily comes to birdtables in winter and is especially fond of sunflower seeds. The coal tit's toes and claws are long and are specially adapted to a life in conifers; it shows greater agility than other tits when foraging in the foliage. When viewed from below it is very like other black-capped tits; from this angle, the extent of the black bib and its calls are the most important features.

Voice: Call piping 'tsee'; song loud and clear 'teechu, teechu, teechu'
Length: 11.5cm
Wingspan: 17–21cm
Weight: 9–10g
Habitat: Typically coniferous forest and woodland, but now anywhere with firs,
including cemeteries and parks
Nest: In hole in tree-stump, tree, wall or rock; of moss, lined with hair and wool
Eggs: 8–9; white, finely speckled with red-brown
Food: Adult and larval insects and spiders; seeds in autumn and winter

Slightly smaller and shorter-tailed than blue tit. Adult has glossy black cap and white cheeks; large, white patch on nape is diagnostic. Cap extends down to level of eye; chin, throat, upper breast black, joined to cap by black collar. Underparts buff,
paler towards the centre. Upperparts, wings and tail olive-grey. Median and greater wing coverts have white tips, forming two wingbars. Bill rather fine, black. Legs lead-blue. Sexes similar but female has less extensive bib. Juvenile similar to adult but markings less distinctive.

Distinctive double wingbar is often easier to see than nape patch; at close range wingbars show as separate white spots

Siberian Tit

Parus cinctus

THE Siberian tit is a rather sedentary resident, but juveniles are sometimes nomadic outside the breeding season. In winter it visits the houses of foresters to feed on birdtables and rubbish-tips, and will even land on foresters who are having a meal to pick up crumbs. This tit is territorial, pairs for life, and is gregarious in winter, when small flocks follow the same route each day through the forest. Unusually for a tit, the Siberian tit does not have a far-carrying song, and it can therefore be hard to find.

Voice: Call 'sip' and 'tchay' similar to willow tit; song unmusical repetition of calls
Length: 13.5cm
Wingspan: 19.5–21cm
Weight: 11–14g
Habitat: Coniferous taiga, tree-lined river banks, virgin coniferous forest
Nest: In tree-hole or nest box; moss and grass base with cup of hair
Eggs: 6–10; white with sparse brown spots over olive-brown and grey spots
Food: Small invertebrates and seeds; at birdtables in winter

Rather large, often fluffy-looking tit, a little smaller than great tit. Sexes alike. Adult has sooty-brown cap and nape, with darker line through eye. White face. Large sooty-black bib with broken edge. Upperparts warm
brown. Wings dark brown and all flight feathers clearly edged with greyish-white, making biggest contrast between wings and back of all black-capped tits. Tail grey-black with dull-white outer feathers. Underparts two-toned: breast and belly dull white, while sides of breast and flanks rusty red. Bill black. Legs grey. Juvenile similar to adult.

Very confiding, even at nest site

Sombre Tit

Parus lugubris

ALTHOUGH it is as large as a great tit and is easy to identify, the sombre tit is hard to find because it spends so much time in the foliage of the woods and open forests it inhabits. Its song is not striking, having a repetitive, buzzing quality, but it does have a characteristic call of alarm or excitement, a deep 'churrrr', not unlike a sparrow's alarm. The sombre tit comes to ground much less often than other tits and over 90 per cent of its time is spent foraging in the crown of deciduous trees.

Voice: Call loud 'churrrr'; song unmusical repetition of a single note
Length: 14cm
Wingspan: 21.5–23cm
Weight: 15–19g
Habitat: Open forest, orchards, vineyards, conifers, scrub
Nest: In hole in a tree; cup of plant materials (not moss), lined with feathers
Eggs: 5–7; white with fine reddish speckles
Food: Mainly small invertebrates, especially their larvae

Dull plumage pattern similar to marsh tit's. Adult has sooty-black, long cap. Sooty-black chin and throat appear as large
bib. Cheeks, ear coverts and sides of neck white. Upperpart, wings and tail ashy brown, with distinct greyish-white fringes to tertials and inner secondaries. Underparts dull, creamy white with ash-brown wash on the sides. Bill strong, black. Legs grey. Female similar to male but with less contrasting cap. Juvenile is similar to adult female, but cheeks look grubby.

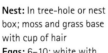

Has heavy bill to split large seeds

Adult male

Blue Tit

Parus caeruleus

Male glides slowly towards a possible nest site to attract female to it; at other times flight action is fluttery

Adult

Blue tits readily take to nest boxes but prefer ones sited in oak trees if available

Blue tits are known to exploit the nectar in willow catkins and cherry flowers, a rich food source little used by other European birds

Fledglings have same patterning as adults but yellower face

Blue tits are extremely acrobatic, and unlike great tits are light enough to forage at the tips of even the thinnest twigs

In Britain blue tits sometimes rip open tops of newly delivered milk bottles to drink the cream

THE blue tit is abundant in most habitats with trees, although it avoids conifers, and outside the breeding season even wanders to reedbeds and clifftops. It tends to feed high up in broad-leaved trees, foraging on twigs, buds and leaves, but will visit birdtables in winter. Blue tits are inquisitive and agile birds: they tap reed stems to locate hidden prey and open only those stems that contain larvae. They are occasionally known to hang by one foot and grab food with the other and routinely hold hard seeds underfoot and hammer them with their bill; they can also solve birdtable puzzles in order to reach food.

Voice: Call 'tsee-tsee;. alarm 'chirr.r.r'; song tremolo 'tsee-tsee-tsee-tsuhuhuhu'
Length: 11.5cm
Wingspan: 17.5–20cm
Weight: 10–12g
Habitat: Anywhere with trees, even inner-city parks and gardens
Nest: Hole in tree or wall, nest box; pad of moss, cup lined with hair and fine grass
Eggs: 6–16; white with fine, reddish spots
Food: Chiefly adult and larval insects and spiders; fruits and seeds in winter

Adult is the only European tit with bright-blue crown, bordered with white. Sexes similar. Has dark lines from bill through eye, around back of head and around otherwise white cheeks. Upperparts yellowish-green, underparts sulphur-yellow, with small blackish central streak. Wings dark blue with white wingbar. Tail dark grey-blue. Bill short, black. Legs dusky blue. Juvenile washed yellow and lacks blue in plumage but similar to adult in other respects.

Azure Tit

Parus cyanus

THIS stunning forest bird is resident across central Asia as far west as the borders of Europe; from time to time it breeds in Finland and there are indications that the species' range is expanding somewhat. Azure tits also occur as rare vagrants to Europe, especially in the east. Azure tits appear to favour broad-leaved woods throughout most of their range, often occurring in areas where these grade into wetland habitats. They can be surprisingly difficult to locate as they are generally retiring in their habits. During the winter months, azure tits will also visit reedbeds to forage for food. The species could potentially be confused with long-tailed tits with damaged and shortened tails or partially leucistic blue tits and great tits.

Voice: Utters a trilling song; calls include a nasal 'tzee-tzee'
Length: 13cm
Wingspan: 19–20cm
Weight: 12–13g
Habitat: Mainly broad-leaved woodland
Nest: In tree-holes and nest boxes
Eggs: 9–10; white with faint speckling
Food: Mainly insects and other invertebrates

Attractive tit, unmistakable when seen well. Sexes similar. Adult and juvenile have largely white plumage. Head shows narrow black stripe running back from eye to join black nape band. Back pale blue-grey and wings blue with white wingbar and white tips to secondary feathers. Tail proportionately long; blue with white feather tips. Bill stubby and dark and legs dark.

Voice: Call loud 'tink, tink, tink'; song far-carrying 'teacher, teacher, teacher'
Length: 14cm
Wingspan: 22.5–25.5cm
Weight: 16–20g
Habitat: Almost anywhere with trees, except coniferous forest; even in cities
Nest: In hole in wall or tree, or nest boxes; moss base, cup lined with hair, wool and feathers
Eggs: 5–12; white, speckled reddish-brown, larger than blue tit's markings
Food: Great variety of adult and larval insects; spiders; seeds and fruits in winter

The largest common tit, with quite a long tail. Adult is basically yellow-green above and yellow below. Wings have black flight feathers, blue-grey coverts and black tertials, tipped white. Shows white wingbar and white outertail feathers. Distinctive head pattern comprises glossy blue-black cap with triangular white cheek patch. Black on chin and throat extends into bold, black stripe down centre of underparts, forming a wide black patch

Great Tit

Parus major

THE great tit has the widest distribution in the world of all the tits. Birds from western and southern Europe are mostly sedentary but northern and central European birds, at times of high population, irrupt into other parts of Europe. Great tits forage for food low down more than other tits. Those resident in beech woods may spend as much as 45 per cent of their time on the ground in late autumn searching for beech-mast. By contrast, in an oak wood they may spend 60 per cent of the time on low branches in search of insects. In winter they regularly come to birdtables.

between legs on male, and much narrower one on female. Bill strong and black. Legs blue-grey. Juvenile similar to adult but has sooty crown, browner back, cheeks washed yellow and underparts duller yellow.

Scientists at Oxford University have been conducting long-term ecological studies of the great tit since 1947, making this one of the most investigated species in Europe

Large size and striking combination of colours make great tit unmistakable

Song is vary varied, often leading to misidentification

Juveniles look very washed out and have yellow cheeks rather than white

Adult male

On the forest floor great tits will toss leaves aside and rip up fungi and moss in their search for food

Wings and tail are held fanned in threat posture

Crested Tit

Parus cristatus

THE crested tit is the only small European bird with a crest. It is a very sedentary bird, only very rarely wandering as far as 50km. The crested tit is an undemonstrative tit with a limited vocal repertoire. Most of the work of excavating the nest hole and building the actual nest is done by the female; a new hole is prepared each year, even if it is made in the same stump as last year's hole. Unusually among the tits, the young are not fed extensively on moth larvae, receiving instead many spiders and pine seeds. In common with their relatives, however, crested tits store food in autumn for use in winter.

Crest can be very difficult to see, particularly if bird is overhead

The crested tit's range is confined by its need for rotten wood in which to excavate its nest hole

Crested tits often feed clinging to a tree-trunk

Voice: Call low-pitched purring trill; song makes repeated use of calls
Length: 11.5cm
Wingspan: 17–20cm
Weight: 10–12g
Habitat: Pine forest in the north; mixed woods; also in beech or cork oak woods in south
Nest: Moss, lined with hair and wool, in an excavated tree-hole
Eggs: 6–7; white, spotted and blotched rusty-red, usually more at large end
Food: Insects and spiders; seeds outside breeding season

Small tit with backward-pointing black crest, with the feathers tipped white. Sexes similar. Adult has very distinctive face pattern of black line on a white face, running behind eye and around rear of ear coverts; another black line starts at end of crest and runs down side of neck to join black bib. Upperparts buff-brown, wings and tail grey-brown. Bill black, quite long for a small tit. Legs olive-grey. Juvenile has shorter crest than adult but otherwise similar.

Long-tailed Tit

Aegithalos caudatus

THE long-tailed tit is mainly sedentary, but at times of high populations many irrupt from their breeding grounds. Long-tailed tits are territorial in the breeding season, after which they are gregarious, forming small flocks of around ten birds. These flocks defend a winter territory against others, and consist of parents, their offspring and helpers related to the male. A flock keeps together with the help of a constant 'conversation' of 'tsirrrup' calls, as its members restlessly hunt for food. The flock roosts communally, in a thick bush, huddled together on one horizontal perch.

Western European race adult

Unusual oval nest takes the male and female three weeks to build

Tiny-bodied, long-tailed bird, not related to true tits

Adult of Scandinavian race

Voice: Call low, repeated 'tsupp'; alarm trilled 'tsirrrrup'; song rapid repetition of calls
Length: 14cm
Wingspan: 16–19cm
Weight: 7–9g
Habitat: Deciduous woodland; for nesting, thick scrub like gorse, bramble or briar
Nest: Usually in a thorny bush; domed nest of moss, lichen and feathers
Eggs: 8–12; white, unmarked or with minute reddish speckles

Food: Insects, especially eggs and larvae of butterflies and moths

Sexes similar. Adult birds from most of Europe have head and underparts whitish, washed with dusky pink on nape, and from belly to undertail coverts; black bands extend from bill, above the eyes to the mantle. Upperparts, wings and tail dull black, with pink scapulars and rump, and white tips and edges to graduated tail feathers. Pink tones wear off. Adult of subspecies from northern and eastern Europe has pure white head and noticeably white-edged tertials and secondaries; birds of southern subspecies have grey backs, darker faces, and little or no pink. Eyering reddish in all birds. Juvenile shorter and darker than adult, with little pink.

Bearded Tit

Panurus biarmicus

THE Netherlands are Europe's bearded tit stronghold with up to 55,000 pairs but, as elsewhere in Europe, populations suffer in hard winters. The bearded tit is very dependent on reedbeds. Here it is very gregarious outside the breeding season and confiding at nesting time. The birds are restless and regularly fly out low over the reeds, with whirring wings and long, waving tail. The birds are not territorial, and nests are often concentrated in one place, leaving large, communal feeding areas. Juveniles form flocks of up to 200 soon after independence.

Female (right)

Adult male

Voice: Call explosive, metallic 'ping'; song quiet and easy to miss
Length: 12.5cm
Wingspan: 16–18cm
Weight: 14–19g
Habitat: Large reedbeds
Nest: Low down; deep cup of dead reed leaves, lined with reed flowers and feathers
Eggs: 4–8; white or creamy white, finely marked with dark brown
Food: Chiefly invertebrates in summer; seeds in autumn and winter

Short-winged, very long-tailed, unmistakable bird with predominantly tawny-russet plumage at all times. Adult male has grey head and striking black 'moustaches' of loose feathers highlighted by white chin and throat. Tail graduated, with white tips to feathers forming ladder effect. Undertail coverts black. Closed wing appears banded: white on outer flight feathers, rufous centre panel, black and white tertials. Stubby yellow bill, orange eye, black legs. Female lacks male's head pattern, is duller and less russet; undertail coverts warm buff but similar to male in other respects. Juvenile resembles female but has obvious black back and wing coverts.

In the breeding season, from April to August, bearded tits regularly rear two broods and sometimes three

Most populations are sedentary but when numbers are high birds disperse to nearby lakes and marshes

Penduline Tit

Remiz pendulinus

THE penduline tit is migratory in the north of the range, and resident in the south. The migrants winter in southern Europe within the species' overall breeding range. Adult penduline tits are gregarious, active little birds and both adults and juveniles will allow close approach. A family stays together in a flock after breeding and attracts attention with its soft, repeated calls. The penduline tit's amazing nest is started by the male, who twists plant fibres into a ring dangling from a forked twig on a tree that hangs over or is near water. Once mated, the pair build a cup, which is then roofed; finally a little tunnel is made for an entrance near the top.

Plant fibres of hop and nettle are the main nest materials, woven tightly to a felt-like consistency with plant down and wool

Voice: Call soft drawn out 'tseeoo' and tit-like 'tsi-tsi-tsi'; song finch-like trill
Length: 11cm
Wingspan: 16–17.5cm
Weight: 8.5–10g
Habitat: Luxuriant vegetation by fresh or brackish water
Nest: Large, hanging, domed pouch with entrance tube at top
Eggs: 6–8; white
Food: Mainly larval insects and spiders; seeds outside breeding season

Smaller than blue tit, but with relatively longer tail. Adult has pale-grey head with black mask. Mantle, scapulars and wing coverts chestnut. Flight feathers black, fringed with buff. Back and rump greyish, contrasting with nearly black tail, which has off-white feather margins. Underparts off-white with chestnut smudges on sides of breast and flanks. Bill black. Legs bluish-black. Sexes similar, but female less bright than male. Juvenile lacks black face mask of adult and has cinnamon back.

Males build throughout the breeding season as part of a complex mating system: both males and females usually have more than one mate

Nuthatch

Sitta europaea

Western European race adult

THE nuthatch is the only widespread member of its family in Europe. It is a resident and very sedentary. Birds pair for life and live in the same territory throughout the year, and most juveniles settle within 10km of where they hatched; all ages are tolerant of humans and regularly visit birdtables in winter. The nuthatch searches for food on tree-trunks; a seed is fixed in a crevice of bark in a tree and hammered open with blows of its bill. It stores food in the winter in the same way that tits do. Sometimes an observer is attracted to a nuthatch by hearing the ringing blows high up in a tree.

This small, woodpecker-like bird is always on the move

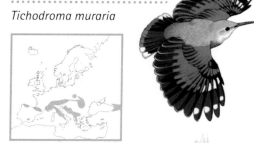

The only European bird that can move head first down a tree-trunk in search of food

Scandinavian race adult

Weight: 22–25g
Habitat: Broad-leaved and mixed woods, open parkland, avenues of older trees
Nest: Hole in tree or nest box; flakes of bark on wood chippings
Eggs: 6–8; white, sparsely marked reddish-brown or purple
Food: Invertebrates; seeds in autumn and winter

Voice: Call loud 'chwit-chwit'. Song rapid 'chu-chu-chu', slow 'pee, pee, pee'
Length: 14cm
Wingspan: 22.5–27cm

Easily recognised by plump body, short tail, long head and woodpecker-like bill. Sexes similar. Adult upperparts all blue-grey. Cheeks and throat white. Rest of underparts orange-buff merging into orange in birds from central, southern and western Europe but much paler in Scandinavian race. Has chestnut markings on flanks and white-centred chestnut undertail coverts. Broad, black eyestripe. Outertail feathers black with white sub-terminal spots. Bill long, pointed, greyish-black. Legs yellowish-brown. Juvenile similar to adult but duller below.

Wallcreeper

Tichodroma muraria

WALLCREEPERS are often found near torrents, caves and scree. Some birds are sedentary, but most are short-distance migrants, retreating before the winter snows. The species is a very rare vagrant to northwest Europe. The wallcreeper looks much bigger in flight than perched because its wings are broad and a third longer than the wings of other species of similar length. It is constantly on the move, flicking its wings as it searches for insects. Wallcreepers move quite fast as they forage, in short flights like jumps, or hopping supported by their wings. They are fairly confiding throughout the year, and will allow careful approach to within 10–20m.

It seems likely that the spectacular crimson coverts and white spots evolved as visual signals, this form of communication being more effective in mountainous terrain than sound

Voice: Call short chirp; song comprises clear whistles in crescendo, rising in pitch
Length: 16.5cm
Wingspan: 27–32cm
Weight: 17–19g
Habitat: Rocky, broken, precipitous mountain terrain, 1,000–2,000m
Nest: In a cleft in rock or scree; of moss, grass, roots; lined with hair and wool

Eggs: 4–5; white with sparse, fine, deep-red speckles, mostly at large end
Food: Small insects and spiders found mainly on rock faces

Unmistakable. Breeding male upperparts from forehead to uppertail coverts grey. Lower face, throat and upper breast black, shading to dusky grey on rest of underparts. Undertail coverts white-spotted. Large butterfly-like wings. Wing coverts crimson. Flight feathers sooty black with crimson bases. Outer four primaries have grey tips with two white spots behind. Tail black, tipped grey with a white spot on outertail feathers. Male moults between July and September. Tail and flight feathers then look blacker but face and upper breast lose black, becoming white, shading to grey. Legs black at all times. Bill black, needle-like, long and decurved. Female and juvenile similar to non-breeding male.

Corsican Nuthatch

Sitta whiteheadi

THE Corsican nuthatch is one of Europe's rarest birds. It is chiefly sedentary, although snow in the mountains will force birds down below 1,000m. Corsican nuthatches are not shy, and will tolerate human presence provided that their habitat is secure. They feed and move like nuthatches, and cache seeds of Corsican pine for the winter. This nuthatch commonly uses the holes of great spotted woodpeckers to nest in, but will also excavate its own in rotten sapwood.

Voice: Call quiet 'yip'; song trill of short notes, ascending in pitch
Length: 12cm
Wingspan: 21–22cm
Weight: 12–14g
Habitat: Tall, old, unmixed, unmanaged pine forest at 1,000–1,500m above sea-level
Nest: Often in old woodpecker hole; cup of pine needles, wood chips, lined with hair and moss
Eggs: 5–6; white with pale and dark red speckles mostly at large end
Food: Insects and spiders in breeding season; mainly pine seeds otherwise

Noticeably small nuthatch. Finest bill, longest-looking head and shortest tail of the European nuthatches. Adult essentially grey-blue above, dull white below. Male has head pattern of jet-black crown and long, white supercilium, underlined with long, black eyestripe. Female has black crown replaced by dusky blue. Both sexes show dark primaries. Outertail feathers black with white tips. Bill black, greyish at base. Legs lead-grey. Juvenile similar to adult female but with buff wash to all underparts except throat.

Rock Nuthatch

Sitta neumayer

THE rock nuthatch is a sedentary bird, but in some areas birds retreat down to valleys at the onset of snow, and may be found in wayside shrubs and even in gardens. Rock nuthatches mostly hunt on the ground and in rock crevices. When feeding, one of the pair will continually break off from foraging to check for predators. They are lively birds and call frequently. The rock nuthatch builds an amazing nest under an overhang of rock or in a slight depression on the rock face. This flask-shaped structure is made of mud and animal excrement, built against the rock, with a tunnel-like entrance.

Voice: Call excited trill; song is a loud trill, variable in tempo
Length: 13.5–14.5cm
Wingspan: 23–25cm
Weight: 25–35g
Habitat: Sunny, rocky slopes with poor shrub vegetation up to 1,000m
Nest: On a rock face, usually facing north; mud nest with lining of feathers, hair, wool
Eggs: 6–10; white with speckles and blotches of reddish colours
Food: Mainly insects in summer; mostly seeds, some snails in winter

Similar in appearance to nuthatch but much paler. Adult is basically blue-grey above from forehead to tail, and dirty white below. Underparts change from white on face and throat, to buff belly; darkest on undertail coverts. Long, broad, black eyestripe separates grey crown and white face. Grey tail is unmarked. Bill black with paler base to lower mandible. Legs dark grey. Sexes alike. Juvenile similar to adult but duller and with less distinct eyestripe.

Treecreeper

Certhia familiaris

Underparts can become stained as they drag on bark, moss and lichen, and should not be confused with short-toed treecreeper's duller underparts

THE treecreeper is mostly a sedentary bird, but northern populations overwinter further south in the species' breeding range. It is hard to find in the woods because of its camouflaged plumage and high-pitched voice, which is beyond the hearing of many observers. The treecreeper spirals up and around tree trunks and under branches, and when it has searched up one tree it flies to low down on another. It creeps close to the trunk on its short legs, supported on its tail feathers. Treecreepers are known to roost, sometimes communally, in bark crevices in the winter months.

Voice: Call thin 'tsiew'; song high-pitched cadence lasting 2.5–3 seconds
Length: 12.5cm
Wingspan: 17.5–21cm
Weight: 8.5–10g
Habitat: Predominantly in mature broad-leaved trees, but also conifers
Nest: Commonly behind loose tree-bark; cup of grass on twigs, lined with hair
Eggs: 5–6; white with fine reddish-brown speckles
Food: Insects and spiders throughout the year; some winter seeds

Sexes alike. At a distance adult appears brown above and silky white below. At close range shows rufous rump, long, white supercilium and white-mottled and streaked back. Complex pattern on wings comprises two pale-buff wingbars on coverts, buff band across secondaries and primaries, and white-spotted tertials. Tail is long and brown with dark shafts; feathers are stiff and pointed, and when spread the tail looks frayed. Bill quite long, gently decurved (rare in European passerines) and dark brown. Legs pale brown. Juvenile very similar to adult but upperparts appear spotted. See entry for short-toed treecreeper, which is almost identical, for details of spearation of the two species.

Short-toed Treecreeper

Certhia brachydactyla

THE short-toed treecreeper is very similar to the treecreeper to look at and its most reliable field characteristic is its voice. Its calls are louder and less sibilant than its relative's and include a diagnostic, shrill, loud 'tseep', rather like a dunnock's call. This is used as an alarm or rival-call, either singly or in a series. The song is a rapid, short phrase, lasting a second or so, of about six notes; 'teet-teet-teetero-tit'. Its short duration, loudness, lower pitch, and short and clear introductory notes make it clearly distinguishable from the treecreeper's song.

Voice: Call shrill 'zeet', and 'srriih'; song comprises short, loud phrase
Length: 12.5cm
Wingspan: 17–20.5cm
Weight: 8.5–11g
Habitat: Tall trees with rugged bark in parks, avenues, orchards, forest edge
Nest: Often behind loose bark; like treecreeper's
Eggs: 6–7; white spotted with shades of red chiefly at larger end
Food: Mainly insect larvae and pupae and spiders throughout the year

Very similar to treecreeper and often best distinguished by voice. Sexes alike. Adult is brown above and white below. Compared to treecreeper sustained observation should reveal these differences: (a) upperparts and wings are duller, browner and less obviously spotted; (b) dull brown rump; (c) shorter, duller supercilium often not showing in front of eye; (d) breast and rest of underparts washed grey or brown, most noticeably on the flanks; (e) bill usually looks longer and more slender, and bent at tip rather than gently decurved. Juvenile similar to adult but upperparts appear more spotted.

Attractive woodland bird; adult has delicately marked brown upperparts and white underparts

Like treecreeper, usually solitary outside the breeding season, but will associate with foraging tit flock

Golden Oriole

Oriolus oriolus

GOLDEN orioles are summer visitors to Europe, overwintering in sub-Saharan Africa. Orioles are secretive, arboreal birds and although not abundant, are well known because of the male's far-carrying song. Although the male is unmistakable the female may be confused with the green woodpecker, but that is a heavier bird and has a red bill. The golden oriole's nest may take the female 6 to 12 days to build on her own. A hammock of plant fibres, tied by 20–40cm long loops of grass to the twigs, first looks like a net, but is filled in with more grasses, feathers, down and wool. It is so well made that it may last, be repaired and used the following year.

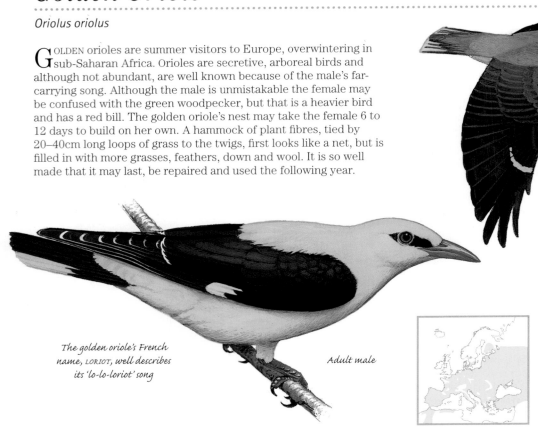

Adult female

The golden oriole's French name, LORIOT, *well describes its 'lo-lo-loriot' song*

Adult male

Voice: Call cat-like; alarm rattle; song is a melodious, flute-like whistle
Length: 24cm
Wingspan: 44–47cm
Weight: 55–80g
Habitat: Tree-loving but not a forest bird; parks, large gardens, copses, open woods
Nest: Slung like a hammock from a fork in a tree
Eggs: 3–4; white or cream, with scattered black spots
Food: Insects, especially large larvae; berries and fruits from late summer onwards

Adult male has bright-yellow head and body, black wings and tail. Head marked by black lores. Black-centred tail has yellow corners. Wings black with short yellow bar across tips of primary coverts. Eye crimson. Bill strong, dark pink. Legs dark grey. Female has yellowish-green body, greenish-brown wings and brownish-black tail with yellow corners. Underparts palest on chin to upper-breast; all underparts streaked dull brown. First-year male is streaked and has bright-yellow plumage replaced by dull olive-yellow. Some mature females appear almost as yellow as male but lores always grey. Juvenile like female but has dark-brown eye and slate-grey bill; takes two years to attain adult plumage.

Red-backed Shrike

Lanius collurio

At rest frequently fans tail or swings it from side to side

Adult female

Now essentially extinct as breeding bird in Britain and northwest Europe, but may be seen on passage

Male

Juvenile

Adult male (above)

RED-BACKED shrikes are summer visitors to Europe, wintering in eastern tropical and southern Africa; sadly, their numbers have declined in many parts of Europe. Most of a shrike's prey is hunted using a 'wait-and-see' strategy from a perch with a good all-round view. When an insect passes by, up to 30m away, the shrike will dive on to it, seize it in its bill, and return to a bush with a characteristic, abrupt sweep upwards to the perch. In the breeding season an average of 34 sorties an hour has been noted. Extra prey is often impaled on thorns and barbed wire to guarantee a food supply.

terrain with bushes and small trees for lookouts
Nest: In a bush, about 1m up; loose cup of plant materials, with compact lining
Eggs: 3–7; very variable ground colour with multicoloured spots at larger end
Food: Mainly insects, especially beetles; some small birds and animals

Voice: Call harsh 'chack, chack'; song subdued, lengthy, with mimicry
Length: 17cm
Wingspan: 24–27cm
Weight: 25–36g
Habitat: Sunny, open

Adult male has blue-grey crown and nape, chestnut back, blue-grey rump and black tail with white outer feathers. Underparts pinkish-white. Shows narrow, black band across forehead extending into broad, black mask through eye and across ear coverts. Flight feathers, tertials and greater coverts brown-black with chestnut margins. Bill black, distinctly hawk-like with hooked tip. Legs grey-black. Female has rufous-brown upperparts, reddish tail, pale-buff supercilium and cream underparts with brown crescent markings. Juvenile similar to female with close barring to black crescents on upperparts.

Great Grey Shrike

Lanius excubitor

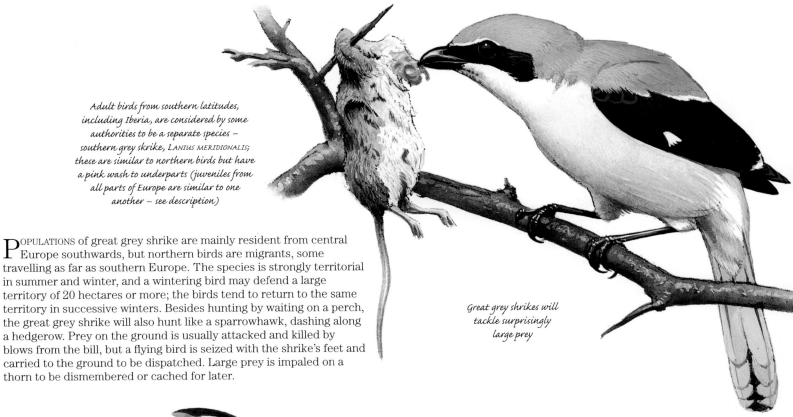

Adult birds from southern latitudes, including Iberia, are considered by some authorities to be a separate species – southern grey skrike, LANIUS MERIDIONALIS; these are similar to northern birds but have a pink wash to underparts (juveniles from all parts of Europe are similar to one another – see description)

Populations of great grey shrike are mainly resident from central Europe southwards, but northern birds are migrants, some travelling as far as southern Europe. The species is strongly territorial in summer and winter, and a wintering bird may defend a large territory of 20 hectares or more; the birds tend to return to the same territory in successive winters. Besides hunting by waiting on a perch, the great grey shrike will also hunt like a sparrowhawk, dashing along a hedgerow. Prey on the ground is usually attacked and killed by blows from the bill, but a flying bird is seized with the shrike's feet and carried to the ground to be dispatched. Large prey is impaled on a thorn to be dismembered or cached for later.

Great grey shrikes will tackle surprisingly large prey

Flight is low and deeply undulating, with a sweep up to the perch

Northern race adult

An overwintering bird may, on establishing a territory in autumn, still feed on insects, but increasingly it will turn to voles and shrews, and finally to small birds

Conspicuous bird that likes to perch on bushes, trees or telephone wires, and so is comparatively easy to find

Voice: Call harsh 'sheck, sheck'; song is a quiet, rambling warble with mimicry
Length: 24–25cm
Wingspan: 30–34cm
Weight: 60–75g
Habitat: Open country with plenty of bushes and trees
Nest: In a tree, usually 3–7m up; bulky nest of twigs and grasses, softly lined
Eggs: 4–7; colour variable even in one clutch, heavily blotched with darker colours
Food: Large insects, especially beetles; small reptiles, birds and mammals

The largest shrike. Northern European adult is tricoloured, with black face mask, wings and tail, grey upperparts and white underparts. Adult has white supercilium, white patch on scapulars, white-edged tail (which is long and graduated) and white, narrow bar across base of primaries. Bill quite long, hooked, black. Legs black. Sexes alike, but female has faint brown barring on breast in winter. Juvenile has brownish-grey upperparts and brownish-white underparts with faint, brown, wavy bars from throat to breast and flanks.

Woodchat Shrike

Lanius senator

Juveniles can be hard to separate from juvenile lesser grey and red-backed shrikes but can usually be identified by their white shoulder patches

Adult birds are easily recognised by their black, white and chestnut plumage

THE woodchat shrike is a summer visitor to Europe, overwintering in Africa; it is a rare spring and autumn passage migrant to northwest Europe. Woodchat shrikes prefer less open perches in trees than other shrikes, from which they drop or glide on to ground prey or chase flying insects. As with other shrikes, indigestible food such as chitin, hair and bones is regurgitated in small, hard pellets. Woodchat shrikes are usually paired by the time they arrive in Europe. Males have the best song of all European shrikes: a single bird may include imitations of seven to eight other species, often singing a copied song in quite a long burst.

Adult male

Numbers of woodchat shrike have declined seriously in the north and west of its European range

Habitat: Woodland margins, old orchards, roadsides, maquis
Nest: On horizontal tree branch below 5m; strong cup of leafy material, roots, lined
Eggs: 5–6; greenish with brown and olive speckles at larger end
Food: Mainly insects, especially beetles; some small vertebrates

Voice: Call 'kiwick, kiwick'; song is a rich sustained warble with mimicry
Length: 18cm
Wingspan: 26–28cm
Weight: 30–40g

Small pied shrike with chestnut rear crown, nape and upper mantle in all adult plumages. Adult male has black forehead, which continues as broad, black patch through eye and ear coverts, and black wings and tail. Shows white outertail feathers, rump (conspicuous in flight), scapulars (forming two oval patches when perched) and underparts. Back grey. Bill short but strong, hook-tipped, black. Legs black. Female similar to male but colours duller and shows chestnut flecks in black forehead, white at base of bill, browner back and variable markings on breast. Juvenile has mostly grey or buff upperparts with pale whitish-buff scapulars, all barred with dark brown. Rump rufous and underparts dull white with many crescent-shaped bars. Whitish supercilium. Wings brownish-black with paler feather edges. Tail brownish-black with white edges.

Lesser Grey Shrike

Lanius minor

Juvenile has creamy-white underparts and a much smaller face mask than adult

Generally perches conspicuously on wires and bushes

Adult

DESPITE its superficial similarity to the great grey shrike, the two species should not be confused for there is little overlap in their distribution. The entire population of this summer visitor overwinters in southern Africa. It is a rare visitor to northwest Europe in spring and autumn. The lesser grey is shorter than the great grey shrike, but its proportionately longer wings allow it to chase prey rapidly, glide well, and hover and pounce like a kestrel. It will use many perches in its breeding territory, each one having a good all-round view and clear sight of the ground, on which it can spot large insects up to 15m away. It rarely caches food.

Voice: Calls variable; song is a soft, musical, chattering ramble with mimicry
Length: 20cm
Wingspan: 32–34.5cm
Weight: 45–65g
Habitat: Warm, open country with scattered or grouped bushes and trees
Nest: Usually about 5m up in small tree; well-made cup of plant materials, often unlined
Eggs: 5–6; pale bluish-green with olive and lavender-grey spots
Food: Almost wholly insects, especially beetles

Adult male has broad black band across forehead, over and through eyes and ear coverts. Rest of upperparts blue-grey. Male underparts white, with breast and flanks washed pink. Wings black with broad, white bar across base of primaries.

Tail black with wide, white outer edges. Bill black, short and stubby. Legs brown. Female very similar to male but shows grey speckles on forehead, less pink below, and less blue above. Juvenile has black and white patterns of adult on wings and tail but underparts creamy white and upperparts brownish-grey with fine, close, darker brown bars. Face mask reduced to broad, black eyestripe. Bill grey.

Masked Shrike

Lanius nubicus

THE masked shrike has less of a hawk-like bill than other shrikes in Europe. It hunts more from the inside and lower branches of trees, and less from exposed perches; it does, however, employ a similar perch-and-pounce strategy. It is the most agile on the wing of the European shrikes; its actions are then like those of a flycatcher. Although its behaviour often seems to be skulking, the masked shrike shows little fear of people when feeding, and has even been known to follow people closely to catch grasshoppers disturbed as they walk through grass.

Voice: Calls hard 'tsr' and reedy 'keer'; song is a vigorous warble
Length: 17–18cm
Wingspan: 24–26.5cm
Weight: 20–25g
Habitat: Almost any wooded country, including citrus and olive groves
Nest: In tree or dense, thorny bush, mostly over 5m; carefully made
Eggs: 4–7; creamy or yellowish, blotched pale grey, speckled brown at larger end

Food: Insects, especially beetles and grasshoppers; some small birds

Small shrike, more slightly built than woodchat shrike, and with proportionately the longest tail of the region's shrikes. Male distinctively pied: generally black above and white below with reddish-orange flanks. Has white forehead and supercilium, white outertail feathers, white scapulars and broad, white bar across base of primaries. Bill slight, black. Legs black. Female similarly patterned to male but has greyer head, browner wings and less rusty underparts. Juvenile plumage scaly grey-brown; very hard to separate from young woodchat shrike but has longer tail and greyer upperparts.

Very confiding and approachable even during the breeding season

The masked shrike is a summer visitor to its breeding range, overwintering in Africa, south of the Sahara

Adult male

Isabelline Shrike

Lanius isabellinus

THE charming isabelline shrike occurs as a breeding species across much of central Asia and overwinters in east Africa, southern Arabia and northwest India. Like other medium-sized shrikes, this species is a voracious hunter of insects. These are often located on the ground from a vantage point such as a bush, the bird gliding down and seizing the prey in its beak. At one time the isabelline shrike was considered to be a race of red-backed shrike, the species with which it most easily confused when seen as a vagrant to Europe. Nowadays it is recognised as a species in its own right but identification of immature birds remains a problem. Important features to look out for on a first-winter bird are the colour of the crown, nape and back (grey-brown in isabelline but reddish-brown in red-backed) and the presence or otherwise of scaly feathering on the upperparts (conspicuous in red-backed but very faint or absent in isabelline). The reddish-brown tail of an isabelline shrike always contrasts with its greyer back while the brown tail of a first-winter red-backed shrike is normally the same colour as the rest of the upperparts.

Voice: Calls include a harsh 'tchak'
Length: 17–18cm
Wingspan: 26–27cm
Weight: 28–32g

Habitat: Open grassy areas with scrub
Nest: Does not breed in region
Eggs: Does not breed in region
Food: Mainly insects

Distinctly pale shrike. In most plumages contrast between grey-brown back and reddish-brown lower rump and tail is distinctive. Adult male has mainly grey-buff upperparts, warmest brown on crown; lower rump and tail reddish-brown. Underparts whitish but with buff wash to breast and flanks. Head has black mask through eye. Wings have striking pale patch at base of primaries. Female similar to male but has more subdued plumage colours, pale patch at base of primaries usually absent and eye mask brown not black; shows faint scaly markings on underparts. First-winter bird (plumage most likely to be encountered in Europe) similar to female but scaly markings more extensive and present on face as well. All birds have dark bill and dark-grey legs.

Immature, first-winter plumage

225

Jay

Garrulus glandarius

WESTERN and southern European jays are sedentary, but other populations are irruptive migrants when the acorn crop fails. Jays are commonest in deciduous woodlands but are rarely heard except for their loud, raucous screech. Acorns are the jay's staple winter diet. They are picked from the tree and many are hidden in soil, turf and moss in September and October. One bird can carry up to nine acorns in its gullet and may bury around 4,000–5,000 during the autumn. Their visual memory is good and most acorns eaten in winter are from caches, even from those under snow.

Most likely to be seen flying away from observer, showing rounded wings and striking black and white pattern of rump and tail

Juvenile (right) has fewer streaks on crown, smaller moustache and shorter tail than adult

 Voice: Loud, harsh, raucous calls, including 'skaaak skaaak' – far-carrying even in dense woodland
Length: 34–35cm
Wingspan: 52–58cm
Weight: 150–180g
Habitat: Fairly dense cover of trees, usually broad-leaved, but also conifers
Nest: In tree or bush, close to trunk; foundation of twigs, lined with roots, grass and hair

Eggs: 5–7; pale green or blue or olive, speckled brown and olive all over
Food: Invertebrates, especially beetles and larvae; fruits and seeds, especially acorns

A small crow, the most colourful in Europe. Sexes alike. Adult body pinkish-brown with white rump and undertail coverts, white forehead, crown streaked black, and broad, black moustachial stripe. Wings black with white at base of outermost secondaries forming short bar on closed wings; outer greater coverts, primary coverts and bastard wing have shiny blue bars. Bill dark. Legs pale flesh-brown. Juvenile similar to adult, but plumage more red and crown less streaked.

Siberian Jay

Perisoreus infaustus

THE Siberian jay is generally a sedentary resident and is very faithful to its chosen territory. It is a secretive bird in the breeding season and is hard to find at this time of the year. Nevertheless, it is not afraid of people and is quite prepared to approach houses or people for scraps, especially outside the breeding season. Siberian jays pair for life and are territorial throughout the year. The winter feeding territory may be as large as 150 hectares, but the breeding territory is much smaller. The breeding season is early: eggs are regularly laid in early April when everywhere is covered with snow.

Red in plumage is diagnostic for a bird of this size

The nest lining of feathers and reindeer hair and the bird's fluffy plumage help to insulate the bird and the eggs against temperatures ranging from -20 to -30°C

Voice: Calls 'tchair', 'kook kook' and 'kij kij'; mewing like buzzard
Length: 30–31cm
Wingspan: 40–46cm
Weight: 80–95g
Habitat: Natural, dense coniferous forest
Nest: Close to conifer trunk; cup of lichen lined with feathers and hair, on base of twigs
Eggs: 3–4; very pale bluish, spotted and blotched grey and olive brown
Food: Omnivorous all year round, including carrion and scraps

Smallest member of the crow family in Europe, with proportionately longer tail than jay and shorter, pointed bill. Adult has sooty-brown crown, nape and upper face. Dense pale-buff bristles at base of bill. Back and underparts brown-grey, becoming foxy-red on rump, upper and lowertail coverts and belly. Wings sooty brown with foxy-red coverts and bases to flight feathers. Bill and legs black. Sexes similar and juvenile similar to adult.

Azure-winged Magpie

Cyanopica cyanus

In the breeding season, April to June, the azure-winged magpie is secretive and keeps to tree cover much of the time; in a fleeting view it could be confused with the common magpie. At other times it is noisy and bold. Outside the breeding season a flock, consisting of breeding pairs and their young, defends its territory, forages and roosts together. Pairs are faithful, but in the breeding season non-breeding members of the flock help breeding pairs build their nest and care for their young.

Voice: Main call is a husky whistling 'zhreee', rising at end
Length: 34–35cm (nearly half is tail)
Wingspan: 38–40cm
Weight: 70–75g
Habitat: Groups of trees, cork oak and olive groves, pine and eucalyptus plantations
Nest: In fork, near the tree crown; of twigs, with mud cup, soft-lined 1cm thick
Eggs: 5–7; pale cream to brownish-olive, with sparse brown spots
Food: Invertebrates, especially beetles, but will scavenge almost anything

Small, elegant, long-tailed crow. Adult has forehead, crown and nape velvet black to a line below the eye. Back, rump and uppertail coverts grey-brown. Underparts off-white, with pale tinge of ashy colours on flanks and undertail coverts. Wings azure blue, with inner webs of tertials, greater coverts and primaries black. Tail noticeably graduated, blue above, dark grey below. Bill and legs black. Juvenile similar to adult but plumage duller.

Nutcracker

Nucifraga caryocatactes

THE nutcracker's distribution is dictated by its food supply; western birds are chiefly resident, but birds from further east are subject to irruptive movements when the conifer seed crop fails. Nutcrackers are secretive in the breeding season, which often begins when snow is still on the ground, but they do favour conspicuous perches in treetops. Irruptive migrants, searching for food, sometimes enter human settlements and become very tame. The survival of nutcrackers in winter depends on their being able to cache enough food to last from September to May.

Voice: Utters a far-carrying 'kraak'; spring call 'kerr-kerr'; alarm call 'churr'
Length: 22–23cm
Wingspan: 52–58cm
Weight: 120–170g
Habitat: Cool forests of spruce or pine, in northern lowland and southern mountains
Nest: Almost always in a conifer; compact, well made, well lined
Eggs: 3–4; whitish to deep green, with near-invisible or dense olive and grey spots

Food: Very dependent on conifer seeds and hazelnuts; some invertebrates

Sexes alike. Adult body plumage chocolate-brown with teardrop-shaped white spot at tip of most feathers. Forehead and crown very dark brown, nasal bristles and lores creamy white. Wings brown-black, glossed bluish-green, with white spots on lesser and median coverts. Tail brownish-black with blue-green gloss above and feathers tipped white, becoming progressively wider from centre outwards; tail appears mostly dark from above but mostly white from below. Undertail coverts white in contrast to black base of tail and brown body. Bill long and black. Legs black. Juvenile paler than adult, with less well-defined white spots.

Hammers open cones with its bill, eats some seeds and buries many more

Each bird caches some 100,000 seeds in autumn, and needs 27,000 to survive

---

Magpie

Pica pica

ALTHOUGH the magpie is predominantly a bird of lightly wooded open country, it has now moved into suburban and urban habitats in several countries. It is widespread throughout Europe except in treeless areas. Adults may spend all their lives in the same territory but first-year birds disperse to find their own territories. The magpie finds almost all its food on the ground, where it moves in bold steps and hops, with a raised tail. Magpies are gregarious, especially in early spring at the 'great magpie marriage', a gathering that helps to establish pairs, which strongly defend their territory afterwards. Magpies roost communally; winter flocks may contain over 300 birds.

In flight short bursts of rapid wingbeats alternate with glides

Voice: Commonest call is a staccato chatter 'chacker chacker chacker chacker'
Length: 44–46cm
Wingspan: 52–60cm
Weight: 190–240g
Habitat: Mainly a lowland bird in lightly wooded country
Nest: Near top of tree; of twigs, with a roof, lined with mud then softer materials
Eggs: 5–7; variable, blue or olive or greenish, heavily speckled olive-brown
Food: Mostly invertebrates in summer; vertebrates and seed in winter; also carrion and scraps

An unmistakable pied bird with a long, graduated tail. Sexes similar. Adult scapulars, belly and flanks white. Rest of plumage black with beautiful iridescence when seen closely in sunlight: purple on most of head and body, green on crown and scapulars, blue-green on wings, and brilliant bronze-green on tail with bands of several shades of purple near tip. Bill and legs black. Juvenile similar to adult but has shorter tail, duller plumage and less iridescence.

Long, graduated tail and black and white plumage distinctive even at a distance

227

Chough

Pyrrhocorax pyrrhocorax

THE chough has a very fragmented distribution in Europe: it nests in Switzerland as high as 1,500m but is also found on sea cliffs in the British Isles. It is sedentary and rarely leaves its breeding areas. In the British Isles and elsewhere the chough has been in decline for many years, probably because of the destruction of traditionally grazed grassland, which supported the choughs' summer food supply of ants. These and other insects are probed for in the turf using the long bill. Choughs are masterful fliers: they can glide, soar on thermals and perform aerial manoeuvres, all to the accompaniment of many contact calls.

When a perched bird gives a call it often conspicuously flips its wings and tail to help advertise its presence

Choughs are gregarious even in the breeding season, and small flocks can be seen flying along the cliffs

Glossy plumage is entirely black

Voice: Common call is a yelping 'cheeow' or 'kiaa'
Length: 39–40cm
Wingspan: 73–90cm
Weight: 230–350g
Habitat: Inland crags or coastal cliffs (for nesting) near grassy swards (for feeding)

Nest: In crevice in cliff or on ledge in cave; large pile of twigs, lined with wool
Eggs: 3–5; very pale buff or green, with small olive and green markings all over
Food: Soil-living invertebrates; grain; berries in winter

Adult plumage all black; most parts have a blue gloss, although tail, tail coverts and flight feathers have a greener iridescence. Bill red and downcurved. Sexes alike. Juvenile duller than adult, with shorter, dull-pink bill. Adult chough separable from adult Alpine chough by length of bill, shorter tail, about as long as primary tips when bird is standing, five to six primary 'fingers' (in flight), and distinct call.

Alpine Chough

Pyrrhocorax graculus

ALPINE choughs are masters of the air. They fly fast and with great skill, manoeuvring near cliffs and in fierce air currents. Their broad, fingered wings and often-fanned tails enable them to twist and turn, spiral and dive with ease. In summer Alpine choughs feed on the grassland above the tree-line, but in winter they come down to the valleys, into towns, or scavenge at ski resorts. The Alpine chough is gregarious all year round. It is found in pairs, family parties, or winter flocks that may be as big as 300 birds. Flocks are very vocal throughout the year.

A small flock in aerial display, calling the diagnostic 'chree', is a memorable sight

smart, glossy black plumage; has more jackdaw-like silhouette than chough

Voice: Calls include a frequent 'chirrish'; in chorus often utters a piercing 'treee'
Length: 38cm

Wingspan: 75–85cm
Weight: 190–240g
Habitat: Strictly montane, ranging from tree-line to snow-line
Nest: On ledge, crevice in cave, cliff, tunnel, building; bulky mass of twigs, with soft lining
Eggs: 3–5; whitish, profusely marked with shades of brown
Food: Insects from spring to autumn; berries and human scraps in winter

Adult has all-black plumage with a sheen: blue-green gloss, particularly on wings. Sexes alike. Bill pale yellow. Legs orange. May be distinguished from chough by its yellow, shorter bill, duller plumage, longer tail, only four separated primaries in flight and straight leading edge to the wings. Juvenile similar to adult.

Jackdaw

Corvus monedula

JACKDAWS tend to move more outside the breeding season than other members of the crow family and vacate cold, bleak uplands for lowlands in the west. The species has declined in many parts of Europe where its habitat requirements of nest sites near grass grazed by sheep or cattle are not met. Jackdaws are very gregarious: they feed together in pairs or small flocks, roost communally at traditional sites (winter flocks may number many hundreds or even thousands), and nest in small colonies. Jackdaws often associate with rooks on feeding grounds and are given to sudden 'dreads' when the whole flock will fly up in a panic, then break up, circle and drift down again to feed. Jackdaws are wary in the countryside, but quite approachable in towns and villages.

Voice: Short, loud 'kjack' is the common contact note; many other short call notes
Length: 33–34cm
Wingspan: 67–74cm
Weight: 200–250g
Habitat: Groups of old trees, avenues in town or country; sea cliffs, mountain crags
Nest: Colonial. In hole in cliff, tree, building or nest box; messy pile of twigs, with soft lining

Eggs: 4–6; light blue or greenish-blue, with very variable speckles and blotches
Food: Omnivorous; almost all gathered on the ground

Sexes alike. At a distance adult appears black with grey nape and ear coverts. Close views reveal purple gloss on black crown, some blue gloss on wings and back, and greyish cast on underparts. Eyes of adult pale grey, very distinctive. Bill short and black. Legs black. Juvenile duller than adult, grey patch less contrasting; eyes brown, taking a year to become grey.

One of the smallest members of the crow family in Europe

The jackdaw will choose almost any nest site so long as it is a hole – from sea cliffs to old mine shafts and church towers

Rook

Corvus frugilegus

MANY rook populations, such as those in Britain and France, are resident; elsewhere rooks are migrants, especially in cold winters. The rook is gregarious at all times; after the breeding season family groups join other families for feeding, roosting and migrating. They migrate by day, following valleys and coasts. Winter roosts may be huge, often of thousands of birds. Rooks nest colonially, close together in a 'rookery'. As populations in western Europe have declined, so have the number of nests per colony, but there are still large rookeries across the range; the biggest ever known was around 16,000 nests in Hungary.

Voice: Commonest call is a prolonged 'kaah'
Length: 44–46cm
Wingspan: 81–99cm
Weight: 400–500g
Habitat: Wherever tall trees border agricultural land
Nest: Colonial; in topmost branches of tree; base of twigs and mud, with soft lining
Eggs: 2–6; light blue or green, with specks and blotches of shades of olive
Food: Especially earthworms and beetles (from pasture) and cereal seed (from arable land)

Adult all black except for whitish-grey skin around base of bill, from lower forehead, behind the gape, and on upper throat. Black is iridescent in sunlight with shades of greenish – and reddish-purple. Separable from carrion crow by whitish face, steep forehead, narrower bill, more fingered wingtips in flight, round-tipped tail, glossier plumage and loose thigh feathers. Juvenile has black nasal bristles and no bare grey skin.

Face and chin are pale grey and unfeathered

Long, loose thigh feathers give 'baggy trousers' effect

Noise and activity at the rookery peak in early spring, as birds quarrel over territory and males display

229

Hooded/Carrion Crow

Corvus corone cornix (hooded)/*Corvus corone corone* (carrion)

WESTERN crow populations are black and referred to as carrion crows, while central and eastern populations are grey and black and are called hooded crows. Crows of both subspecies are migratory in the north of their range but sedentary in the south and west. All migrants winter within the species' overall breeding range. Crows are less gregarious than rooks but not as solitary as jays. Flocks gather in flocks for springtime displays and winter roosts, and at rich food sources such as rubbish tips and tidal estuaries. In these estuaries the birds feed on dead fish and shellfish; they open the latter by flying up and dropping them. Crows are paired throughout the year and occupy a range of around 53 hectares.

Voice: Call is an abrupt 'kawr', often three together; also a range of other short, hard calls
Length: 45–47cm
Wingspan: 90–100cm
Weight: 450–600g
Habitat: Open country with scattered trees, hedgerows; also in towns
Nest: High in a tree, or bush if no tall trees; substantial nest of twigs with soft lining
Eggs: 3–6; light blue or green, variably spotted with olive and brown
Food: Omnivorous; many invertebrates, much cereal grain, carrion, scraps

Occurs as two clearly distinguishable subspecies. Carrion crow has all-black plumage, bill and legs. Hooded crow has back of neck, mantle, back, rump, scapulars, lower breast, belly, flanks, axillaries and undertail coverts ash grey. Rest of plumage black. Bill and legs black in both races. Sexes alike in both races. Juvenile carrion crow similar to adult. Juvenile hooded crow similar to adult but grey element of plumage has buffish tinge.

Hooded crow has grey back and undersides and grey on innerwing

The two crows are so different that for a long time they were considered to be separate species

Hooded crow

Carrion crow

Both races often mob birds of prey, such as buzzards, and usually succeed in driving them away

Powerful, dagger-like bill can tear flesh with ease

Juvenile (below) follows parents for several weeks after leaving nest, depending on them for food

Carrion crow can be confused with rook and raven, although latter is much bigger, has long throat feathers and noticeably wedge-shaped tail

Where carrion and hooded crow populations meet, they interbreed; their young have intermediate plumage patterns

Raven

Corvus corax

IN EUROPE ravens occur where they can find eyrie-style nest sites overlooking a large foraging area. Most ravens are sedentary; some may disperse southwards in winter. In flight, overhead, the raven's cruciform shape is distinctive. Ravens are at their most active at the start of the breeding season (from February onwards), when pairs indulge in spectacular aerial displays of dives, tumbles, and rolls. Ravens pair for life, and although solitary in the breeding season, flocks of 50 to 60 are frequent at winter roosts and where there are plentiful supplies of food. Nests are often reused, may be very large, and are built in layers from a base of twigs and small branches to a cup of wool and hair.

Voice: Typical call is a deep, resonant 'karronk'; also utters a deep 'prruk' and 'toc-toc-toc'
Length: 64cm
Wingspan: 130–150cm
Weight: 900–1,400g

Habitat: From coast to 3,000m, but not dense forest, dense settlement or cultivation
Nest: Usually high in a tree or on a cliff ledge; huge pile of sticks with cup of wool and hair

Eggs: 4–6; light blue to blue-green, variable olive and dark-brown markings
Food: Much carrion; seeds and fruit; scavenges at settlements; kills animals and birds

Large, entirely black crow with evocative, deep 'prruk, prruk' call

A pair defends a large territory of between 7 and 67sq km (depending on food supply), which may contain two to seven nest sites that are rotated irregularly

The raven's principal food is dead sheep, but it will also eat live small animals and seeds and fruit

The largest member of the crow family, one-third bigger than rook and crow, and as big as a buzzard. Sexes similar. All-black, iridescent plumage; purple-blue on wings, reddish-purple on tail. Shaggy throat feathers and wedge shape to tip of tail are distinctive. Black bill is massive, especially deep upper mandible, markedly curved towards the tip. Legs black. Juvenile similar to adult.

Long throat feathers give bearded appearance; this and heavy bill help distinguish raven from carrion crow

Starling

Sturnus vulgaris

song is long, unmusical mixture of trills and rattles, delivered with great energy; many starlings mimic other birds and mechanical sounds

STARLINGS from northwest and central Europe are mostly resident, and their numbers are swollen in winter by visitors from northeastern and eastern Europe. The starling is gregarious throughout the year. Winter roosts in evergreens, reedbeds or on buildings commonly comprise 100,000 or more birds, and they nest in loose colonies. Starlings generally have a direct flight, with a silhouette like a delta-winged fighter, but in summer many will twist and turn high in the sky to catch flying ants. A colony or winter feeding group will suddenly rise in a tight flock, giving a distinctive predator alarm, 'chip chip chip', to mob a raptor.

Voice: Calls include characteristic 'tsiew', 'tcherr'; song is a lively medley of whistles, gurgles and mimicry
Length: 21.5cm
Wingspan: 37–42cm
Weight: 75–85g
Habitat: Almost anywhere; very ready to live with man; needs holes to nest in, open ground to feed on
Nest: Hole in a tree, cliff, building or nest box; bulky, grassy base
Eggs: 5–7; shades of pale blue
Food: Mostly insects and larvae in breeding season; also seeds, fruit, nectar

Male in winter has glossy black plumage, with buff tips to feathers of upperparts, buff edges to wing feathers and white tips to feathers of underparts from throat to belly. Bill grey-brown with yellow base. Legs reddish-brown. Eyes brown. Male in summer loses buff and white feather tips, and due to wear the bird looks darker and very glossy, with green, purple, bronze and blue iridescence. Lemon-yellow bill. Female has broader spots in winter than male, keeps some spots all year and is less glossy. Bill has pinkish base in breeding season, eye has a whitish ring on the iris. Juvenile looks like a different species with mouse-brown plumage, darker above than below. Shows whitish chin and grey-brown bill. Moults in autumn and attains first-winter plumage similar to adult; bill black.

Breeding-plumage male is very glossy and colourful, and beak has blue base

The starling has expanded its range north and south but decreased in numbers, especially in northern and central Europe

After autumn moult adult has fresh, creamy tips to body feathers, while wing feathers are edged orange-brown

Juvenile just out of nest is mouse brown

Feeding parties on grass have a bustling, jaunty walk and are often quarrelsome

Juvenile in late summer

When moult is almost complete young birds are all spotted except for pale heads

Juvenile

Immature, first autumn

Immature, first winter

Adult, summer

Adult, winter

Summer adult

Juvenile

THE rose-coloured starling breeds across central Asia, and erratically in Greece, Bulgaria, the former Yugoslavia and the former Czechoslovakia; it mostly overwinters in India. After breeding but before autumn migration, the birds form flocks that wander in search of food. Vagrants seen in northwestern and western Europe mostly occur at this time and are often juveniles; they often spend weeks visiting garden bird feeders with starlings.

Voice: Calls include a thin 'kri'; song varied and twittering
Length: 21cm
Wingspan: 38–40cm
Weight: 70–80g
Habitat: Typically arid grassland and semi-desert
Nest: Nests colonially in holes in stony cliffs and buildings
Eggs: 3–6, pale blue
Food: Mainly insects but also berries and fruits

Adult male's head, crest, neck and upper breast dark with purple sheen. Wings black with greenish sheen and tail and undertail coverts black. Mantle, back, lower breast and belly pink. Pink elements of plumage appear grubby in winter and black lacks sheen. Bill and legs pink. Female like male but plumage duller at all times. Juvenile has essentially pale sandy-brown plumage, darkest on wings and tail. Bill yellow and legs dull red.

Spotless Starling

Sturnus unicolor

IN THE western Mediterranean this starling fills the same niche as its commoner relative, feeding and breeding in a wide variety of habitats, including inner cities. Spotless starlings commonly feed in similar places to the starling, and have a similar feeding method, probing into the ground with an open bill to find invertebrates. They are wary at all times, but are more approachable in villages or towns, especially in winter. In Spain, where it is common and increasing in numbers, the spotless starling prefers open woodland with easy access to short grass on which to forage and is often found near cattle all the year round.

Voice: Similar to starling, but song louder, especially introductory whistles
Length: 21–23cm
Wingspan: 38–42cm
Weight: 80–90g
Habitat: Open woodland, near short grass for foraging; fields and marshes in winter
Nest: In hole in tree, building or other nest; foundation of grass and twigs, soft lining

Eggs: 4–5; pale blue
Food: Invertebrates in spring and summer; seeds and fruit at other times

Male in summer has all-black plumage, glossed purple (not green as in starling and without pale edges to wing feathers). Feathers of throat are long and bird looks bearded (more so than starling). Bill pale yellow with bluish-black base. Legs pale pink. In early winter, shows pale tips to feathers on head, mantle and underparts; bill dark. Female similar to male but less glossy; has small, white spots on fresh undertail coverts and pale-yellow margins to larger

wing feathers. Juvenile similar to, but darker than, juvenile starling. First-winter birds have whitish tips to body feathers.

Summer adult has bearded appearance

The spotless starling is generally a resident in its range, but in winter some birds disperse or undertake short-distance migrations

Winter bird shows pale tips to feathers

House Sparrow

Passer domesticus

Adopts perky
stance when
perched, with
chest puffed and
tail cocked

THE house sparrow is widespread and common throughout Europe, although it is almost entirely restricted to habitats close to human habitation. It is generally a sedentary resident, juveniles rarely wandering more than a few kilometres. Birds rapidly become very tame around outlets where food is provided; at open-air cafés they will visit occupied tables and even perch on customers to take food. Most pair for life, and will use a good nest site several years running. This species hybridises with the Spanish sparrow round the Mediterranean, and stable hybrid populations of 'Italian sparrows' occur in Italy.

House sparrows are gregarious, nesting in loose colonies and forming flocks for roosting, feeding and dust-bathing

Drab female (below) and juvenile have distinctive pale band over eye

Male

Voice: Calls include familiar 'cheep' or 'chirrp'; song is a succession of chirps
Length: 14–15cm
Wingspan: 21–21.5cm
Weight: 28–32g
Habitat: Almost invariably associated with human habitation
Nest: In a hole, mostly in a man-made structure; loosely made of grass, with softer lining
Eggs: 3–5; white or faintly greyish, variably marked in shades of grey and brown
Food: Principally seeds; household scraps; animal feed; young fed on invertebrates

Male warm brown above and greyish below, with grey crown, black eyestripe, black bib with broken bottom edge, dull-white cheeks, grey rump, black-brown, square-ended tail and white wingbar. Bill black in breeding season, grey at other times. Legs pink or brown. Female lacks strong plumage pattern. At a distance appears dull brown above and dingy white below. Shows broad, pale-buff supercilium and lighter brown or buff edges to wing feathers. Bill grey, legs pink. Juvenile similar to female.

Tree Sparrow

Passer montanus

IN EUROPE the tree sparrow is much less associated with settlements than its commoner relative, the house sparrow, and is more shy and retiring. It is particularly fond of lightly wooded farmland, but is an urban bird in the far east where it is not in competition with the house sparrow. The tree sparrow is a sociable species that forages in flocks with finches and buntings in winter, and in summer breeds in loose colonies. Four or five pairs may nest in the foundations of a heron's or crow's nest. Local populations can be increased by the provision of nest boxes.

Voice: Distinctive, repeated 'chet' or 'teck' is characteristic of birds taking flight
Length: 14cm
Wingspan: 20–22cm
Weight: 20–24g
Habitat: Small woods, roadside trees, ivy-covered cliffs, parks, wooded suburbs
Nest: In hole in tree, earth bank or building; untidy, of plant materials, softly lined
Eggs: 4–6; white or pale grey, heavily marked, usually with dark brown
Food: Seeds and invertebrates, mostly taken on the ground

Smaller and more trim than house sparrow. Sexes alike. Adult distinguished from male house sparrow by rich, dark-chestnut crown and nape, and whiter cheeks, which almost form a white collar contrasting noticeably with crown and black bib (smaller than house sparrow's); the cheek shows a conspicuous black patch below and behind the eye. Back and rump yellowish-brown. Tail dark brown. Wings show two pale wingbars. Underparts whitish, palest on belly, and washed buff on flanks. Bill black. Legs pale brown. Juvenile as adult but duller.

Unlike house sparrows, male and female tree sparrows share incubation of the eggs

In flight shorter tail and more bouncy flight action distinguish tree sparrow from house sparrow

Spanish Sparrow

Passer hispaniolensis

SPANISH sparrows breed colonially, and outside the breeding season the species is very gregarious. In Spain, in autumn, flocks of up to 4,000 form to forage for food and to roost. Some breeding colonies are huge and closely packed; in these colonies a pair's territory is simply the immediate area around the nest. In southern areas, where the birds are sedentary, the same site may be used every year. Spanish sparrows often build their nests into those of white storks, raptors and crows.

Voice: Call distinct, contralto 'chup'; song similar to house sparrow's but richer
Length: 15cm
Wingspan: 23–26cm
Weight: 25–30g
Habitat: Cultivated land, settlements; also arid regions, and woods and thickets
Nest: Free-standing on a branch fork; untidy, domed, of grass and straw, with finer lining
Eggs: 4–6; white or faintly tinted blue or green, speckled in shades of grey
Food: Seeds and invertebrates, taken mainly from the ground

Male has chestnut crown, nape and sides of neck. Black bib extends to unique arrowhead streaks on breast and flanks. White cheeks very noticeable. Short, white, broken supercilium. Mantle and rump grey. Wings brown with two pale wingbars, and tail dark brown. Bill black in breeding season, paler at other times. Legs light brown. Female and juvenile dull brown and dingy white below; almost indistinguishable from equivalent plumages of house sparrow.

Rock Sparrow

Petronia petronia

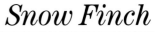

ROCK sparrows are sociable birds and form flocks of up to several hundred from late summer to spring. They readily associate with foraging finches, feeding on the ground on seeds throughout the year, on berries in autumn, and on caterpillars and other invertebrates in the breeding season. This is a nervous species and is often the first in a mixed flock to fly up in alarm, though it can become fairly tame in the breeding season. Rock sparrows generally breed in small, loose colonies, sometimes quite close together, such as in a big cave with many crevices. The males defend a small territory and, once mated, many attempt to get a second mate.

Voice: Characteristic call is a nasal 'pey-ee'; song comprises a repetition of calls
Length: 14cm
Wingspan: 28–32cm
Weight: 30–35g
Habitat: Treeless terrain with sparse vegetation; sometimes vineyards, olive groves
Nest: In a natural hole, a building, in another species' nest hole; untidy, like house sparrow

Eggs: 5–6; white, variably blotched and spotted brown and grey
Food: Mostly seeds taken on the ground, berries in autumn; feeds young on caterpillars

Adult is superficially like female house sparrow, but has longer wings, shorter tail and heavier bill. Upperparts and wings dusty brown, heavily streaked with brown-black.

Underparts buffish-white, streaked and spotted brown especially on flanks and undertail coverts. Tail dark brown with white terminal spots, which show clearly in flight. Both sexes have distinctive striped head pattern: creamy-coloured central crown stripe, dark-brown lateral crown stripes, broad off-white supercilium and dusky ear coverts. Bill large, deep and greyish. Legs brownish-yellow. In spring male has bright-yellow patch on upper breast. Sexes otherwise similar. Juvenile similar to adult but without yellow on throat.

Runs around on ground like a pipit rather than hopping and jumping like a house sparrow

Snow Finch

Montifringilla nivalis

ALTHOUGH superficially similar to the snow bunting, the snow finch is not closely related to this species, and has a different geographical range. During the summer months, snow finches are found between 2,000m and nearly 3,000m; in winter, however, they may be forced to descend to lower levels in adjacent valleys. Snow finches are often found in the vicinity of ski-lifts and paths, where they are usually completely tolerant of man's presence, on occasion even searching for crumbs; small flocks sometimes aggregate during the winter months. When seen closely, their shuffling and hopping gait recalls that of both chaffinches and house sparrows.

Voice: Sparrow-like song includes chaffinch-like 'pink'
Length: 17cm
Wingspan: 34–38cm
Weight: 35–40g
Habitat: Bare, stony sites, above the tree-line in summer
Nest: Grassy nest built in rock crevice
Eggs: 4–5; white
Food: Seeds and invertebrates

Snow finches are birds of mountaintops and Alpine slopes; in Europe they are found in the Pyrenees, Alps and more locally in the Italian Abruzzi Mountains and in the Balkans

Finch-like member of the sparrow family with considerable amount of white in plumage. Adult has blue-grey head, white underparts and brown mantle. Wings white with black tips, extremely striking in flight. Tail white with black central bar. Male has black bib and dark bill in summer but has yellow bill and loses bib in winter. Female similar to winter male. Juvenile similar to winter male but with dull bill.

similar to snow bunting, but has a quite different range

summer male

Chaffinch

Fringilla coelebs

THE chaffinch is one of the commonest and most widespread of all birds in western Europe, breeding wherever there are bushes or trees. Most birds in northwest Europe are rather sedentary; other populations are migratory, moving generally southwest. Spring migration is in March and April, when flocks of winter visitors may gather on farmland where resident males are already singing and defending territory. The chaffinch is gregarious outside the breeding season. Although a chaffinch's song has a generally recognisable form, each male in fact has up to six song-types; he sings a series of one type before going on to another.

In continental flocks one sex often predominates, but flocks of British birds generally have an equal sex ratio

Female

Male's contrasting plumage highlighted by pink breast

Juvenile

Male, March

Male, May

Male, September

Male, November

Voice: Call 'chink;. male's call in spring, 'wheet'; song is an accelerating phrase ending in a flourish
Length: 14.5cm
Wingspan: 25–28cm
Weight: 20–28g
Habitat: Woods, forest, coniferous plantations; also in farmland, parks and gardens
Nest: In fork of tree or bush; beautiful cup of moss, lichen and spiders' web; lined with hair
Eggs: 4–5; variable, bluish, or reddish-grey with purple-brown blotches and scrawls
Food: Mostly seeds from the ground; invertebrates, especially caterpillars, for young

Male very distinctive, with pink face, breast and belly. Crown, nape, upper mantle blue-grey; lower mantle chestnut brown. Greenish rump, white undertail coverts and black forehead. Tail black with white outer feathers. Wings black with pale fringes to flight feathers; shows broad, white wingbar across tips of greater coverts, and long, deep, white blaze from shoulder to scapulars on lesser and median coverts. Bill blue in breeding season but dull pinkish-grey at other times. Legs grey or brown. Female plumage pale olive-brown above and greyish-white below; has same diagnostic tail and wing patterns as male. Bill pinkish-grey and legs reddish-brown. Juvenile similar to female.

Brambling

Fringilla montifringilla

Breeding male's black head and bright breast unmistakable

IN AUTUMN all European bramblings eventually migrate south and west, but many birds remain in the northeast of their wintering range as long as possible while good stocks of beech-mast last. When these fail they move on, often in huge numbers: several million birds may reach western Europe in hard winters. In winter, at the edge of its range, flocks may contain between a few dozen and several hundred birds, but in central European beech woods there may be hundreds of thousands. In the breeding season, bramblings forage mainly in trees, feeding on caterpillars. They often associate with chaffinches and will sometimes visit garden feeding stations.

Winter female

In flight white rump is key identifying feature

Winter male

Eggs: 5–7; variable, greenish, blue, olive with few or many rusty spots
Food: Summer and winter diets different

Voice: Call a wheezy 'tsweep'; song a monotonous, repeated 'dwee'
Length: 14cm
Wingspan: 25–26cm
Weight: 20–28g
Habitat: Birch and mixed forest; woodland, and open ground in winter
Nest: High in a tree; cup of moss, lichen and grass; lined with feathers, hair and fur

Identified at all times by buffish-orange breast and shoulder, diagnostic long, white rump and black, slightly forked tail. Breeding male has glossy black head and mantle, orange throat, breast and shoulders; rest of underparts white. Wings black with narrow white bar across tips of greater coverts and white patch below orange shoulder. Bill blue-black. Legs brownish-flesh. In winter male's head and mantle mottled with brown; bill yellowish with black tip. Female has underparts and wing pattern of male but in washed-out colours. Head has dark-brown crown, greyish nape with brown lateral stripes, buff supercilium and ear-coverts, whitish chin and throat. Bill grey in summer, blue-black in winter. Juvenile as female.

Goldfinch

Carduelis carduelis

The breeding territory is small, just around the nest, and the pair forages for food up to half a mile away

MOST goldfinch populations are migratory, wintering within the species' breeding range, especially round the Mediterranean. A serious decline in numbers in the 1980s in parts of its range was probably caused by the increasing scarcity of weed seeds, but some recovery has taken place since. Generally the goldfinch feeds on seeds taken directly from the plant, and birds can often be seen acrobatically extracting thistle seeds or swinging on alder or birch catkins: the relatively long, pointed bill acts like a pair of tweezers. Goldfinches are gregarious outside the breeding season, forming nomadic flocks.

Voice: Call a liquid 'tswitt-witt-witt'; song a characteristic, cheerful tinkling
Length: 12cm
Wingspan: 21–25.5cm
Weight: 15–22g
Habitat: Orchards, parks, gardens, scrub, thickets, rough grassland, overgrown sites
Nest: Well hidden in outermost twigs of tree; very neat cup of moss and grass, thickly lined
Eggs: 4–6; very pale bluish-white, spotted and scrawled reddish or purplish

Food: Small seeds, especially daisies, dandelions, groundsel, thistles, teasel, burdock

Adult unmistakable with golden-yellow panel along centre of black wing and head patterned vertically in bands; red from bill to eye, white behind eye, black crown and nape. Sexes similar. Mantle, back, breast band and flanks pale rufous, rump whitish. Tail black. White spots to tips of flight and tail feathers. Bill noticeably pointed, pinkish with dark tip. Legs pale flesh. Juvenile reveals yellow on wings in flight but head and body plumage greyish-brown, spotted and streaked brown until autumn moult.

Young birds lack the adult face pattern on leaving the nest, but acquire it within two months

Greenfinch

Carduelis chloris

Juvenile

Winter flocks will stay at a food source until it is exhausted

THE greenfinch is widespread in Europe from close to the Arctic Circle to the Mediterranean. It is mainly a lowland species closely allied to its habitat of trees and open ground, on which it forages for seeds. Increasingly it has learned to live with man in towns and around farms, especially where cereals and seeds of plants of the cabbage family are found. Most greenfinches winter southwest of their breeding range. Birds from northwest Europe are partial migrants, tending to move to milder lowland and coastal districts. Greenfinches defend only a small area around the nest, often in neighbourhood groups of four to six pairs, and travel up to 3km to find food. Unlike chaffinches, greenfinches even feed their young on seeds. A striking feature of spring and summer is the male greenfinch's erratic, circular song-flight on slow wingbeats that do not seem strong enough to keep him airborne. At a birdtable dominant birds will get most of the food, quarrels are frequent and birds low down the pecking order will wait or fly off to find other food. Garden fruits like rose-hips and cotoneaster are nibbled to get the seeds, leaving the broken flesh on the plant.

Adult male (right) has brighter colouring than adult female (far right)

Voice: Call loud nasal 'tsweee'; flight call rapid twitter; song strong, twittering trill
Length: 15 cm
Wingspan: 25–27cm
Weight: 25–30g
Habitat: Densely leafed trees in woodland edge, orchards, parks, graveyards, gardens

Nest: In fork of dense bush or small tree; bulky cup of grass, moss and twigs; soft lining
Eggs: 4–6; greyish- or bluish-white, sparsely spotted red, purple, black
Food: Fairly large seeds of wide variety of plants, taken on bush or ground

Male is striking olive-green and yellow, darker olive above and yellower below. Tail and flight feathers brown-black, with brilliant yellow fringes to primaries (forming bold patch on bottom edge of folded wing), and brilliant yellow on bases of outer four pairs of tail feathers. Underwing yellow. Yellow patterns very noticeable in flight. Tail short, distinctly forked. Bill stout, conical, pale flesh. Legs pale flesh. Female similar to male but duller overall, with indistinct streaks on crown and mantle. Juvenile even duller than female and more distinctly streaked above and below.

Serin

Serinus serinus

Adult male

Adult female

Breeding birds defend small territories, may form neighbourhood groups and are often very tame; the density of these groups varies markedly from a few pairs to over a hundred pairs per square kilometre

ORIGINALLY a Mediterranean species, the serin spread north during the 19th century. It is vulnerable to cold, wet weather, however, and so northern populations migrate south to winter within the species' breeding range. Outside the breeding season serins form small flocks, but often migrate in their hundreds. Serins sing throughout the year. Small, post-breeding flocks keep up a continuous jingling, chirping twitter, while a breeding male sings from a high perch on a tree or telegraph line, or in a spectacular song-flight in an erratic course with slow, deep wingbeats; he may sing all day when the female is building the nest.

Voice: Call a distinctive 'tirlillillit'; song a rapid succession of chirps, jingles and twitters
Length: 11.5cm
Wingspan: 20–23cm
Weight: 11–13g
Habitat: Forest edge, clearings, parkland, orchards, vineyards, gardens
Nest: Often in conifer or fruit tree; small cup of stalks, moss and lichen; thick, soft lining
Eggs: 3–4; bluish-white, sparsely spotted and streaked rusty, mostly at large end
Food: Mostly small seeds from plants such as the daisy and cabbage families and catkins

A tiny finch, as small as a blue tit. Male is streaky, greenish-brown above with bright-yellow head, breast and rump. Male's blackish-brown wings have pale fringes to wing coverts showing as pale wingbars. Tail deeply forked. Black eye looks beady on yellow face. Stubby grey bill. Legs brown. Female has same basic pattern as male, but browner above with duller yellow parts. Juvenile resembles dull female. Confusion with female or juvenile siskin likely, but distinguished by small bill, narrow wingbars and uniformly streaked underparts.

Citril Finch

Serinus citrinella

Citril finches eat more grass seeds than most finches and are quite adept at bending over a stalk and holding the seed head underfoot in order to peck out the seeds

THIS small finch favours a high-altitude habitat in the mountain ranges of southern Europe, although it may move into sheltered valleys in winter. The resident birds of Corsica and Sardinia are exceptional in breeding from sea-level to above the tree-line, nesting in bushes of tree heathers and broom. Elsewhere it is a rare vagrant. The citril finch has not moved into man-made habitats as much as the serin has, but it does forage in mown meadows, beside ski-runs and roads, on wasteland and in gardens. Citril finches are gregarious outside the breeding season, forming flocks of up to several hundred, pairs keeping together. Breeding is often in small neighbourhood groups of three to five pairs, with apparently suitable habitat left unoccupied between groups.

Voice: Call a metallic 'chwick; flight call 'didididid'; song a fast tinkling twitter
Length: 12cm
Wingspan: 23–24cm
Weight: 11.5–13g
Habitat: Woodland, especially spruce bordering Alpine meadows between 700m and 3,300m
Nest: Almost always in a conifer; cup of grass, roots, lined with hair, feathers and wool
Eggs: 3–5; pale blue, sparsely marked at large end with reddish spots
Food: Small and medium-sized seeds, including grass seeds

Adult plumage mainly yellow-green, with slate-grey nape and sides to neck, yellow rump and unstreaked underparts. Tail and wings black, latter with yellowish-green lesser coverts and ends of greater coverts, forming broad bars in flight. Bill greyish with dark tip. Legs brownish. Female similar to male but duller. Juvenile buff-brown above, whitish-buff below, with dark-brown streaks on crown, mantle and all underparts except belly.

Siskin

Carduelis spinus

THE siskin breeds widely in Scandinavia and eastern Europe, and has spread in the British Isles and western Europe thanks to afforestation. Most populations are migratory, moving south and west outside the breeding season. Siskins are particularly fond of spruce, alder and birch seeds, which they extract with their tweezer-like bills. They feed mostly in the trees, hanging acrobatically on to cones and twigs, and using both bill and foot to reach for and hold food. They have also learned to feed on peanuts at garden birdtables, a habit that began in southeast England and is now widespread.

Voice: Calls include 'dluee' and 'tsüü', often given in flight; song a sweet twitter with wheezy ending
Length: 12cm
Wingspan: 20–23cm
Weight: 12–15g
Habitat: Especially coniferous forest; alders, birches by streams; gardens in winter
Nest: High in outer twigs of conifer; cup of conifer twigs, grass and moss; lined with hair and wool
Eggs: 3–5; bluish with dark purplish or brown spots over reddish blotches

Food: Seeds, especially of spruce, alder, birch, and herbs; peanuts

Both sexes have black wings with broad, yellow wingbar across tips of greater coverts and inner primaries. Adult male green above and yellow below, with diagnostic black forehead, crown and chin. Tail forked, black, edged along basal two-thirds with brilliant yellow. Belly and undertail coverts white, the latter streaked black. Tapered, pointed bill, yellowish. Legs dark brown. Female lacks male's black crown. Breast yellow, rest of underparts white, streaked black. Yellow on wings and tail patterned like male but less obvious. Juvenile similar to female but browner and more streaked.

Winter flocks are nomadic, and ringing has shown that many birds overwinter in different areas of Europe in successive years, although a few may be faithful to a previously used site

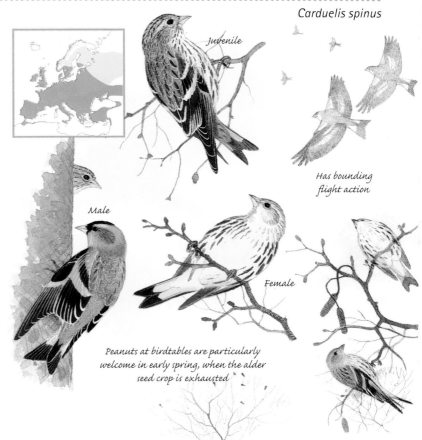

Juvenile

Has bounding flight action

Male

Female

Peanuts at birdtables are particularly welcome in early spring, when the alder seed crop is exhausted

Linnet

Carduelis cannabina

THE linnet eats almost exclusively seeds, its favourites being the seeds of chickweed, persicaria, fat-hen and charlock. The increase in cultivation of oil-seed rape has proved to be a help to the linnet, which feeds on it avidly, and 'set-aside' fields are providing more weed seeds. Even so, the population in many parts of Europe is probably still around 50 per cent below numbers in the 1960s and 1970s. Linnets often form large winter flocks for feeding, roosting and migrating. In the summer they breed in neighbourhood groups of between two and several dozen pairs, with nests only a few metres apart.

Voice: Alarm call 'tsooeet'; flight call 'tihtihtihtit'; song a musical, soft warbling twitter
Length: 13.5cm
Wingspan: 21–25cm
Weight: 15–20g
Habitat: Scrub, heath, hedges, vineyards, maquis, uncultivated fields
Nest: Low in thick, often thorny, bush; cup of twigs, grass; lined with hair and wool
Eggs: 4–6; very pale blue with reddish blotches under pink and purplish spots
Food: Almost completely seeds

Male has chestnut mantle, scapulars and wing coverts. Wings and tail dark brown with white edges to some flight and tail feathers, showing as indistinct wingbar on perched bird and as greyish patches in flight. Bill greyish-brown and head grey except for crimson forehead. Bill greyish. Legs dark brown. Female lacks male's crimson breast and forehead. Brown back streaked darker than on male and underparts streaked buff-brown. Like male, female shows distinctive whitish wing and tail patches. Juvenile similar to female but more heavily streaked, so shows less contrast between upperparts and underparts. Wing and tail patches indistinct.

Young males resemble females; acquire crimson after one year

Adult male

Female

Breeding birds perch very openly on the tops of low bushes

Feeds on bushes in summer, but on ground in winter

Twite

Carduelis flavirostris

Pink rump prominent in flight; shows very little white on wings

ALTHOUGH twites look very much like linnets or redpolls, their choice of habitat and distinctive alarm and contact calls should help to identify them. The twite is gregarious outside the breeding season and often winters on saltmarshes or on coastal grassland. The birds in Britain are described as a separate subspecies, and are considered to be in special need of conservation. In many parts of its range, and especially in Britain, the twite has declined recently, probably because of overgrazing and afforestation of its moorland breeding grounds.

Voice: Call nasal 'chweek'; constant twitter in flight; song hoarse and twanging
Length: 14cm
Wingspan: 22–24cm
Weight: 13–16.6g
Habitat: Almost treeless countryside in cool and often rainy climate
Nest: Close to ground in herbage or crevice; deep cup of twigs and bracken; warmly lined

Eggs: 4–6; blue, with spots, speckles and scrawls of reddish- or purplish-brown
Food: Small seeds gathered on the ground

Adult is liable to be confused with female or juvenile linnet but plumage is generally darker, more tawny above and more heavily streaked below; the ground colour is warm buff. Shows white wing patches and tail sides but these features less noticeable than on linnet. Sexes similar but male has rose-pink rump, that of female being same colour as mantle. Both sexes have yellow bill in winter but grey bill in summer. Juvenile similar to winter adult.

Redpoll

Carduelis flammea

REDPOLLS are perhaps easiest to see during the winter months when they gather together in flocks, and the trees in which they feed have lost their leaves. Favouring alder and birch, the seeds of which they relish, wintering flocks of redpolls frequently associate with siskins and the calls of both species are usually the first clue to their presence. Migrating flocks in spring and autumn are sometimes found in surprisingly short vegetation, replenishing their food reserves for their onward journey.

Voice: Trilling, unmusical song delivered in flight; utters fast 'chuchuchuh-uh' call
Length: 13–14cm
Wingspan: 20–25cm
Weight: 10–13g
Habitat: Favours birch and alder woodland; will also nest in conifer plantations and forests
Nest: Twig and grass construction, usually high in tree
Eggs: 4–5; blue, spotted and streaked
Food: Mainly seeds

Plumage variable but generally has brown, streaked upperparts, pale underparts streaked on flanks, and streaked rump; shows two white wingbars. Male has black chin, red forecrown and narrow band of white running from base of forecrown above eye; shows pinkish flush to breast, most apparent in breeding season. Female similar to male but shows less extensive red on forecrown, base of which is black not white, and lacks pink flush to breast. Bill short, triangular in profile, and yellowish with curved culmen in all birds. Juvenile similar to female but lacks red on forecrown.

Juvenile (left) and female lack pinkish flush to breast shown by male (far left)

Arctic Redpoll

Carduelis hornemanni

ARCTIC redpolls often remain in the vicinity of their breeding grounds throughout the year, only moving south in the severest of conditions; even then, they seldom move far. Outside the breeding season distinguishing Arctic redpolls from redpolls is invariably a challenge. Given the birds' small size and feeding habits, neither species makes it easy to see the most diagnostic feature, the rump. Unlike their more arboreal cousins, however, Arctic redpolls are more inclined to feed on the ground or in low scrub. A few birds are gleaming white and easy to identify.

Voice: Chattering flight call similar to redpoll's but slower
Length: 13–14cm
Wingspan: 21–27cm
Weight: 12–14g
Habitat: Breeds on Arctic tundra; in winter, most remain in northern latitudes
Nest: Twig and grass construction, usually in dwarf willow scrub
Eggs: 4–5; pale blue with dark markings
Food: Mainly seeds of birch, alder and willow

Can be difficult to distinguish from redpoll. Plumage generally much paler, in some races almost white, and rumps of adult birds always unstreaked. Bill triangular in profile and yellowish with straight, not curved, culmen. Male has pale buffish-brown, streaked upperparts and pale, usually white underparts with faint streaking on flanks. In breeding season may have pink flush on breast. Shows black bib and red forecrown, base of which is white and continues above eye; white on forecrown more extensive than on redpoll. Female similar to male but upperparts usually darker; lacks pink flush on breast. Juvenile similar to female but has buffish plumage and lacks red forecrown.

Adult male

Two-barred Crossbill

Loxia leucoptera

THROUGHOUT their range, two-barred crossbills are year-round residents so long as food supplies hold out; in most years the conifers on which they feed produce an abundance of seeds, but in some years almost the entire crop can fail. This is a problem for the two-barred crossbill, because its bill has evolved specifically to extract the seeds of larch in particular. Although they will tackle other conifer species and berry sources, the birds are sometimes forced to move *en masse* in search of new food sources.

Voice: Rattling and buzzing song; utters chattering call in flight; occasionally toy trumpet call heard
Length: 15cm
Wingspan: 26–29cm
Weight: 29–34g
Habitat: Conifer forests, especially larch
Nest: Twig platform, built close to trunk of conifer
Eggs: 3–5; pale bluish-white with faint markings
Food: Mainly larch seeds but sometimes seeds of other conifers or berries

Adults of both sexes distinguished by relatively long, slender bill with overlapping mandible tips and two striking white wingbars. Male has pinkish-red plumage, while that of female is yellowish-green. Juvenile shows double wingbars but has grey-brown, streaked plumage and lacks adult's white tips to tertial feathers.

Adult male

White wingbars impressive at rest and in flight

Crossbill

Loxia curvirostra

UNLIKE its near relatives, the crossbill is widespread throughout much of Europe wherever suitable habitats occur. Its bill is superbly adapted for extracting seeds from the cones of conifers, particularly spruce trees, and in this choice of food it has no bird competitors. Although generally sedentary, crossbills will often make post-breeding forays, presumably in search of new feeding and nesting areas. In years when the conifer seed crop fails, flocks make long irruptive journeys, sometimes covering hundreds of kilometres.

Voice: Loud, persistent 'chip chip' flight call; song comprises trilling notes followed by greenfinch-like calls
Length: 17cm
Wingspan: 27–30cm
Weight: 34–38g
Habitat: Conifer forests, mainly pine and spruce

Nest: Twig platform, built near trunk of tree
Eggs: 4; off-white with bold spots
Food: Conifer seeds, especially spruce

Adult male has mainly bright-red plumage except for the dark wings. Adult female is green except for the dark wings. Juvenile has brown, heavily streaked plumage; sometimes shows faint wingbars but these

much less conspicuous than on juvenile two-barred crossbill.

Male

Female

Dumpy finch with robust bill; mandible tips cross

Scottish Crossbill

Loxia scotica

ONCE considered by many experts to be a race of crossbill, it is now generally agreed that the Scottish crossbill should have species status. This makes it the only bird that is endemic to Britain: that is, it occurs nowhere else in the world. Its fate is inextricably linked to that of the remaining forest stands of Scots pine: the shape of the Scottish crossbill's bill has evolved specifically for this tree. All crossbills make regular visits to water to drink: trackside pools are frequently used, affording the observer good views of these rather confiding birds.

Voice: Loud 'chip chip' flight call; song includes trilling and greenfinch-like notes
Length: 16cm
Wingspan: 28–30cm
Weight: 40–46g
Habitat: Conifer forests
Nest: Twig platform, usually close to tree trunk
Eggs: 4; off-white with bold spots

Food: Conifer seeds, mainly Scots pine

Out of range, could easily be confused with small-billed parrot crossbill or large-billed crossbill. Bill is heavy with tips of mandibles

overlapping. Adult male has bright-red plumage, except for darker wings. Adult female has green plumage except for darker wings. Juvenile has grey-brown, heavily streaked plumage with same bill shape as adult.

Adult male

Has larger, blunter bill than crossbill

Parrot Crossbill

Loxia pytyopsittacus

PARROT crossbills are generally rather sedentary birds. In years when the pine seed crop fails, however, they can be forced to irrupt in search of new sources of food. At such times, sometimes sizeable flocks have spread as far as Scotland and the east coast of England. Like other crossbill species, parrot crossbills spend much of their time feeding on pine cones in trees. They are, however, not averse to feeding on fallen seeds on the ground, so views are less neck-breaking than those of their more arboreal cousins.

Voice: Utters 'chip chip' flight call, lower pitch than crossbill's; song comprises greenfinch-like elements, lower pitch than crossbill's
Length: 17.5cm
Wingspan: 32cm
Weight: 48–62g
Habitat: Conifer forests, mainly pine
Nest: Twig platform, built close to tree trunk
Eggs: 3–4; pale yellowish-green with brown markings
Food: Mainly pine seeds

Superficially very similar to crossbill. Generally shows larger and heavier bill, the

mandible tips of which cross but cannot be seen to project in silhouette. Head and neck also appear proportionately larger. Male has red plumage with dark wings. Female has yellowish-green

plumage with dark wings. Juvenile has grey-brown, streaked plumage.

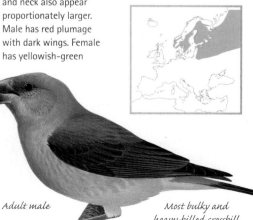
Adult male

Most bulky and heavy-billed crossbill

Scarlet Rosefinch

Carpodacus erythrinus

The breeding male's smart colours are a fitting complement to his tuneful song, which contains elements reminiscent of the golden oriole

The breeding range of the scarlet rosefinch has spread north and west since the late 20th century, and it now nests in significant numbers as far west as southern Scandinavia

Female (below) much duller than male

S CARLET rosefinches are summer visitors to Europe, present from May to September; the winter months are spent in the Indian sub-continent and parts of southeast Asia. Even where they are common, scarlet rosefinches can be difficult to see. Although not especially shy, they are rather unobtrusive and spend considerable periods of time either feeding or just resting in cover; their usual reaction when alarmed is to retreat into dense foliage. When seen in the open, the birds appear slightly ungainly as they clamber among the twigs and leaves. The majority of birds seen are either immatures or females, with rather nondescript plumage.

Voice: Male has distinctive, far-carrying, whistling song
Length: 14.5cm
Wingspan: 25cm
Weight: 21–25g
Habitat: Scrub and forest edge
Nest: Twig and grass structure built in dense cover
Eggs: 4–6; pale green with brown spots and streaks
Food: Seeds and other plant material, with some insects

Medium-sized finch with large, stubby bill; all ages and plumages show two pale wingbars. Mature adult male distinctive with red head, breast and rump; wings brown with wingbars tinged pink and underparts white. Immature male and adult male in winter have less intense colour. Female and juvenile have undistinguished brown plumage with underparts pale and streaked.

Pine Grosbeak

Pinicola enucleator

P INE grosbeaks are generally rather sedentary and move little throughout the year. In some winters, however, they range further south, and from time to time irruptions occur south and west of the usual range. They feed on the ground, where they hop and walk, and among branches, where their progress can be rather cumbersome. They are seldom particularly numerous, however, so finding this species can be something of a challenge. Pine grosbeaks are adapted to make best use of the often meagre supplies of food in their environment. In spring they favour the growing shoots of trees such as birch; in summer they feast on bilberries, other fruits and some insects. The winter months are spent foraging for fallen seeds and the persisting berries of trees such as rowan.

Breeding-plumage male

Voice: Loud, fluty and yodelling song
Length: 18.5cm
Wingspan: 31–35cm
Weight: 50–60g
Habitat: Northern taiga forest
Nest: Twig nest in conifer, usually near trunk
Eggs: 3–4; greenish-blue with dark markings
Food: Mainly shoots, buds, seeds and fruits

Comparatively large, dumpy finch with large head and stout bill. Both sexes show two conspicuous pale wingbars, those of male tinged pink. Wings of both sexes appear dark grey and show grey feathering on undertail and lower belly. In flight tail looks relatively long. Adult male has pinkish-red plumage, while that of adult female is mainly greenish-yellow. First-year male and female resemble dull version of adult female. Juvenile plumage is dull grey-brown.

Although unobtrusive, pine grosbeaks are not shy and can often yield very good views when found

Trumpeter Finch

Bucanetes githagineus

Breeding male

T RUMPETER finches are adapted to life in extremely arid climates, but they do need a daily drink. To this end they will visit seasonal pools or even dripping irrigation pipes, where they can be easy to see. At other times, birds can be rather elusive, since they feed unobtrusively in broken ground. When alarmed, they sometimes crouch, but will on occasion adopt a more upright posture, usually just before taking to the wing. During the breeding season trumpeter finches are rather solitary birds, but in the winter months small flocks may gather in suitable feeding areas.

Voice: Song recalls sound of a toy trumpet
Length: 12.5cm
Wingspan: 25–28cm
Weight: 19–23g
Habitat: Arid semi-desert
Nest: Grass structure built in rock crevice
Eggs: 3–4; pale blue with dark speckling
Food: Mainly seeds but some insects

Small, compact finch with proportionately large, stubby bill; this is red in summer male but pinkish-buff in winter male and in female. Plumage is mainly uniform buffish but that of male has pinkish flush to underparts and wings. Legs pinkish in both sexes. Juvenile similar to female.

Bullfinch

Pyrrhula pyrrhula

A RATHER shy and retiring species, the bullfinch is heard more often than it is seen: its soft, piping calls carry a surprising distance through the undergrowth. In areas where fruit trees are grown commercially bullfinches have a bad reputation, since they are extremely fond of the nutritious developing buds that appear in spring. In more natural habitats, bullfinches can survive perfectly well on nature's harvest, ash-keys in particular being an important source of food from autumn through to early spring. Insects are eaten by adult birds as well, but feature particularly as an appreciable part of the macerated food fed to the young in the nest.

White rump shows well in flight

Most birds winter within the species' breeding range; some migrate to southern Europe

Male

Juvenile (above)

Female

Voice: Call is a distinctive, low piping 'teu'
Length: 15cm
Wingspan: 25cm
Weight: 21–27g
Habitat: Undergrowth near woodland edge, hedgerows and gardens
Nest: Twig platform, built in deep cover
Eggs: 4–5; clear greenish-blue
Food: Buds, berries and seeds; some invertebrates

A dumpy finch with a stubby, black bill and conspicuous white rump, seen in flight. Male has black cap, blue-grey nape and mantle, and pinkish-red underparts, except for white undertail feathering; hue of red underparts distinctly different from other birds found in same habitats. Wings black with broad white wingbar; tail black. Female has similar patterning to male but more sombre, muted colours, appearing pinkish-buff. Juvenile similar to female but lacks black cap.

Hawfinch

Coccothraustes coccothraustes

T HROUGHOUT much of their range, hawfinches go undetected because of their shy nature and habit of favouring dense foliage in tall trees during the breeding season. They are widespread in central and southern Europe although, in the west of their range, their precise distribution is rather patchy; in Britain they occur as far north as southern Scotland. Hawfinches are generally resident but birds from the east of the range migrate south and west in autumn. They are perhaps easiest to see during the winter months, when the leaves are off the trees and their distinctive profile is recognisable even in silhouette. Small flocks sometimes gather in good feeding areas, the seeds of hornbeam being perhaps their favourite food; areas of parkland or coppice planted with this species are well worth investigating. During the summer months, insects, particularly caterpillars, become an important part of the diet.

Easily recognised by profile and white band on wings

Voice: Loud, robin-like 'tic' call
Length: 18cm
Wingspan: 29–33cm
Weight: 48–62g
Habitat: Mixed woodlands, mainly deciduous
Nest: Twig construction built in tree
Eggs: 4–6; bluish-green, spotted
Food: Large seeds and fruit stones; some insects in breeding season

Large and unmistakable finch with distinctive profile, both when perched and in flight. Bill proportionately massive and triangular in outline. Bird looks top-heavy and large-headed when perched; in flight shows a considerable amount of white and looks short-tailed with proportionately large head and neck. Male has mainly orange-buff and pinkish-buff plumage. Shows black around base of bill and on bib. Mantle reddish-brown and wings dark but showing broad, white band on coverts. Undertail feathering and tip of tail white. Female similar but with duller colours. Juvenile has brownish plumage and spotted underparts.

Because of its huge bill, the hawfinch is the only European bird that can successfully tackle hard-cased hornbeam seeds, and it can also crack open cherry stones

243

Snow Bunting

Plectrophenax nivalis

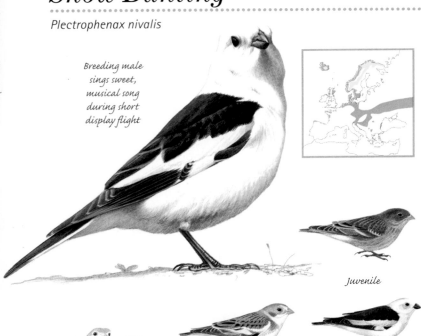

Breeding male sings sweet, musical song during short display flight

Juvenile

Immature, first autumn

Immature, first winter

Adult male, summer

Adult male, winter

Plumage of winter birds variable but bill always yellow

IN EUROPE the snow bunting nests commonly in Scandinavia and Iceland, and rarely but regularly in Scotland. In winter its range is more extensive and it is widespread in northwest Europe from October to March; it is also found in a broad band from central eastern Europe across Asia. Flocks of snow buntings are sometimes called 'snowflakes': one moment the birds will be feeding unobtrusively on the ground; the next they are in the air, their wings and tails a blizzard of flashing white. Birds on migration in autumn are often confiding and even later in the winter the birds afford closer views than many other passerines. On the ground snow buntings usually adopt a rather horizontal stance and run as if powered by clockwork.

Length: 16cm
Wingspan: 32–38cm
Weight: 30–40g
Habitat: Breeds on Arctic tundra; in winter, on grassland, often coastal
Nest: In rock crevice
Eggs: 4–6; off-white, blotched brown
Food: Seeds and invertebrates

 **Voice:** Song a rapid trilling, sung either from perch or in flight; tinkling calls

 Breeding-plumage male unmistakable, with striking black and white plumage and black bill. Breeding female has white plumage tinged with orange-buff wash and black elements of male's plumage replaced by brown. Bill dark. In autumn and winter, plumage of adults and juveniles rather variable but back and nape usually appear orange-brown. Often shows buffish-orange on cap and cheeks and as breast band. Underparts always white and bill yellow. In flight shows considerable amount of white on wings and tail in all plumages.

Lapland Bunting

Calcarius lapponicus

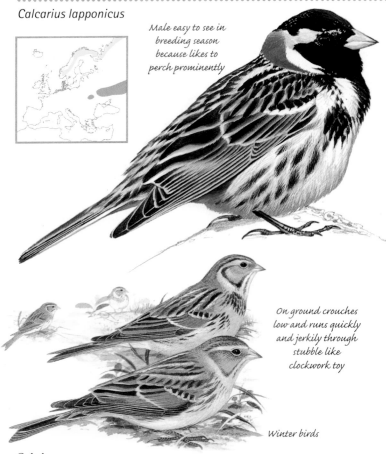

Male easy to see in breeding season because likes to perch prominently

On ground crouches low and runs quickly and jerkily through stubble like clockwork toy

Winter birds

IN EUROPE the Lapland bunting breeds in northern Scandinavia. In winter most Eurasian birds are found in central Asia; in Europe the species is most reliably seen in the northwest, mostly in countries bordering the North Sea. The stunted tundra vegetation and the boldness of the bird's plumage often make the Lapland bunting conspicuous and easy to see in the breeding season. In winter it is far otherwise. Even when present in small flocks, Lapland buntings are unobtrusive and it is a challenge to to obtain a good view before they are flushed into flight. As they feed in stubble fields or coastal grassland, views are often confined to their backs and heads. When alarmed, the flock will take to the air, where flight calls and wing patterns offer the best clues to their identity.

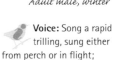 **Voice:** Calls include dry, quick rattle, 'tik-ik-ik-it' and liquid 'tew'; song is a rapid trill, sung either from perch or in flight
Length: 15.5cm
Wingspan: 26–28cm
Weight: 25–28g
Habitat: Nests on Arctic tundra; on migration seen on coasts; in winter favours open, often cultivated land, sometimes coasts
Nest: In tussock of grass
Eggs: 4–5; variable but often pale green with dark markings
Food: Mainly seeds but invertebrates important during breeding season

Male in breeding season unmistakable. Head has striking black, white and chestnut markings and black-tipped yellow bill. Underparts white and back brown with bold streaks. Female in breeding season similar to male but has black on face replaced by worn-looking brown feathering. Both male and female non-breeding birds lose bold markings on head but usually retain hint of chestnut on nape; chestnut wing coverts bordered by two white wingbars are good features for identification. Juvenile recalls winter female but lacks chestnut on nape. Gait of Lapland bunting rather characteristic: crouches low and runs rather quickly and jerkily like clockwork toy.

Yellowhammer

Emberiza citrinella

Breeding male (right) much more colourful than female and non-breeding birds

Often feeds on ground in winter

I N MUCH of western Europe, yellowhammers are rather sedentary; birds from upland regions and from the north and east of their range are migratory, however, moving south and west in September and October. During the breeding season, males frequently announce their presence by singing from the top of a bush or an exposed branch. They often continue to sing well into the summer, long after other songbirds have become silent. When disturbed, a bird will often make a long, circular flight, returning to a point close to where it took off. Outside the breeding season, yellowhammers tend to gather in small flocks, especially in areas of good feeding such as grain spills or newly ploughed fields. At this time, they sometimes mix with other species, such as corn buntings, reed buntings and chaffinches.

Voice: Chirping song, often rendered in English as 'a little bit of bread and no cheese'; rasping call
Length: 16.5cm
Wingspan: 23–29cm
Weight: 25–30g
Habitat: Farmland, heaths, scrub
Nest: Bulky platform of grass and straw, low down or on ground in clump of grass
Eggs: 3–5; pale with dark 'scribbling' and spots
Food: Cereal and grass seeds; invertebrates during summer months

Male in summer is attractive, with mostly lemon-yellow plumage on head and underparts. Plumage often has suffusion of chestnut forming breast band and chestnut on wings, mantle and rump; bright, unstreaked rump striking in flight. In winter male's plumage is duller, the feathers having greyish-green tips. Female much duller than male in all plumages and with more of a suggestion of facial stripes. Juvenile similar to female but with extensive streaking on head and breast in particular.

Black-headed Bunting

Emberiza melanocephala

I NVARIABLY associated with hot, dry regions, the black-headed bunting is common in lowland mainland areas in the eastern Mediterranean between May and August; thereafter, it migrates to the Indian sub-continent. With their distinctive song and habit of singing from an exposed perch, male black-headed buntings are usually easy to locate at the start of the breeding season. Despite their coloration, feeding birds are unobtrusive, however, and are often found foraging on the ground. Seeds are an important part of the diet but, during the breeding season in particular, insects and spiders are also favoured items of food, especially for nestlings.

Voice: Song comprises initial harsh phrases followed by series of notes with tinny ring; flight call a sharp 'tsit'
Length: 17cm
Wingspan: 26–29cm
Weight: 26–30g
Habitat: Olive groves, orchards and maquis
Nest: Low down in dense vegetation
Eggs: 4–5; pale green with brown speckles and streaks
Food: Mainly seeds and invertebrates

Comparatively large bunting with robust, grey bill. Male unmistakable with black head, bright-yellow underparts, yellow sides to neck and chestnut back; wings and tail dark. Female has much more subdued colours, head being greyish-brown. Underparts very pale dirty yellow, and back shows hint of male's chestnut colour. Juvenile superficially resembles corn bunting; has rather plain, buffish-brown plumage with streaking on crown and back.

Male

Female

Yellow-breasted Bunting

Emberiza aureola

T HE yellow-breasted bunting's main breeding range extends across central Asia; in Europe a few hundred pairs nest in Finland. It is present in the breeding range from late May to August. Thereafter, this migratory species flies south to overwinter in southeast Asia; it is a rare vagrant to northwest Europe, being seen mainly in late autumn. Although feeding birds and individuals on migration are unobtrusive and have retiring habits, male yellow-breasted buntings are usually conspicuous and easy to see: perched on exposed branches, they are keen songsters. If unduly disturbed, however, they soon retreat to the cover of dense vegetation.

Voice: Jingling song recalling that of Ortolan bunting; call a sharp 'tsee'
Length: 14cm
Wingspan: 22–24cm
Weight: 21–24g
Habitat: Flooded woodland and wetland scrub
Nest: On ground, usually in grass tussock
Eggs: 4–5; greenish with purple markings
Food: Seeds and invertebrates

and two white wingbars – one broad, one narrow. First-summer male has incomplete markings on head. Female has striped head with white throat and white stripe above and behind eye. Underparts pale yellow, and upperparts streaked brown; wingbars less conspicuous than on male. Juvenile has buffish-brown plumage, broad pale supercilium and dark-brown streaked rump.

Mature summer male has black face and chestnut cap, nape, back and breast band. Underparts and partial throat band yellow; shows white undertail feathering

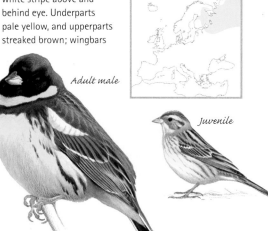

Adult male

Juvenile

Rock Bunting

Emberiza cia

Female

Characteristically feeds on broken ground, searching for seeds and insects, but progress usually remarkably slow

Male

THE rock bunting invariably favours stony or rocky ground – ideally on sunny, south-facing slopes. In much of its range it is sedentary and a year-round resident, but birds that breed in colder, more mountainous districts show some degree of altitudinal migration in the winter. Rock buntings are usually relatively easy to see in southern Europe since suitable habitats are often provided by the broken ground found beside roads in the region. In a more natural setting, terraced vineyards and stony arable land are also favoured. Outside the breeding season small flocks sometimes gather and occasionally mix with other bunting species.

Voice: Male has dunnock-like song; calls include a sharp 'tsee'
Length: 16cm
Wingspan: 22–27cm
Weight: 23–25g
Habitat: Sunny slopes with broken ground
Nest: Grass and moss, built in bush or rock crevice
Eggs: 4–5; pale bluish-white with dark streaking
Food: Seeds and insects

Attractive bunting with triangular, silvery-grey bill in all plumages. Male is a distinctive and attractive bird, with grey head boldly marked with black stripes. Underparts orange-brown and upperparts, including rump, reddish-brown. Female rather similar to male but plumage always washed-

out and less distinct. Juvenile has brown, streaked plumage.

Ortolan Bunting

Emberiza hortulana

THE Ortolan bunting is in its European breeding range from May to September; it overwinters in sub-Saharan Africa. Its choice of breeding habitat is unusually catholic but it generally favours comparatively sunny, dry regions. Ortolan buntings are typically rather unobtrusive birds that feed on the ground. On migration they are often found in ploughed or harvested fields.

In first-winter plumage (above) shows pale 'moustache' and throat markings and pinkish bill

Adult male

Voice: Male has ringing 'see-see-see-see' song; 'chip' flight call
Length: 16cm
Wingspan: 23–28cm
Weight: 20–25g
Habitat: Variety of habitats, including agricultural land and rocky slopes
Nest: Grass and moss construction, in dense vegetation
Eggs: 4–5;

pale blue with dark blotches and speckles
Food: Invertebrates and seeds

Attractive bunting with rather subdued colours and pinkish bill and legs. Male has greenish-grey head with pale-yellowish eyering, 'moustache' markings and throat. Underparts orange-red and upperparts mostly reddish-brown. Female has less intense colours on head than male and streaking on breast, but otherwise similar. Juvenile has mostly sandy-brown plumage.

Cretzschmar's Bunting

Emberiza caesia

CRETZSCHMAR'S bunting is present in warm Mediterranean habitats from April to September; stray migrant birds are very rare outside their normal range. The species is usually tolerant of humans, but it can be difficult to find since it spends a great deal of time feeding unobtrusively on the ground, and, when alarmed, retreats to the cover of ground vegetation. The species is most easily confused with the Ortolan bunting; the warmer, reddish plumage of Cretzschmar's, particularly evident on the underparts, throat and 'moustache' stripes, is the best feature for sure identification.

Voice: Song a ringing 'tsee-tsee-tsee'; flight call a sharp 'chit'
Length: 16cm
Wingspan: 23–26cm
Weight: 20–23g
Habitat: Dry, sunny slopes
Nest: On ground, usually among rocks or vegetation
Eggs: 4–5; pale bluish-white with dark speckles and streaks
Food: Invertebrates and seeds

stripes and throat; eyering buffish. Underparts reddish-orange and back and wings reddish-brown. Female similar to male but with more subdued colours and some streaking on head. Juvenile very similar to juvenile Ortolan but plumage has reddish, not sandy-olive, tone.

A well-marked and colourful bunting, superficially rather similar to Ortolan, with reddish bill and legs. Male has blue-grey head with reddish-orange 'moustache'

Adult male

Little Bunting

Emberiza pusilla

THE smallest member of the bunting family in the region, the little bunting nests in Finland with a few hundred pairs also present in northern Norway. The species is present in its breeding range from May to August, the vast majority of birds then migrating to winter grounds in eastern Asia. In northwest Europe little buntings are known as rare passage migrants, mainly occurring in the autumn, although there are several records of overwintering birds. Periodically birds will perch in nearby shrubs or bushes, usually if alarmed by some apparent danger on the ground. When not actually nesting, little buntings sometimes form small flocks and mix with other buntings or finches when feeding; under these conditions they are hard to distinguish from non-breeding plumage reed buntings.

Seen on the ground, the little bunting often moves like a pipit, although it will hop on occasion as well; it spends much of its time feeding in this unobtrusive manner, often in comparatively tall or dense vegetation

Voice: Song a series of sharp phrases; call a metallic 'tik'
Length: 13cm
Wingspan: 20–22cm
Weight: 13–18g
Habitat: Favours swampy forests during breeding season
Nest: On ground, usually in tussock of grass
Eggs: 4–6; pale green with dark speckles and streaks
Food: Seeds and invertebrates

Superficially similar to non-breeding reed bunting but appreciably smaller and with proportionately longer, finer bill, the culmen of which is straight, not curved. Breeding male has rusty-brown head with white supercilium and black stripe above eye defining rusty crown stripe. Shows thin, dark stripe running from behind eye and around ear coverts; small pale spot conspicuous on otherwise rusty-brown ear coverts. Underparts white, streaked on breast and flanks, and upperparts streaked brown. Female, non-breeding male and juvenile similar to breeding male but with subdued colours and less distinct markings on head.

Rustic Bunting

Emberiza rustica

THE rustic bunting reaches the western limit of its worldwide breeding range in Scandinavia; it is present there from May to August, birds then migrating to their overwintering grounds in eastern China and Japan. In northwest Europe, rustic buntings occur as rare passage migrants, mainly in September and October. During the breeding season, rustic buntings favour damp, boggy woodland with ground vegetation that often includes bog moss and bilberry. They are usually fairly tolerant of human intruders in their territories; feeding on the ground or perched in trees, they allow good views to be obtained. If a rustic bunting feels threatened, it usually starts to flick its tail and raise its crown feathers before flying off.

Voice: Song a ringing 'see-see-see-see'; call a sharp 'tik'
Length: 15cm
Wingspan: 21–25cm
Weight: 18–21g
Habitat: Breeds in northern woodlands
Nest: On ground, usually among moss or grasses
Eggs: 4–5; pale bluish-white with olive-grey streaks and speckles
Food: Invertebrates and seeds

A well-marked bunting. In some plumages, superficially similar to reed bunting, but has proportionately longer bill with straight, not curved, culmen; in all plumages, has pale spots on otherwise dark ear coverts. Male in breeding plumage has bold black and white stripes on head, which has rather peaked appearance. Has rusty-chestnut nape, back and breast band with chestnut streaks on flanks and white underparts. In breeding plumage, female similar to male but black on head replaced by brown. For description of non-breeding adult and juvenile see caption.

The summer diet includes numerous adult and larval stages of aquatic and waterside insects, as well as fruits and seeds as the season progresses

Breeding-plumage male

Juvenile (left) and non-breeding adult best identified by bill proportions and rusty-chestnut tone to back, breast band and streaks on flanks

247

Reed Bunting

Emberiza schoeniclus

THE reed bunting nests throughout northern and central mainland Europe, being a resident in the west but a summer visitor in the north and east; these migratory populations move south and west in autumn. Although somewhat subdued, the call of the reed bunting, once learned, is distinctive. During the breeding season, males in particular often perch on prominent twigs or barbed wire fences, affording excellent views to the observer as they sing their tirelessly repetitive songs. During the winter, when birds sometimes form small flocks and mix with other species, they can, however, be easy to overlook. In some parts of their range, notably Britain, reed buntings visit gardens and bird feeders in the winter.

Voice: Song a short series of chinking phrases; call a thin 'seep'
Length: 15–16cm
Wingspan: 21–27cm
Weight: 18–21g
Habitat: Favours wetland habitats, but sometimes found in drier terrain
Nest: Usually on ground, among vegetation
Eggs: 4–5; pale bluish-grey with dark spots and scratches
Food: Invertebrates and seeds

In breeding season male is distinctive, with black bill and black head. White on underparts extends around nape as narrow collar and as moustachial stripes to base of bill. Back brown with dark streaking and rump greyish. In non-breeding male, pale feather tips on head make black elements of plumage appear brownish. Female has stripy-headed appearance with black 'moustache' being prominent; plumage otherwise similar to that of male. Juvenile similar to female but with even less distinct markings on head.

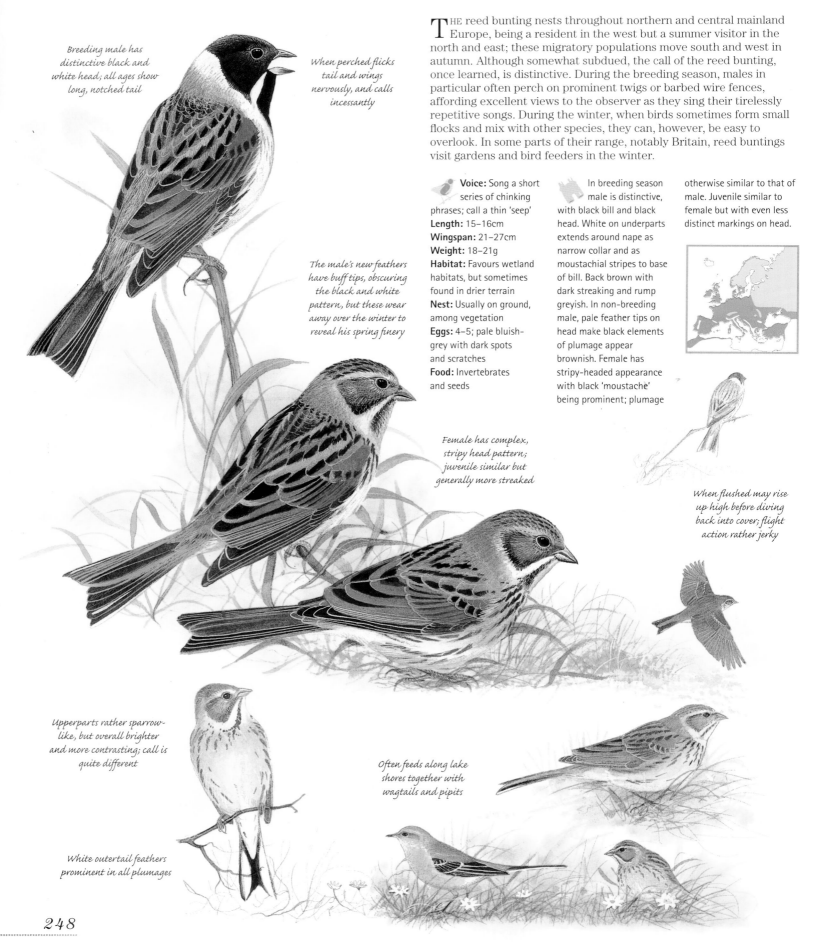

Breeding male has distinctive black and white head; all ages show long, notched tail

When perched flicks tail and wings nervously, and calls incessantly

The male's new feathers have buff tips, obscuring the black and white pattern, but these wear away over the winter to reveal his spring finery

Female has complex, stripy head pattern; juvenile similar but generally more streaked

When flushed may rise up high before diving back into cover; flight action rather jerky

Upperparts rather sparrow-like, but overall brighter and more contrasting; call is quite different

White outertail feathers prominent in all plumages

Often feeds along lake shores together with wagtails and pipits

Cirl Bunting

Emberiza cirlus

RESIDENT throughout the year within its European range, the cirl bunting is primarily a bird of warm climates, whose range includes most of southern Europe. In western Europe it is more widespread, reaching its northern limit in southwest England, where 150 pairs or so are confined mostly to Devon. Although generally retiring in nature, cirl buntings are sometimes conspicuous in early spring, when the male sings his lesser whitethroat-like rattling song from a prominent perch. The song period often continues, off and on, well into late summer, although the frequency at which it is performed gradually diminshes. With practice, the cirl bunting's soft, penetrating 'ssi' call gives a clue to their identity but perhaps the most diagnostic feature for juveniles and females is the greyish rump seen in flight.

Voice: Male's song is a metallic rattle on one note
Length: 16cm
Wingspan: 22–25cm
Weight: 22–26g
Habitat: At least partly wooded Mediterranean habitats, hedgerows, scrub and farmland
Nest: Neat and well-concealed construction built of moss and grass
Eggs: 3–4; bluish-white, boldly marked
Food: Seeds, insects

Superficially yellowhammer-like in size and shape. Adult male has striking head pattern with black throat and black through eye. Underparts mainly yellow but shows grey and chestnut breast band. Upperparts mostly chestnut but rump grey-brown. Female lacks male's bold head markings and rest of plumage is washed-out version of his. Juvenile similar to female

but plumage generally buffish-brown.

Female distinguished by olive-grey rump and buff breast with neat streaks

During the winter cirl buntings sometimes gather together in small flocks, although pairs often keep their own company within their territories

Corn Bunting

Miliaria calandra

A LOCALLY common bird of farmland, the corn bunting is widespread throughout most of mainland Europe as far north as the Baltic coast, being absent only from some of the larger mountain ranges. Throughout most of their range corn buntings are year-round residents, birds gathering in flocks during the winter months; in the far northeast, however, the species is a summer migrant. The song of the corn bunting has been likened to jangling keys; birds sing with head thrown back from a wire fence or exposed branch, and the sound is a familiar one throughout most of Europe. Were it not for this unique and diagnostic song, however, the species might be more tricky to identify since it lacks any really distinctive features.

Voice: Song a unique, discordant jangling; flight call a low-pitched, loud 'kwit' or 'quilp kwit-it'
Length: 18cm
Wingspan: 26–32cm
Weight: 44–54g
Habitat: Farmland with hedgerows
Nest: Large, loose construction of coarse grasses, often in a scrape on the ground
Eggs: 3–5; usually pale with bold, dark, scribbles and blotches

Food: Seeds and invertebrates

Large, dumpy bunting with rather plain plumage. Bill large and pinkish and dark eye proportionately large. Upperparts buffish-brown and heavily streaked. Underparts whitish and also heavily streaked, particularly on breast. Often flies on fluttering wings and with legs dangling. Sexes similar, and juvenile similar to adult.

Both males and females are promiscuous, mating with several partners

Flies short distances with legs dangling, on fluttering wings

The male's distinctive song is one of the most characteristic sounds of agricultural land in southern Europe

One of the few species at home in modern agricultural 'prairies'

Comparing Immature Buntings

As with many other passerines, buntings are easiest to identify in the spring. The males of most species are colourful or distinctive and all sing unique songs, which can be recognised with comparative ease. Even adult females are relatively easy to identify, not least because of their association with males of the same species. In the autumn, however, problems of identification do arise, with many immature buntings looking confusingly similar and, in the case of migrant birds, often occurring outside their normal range in unexpected habitats.

SNOW BUNTING: Has characteristic orange-buff elements to plumage with whitish underparts and striking black and white wing pattern; bill yellowish

LAPLAND BUNTING: Plumage generally rather nondescript streaked brown with rather clean, pale belly; always shows chestnut panels on wings (greater coverts) bordered by pale wingbars

YELLOW BREASTED BUNTING: Plumage recalls female yellowhammer, with sandy-brown, streaked upperparts and yellowish tinge to paler underparts; shows broad, pale supercilium and streaked, rather rufous rump; bill dull pink

ORTOLAN BUNTING: Head and back olive-brown while underparts and wings suffused with pale rufous or sandy tints; has white eyering and pink bill; moustachial stripe and throat pale, sometimes appearing yellowish

CIRL BUNTING: Superficially similar to immature yellowhammer but lacking that species' yellow wash to head, throat and underparts; throat and supercilium appear particularly pale; rump greyish-brown and only faintly streaked; bill grey

ROCK BUNTING: Plumage overall pale rufous-brown; grey elements of adult plumage absent or much reduced in intensity; black facial markings less distinct than on adult and white wingbars rather indistinct

CRETZSCHMAR'S BUNTING: Warm sandy-brown plumage, including rump, moustachial stripe and throat; shows white eyering and pink bill

Comparing Immature Buntings

YELLOWHAMMER: Has yellowish-buff head, throat and underparts and dull rufous-brown back and wings; rump is rufous-brown and unstreaked; bill dull pinkish-grey

REED BUNTING: Plumage recalls adult female but facial markings less intense; ear coverts uniformly dark, lacking pale spot seen on rustic buntings of similar age; moustachial stripe and throat white and streaks on breast and flanks blackish

RUSTIC BUNTING: Well-marked plumage with chestnut-brown upperparts and chestnut streaks on breast and flanks of otherwise pale underparts; head markings distinctive with pale yellow-buff supercilium, moustachial stripe and throat, and pale spot on rear of ear coverts

LITTLE BUNTING: Plumage similar to that of adult but chestnut on ear coverts and supercilium less intense; shows characteristic pale spot on rear of ear coverts

CORN BUNTING: Relatively large, plump bunting; plumage essentially indistinguishable from adult in the field – streaked sandy-brown upperparts and paler underparts; bill more substantial and conical than other buntings'

BLACK-HEADED BUNTING: Plumage rather uniform sandy brown, palest on underparts, which have only faint streaking; shows pale lemon-yellow undertail coverts; bill dull pinkish-grey

Vagrant Passerines from North America

ALL birds are shown here in first-autumn plumage, the form most likely to be seen in Europe.

RED-EYED VIREO (VIREO OLIVACEUS): All birds have red eye and stout bill; sexes similar; adult has greenish-brown upperparts, striking head pattern and whitish underparts; first-autumn bird has pale-yellowish wash to flanks

YELLOW-RUMPED WARBLER (DENDROICA CORONATA): All plumages show diagnostic yellow rump; breeding male streaked blue-grey; female and first-winter birds much duller with warm-brown upperparts

AMERICAN REDSTART (SETOPHAGA RUTICILLA): Adult male upperparts slaty black with red patches on sides of breast; female and juvenile grey-brown with yellow patches

BLACKPOLL WARBLER (DENDROICA STRIATA): In all plumages shows two conspicuous white wingbars, and white spots on outertail feathers; female heavily streaked and washed buffish-yellow; first-autumn bird similar to female but less streaked

COMMON YELLOWTHROAT (GEOTHLYPIS TRICHAS): Adult male has striking black mask, olive-brown upperparts and bright yellow throat and upper breast; female and juvenile lack black mask, having greyish lores and ear coverts

SCARLET TANAGER (PIRANGA OLIVACEA): Breeding male bright red with black wings and tail; winter male olive-brown; female and first-winter male olive-yellow

NORTHERN PARULA (PARULA AMERICANA): Adult male has blue-grey upperparts, yellow throat and flush of orange on breast; female and first-winter male similar but breast markings less conspicuous and flight feathers fringed green

NORTHERN ORIOLE (ICTERUS GALBULA): Adult male has black head, breast and upperparts, and orange rump and underparts; female and juvenile brown instead of black and dull orange-buff rather than orange

Vagrant Passerines from North America

ROSE-BREASTED GROSBEAK (*PHEUCTICUS LUDOVICIANUS*): Large-headed, large-billed bunting-like bird; female streaked brown with white wingbars and white supercilium and moustachial stripe; first-winter male similar to female but with faint pink flush to breast

SONG SPARROW (*MELOSPIZA MELODIA*): Sexes similar; adults and juveniles have streaked dark grey-brown upperparts and white underparts with brown or black streaks; head markings grey and rufous-brown

BLACK-AND-WHITE WARBLER (*MNIOTILTA VARIA*): Plumage entirely black and white; all plumages similar except that first-autumn males have buffish wash to sides of neck and flanks and have greyish, not black, ear coverts

NORTHERN WATERTHRUSH (*SEIURUS NOVEBORACENSIS*): Superficially thrush-like warbler; bobs up and down like a dipper when feeding; sexes similar and juvenile resembles adult; upperparts olive-brown and underparts off-white marked with black spots

BOBOLINK (*DOLICHONYX ORYZIVORUS*): Bunting-like but with pointed-tipped, triangular bill and sharply pointed tail feathers; breeding male black with buff nape and white on scapulars and rump; female and non-breeding male buffish-brown and streaked; juvenile similar to female but less streaked on underparts

DARK-EYED JUNCO (*JUNCO HYEMALIS*): Adult male has slaty-black head, neck, breast, wings, tail and back; outertail feathers white; underparts white; female similar but grey-brown rather than black; first-winter birds similar to adults but show brown fringes to tertials and wing coverts

BUFF-BELLIED PIPIT (*ANTHUS RUBESCENS*): Superficially similar to water pipit; underparts washed buff at all times; breeding adult has streaked grey-brown upperparts; autumn birds similar but upperparts warmer brown and underparts more streaked

GLOSSARY

Abrasion Wear and tear on feathers, which can change a bird's appearance dramatically. Pale parts wear more easily than dark; for example, white spots on gulls' wingtips wear off to leave a uniform dark colour

Barring Narrow bands or stripes on a bird's plumage

Basal knob Swelling seen at the base of the bill in some species of wildfowl

Boreal Northern

Brood Set of offspring

Calls Sounds uttered by bird other than song. In some non-passerines these may fulfil the same role as song, but generally they are concerned with contact and alarm functions

Carpal Area of feathers at wrist joint of wings, contrastingly marked in some birds of prey

Carr Type of woodland; occurs in damp situations and normally comprises alder

Cere Naked wax-like membrane at base of bill in some species

Courtship In order to mate and rear young successfully pairs of most species must first break down their natural instinct to keep their distance, must reduce aggression and maintain a firm relationship, or pair bond, which is created and reinforced by courtship behaviour

Coverts The name given to a group of feathers covering a particular part of a bird's body. Thus ear coverts cover the ear, undertail coverts are found on the undertail area and underwing coverts are found lining the inner part of the underwing. Those feathers on the upperwing not concerned with flight are also referred to as coverts; they are arranged in zones which are, from the leading edge backwards, referred to as greater, median and lesser coverts; those covering the bases of the primary feathers are called primary coverts

Culmen Upper ridge of the bill

Display Behaviour designed to demonstrate a bird's presence

Diurnal Active during the day

Eclipse A dull plumage, notable of male duck, acquired after breeding to reduce conspicuousness (ducks moult all their flight feathers and lose the power of flight for a short period while 'in eclipse')

Extralimital Outside the normal range

Feral Precise definition means 'wild', but is used to describe a species or individuals once domesticated or captive but since released or escaped and living wild

Flank Side of breast and belly

Gape The opening or the corners of the mouth; 'to gape' is to hold the bill wide open

Garigue Sparsely vegetated habitat characteristic of arid, stony terrain in the Mediterranean region

Gliding Effortless and usually level flight where wingbeats are not involved

Hirundines Swallows and martins, members of the family Hirundinidae

Immature Not old enough to breed. With birds this usually refers to a certain stage of plumage, so some birds, such as eagles, are confusingly said to 'breed in immature plumage'. Others, like the fulmar, may not breed for several years even though visually indistinguishable from an adult

Irruption The sudden large-scale movement out of one area and their arrival into another; generally occurs in response to food shortage

Jizz Field characteristics that are unique to a species

Juvenile A bird in its first set of feathers, or juvenile plumage

Lek Communal display ground

Lores Region of feathers between the eye and the bill

Malar stripe A marking originating at the base of the lower mandible of the bill

Mandible One half of the bill

Maquis Shrub-dominated vegetation typical of many parts of the Mediterranean region

Migration Regular, seasonal movements of species; more or less predictable, with a return trip. Irregular movements caused by, for example, hard weather or food shortage also occur (see fieldfare). Young birds invariably spread away from breeding areas in autumn – this type of movement is termed dispersal

Mimicry Vocal mimicry is copying other sounds, natural or man-made; the precise reason for it is unknown

Mobbing Small birds that discover a roosting owl or bird of prey, or sometimes a mammalian predator or snake, will flutter around or dive at it with loud calls, attracting mixed species to join in. The purpose is uncertain

Moult Shedding and replacement of feathers or plumage in a regular sequence, which may or may not affect the appearance of the bird. Many species have feathers with dull tips that crumble away in spring to reveal brighter colours beneath. This is sometimes referred to as moulting by abrasion

Nest Usually thought of as a structure to hold eggs. Some birds, however, dispense with nests and lay their eggs on the ground or on a ledge

Nocturnal Active at night

Partial migrant A species where only some individuals migrate

Passage Refers to migrants and migration – a bird 'on passage' is en route to its winter or summer grounds. A 'passage migrant' is a species that appears in the spring and/or autumn but does not breed or spend the winter, such as a little stint or black tern in Europe

Passerine One of a large order of birds called the Passiformes, all members of which can perch (although many other birds can perch as well).

Pelagic Found in the open sea

Plumage The whole set of feathers covering a bird. Also used to describe different combinations of colour and pattern according to sex, season or age (for example, summer plumage, adult plumage etc)

Predator An animal that eats other animals. Among birdwatchers the term is often used to describe an avian predator of other birds

Preening Using the bill to clean and adjust the feathers

Puszta East European grassy plain

Raptor Bird of prey

Resident A species that remains in a given area all year round

Roost Rest or 'sleep', or the place where a bird or birds do this

Scapulars Region of feathers between the mantle and the wing coverts

Scrape Nest site of some wader species, where small stones form a small depression

Secondaries Inner flight feathers

Sedentary A non-migratory, non-dispersive species

Soaring Effortless flight by broad-winged birds rising on heat thermals and updraughts

Song Voice of a bird in a recognisable pattern for its species, be it an irregular flow or a repetitive phrase; intended to identify the individual and its species, to proclaim ownership of territory and/or attract a mate. Other vocal sounds are usually termed 'calls'

Species A 'kind' of organism, basically isolated from others by its inability to cross-breed and produce fertile young. A subspecies is a recognisably different group (because of size or colour) within a species in a defined area. Apart from subspecies the remarkable feature of a bird species is the lack of variation within it, in terms of size, colour, pattern, voice, behaviour, food, nest and many other factors, which remain remarkably constant

Speculum Coloured patch on a duck's wing, often used in display

Steppe Treeless, grassy habitat associated mainly with Russia and eastern Europe

Supercilium Stripe above the eye

Taiga Forest type found at northerly latitudes, just before the tree-line is reached; often comprises spruce and birch

Territory An area (or 'home range') occupied by a bird (or a pair), and which is defended against other individuals of the same species

Thermalling Method of flight employed by broad-winged birds, including raptors and storks, where lift is provided by currents of hot air

Tundra Northern, treeless habitat; normally characterised by the presence of permafrost

Vagrant Usually a migrant that appears outside its normal range. During spring migration, southerly winds often induce migrants to overshoot. On autumn migration inexperienced juveniles are sometimes blown off course by strong winds or engage in 'reverse migration' (flying in the wrong direction)

Vermiculation Feather pattern where numerous worm-like lines create a close-packed pattern

INDEX

ACKNOWLEDGEMENTS

The Automobile Association would like to thank the following illustrators and libraries for their assistance in the preparation of this book.

All illustrations are held in the Association's own library (AA Photo Library)

R Allen 36; N Arlott F/Cover b, 47, 48b, 52c, 76c, 77, 78b, 79b, 80a, 81a, 94a, 95–101, 105–111, 142a, 153, 154c, 156b–160a, 161a, 162a, 164a, 166a–169, 173b–175b, 176a, 176b, 176c, 177b–180, 186b, 210–211, 222c, 223b, 252-253; T Boyer 39, 40a, 41–42, 43b–46a, 46c, 48a, 50, 51c, 52a, 52d–53, 134, 135c–137, 144a, 144b, 146b–147, 150, 182a, 184a, 184c, 185b, 185c, 186a, 190–192a, 192c, 226a, 227e, 228a, 229–232; H Burn F/Cover d, 6e, 30–34a, 35a, 35b, 38, 40b, 43a, 46b, 49, 51a, 51b, 52b, 88a, 88b, 89–92; J Cox 17a, 37, 80b, 80c, 80d, 86a, 86b, 87, 143, 160b, 161b, 162b–163, 164b–165, 220b–222, 223a, 224–225a, 233a; D Daly 102–104, 112–113; J Gale 11a, 13a, 14b, 15b, 16b, 19–20a, 20c–27, 48c, 79a, 82c, 83b, 83c, 84b, 85b, 86c, 88c, 94b; R Gillmor 13b, 16c, 17b–18, 20b, 28, 29a, 29c; P Hayman 13c, 14a, 15a, 29b, 29d, 76a, 76b, 76d, 78a, 79c, 81c, 213–216, 217b–219, 234–243, 244b, 244g, 244i, 245a, 248–249; I Lewington B/Cover a, 154b, 155, 181a, 181c, 182b, 183a, 186c, 187b, 187c, 189, 192b, 193, 233c, 244a, 244b, 245b–247; D Quinn 5b, 6d, 7b, 7c, 114c, 115, 116b–117, 118b, 119b, 119c, 119d, 120b, 121b–121f, 123b, 123d, 124b–127, 128b, 129a, 132–133, 135a, 135b, 217a, 250–251; D Rees 194b, 195b–197a, 199–200, 201b–203, 206, 226b–227d, 228b, 228c; C Rose F/Cover a, c, Spine, B/Cover b, 7a, 8–10, 11b–12, 14c, 15c, 15d, 16a, 34b, 35c, 54–75, 82a, 82b, 83a, 84a, 85a, 114a, 114b, 116a, 118a, 118c, 119a, 120a, 121a, 122, 123a, 123c, 124a, 128a, 129b, 130–131, 138–141, 144c–146a, 148–149, 151–152, 154a, 156a, 170–172, 181b, 194a, 195a, 197b–198, 201a, 204–205, 207–209, 212, 220a; C Schmidt 142b, 173a, 175c, 177a, 183b, 184b, 185a, 187a, 188, 225b, 233b; Nature Photographers Ltd 6c (P Sterry)